The Long View and the Short

The Long View
and the Short

STUDIES IN ECONOMIC THEORY AND POLICY

by Jacob Viner

PRINCETON UNIVERSITY

The Free Press, Glencoe, Illinois

Preface

THESE ESSAYS by Jacob Viner, which have appeared at various times and in various places, have been collected for publication by a group of his students and other friends on the occasion of his sixty-fifth birthday to express the gratitude, admiration, and warm affection of the members of our discipline. No member of our craft more clearly merits such an expression.

The usual Festschrift formula has been abandoned in this volume because it was strongly felt that a collection of his own writings would be not only a better tribute to Professor Viner but a welcome contribution to economic literature. It is unfortunate that the written word cannot also convey the agility and penetration of Professor Viner's oral argument and his power of stimulation as a teacher and colleague.

Of the papers included in this volume, none lies primarily within the area of international trade, to which Professor Viner has devoted so much attention, because of the recent appearance of several books by him on this subject. Even the present selection does less than justice to his remarkable versatility and the breadth of his interests and his knowledge.

Sincere thanks are due to the following publishers, who readily granted permission to reprint material they had originally published; Addison-Wesley Publishing Company; American Economic Association, publishers of *The American Economic Review*; American Statistical Association, publishers of *The Journal of the American Statistical Society*; Augustan Reprint Society; Brown University; Cambridge University Press, publishers of *Economic History Review*; the Chamber of Commerce of the United States; Harvard University Press, publishers of *The Quarterly Journal of Economics*; Richard D. Irwin, Inc.; The London School of Economics and Political Science, publishers of *Economica*; *The New York Times*; Northwestern University School of Law, publishers of *Illinois Law Review*; Princeton University Press, publishers of *World Politics*;

Royal Economic Society, publishers of *Economic Journal;* Springer-Verlag, publishers of *Zeitschrift für Nationalokonomie;* University of Chicago Press, publishers of *The Journal of Modern History,* *The Journal of Political Economy,* and *Modern Philology.* Thanks are also due to Frank H. Bauer for permission to use his photograph of Professor Viner.

The friends of the author who arranged for the publication of this volume are responsible for the selection of the essays which have been included, the preparation of the bibliography, the preparation of the book for the press, and the indexing of the volume.

Contents

PART I

Economic Theory and Policy

Price Policies: The Determination of Market Price*

ONE OF THE MOST important problems which confronts every business man is the question of what price he can obtain for his product. Many factors co-operate to determine the market price, and many of these factors are beyond the power of the producer to control. The mechanism of price determination varies with the degree of power of price control possessed by the producer and with the character of the market.

Economic theory has confined itself very largely to the exposition of the method of determination of market price in what economists call a perfect market, namely, a market in which there are many alert and experienced buyers and sellers; in which there is an effective organization for the purpose of mediating purchases and sales, recording prices, and diffusing important information with respect to present and prospective production and consumption and other factors bearing upon price; and in which there is no agreement among buyers or sellers, formal or informal, with respect to the prices to be bid or asked. Very few commodities have markets which possess all of these characteristics. It is not far from the truth to say that a few basic foodstuffs and raw materials produced under small-scale conditions and important securities widely held and traded on the stock exchanges in large amounts are the only commodities having perfect markets.

Market price, regardless of the character of the market, is always determined by demand and supply, i.e., by the willingness of buyers to buy and sellers to sell. In the perfect market, the buyers will stand ready to buy but in amounts varying inversely with variations in the price, and the sellers will stand ready to sell, but in amounts varying directly with variations in the price. If the price settles tem-

*Reprinted from L. C. Marshall, ed., *Business Administration*, Chicago, University of Chicago Press, 1921, pp. 343-347, by the courtesy of the publisher.

porarily at a point at which the offers to sell are greater in volume than the bids to buy, price-cutting competition between sellers in their eagerness to make sales will force the price down. If, on the other hand, the price settles temporarily at a price at which the offers to sell are smaller in volume than the bids to buy, price-raising competition between buyers in their eagerness to buy will force the price up. The market price tends to settle at that point at which all buyers will be able to buy all they are willing to buy at that price, and all sellers are able to sell all they are willing to sell at that price.

Any change in the demand or the supply, however, will change the location of this point of equilibrium. In a typical perfect market, such as the wheat market, the point of equilibrium is rarely constant even for an hour. News about the growing crops, of an impending war, of government plans to change the scheme of taxation, of heavy shipments of grain to market by farmers, affect demand and supply or the willingness of traders to buy or sell. Since, in a wholesale market, most of the purchases either are made by middlemen who expect to resell to the actual consumer, or, if made by the consumers themselves, are in anticipation of future needs, any factor which affects the prospects of future prices will be reflected in a change in their present willingness to buy. Traders in the perfect market are constantly on the alert to get wind of prospective changes and any scrap of news, very often any rumor, will affect their willingness to buy or sell, and will, therefore, affect the market price. Since valuable information may reach some traders before others, they constantly watch each other's bids and offers. If a group of traders bid prices up and make large purchases at the higher prices, other traders, confident that there must be some good reason as yet unknown to them for this anxiety to buy, will also buy and thus force prices up still further. Similarly, a disposition to sell on the part of some traders will spread to others and lead to a fall in price.

A commodity is not suitable for large-scale and smoothly organized competitive trading unless it is by its nature homogeneous or is artificially standardized by careful and authoritative grading, so that it can be traded in by name without necessity of samples or bulk inspection. Price policy for the producer of a commodity which has a perfect market is a comparatively simple matter. He can sell only at the current market price, which is determined by the concurrence of a great many buyers and sellers. In the short run he has only two alternatives, to sell at the current price or to hold for a rise. In the long run, he must make guesses as to what the average future price will be and adjust his production to the scale which would be most profitable at that average price. The outstanding characteristics of the perfect market price are, therefore, its quick responsiveness to changing conditions, its freedom from control by individual producers or buyers, and its uniformity at any one moment over the entire area of the market, if allowance is made for transportation costs.

The most complete contrast to the perfect market is presented by the monopoly market. In the strict sense of the term monopoly, a commodity has a monopoly market when supply is controlled by a single producer or combination of producers. The monopoly producer has much greater control over price than does the producer for a perfect market. Within a wide range of prices, the monopoly producer will continue to make sales, although in varying amounts, if he varies his prices, whereas the producer for the perfect market will see his sales drop to zero if he demands a price higher only by a small fraction than that demanded by his competitors. It is not accurate to say, however, that the monopolist has complete control over price. As he raises his price, sales will fall somewhat. As he lowers his price, sales will increase somewhat, the degree of change in the volume of sales, as price changes, varying with the character of the demand for the commodity and the availability of substitutes. The monopolist is able to determine the price at which his product will sell, but if he is an efficient business man, he will endeavor to find the price at which profit per unit times total sales will yield him the greatest amount of total profit. He will also give consideration to the possibility that a price yielding a high profit will attract competitors into the industry or will lead to a demand for government interference with his industry. Monopoly price normally will remain constant for comparatively long periods and will be adjusted to changing conditions of costs of production or of demand by sharp changes at infrequent intervals. The outstanding characteristics of monopoly price are, therefore, its slowness of response to changing conditions and the great degree of control over price exercised by the producer.

Between the perfect market and the monopoly market there is for wholesale markets a gradation from those which closely resemble but do not fully approach free and energetic price competition to those which closely resemble but do not fully approach complete monopoly control over price. Producers always desire as full a measure as possible of control over the prices of their products. They fear price competition, because with the importance in modern industry of indirect or overhead costs, price-competition always threatens to become cut-throat competition. Moreover, they dislike frequent fluctuations in price. They seek every possible means, therefore, of withdrawing their products from the field of keen price competition, and in pursuit of this end they use a variety of devices such as special brands, trade marks, patents, style differentiation, even different methods of wrapping or different containers, to differentiate their products from those of their competitors. If they succeed in developing a special demand for their products, such producers find that to some extent they can determine their prices independently of the prices of their competitors and still maintain their sales. The importance of advertising to producers of commodities only slightly differentiated from competing articles is obvious. Competition between such producers tends more and more to become competition in sales efforts, such as special displays, number of salesmen, volume of advertising, and tends to refrain from price-cutting as a means of stimulating sales. Specialized commodities of this kind tend to be less responsive in their price to changing conditions of production or consumption than perfect market commodities, more responsive than monopoly products; their producers can exercise more control over their prices than producers of commodities for a perfect market, less control than producers for a monopoly market; the products are not standardized as between producers as compared with perfect market commodities; they are not as much differentiated from rival commodities as are monopoly commodities.

The methods of differentiation—or specialization—of products discussed in the preceding paragraph generally can be applied successfully only to consumers' goods, where the purchasers are not sufficiently skilled or sufficiently interested purchasers to discover the substantial identity between rival products. Industries producing fairly standardized raw materials or intermediate products often avoid keen price competition by another method which may be called the follow-the-leader method of price determination. This method is most likely to occur in industries where one producer controls a large fraction of the total production and enjoys strong financial backing. The leading producer will determine the prices for his own products, and will issue a price list several times a year. The smaller producers, without any formal or informal agreement, will adopt this price list as their own. If they should not do so but should charge higher prices, they will make no sales so long as the leading producer and other producers adopting its scale of prices are able to accept additional orders. If they charge lower prices, they face the danger that the leading producer will under-cut their prices, and with his greater financial resources will be able to force them into bankruptcy. The smaller concerns will often welcome the leadership of a strong producer in setting prices, as they are glad to escape price competition and feel that they can rely on the superior facilities of the leading producer for gathering information to make the prices fixed upon those most profitable for the industry as a whole. The leading producer by this method gains most of the advantages of monopoly control while avoiding the expense of eliminating competitors and the danger of governmental interference and of public resentment.

The retail market differs from all of these markets in that owing to its lack of organization and to the lack of skill, alertness, and information on the part of both buyers and sellers, prices differ from store to store on the same day for absolutely identical articles, and reflect only slowly and imperfectly changing conditions of production and consumption.

The Relation between Economics
and Ethics (Discussion)*

THE SCRUPULOUS CONCERN lest they encroach upon the fields of other sciences which economists often express in their theoretical discussions of the proper relations between economics and ethics is, fortunately for the value of their work, not greatly in evidence in their actual research and teaching. Over-lapping is inevitable in the social sciences in their present stage of development. Economics, although most outspoken as to its dangers, is no less enterprising than the allied sciences in extending the range of its activities extensively as well as intensively. Economics, it is true, has no direct concern with the analysis of the processes whereby men acquire a consciousness of moral obligation, and it is in this limited field that ethics finds the bulk of its subject matter. All the social sciences, however, take into account "ethical considerations" in the ordinary meaning of the term; they appraise and they judge as between conflicting programs and policies affecting human welfare. Economic welfare, as an integral and important part of general welfare, is the peculiar concern of economists; and to the extent that the final determination of the rightness or wrongness of given human activities rests upon economic considerations, the economist is in the position to guide opinion.

The fact that in the physical sciences ethical considerations play no part has little bearing for the economist. "Scientific method" connotes different things in the field of the social sciences from those in the field of the physical sciences, for these latter are not value sciences, and are not immediately concerned with the evaluation of human behavior. The economist should not refrain from making his special contribution to decisions of public importance

*Reprinted from *The American Economic Review, Supplement*, Vol. 12, March 1922, pp. 198-200, by the courtesy of the American Economic Association.

because of a doctrinaire adherence to an academic standard of scientific uninterestedness more appropriate—or less wasteful—in the physical laboratory than in the field of the social sciences. The whole problem now under discussion is virtually of little importance, however, because, regardless of how vociferous the economist may be in his methodological discussions of the need for "purification" of his science, in his practice he continues to strain every effort to make it socially useful.

Another point of view, not given its due attention in the discussions by economists of the proper relations between their science and ethics, may throw new light on the problem. The range of data, problems, and points of view of economic significance is too great to be subjected to complete and thorough analysis and investigation, and selection becomes necessary. The basis of selection, and subsequently the distribution of emphasis, must rest on some system of values derived from some concept as to the function, not of economics—for it may have many functions or may not require any functional justification for its existence—but of the economist. There suggest themselves at the moment three possible bases of selection of data and problems for consideration, arising in each case from a different conception of the role of the economist.

The economist may select his data for consideration wholly or mainly on the basis of their intellectual appeal, their challenge to his mental powers, and may distribute his limited energy in proportion to the degree of intellectual tickle the various problems afford. This basis of choice leads normally to a scholastic economics, largely mathematical in character, resting on a few general assumptions of questionable factual validity, finding its chief interest in the construction of new permutations and combinations of syllogistic legerdemain, and having little ascertainable relationship to actual human problems. Such is the non-ethical economics par excellence. It is by no means worthless. Its satisfaction of the sophisticated craving for mental exercise is itself a distinct contribution, although to a very limited group. Its incidental training in the technique of deductive logic becomes valuable when applied to problems of actual current significance. Its conclusions often afford starting points for the investigation of real problems. Even aside from all other considerations, it can find weighty justification for its existence in the historical fact that the long-run pragmatic value of scientific contributions to knowledge is not adequately measured by the degree of immediate recognition of their practical significance.

Or the economist may choose his problems for investigation and select his material for instruction on the basis of their probable value in training the young idea how to do well for itself in industry, or, more generously, how to do well for industry as cogs in its machinery. Such is the logical basis for the selection of subject material and the distribution of emphasis in vocational economics. Here at least one ethical consideration appears to demand constant and careful attention: namely, that arising from the conflict between private economic interest and public economic welfare.

Finally, the economist may be guided in his selection of subject matter for investigation and in his distribution of emphasis primarily by frank and avowed consideration of their significance in the determination of public policy with respect to questions affecting general economic welfare. Such a basis of selection leads to what may be called without apology welfare economics, and it is in this field that general economics can render its chief service. If in the course of his investigations the economist finds it essential to give attention to ethical considerations, or to take into account the ethical aspects of human behavior, he need only remember that important problems of public policy may be none the less economic because they are ethical problems, to find sufficient justification for making appraisals and delivering judgment. That he must endeavor to free himself from personal or class bias it is gratuitous to mention. But he need not fear for the purity of the science. There can be no realistic "pure economics" until economic phases of human behavior and of man's environment are purified from contact with the remaining texture of reality.

Taxation and Changes in Price Levels*

CHANGING PRICE LEVELS give rise to important theoretical and practical problems of taxation which have received no systematic treatment and only occasional mention in the economic literature on taxation and on price levels. The adequate theoretical presentation of the case for or against a particular tax often demands consideration of the special conditions resulting from the upward or downward swing of the general price level. Tax laws are almost invariably written in pecuniary terms. They may not operate in the manner intended by the legislators or they may even operate in a manner directly contrary to that anticipated by the legislators and productive of gross inequalities if provision is not made therein for changes in the value of the monetary unit. The relation of taxation to price levels is a problem of sufficient importance to merit a greater measure of attention from students of government finance than has been vouchsafed to it in the past. This article is an attempt to open up the subject in the hope that it will lead to further discussion of the general problem and its detailed manifestations.

Income Taxes

To take up first the bearing of fluctuating prices on income taxation, a careful reading of a number of current income-tax laws has not disclosed to the writer a single important instance of deliberate provision for adjustment to changing price levels. In a few instances, isolated provisions in these acts permit of some degree of adjustment, but this effect appears to be a happy coincidence not anticipated by the drafters of the acts.

Exemptions. First, and most obviously, the specific amounts granted as exemptions to small incomes and for dependents have

*Reprinted from *The Journal of Political Economy*, Vol. 31, August 1923, pp. 494-520, by the courtesy of the University of Chicago Press.

no rational basis unless they take into account the purchasing power of monetary incomes. The degree of adequacy for its intended purposes of a given exemption will vary inversely with fluctuations in the general price level.

Progression. If the rates of an income tax are progressive the severity of the tax will increase as prices rise and will decrease as prices fall, even though the statutory rates remain unaltered, provided that monetary incomes in general vary in some degree of conformity with variations in the purchasing power of the monetary unit. The table presented below gives in Column I the schedule of rates of a hypothetical progressive tax, and in Columns II and III a series of incomes in the years 1915 and 1920, respectively, and the taxes payable thereon, constructed on the assumptions that between 1915 and 1920 there was a 100 per cent rise in the general price level and that monetary incomes were exactly adjusted to this rise in prices, so that real income for all individuals remained unchanged.

I		II			III		
Tax Rates on Amount of Income		Total Income, 1915	Tax	Percentage of Total Income	Total Income, 1920	Tax	Percentage of Total Income
Not exceeding $1,000—exempt	A.	$ 5,000	$ 200	4.0	A. $10,000	$ 450	4.5
$ 1,001-$ 10,000— 5 per cent	B.	10,000	450	4.5	B. 20,000	1,450	7.25
$10,001-$ 20,000—10 per cent	C.	20,000	1,450	7.25	C. 40,000	5,450	14.9
$20,001-$ 50,000—20 per cent	D.	50,000	7,450	14.9	D. 100,000	27,450	27.45
$50,001-$100,000—40 per cent	—						

The table demonstrates clearly enough that a rise in the price level increases the severity of a progressive scale of rates, even though the statutory rates are not increased. It can readily be demonstrated by arithmetical illustrations that, with a given progressive series of rates, the degree of increase in the severity of the rates will vary directly (although not necessarily in exact proportion) with the degree of rise in the price level, and that, with a given percentage of rise in the price level, the degree of increase in the severity of the rates will vary directly (although not necessarily in exact proportion) with the rate of progression in the tax law. In other words, the extent to which an increase in prices will increase the severity of progressive taxation depends upon both the percentage of increase in the price level and the rate of progression in the tax law. The greater the rise in prices and the greater the steepness in progression, the greater will be the increase in the severity of the tax. The reverse propositions also hold true: a fall in the general price level accompanied by a corresponding fall in money incomes will result in a decrease in the severity of a given progressive schedule of rates; the steeper the rate of progression in the tax and the greater the fall in prices, the greater will be the decrease in the severity of the tax. It follows that, assuming the national real income and its distribution to remain the same, the maintenance of a given progressive scale of rates in a general income tax during a period of rising prices will bring into the state treasury an increase in money revenue more than proportionate to the increase in the price level, and during a period of falling prices will result in a decrease in the money revenue more than proportionate to the fall in the price level. As a period of rising prices is probably also generally a period of increasing real income, and a period of falling prices a period of decreasing real income, the variations in the monetary revenue yield of a progressive income tax resulting from changing price levels will be still further accentuated.

A proportional income tax, on the other hand, aside from any exemption provisions it may contain, will not vary in its severity with changes in the price level to which money incomes adjust themselves, and the money revenue which it yields to the government will vary in exact proportion to the variations in the purchasing power of the monetary unit. This irregular and arbitrary variation in the severity and the productiveness of progressive income taxation during a period of changing price levels—from which proportional taxation is exempt—must be regarded either as a hitherto unnoticed objection to the progressive principle or as an argument for the frequent adjustment of the schedule of rates to allow for changes in the value of the monetary unit. Even if the latter alternative be chosen, it still remains true that such adjustment would be difficult to establish in practice, whether by statute or by administrative rule, and that it is not needed in connection with proportional taxation.

Capital gains. One of the difficult problems in connection with income taxation is the propriety of including capital gains in taxable income. In general, writers on this topic definitely take either one position or the other, although logically the problem bristles with difficulties which should restrain the attempt to find in theory a categorical answer. Where the capital gain arises from the appreciation in value, as compared with the original cost, of an income-yielding asset, it can reasonably be argued in opposition to its taxation that such gain is the result of the capitalization of future income which will in due time pay its full measure of taxation. This argument does not hold, however, for those gains which are not reinvested by the recipients, but are used as current income. In such cases, failure to tax such gains either when they accrue or when they are realized results in the total escape from taxation of genuine income with full tax-paying ability. Since the income tax is assumed to be a general tax, it cannot be objected that the taxes on the future income yield of the sold capital asset were discounted in the sale price. There will normally be no shifting of a uniform tax upon all kinds of income. If there is a probability of lower tax rates in the future and if consideration is given to the difficulty of tracing the use to which the recipient of a capital gain puts the proceeds, there is ample justification for a compromise, such as is attempted in the American Revenue Act of 1921, between the full taxation of realized capital gains (as in the American Revenue Act of 1919) and the total exemption from taxation (as in the British income tax) by taxing capital gains more moderately than income in general.[1]

An additional reason for the more moderate taxation of capital gains is that apparent capital gains may merely represent the reappraisal of a capital asset in terms of a dollar of less purchasing power. No acceptable concept of income will include as income the rise in monetary value of a capital asset which represents merely the fall in the value of the monetary unit and is not indicative of increased purchasing power in general.[2] During a period of rising prices, a

---

1. The United States Revenue Act of 1921 provides that at the election of the taxpayer realized capital gains may be taxed separately from ordinary income at a rate of 12½ per cent. There is no justification in principle for restricting the relief from full taxation of capital gains to those whose taxable incomes are otherwise large enough to make them subject to rates higher than 12½ per cent. A more equitable method of granting relief would have been to permit a deduction for capital gains of a stated percentage, say 50 per cent, of the amount of tax to which they would have been subject in the absence of the relief provision. This principle holds, even though the object of the relief provision was not to afford a closer approximation of equity, but was to facilitate property deals.

2. "A man who sold an asset in 1920 which he had purchased in 1914, making an apparent profit of 100 per cent and receiving his pay in fifty-cent dollars is, under our statute, subject to tax on his gain, although that gain is only apparent and not real. Moreover, the situation is particularly unjust under our present system. If complete periodical revaluations were used in determining income there would still be relative equality as between different taxpayers. But as the

lower rate on capital gains than on ordinary income can be justified, therefore, as a rough attempt to offset the taxation of fictitious gains resulting from the fall in the value of the monetary unit. This conclusion remains valid even though it be admitted that, given a constant current interest rate, there will probably be a tendency of variations in the value of income-yielding capital assets to lag behind variations in their monetary yield. The owners or buyers of capital assets probably do not at once fully capitalize an increase or a decrease in monetary income, partly because of inertia, and partly on the logical ground that a rise or a fall in yield may prove to be of short duration. Another justification for the taxation of capital gains at specially low rates is suggested by the point made by Professor Powell, that, as capital gains are taxed only when realized, under progressive taxation a ten years' accumulated gain realized in one year will be subject to a greater tax than the same gain realized evenly year by year.[3]

During a period of falling prices, on the other hand, there may be a genuine capital gain, though the market value of the capital asset remains constant or even falls. In a period of rapid deflation of a depreciated currency, a considerable measure of such capital gains may well be concealed by the general downward trend of prices.

Inventories. In the taxation of business incomes, taxable income is generally measured by the increase in net worth between the beginning and the end of the fiscal period plus any intermediate distribution of earnings. Accounting practice generally demands that net worth be estimated on the basis of the cost price minus depreciation of fixed assets; the cost or market value, whichever is lower, of inventories; and the book value of other assets, adjusted, generally, by reserves for possible losses. During a period of rapidly rising prices, market values of inventory will generally exceed cost values, but if the "cost or market, whichever is lower" basis is used

---

situation now stands, the transactions are closed in a haphazard and uneven fashion. A man who happens to sell out at the peak of the price curves is taxed very unequally as compared with the man who continues his transaction until a period of lower price levels."—R. M. Haig, "The Concept of Income," in R. M. Haig, ed., *The Federal Income Tax* ("Columbia University Lectures," 1921), p. 17.

3. Thomas Reed Powell, "Constitutional Aspects of Federal Income Taxation," in *ibid.*, p. 83.

for valuing inventories, the rise in the market values of inventory
will not affect the income as shown by the accounting records
until the profit is actually realized through sale at the higher prices.
The accountant's case for this method of valuing inventory rests
mainly on the argument that the acknowledgment of losses as soon
as they become prospective, and the admission of gains only when
they are actually realized, promotes conservative business practice.

There are four possible basic methods of valuing inventories:
at cost; at market; at cost or market, whichever is lower; or at cost
or market, whichever is higher. Of these, the last-named is rarely, if
ever, employed. It is sometimes held that for purposes of taxation it
does not matter which method is used, since any loss or gain in
market value not reflected in the inventory or any loss or gain in
inventory valuation not reflected in market value will ultimately
be offset by gains or losses shown by sales.[4]

Under ordinary circumstances, however, and especially during
a period of changing price levels, it does make a difference for
taxation, even in the long run, whether one method or another of
inventory valuation is used. To illustrate the significance of choice
of method of taking inventories during a period of changing
price levels, the following hypothetical cases are presented. Case A
applies to conditions of rising prices followed by falling prices;
Case B applies to conditions of falling prices followed by rising
prices.

CASE A

Inventory of Stock Purchased in 1920, as of December 31, 1920	Sale Price in 1921, after Deduction of Selling Expenses, etc.
Cost, $100,000 Market, $150,000	$100,000

In Case A, if inventory were taken in 1920 at market value,
or at cost or market, whichever was higher, there would have been
admitted as income in 1920 a gain of $50,000, and there would
have been deductible in 1921 a loss of $50,000. If the tax was pro-
portional, if the rate was the same for both years, and if there was

---

4. Cf. U.S. Revenue Act of 1916, Form 1031. "In case the annual gain or loss
is determined by inventory, merchandise must be inventoried at the cost price,
as any loss in saleable value will ultimately be reflected in the sales during the
year when the goods are disposed of." Cf. also, A. A. Ballantine, "Inventories"
in *The Federal Income Tax*, p. 172: "The effect of admitting inventory losses,
even wrongly, is merely to postpone profits from one year to another, while
the effect of failure to admit them is to treat as income that which is really
capital."

for the entire business in both years a net taxable income, then, and only then, would these two items offset each other for purposes of taxation. If there was a net loss for the entire business in 1921, there would be no opportunity in that year for the deduction of the tax paid in 1920 on what later proved to have been a fictitious gain.[5] If the tax was progressive, and if total net income in 1921 before deduction of the loss was not in the same taxable grade as total net income in 1920 after inclusion of the inventory gain, the deduction of the $50,000 loss in 1921 would either more than offset or would less than offset for taxation purposes the addition of $50,000 gain in 1920. In any case, the Treasury would have had the use for one year of the tax on the $50,000 temporary inventory gain. Valuation of inventory for taxation on the basis of market, or of cost or market, whichever is higher, tends to hasten the liability to taxation on gains during rising prices. If, as in the case given, a rise in prices in one year is offset by a corresponding fall in the next year, valuation on the basis of market or of cost or market, whichever is higher, tends also to increase the total amount of tax paid in the two years, since taxable income is probably greater in the year of high prices. If the rise in prices continues, inventory valuation according to either of these two methods tends to advance the liability to pay taxes, but under progressive taxation it probably operates to lessen the total amount of tax paid over a period of years, for rising prices generally bring increasing monetary incomes. When incomes are rising and taxation is progressive, the sooner the tax is paid on any particular item of gain, the lower will be the tax rate thereon. During a period of rising prices or rising tax rates, or both combined, these methods of inventory valuation would tend over a number of years to reduce the tax yield to the government.

In Case A, if cost, or cost or market, whichever was lower, was used as the basis of valuing inventory, there would be no taxable gain in 1920, and no loss in 1921. If prices continued to rise in 1921, however, either of these methods of valuing inventory would postpone taxation until the gain was actually realized. During a period of rising prices, if the tax was progressive, and still more if the tax rates were increasing, these methods of inventory valuation, by postponing liability to taxation to the years in which the

---

5. The provision in the Revenue Act of 1921 (Sec. 204) which permits deduction of net loss in one year from net income of the next succeeding two years meets this problem in part, but only in part.

rates were higher, and the net incomes greater, would tend to increase the tax yield to the government.

CASE B

Inventory of Stock Purchased in 1920, as of December 31, 1920	Sale Price in 1921, after Deduction of Selling Expenses, etc.
Cost, $100,000 Market, $50,000	$100,000

In Case B, if inventory were taken in 1920 at cost, or at cost or market, whichever was higher, no loss would be deductible in 1920, and there would be no taxable gain in 1921. If inventory were taken at market, or at cost or market, whichever was lower, a loss of $50,000 would be deductible in 1920, and there would be a taxable gain of $50,000 in 1921. As has been sufficiently demonstrated in connection with Case A, it would be highly improbable that for taxation purposes the loss in one year would be exactly offset by the equivalent gain in another year. If prices, instead of recovering in 1921, continued to fall, business incomes probably would fall also. Inventory valuation on the basis of market, or cost or market, whichever was lower, would tend to hasten the admission of losses. It would thus permit the appropriate tax deductions to be made in the years of higher incomes, and, therefore, of higher taxation.

The British income tax, in general, permits inventory valuations to be made only on the basis of cost or market, whichever is lower.[6] American federal income taxation started out with an attempt to determine income without reference to inventories, proceeded to the cost basis, and finally, when lower price levels were threatened, permitted, in the interest of the taxpayers, the use of the cost or market, whichever is lower, basis. As has already been pointed out, this basis of inventory valuation under progressive taxation tends to reduce the revenue yield during a period of falling prices, and this tendency is further accentuated if the period of falling prices is also marked by reductions in the statutory tax rates. This tendency, it should be noted, is independent of and additional to the similar tendency resulting from the decline in money incomes. On logical grounds this method of inventory valuation is open to criticism from the Treasury point of view, inasmuch as under it inventory gains are reportable only when realized, whereas inventory losses are deductible as soon as they are reasonably certain to accrue. It

6. R. M. Haig, "The Taxation of Excess Profits in Great Britain," *American Economic Review Supplement*, Vol. X, No. 1 (March, 1920), p. 1.

is not practicable, however, to treat losses in any other manner. Many types of losses cannot be definitely proved to be such until long after they are written off the books, and this applies to inventory losses where the sale of the depreciated goods is indefinitely postponed in the absence of a market, or in the hope of a return of better times.

Depreciation. A depreciation reserve which conforms to the standard accounting practice of distributing the original cost of the property minus the ultimate salvage value over the useful life of the property will not be sufficient during a period of rising prices to provide for physical replacement unless replacement costs lag behind the upward trend of prices. Where accounting practice fails also to sanction the periodic re-appraisal of fixed assets during a period of rising prices so as to take account of appreciation, the maintenance of a depreciation reserve inadequate to take care of physical replacement, together with the failure to write up capital investment, will tend to give an exaggerated appearance of prosperity to the concern and will act as a stimulus either to increased distribution of earnings or to over-expansion of plant facilities.

	1915	1920
Capital	$100,000	$100,000
Net income before depreciation	15,000	30,000
Depreciation allowance	5,000	5,000
Net income after depreciation	10,000	25,000

In the foregoing illustration it is assumed that prices rose by 100 per cent between 1915 and 1920, that the fixed assets of the corporation remained unchanged physically except for full replacement of worn-out plant, and that whereas $5,000 was sufficient to provide for such physical replacement in 1915, $10,000 would be necessary in 1920. On the usual accounting basis the data in this illustration would indicate that the firm could distribute $25,000 as dividends in 1920 without encroachment on capital, as compared with $10,000 in 1915. In any case, under the usual income-tax law, the taxable income of the corporation would have to be reported as $25,000. After physical replacement, however, the money income in 1920 would be only $20,000, and in terms of real income there would have been no change from 1915. A fictitious profit to the amount of $5,000 would be taxed as income to the corporation and, if $25,000 was distributed as dividends, a distribution of capital assets to the amount of $5,000 would be taxed as income to the shareholder. There would be no offset when there was actual need of physical replacement at a money cost greater than the original cost and greater, therefore, than could be met from the depreciation reserve, since income-tax laws under such circumstances forbid a readjustment for taxation of earlier depreciation allowances proved in course of time to have been inadequate to provide for physical replacement. Such is specifically the case in the American federal income tax, where the Treasury regulations permit only of such deductions for depreciation as will suffice, with the salvage value, to provide at the end of the "useful life" of the property its original money cost and not its replacement cost.[7]

During a period of falling prices, if the cost of replacement of worn-out capital goods declines with the general price level, a depreciation allowance on the standard original-cost basis will enable the taxpayer to deduct each year from taxable income an amount greater than is necessary to replace his original physical investment. If the monetary income of the concern prior to depreciation falls *pari passu* with the fall in the general price level, the net monetary income after allowance for depreciation will fall more than proportionately with the fall in the price level, and the burden of taxation upon the concern will be lower, even under proportional taxation, in terms of purchasing power, although its real income remains the same. Allowance for depreciation on the original-cost basis tends, therefore, to increase the real burden of taxation during a period of rising prices and to decrease it during a period of falling prices.

War-Profits and Excess-Profits Taxes

Somewhat similar problems arise in connection with war-profits or excess-profits taxes, which use either pre-war income or invested capital as the basis for calculating taxable profits. In the case of the use of pre-war income as a basis for measurement of war-time excess income for purposes of war-profits taxation, if prices from the pre-war year to the given tax year in general rise by 100 per cent, the monetary income of a business representing the same physical investment as before the war should also increase by 100 per cent if the business is merely holding its own. Nevertheless, the British

7. U.S. Treasury Department, *Income Tax Regulations 62*, 1922 ed., Art. 161.

excess-profits tax and the American war-profits tax of March, 1917, both of which used pre-war profits as a basis of measurement, treated increases in monetary income resulting merely from the general rise in prices, and in many cases not fully compensating for the fall in the purchasing power of the monetary unit, as excess profits properly subject to special taxation over and above the general scheme of income taxation. An appearance of justice was given to such taxation by the accepted accounting practice of making no allowance for appreciation of capital assets and by the common impression that any war-time departure from this practice had for its only purpose the illegitimate evasion of legitimate taxation.

In the present American excess-profits tax, which bases the rates of the tax primarily on the percentage of earnings to invested capital, the various items included in invested capital must be valued at their cash value at the time at which they were acquired. Their valuation "is not to be based upon the present net worth of the assets, as shown by an appraisal or in any other manner."[8] If, between the time of acquisition by a firm of its capital assets and the year of taxation, prices in general have risen, and if the monetary earnings of the firm have kept pace with the rise in prices, these earnings will be a correspondingly increased percentage of invested capital at its original cash value, but they will not necessarily show any change in their percentage to actual net worth on a market basis. In other words, the law, in its assumption that the monetary unit has an unchanging significance for taxation and in its refusal to admit appreciation of capital assets for purposes of income or profits taxation, decrees a basis for measurement of percentage of profits to invested capital which, during a period of rising prices, exaggerates the true proportion which the former bears to the latter. On the other hand, during a period of falling prices the failure to require writing down of capital assets for purposes of taxation to adjust them to the increased value of the monetary unit operates to minimize the proportion which profits bear to the net worth of the invested capital, and thus to lessen the burden of the tax. Where the tax system includes both taxes on capital gains and excess-profits taxes, the taxation of capital gains upon an accrual instead of upon a realization basis would have the double merit that it would prevent the lumping of accumulated capital gains in a single year, and that

---

8. *Ibid.*, Art. 831.

by sanctioning the periodic reappraisal of capital assets it would offset, in part at least, the exaggeration of the ratio of earnings to invested capital during a period of rising prices.

Inheritance Taxes

In connection with inheritance taxes, which normally fall upon any particular estate or succession only at long intervals, if prices are changing and if the tax rates are progressive, the proportion of the estate going to the state will be different in one year from what it would have been in the next or the preceding year, even though the statutory rates remain the same. During a period of rising prices the state will be taking an increasing proportion of the estates, and the proportion going to the state will fall with a fall in the general price level. As in the case of progressive income taxation, the revenue productiveness of a progressive inheritance tax will vary with, but more sharply than, the variations in the general price level, and the steeper the progression the greater will be the accentuation of changes in revenue as prices change. A proportional inheritance tax will adjust itself closely, except in so far as exemptions are concerned, in its revenue yield and in its real burden on the beneficiaries of the inheritance, to the changes in the price level. If there is a residuary legatee, and if the tax law or the will provides that the tax shall be paid either out of the estate before distribution or by the residuary legatee, a rise in prices which is reflected in the money value of the estate will proportionately increase the absolute amount of tax on the residuary legatee if the tax is proportional and will more than proportionately increase the absolute amount of tax if it is progressive. On the other hand, if the will was made at a much earlier period and if the shares were defined in absolute and not in percentage terms, the rise in prices, as reflected in the value of the estate, will also increase the relative share of the residuary legatee in the estate.

Property Taxes

The operation of proportional property taxes should not be disturbed by changes in price levels if the taxes are levied on the basis of annual and not of capital values. Other things being equal, the annual value of property should correspond in its fluctuations with the changes in prices in general. Where, as in the United States, the capital value of property is the base for taxation, the effects of changing price levels on the severity of the tax and on its productiveness of revenue may be somewhat different. Aside from the fact that the change in values will probably be reflected in changing assessments only after some delay, the capital value of property will vary in exact proportion with the variation in its income yield and therefore, by assumption, with the changes in general price levels, only if capitalization of income yield is solely on the basis of current annual yield. As this is not the case, and as capital values probably lag considerably behind both upward and downward changes in income yields and in general price levels, the taxation of property on its capital value at a constant proportional rate during a period of changing prices should generally result in the proportion of the tax to the income from the property diminishing during a period of rising prices and rising during a period of falling prices. It should generally result, likewise, in a less than proportionate increase in the revenue to the government from the taxation of property at a constant percentage during a period of rising prices and in a less than proportionate decrease during a period of falling prices, as compared in each case with the variation in the general price level.

Capital Levies

So-called "capital levies" have been the subject of considerable discussion in Europe as means of reducing the burden of war indebtedness, and in a number of instances have been enacted into law. The proposals take two main forms: first, that a special non-recurrent tax be put upon new capital values created during the war period; and second, that such a tax be put upon the entire body of capital in the country.

The first form, that of a special tax on the war-time increase of wealth, is very much like the ordinary tax on capital gains, such as, for instance, under the American income-tax laws. It differs, however, from the latter in two respects. It is levied upon an appraisal basis as of a specified date, regardless of whether the capital gain had been, or could be, realized through sale, and it is a non-recurrent tax, assessed once for all in a specified year, although it may be payable in installments over a series of years. The bearing of price levels on such a tax is covered by the discussion of a general tax on capital gains. The only additional consideration which its special features suggest is that the presumptive severity of its rates and its restriction to a single year make all-important the status of the price level in that year. A capital levy of this sort with a given progressive schedule of rates would impose a burden of very different magnitude if it were levied on the basis of the increase in capital values from 1913 to 1919 as compared, say, with the increase from 1913 to 1922. On the other hand, since the tax is non-recurrent, any allowance made by the legislators for the influence of changing prices on capital values need also be made only once. Such allowance, logically, could take either of the following forms: (*a*) a deduction from the money values of the post-war capital corresponding to the decline from the pre-war period in the value of the monetary unit; (*b*) recognition, in the form of a lower schedule of rates than would otherwise be imposed, of the fact that some of the war-time increase in capital values was more apparent than real.[9]

The second form which proposals for a capital levy take, namely, that of a tax on the whole body of capital in the country, closely resembles a general property tax, except that the former is non-recurrent, and, in the usual proposals, is to be levied at severe and progressive rates. This form avoids the difficulty of a double appraisal, pre-war and post-war, of capital values. It does not give rise, therefore, to the problem of adjustment to changes in price levels. If it be objected that in the assessment year the capital values are inflated, and that these values will later fall, there is the obvious rejoinder, if the tax is payable in the year of assessment or shortly thereafter, that it will be paid in correspondingly depreciated money. If the tax is a severe one, however, payment in a single year would be a serious hardship to many taxpayers. The same

---

9. A progressive tax on the war-time increase of wealth was imposed in Italy in 1919-20. The British Board of Inland Revenue in 1920 vouched for the practicability of such a tax, and declared that the change in the value of the pound afforded "no justification for a general allowance in determining the amount of wealth subject to the proposed duty." ("Increase of Wealth [War]" [Cmd. 594] as reported in *Economic Journal*, June, 1920, p. 260.) The report is not available, and the grounds for this position are not known to the writer, but if in drawing up the schedule of rates the legislators bore in mind the influence on capital values of a fall in the value of the monetary unit, as is pointed out in the text no formal allowance would be necessary.

difficulty is present in connection with levies on war-time increases of wealth. To meet this problem, the advocates of such taxes often concede that the taxpayer should be granted the privilege of paying on the installment plan over a series of years, but with interest added.[10]

When the capital levy is payable in installments, a rise in the value of the monetary unit, such as is to be expected in the post-war period, will force the taxpayer to pay the tax in more valuable money than that in terms of which his capital was assessed. The law may permit compounding of the payments in the first year—the Italian laws do. This does not, however, fully meet the problem. Some types of wealth have a ready market and are easily divisible, so that their owners can dispose of enough of their holdings to pay the full tax at once. Other types of property, however, can be sold only with difficulty and at a great sacrifice, so that to their owners such recourse is scarcely open. This is particularly true of peasant proprietors, who cannot easily divide up their small estates, and who are extremely reluctant to dispose of them altogether, because they thus separate themselves from their only certain means of livelihood.[11]

In the Italian law, which permits the payment of both types of capital levy in installments spread over a long period, the problem is partially met for the general tax on wealth by a provision for the periodic revaluation of the wealth. This, however, raises another problem in its turn. Since the tax is progressive, and there is at least

---

10. The German Capital Levy Tax of December 31, 1919 (*Reichsnotopfer*) provides for the taxation, with minor exceptions, of all wealth on the basis of the assessed valuation as of December 31, 1919, at steeply progressive rates. There is no general privilege of postponement of payment, but in cases where serious hardship would result from the demand for full immediate payment, the tax administrators are permitted at their discretion to grant postponement. (Cf. *Quarterly Journal of Economics*, XXXIV [1920], 545 ff.) The Italian tax on the war-time increase in wealth permits of payment in installments spread over twenty years. The Italian law, in addition, imposes a tax of the second type, namely, a general tax on wealth, also levied at progressive rates, and payable in installments spread over thirty years. This tax provides, however, for revaluation of wealth at stated intervals during this thirty-year period, so that except for the fact that the reassessments are not annual, that the rates are progressive, and that there is a presumption, if not a pledge, that the rates will not be changed, it very closely resembles in its general features the American general property tax. (Cf. *Economic Journal*, XXIX [September 1920], 296 ff.)

11. This is, in essence, the basis of a criticism of the Italian laws made by C. Gini, "A Levy on Capital: Italian Law and Its Precedents," *Economic Journal*, XXIX (September 1920), 296 ff.

an implied pledge that the rates will not be changed, the severity of the tax and its productiveness to the government will diminish with each successive valuation, if the value of the lira rises. As the estates shrink in value in terms of lire, they will fall more and more below the grades subject to the high rates.

Land-Value Taxes

Changing price levels have an important bearing also on the single-tax program for the special taxation of land values. The single-taxer rarely makes proper allowance for the influence of rising prices on the value of improvements as well as on monetary land values. He consequently almost always underestimates the proportion of the total land value at the end of a period of rising prices—and therefore also of the annual land value—which is properly attributable to the improvements. If unimproved value of the land is measured by the total value minus the original cost of the improvements, all of the increase in the monetary value of the land which is due to rising prices is attributed to the unimproved part of the land. This can be justified only on the theory that improvements on—or in—the land are exempt, or for purposes of taxation should be assumed to be exempt, from the price tendencies affecting all other commodities. Granting the logic of the single-tax argument for the appropriation by the state of all the economic rent, for improved land the determination of economic rent should be based on a formula which takes cognizance of the effect of changing price levels on the monetary values of both site and the improvements thereon.

Similar problems arise in connection with the taxation of the future increment of land values. All such taxes, actual and proposed, define the taxable increment for a given piece of land as the increase in its price between some base-date and some future "occasion" for taxation. Many of the laws make no allowance for the influence on land prices of changing price levels. A rise in the price of land will not indicate "unearned increment" of the sort which such taxes are intended to reach if such rise is not in excess of the rise in the general price level. Moreover, during a period of falling prices there may be genuine unearned increment even though the price of the land falls, provided its fall is less than proportionate to the general decline in prices. A law taxing unearned increment of land values on the basis of comparisons with the prices of a basic date, even though the tax is only a fractional one, may take from the landlord much more than the total real increment during a period of rapidly rising prices and, even though the rate of the tax is a full 100 per cent, may permit unearned increment wholly to escape taxation during a period of falling prices. The imperial German increment value tax of 1911 permitted an addition of from ¾ to 2½ per cent per annum to be made to the purchase price of land from which increment is calculated to compensate the landowners for, among other things, a rise of value which may be in part due to a decrease in the purchasing power of money.[12] This arbitrary allowance is not a very scientific adjustment of taxation to the problem here under discussion, but it is at least an attempt in that direction. There is no provision of the law, however, which meets the problem of increments of value being concealed by a rise in the purchasing power of the mark.[13] It would be interesting to know whether this law has survived, without amendment to permit of fuller adjustment to changing price levels, the post-war period of depreciation in the value of the mark. The lack in this German tax of more elaborate provision for adjustment to changing price levels is made more serious by the fact that its rates are progressive, increasing with the increase of the percentage of increment to purchase price, and that the effects of changing price levels on the severity and the productiveness of the tax are thus accentuated.

The need which has been pointed out, in connection with taxes on land values, for caution lest there be attributed solely to the "economic" land an increase in value really due in part to the rise in the monetary value of the improvements applies also to the increment taxes which differentiate between economic land value and the value of improvements and aim to tax only the increase in the former. The New Zealand authorities appear to have worked out most carefully, in connection with the New Zealand tax of this

---

12. "...This whole provision is designed to meet objections urged against the strong retroactive feature of the law. During a period ranging from twenty-six up to a maximum of forty years the monetary standard of value can decline very materially in purchasing power. Relative to a higher general range of prices a large apparent increase in land values may be real only in part or even totally deceptive.... Hence the allowance of a small steady annual rate of interest upon purchase price and improvement costs."—R. C. Brooks, "The German Imperial Tax on the Unearned Increment," *Quarterly Journal of Economics*, XXV (August, 1911), 694-95.

13. This is pointed out by Brooks, *ibid.*

character, rules for the separate assessment of land value and improvement value, respectively, but their rules require that the improvements be valued at cost or market, whichever is lower.[14] In thus attributing all of the rise in the value of improved land to the bare land, the law intensifies the effect of the basic error of accepting as taxable value increment an increase in the price of land which is due to the fall in the value of the monetary unit.

Import Duties

It is only in connection with import duties that taxing authorities and writers on taxation have given much attention to the problems arising out of changes in price levels. Even here, however, the display of interest has been due more to the obvious influence exerted by changing prices on the manner in which import duties achieve their non-fiscal purposes than to their effects on the taxpayer or on the Treasury. Interest has centered particularly about the different manner of operation under changing prices of specific and ad valorem duties. As Gregory points out, "Specific duties do not respond, as *ad valorem* duties do, to changes in the price level. Whether prices rise or fall 20 per cent, the ratio of the duty to the price remains the same with *ad valorem* duties, but changes in the specific duties inversely to the price movement."[15] Gregory states that it is arguable that the specific duty yields a better result, because the ad valorem duty, which fluctuates in its absolute amount with fluctuations in the price of the imported commodity, increases the burden of the duty on the importer when the price burden has increased and decreases the duty burden when the price burden has decreased. But Gregory's entire discussion rests on the implied assumption that only the price of a particular commodity is changing, all other prices and all money incomes remaining the same, and he gives no consideration to the broader problem of the method of operation of specific and of ad valorem duties when *all* prices are changing. During changes in the general price level, an unaltered schedule of ad valorem duties adjusts itself automatically to the

14. "The amount at which improvements are to be valued is defined by the Act as the sum by which they increase the selling value of the land, *provided that the value must not exceed the cost*, although it may be below the cost if their condition warrants it."—A. C. Pigou, *Economics of Welfare* (London, 1920), p. 611. (Italics his.)

15. T. E. Gregory, *Tariffs, A Study in Method* (London, 1921), p. 120.

change in the price levels so as to maintain the same relative degree of severity on the taxpayer and to bring into the Treasury the same amount of purchasing power. Specific duties, on the other hand, become more severe on the taxpayer during a period of falling price levels and less severe during a period of rising price levels; their relative productiveness during periods of rising and of falling prices, respectively, in terms of purchasing power, will be uncertain and will depend on the elasticity of demand for the imported commodities and on the effects on domestic production of the changing severity of the rates on imports. During a period of rising prices, import duties intended to be protective will be more likely to accomplish their purpose of hindering foreign competition if they are ad valorem than if they are specific; specific duties will require constant revision if they are to exert the same measure of protective influence. The French government has endeavored to maintain its system of specific import duties through a period of rapidly rising prices and, at the same time, to maintain its productiveness in terms of purchasing power and its protective effect, not by repeated legislative revision of the rates, which would have been a source of great inconvenience, but by establishing an administrative commission with the power to multiply the specific rates in the statutory tariff by "value coefficients" corresponding to the changes in price of the particular groups of commodities. This is not, at least from the administrative side, a virtual substitution of the ad valorem for the specific method. The valuation is done only at intermittent intervals, and for classes or groups of commodities. Actual imports need only to be classified and need not be valued.

Where tariff rates are a combination of specific and ad valorem duties or are otherwise more complex than the simple specific or ad valorem duty, the effect of changing price levels on their method of operation is also more complex. Only one such type of rate will be given here as illustrative of the general character of the problems which arise. The classification of commodities for purposes of customs taxation at specific rates is sometimes made on the basis of their prices. For example, in the American tariff, sugar candy and confectionery not specially provided for are dutiable, if valued at fifteen cents per pound or less, at two cents per pound; if valued at more than fifteen cents per pound, at 25 per cent ad valorem.[16] If it be assumed that the fixing of the dividing line between the two

16. Tariff Act of October 3, 1913, No. 180.

classes at fifteen cents per pound was at the time of the enactment
of the tariff law not wholly arbitrary, but conformed to some logical plan, this point becomes too high if prices fall, and too low
if prices rise.[17]

Excise Taxes

Excise taxation is affected by changes in price levels in fundamentally the same manner as import duties. Because the main
purpose of excise taxes is a fiscal one, the effect thereon of changing
prices has not, however, been given the same amount of attention.
Ad valorem taxes will respond in their revenue yield to changes in
price levels, and the real burden on the taxpayer will not be affected
by changes in the prices of the taxed commodities which correspond
to changes in the general price level. Specific taxes, on the other
hand, will become more severe in their burden as prices fall, and
lighter as prices rise. The effect of changing prices on the revenue
productivity of specific taxes will depend on the elasticity of demand
for the taxed commodities. It being assumed that the price changes
in the taxed commodities conform exactly, except for the tax element in price, to changes in the general level of prices, a rise in
prices will cause a relative fall in the burden of taxation and will
tend, therefore, to stimulate consumption of the taxed articles.
Conversely a fall in prices will tend to check their consumption.
The monetary yield of specific excise taxes will tend to vary in
partial correspondence with changes in the price level, rising when
prices rise and falling when prices fall, but, in each case, unless the
demand for the taxed commodities is highly elastic and the tax
very severe, the variation in monetary yield will tend to be less
than proportionate to the change in prices. If, as is generally the
case, the commodities taxed have very inelastic demands, the modifications in the severity of specific taxes resulting from changes in
price levels will have but slight effect on the consumption of the
taxed commodities and therefore on the monetary yield of the taxes.
Where an attempt is made to introduce progression into ad
valorem excise taxation by grading the taxed commodities according
to price and imposing higher ad valorem rates on the higher-priced

---

17. Unless, of course, it is intended to conform with some other part of the
tax law. The specific duty of two cents on sugar candy under fifteen cents per
pound may be intended to prevent sugar from entering the United States in
the form of candy at a lower rate than it would be subject to as sugar.

grades, falling prices will tend to counteract the effect of the grading, and rising prices will tend to accentuate it. Where an attempt is made, as in the American excise on tobacco, to modify the regressive character of specific excise taxes by grading the taxed commodities according to price and imposing higher specific duties on the more expensive grades, falling prices will likewise tend to counteract the effect of the grading, and rising prices to accentuate it. A so-called luxury tax which is imposed only on commodities which exceed specified prices will be somewhat similarly affected by changes in the price level. Rising prices will tend to broaden the incidence of the tax, and falling prices to restrict it, for if prices are rising, an increasing proportion, and if prices are falling, a decreasing proportion, of the range of commodities will be found above the basic prices selected as marking the border line between luxury and non-luxury, or taxable and non-taxable, commodities.

The Effects on Taxation of Changes in Interest Levels

In connection with taxes which rest on the assessment of capital values, such as property taxes, taxes of capital gains, inheritance taxes, and land-value taxes, changing interest levels give rise to problems closely resembling those resulting from changes in general price levels. Invested capital will tend to vary in price in inverse proportion to variations in the current rate of interest. A fall in the current rate of interest will result in an increase in the value of such property without increasing the taxpaying ability, on an income basis, of the owners thereof. An increase in the value of property, due to a fall in interest rates, will make the owners subject to increased capital gain and general property taxation, without increasing the flow of income out of which the tax must generally be met. In the same way, the value of an estate will be returnable at a higher figure when the interest rate is low than when it is high, and the amount of inheritance tax payable thereon will vary accordingly, although there will not be a corresponding variation in the income which the legatee will derive from the estate. Conversely, a rise in the current rate of interest will tend to bring about a fall in the value of invested capital, and to reduce the amount of tax payable under taxation resting on capital values, although the income yield of such capital will not be affected thereby.

This tendency of capital goods to vary in value in inverse proportion to variations in the interest rate is of special significance in connection with the taxation of the increment in land values. A fall in the current rate of interest will operate to increase the value of land without increasing the ability of the landowner to pay taxes from the income derived from the land. A subsequent recovery in interest rates will tend to wipe out the increase in value of his land, perhaps after a substantial part of that increase had already been appropriated by the state. On the other hand, a rise in the interest rate will tend to reduce the capital value of land, without reducing the annual income which its owner derives therefrom. These considerations suggest the desirability that attempts to reach unearned increment of land be directed rather to taxation of the increase in rent yields than of the increase in capital values, but with special provision for the taxation of idle land.[18]

Conclusion

This discussion has, with a few minor exceptions, assumed throughout that when the price level changes all prices change in the same proportion. If provisions of general application were introduced into tax laws in order to permit of adjustment to changes in the value of the monetary unit, such provisions would undoubtedly meet only partially, if at all, the problems presented by individual cases of variation from the general price trend. If it could be demonstrated with reasonable certainty that there are always normal well-defined tendencies for certain sectional price levels to move counter to, or only in partial sympathy with, the general trend of prices, it might be necessary to take account of such tendencies in any attempt to adjust taxation to changing prices.

It may be objected that injustices to taxpayers in the application of tax laws resulting from failure to make proper allowances for changes in value of the monetary unit tend, in the long run, to be offset by unintended generosity to them when the price trend reverses itself. It has been sufficiently demonstrated in the foregoing argument, however, that there is in many cases no probability that a reversal in the trend of prices will fully repay either the Treasury or the taxpayers, as the case may be, for the unreasonable losses incurred when prices had been moving in the other direction. Moreover, men may die, or may go out of business, or the basis for taxation

---

18. Cf. F. W. Taussig, *Principles of Economics,* II (1912), 103, 4.

may change, before the scales of justice which had been unduly tipped in one direction acquire a compensatory bias in the other. Reversals in the trend of the price level are not necessarily, or, if only substantial price changes are considered, are not even usually, matters of a few years. The "long run" may be a very long run, too long to permit of substantial compensation being made to the same individuals who have suffered an original injustice, or of additional demands for taxation being made upon those who had in an earlier period unreasonably escaped therefrom. In any case, even though this were a decisive objection to any plan for adjusting the taxation system to the conditions resulting from changing price levels, it would not be an adequate explanation of the absence of such plans in the past. For to the legislator, as to the average taxpayer and to the main body of accounting practice, a dollar is always a dollar, regardless of its purchasing power. There has not been in the past any general recognition of the existence of such problems in taxation as have been discussed above.

The writer has concerned himself mainly with an attempt to define the problems and has not felt any obligation to devise solutions therefor. In the course of the discussion, however, some suggestions were made which might, perhaps, be capable of practical application. Any comprehensive attempt to prevent changes in price levels from affecting the tax system in such a manner as to impose illogical and undesirable burdens on either the taxpayer or the Treasury must, in its general lines, follow one or another of three possible administrative methods. First, the rates in the tax law could be periodically revised, so as to keep them in proximate adjustment with the trend of price levels. Second, there could be embodied in the texts of the laws provisions intended to make automatic allowance for the effects both of rising and of falling prices. Such provisions might, perhaps, provide for the use of price index numbers in the assessment of taxes. Third, a considerable measure of discretion could be given to the officials intrusted with the administration of the taxes, with power to make proper adjustments, whether in defense of the legitimate interests of the Treasury or of the taxpayer, for the effects of changing price levels. Decision between these alternative methods can well await further analysis of the nature of the problem and of the possible devices for meeting it.

Perfect and complete adjustment of taxation to changing price levels is, it must be confessed, an unattainable ideal. It may even be true that any attempt to bring about even a partial though substantial degree of adjustment would meet with insuperable administrative difficulties. The task would unquestionably be far from simple.[19] But new tax proposals have almost always to meet the anticipatory objection that they are beyond the administrative powers of the government.[20] Our leading authorities on taxation appear at the moment to be in almost unanimous agreement that a comprehensive sales tax would involve the government in insuperable difficulties of administration. But in Canada such a tax, under conditions much more unfavorable than those existing in the United States, has been working smoothly from its very inception. There applies to special provisions in tax legislation such as are suggested above, what Sir Josiah Stamp, from his ripe experience as a tax administrator, says of taxes in general:

> It will be found generally that if a tax is believed to be practicable over a considerable part of the field to which it is to be applied, and the impracticability is confined to a minor part, most States will embark upon the scheme, and by a sacrifice of logical principle at the point of difficulty and the adoption of a few conventions, will satisfy the equities roughly.[21]

Even though there be accepted the conclusions of this paper to the effect that the absence in tax legislation of provisions for adjusting taxes to the changing conditions resulting from changing price levels is a source of serious inequities, it must be admitted that there is a strong presumption against adding further to the intricacies and complexities of taxation. In any case, it may be asked, why treat

---

19. Cf. R. M. Haig, "The Concept of Income," in *The Federal Income Tax*, p. 17: "If it were possible to modify the concept of taxable income so as to eliminate this variation [in the value of money] it would certainly be desirable to do so. The prospect for a complete solution of the difficulty pointed out, however, is identical with the prospect for a perfect monetary standard. But an approximate solution might be realized if we were able to evolve a satisfactory index of the level of prices. If it were accurately known what the change in price level in a given year had been, it might be possible to qualify the results shown by a comparison of the balance sheets for the beginning and the end of the period in such a way as to eliminate the influence of the changing standard. But even this refinement is not likely to be introduced soon. Indeed, the desirability and urgency of its introduction is dependent largely upon the complete solution of the accounting problem, which solution is certainly not imminent."

20. "The first argument that is brought against every new proposal departing from conventional lines is nearly always that it is 'impracticable.'"—Sir Josiah Stamp, *The Fundamental Principles of Taxation* (London, 1921), p. 95.

21. *Ibid.*, p. 96.

symptoms instead of causes? If changing price levels prevent ordinary tax laws from working well, why is this not rather an added argument for the search for means of stabilizing prices, instead of an argument supporting further elaboration of tax laws? The answer to this question turns, of course, upon the relative difficulty of stabilizing price levels as compared with adjusting tax laws. Until the development and installation of some scheme for the stabilization of prices is more of a practical possibility than it appears to be at the present, the possibility of adjusting taxation to changing price levels, even at the cost of further complication in tax laws, is at least deserving of more consideration than it has yet received.

Objective Tests of Competitive Price Applied to the Cement Industry*

IN THE LITERATURE on the trust problem, and especially in the studies made by the Federal Trade Commission of various large-scale industries, there frequently recur attempts to determine the existence or the absence of monopoly control by objective study of the behavior of the prices of the products of the particular industries under investigation. Little, if anything, has hitherto been done, however, to develop a systematic and comprehensive formulation of the normal behavior of a truly competitive price structure and to list and analyze the price manifestations which are presumptive of the existence of monopoly control. A recent study by Professors H. Parker Willis and John R. B. Byers,[1] although it was undertaken on behalf of a group of cement producers and has for its object the demonstration that cement prices are competitive, nevertheless makes a significant contribution to the important task of establishing sound generalizations with respect to the normal behavior of competitive prices. The question as to whether or not the cement industry is competitive is of no special concern to the writer of this note, and the following examination of the tests applied by the authors and of the conclusions they derive therefrom is motivated solely by an interest in the theoretical questions raised by their technique and in its general serviceability.

The authors show that Portland cement prices had risen 75 per cent above the 1913 level by December, 1923, as compared to an average rise of 78 per cent in the prices of all building materials during the same period. According to the authors, the price of cement thus meets the test of competitive price, that its upward

---

*Reprinted from *The Journal of Political Economy*, Vol. 33, February 1925, pp. 107-111, by the courtesy of the University of Chicago Press.

1. *Portland Cement Prices: Their Basis, Character and Present Position.* New York: The Ronald Press Company, 1924.

movement should not be much, if at all, in excess of the upward movement of other related commodities. This test is obviously difficult to apply with certainty, since differences in the trends of prices of different commodities may be due to a host of special factors other than differences in the degree of monopoly control. Let it be conceded to the authors that, in the absence of knowledge of the mode of operation of special factors other than the one under particular investigation, it must be assumed that all commodities were influenced in like degree by these special factors. The value of this test in this particular instance is nevertheless very nearly zero in the absence of any demonstration that cement prices were not already monopolistic in 1913 and in the absence on the part of the authors of any attempt to convince their skeptically minded readers that other building materials are good examples of highly competitive commodities. The only conviction that this test brings is that since 1913 the producers of cement have not been more extortionate than the producers of other building materials, and even here the evidence presented allows room for mental reservations.

The authors show, also, that many basic materials other than building materials rose in price from 1913 to 1923 to a greater degree than did cement. While there may well be ground for questioning the competitive character of most of the commodities listed whose prices underwent a greater increase than did the price of cement, the main flaws in this test are the ones already referred to, namely, the absence of any evidence showing: (a) that no special factors were operating in the cement industry which, in the absence of monopoly control, would tend to make cement prices rise less rapidly than the general price level, and (b) that in the base year, 1913, used for comparison of relative increase in prices the price of cement was not already monopolistic. It might even be further objected that the authors' assumption that monopoly control necessarily means a relatively high price and that moderation of price is proof of price competition is unwarranted on a priori grounds.

According to the authors, the data they present show that changes in cement prices occur with somewhat the same frequency as do changes in the prices of other standardized commodities, thus meeting the test of competitive prices that they are quickly responsive to changes in market conditions. This is a good test, perhaps the best single test, of the competitive character of prices. If there is keen price competition, there must necessarily be an almost continuous fluctuation in prices in response to the buying and selling activities of competing operators, as their judgments of the relation of supply to demand change in accordance with the constant stream of new information. But the price statistics presented by the authors fail to support adequately their inference therefrom. New York is by far the most important cement market in the United States. From January, 1913, to December, 1914, inclusive (24 months), the New York price of cement remained at the same level of $1.58 per barrel; from December, 1915, to October, 1916, inclusive (11 months), at $1.67; from April, 1917, to December, 1917, inclusive (9 months), at $2.12; from April, 1919, to April, 1920, inclusive (13 months), at $2.65; from November, 1922, to November, 1923, inclusive (13 months), at $2.70. If it be remembered that these were periods of extraordinarily sharp and substantial fluctuations in the general price level, these data point to manipulated stability rather than to competitive flexibility of cement prices.

The comparisons of the flexibility of cement prices with the flexibility of the prices of other commodities are equally inconclusive in supporting the authors' inference. The detailed data are presented in the mass, without any attempt at a mathematical test of comparative flexibility. The commodities chosen for comparison, moreover, are common brick, wire nails, pig iron, and—save the mark!—gasoline and petroleum! If a real test was sought, why were not unquestionably competitive articles taken instead of articles which are themselves suspect?

The authors claim that in the delivered prices of cement throughout the United States there is as much variation between different parts of the country as for other standardized commodities, and that there is a distinct tendency toward uniformity of prices among mills in a given locality for orders to be delivered in the same locality. Bulky commodities are likely to vary in price in different localities, especially if production is concentrated in a few localities, whether the industry is competitive or under more or less complete monopoly control. But if the industry is actively competitive, there will be a close relationship between the local variations in prices and the local variations in freight costs from the important producing points.[2] The authors make no attempt, as far as I can see, to demon-

2. Cf. L. B. Zapoleon, *Geography of Wheat Prices*, Washington, D. C.: United States Department of Agriculture, Bulletin No. 594, February, 1918.

strate the existence of a close relationship between the local differences in cement prices and the variations in freight costs from the important cement-producing centers. Nor do they present data of a character to demonstrate, except by implication, the uniformity of prices among mills in the same locality for cement to be delivered in the same locality. Since, however, a substantial degree of such uniformity may be expected for any standardized commodity whether it is competitive or under monopoly control, its existence may be taken for granted without strengthening, and without weakening, the authors' case. Absolute and complete price uniformity of any sort is, in fact, more a characteristic of monopoly than of competitive price.

There is, however, a further and important test of competitive price which the authors do not employ, and which, according to the evidence presented in this book, the cement industry fails to meet. For standardized commodities subject to keen competition, the f.o.b. mill price would be uniform as to all buyers from mills in a given location, regardless of the location of the buyers. The continued existence of differentials in f.o.b. mill prices to purchasers according to the location of the purchaser could be consistent with the absence of any agreement or understanding between producers only if the producers were all scattered geographically, so that each producer was protected in his own immediate vicinity by the cost of transportation thereto from the nearest other producer. But the spot map of the cement industry presented by the authors shows that the industry is substantially concentrated in a few localities. Competing mills in the same locality cannot maintain different mill prices for different groups of purchasers (aside from quantity discounts). Under free competition each mill will try to obtain the full-price orders to the maximum of its producing capacity, and with the struggle to obtain the full-price orders and the reluctance to accept the cut-price orders there will be an inevitable tendency toward an equalization of mill prices to all purchasers. This is, of course, the domestic counterpart of the problem of dumping in foreign trade. It is as true of domestic as of foreign trade that systematic regional price discrimination is inconceivable under free and active competition. The presence of such systematic regional price discrimination in the steel industry under the operation of the Pittsburgh-plus practice is the essential item in the finding of the

Federal Trade Commission to the effect that Pittsburgh-plus is a practice inconsistent with the existence of normal competitive conditions.

The authors present evidence to the effect that mills quote varying f.o.b. mill prices to purchasers according to their distance from the mill. They interpret this evidence as confirming the prevalence of price competition in the cement industry, on the ground that the local price-cutting is done to meet the competition of other mills not so distant from the purchasers and therefore having the advantage of lower freight costs. The distant mill, they argue, must "absorb" a part of the freight cost if it is to share in the business. But if the national market for a commodity were divided by agreement or tacit understanding among the producers in such a way that each producer or local group of producers were permitted to monopolize the market in its immediate vicinity at a fixed price and in addition to operate in certain neutral territory, the geographical range of prices would be about as described by the authors for the cement industry. There would be competition in the neutral territories, but monopoly in the restricted zones, and the existence of such local monopoly would be manifested by higher f.o.b. mill prices to purchasers in the restricted area than to purchasers in the neutral area. The practice of charging different f.o.b. mill prices according to the location of the purchaser, if it is common in the cement industry, is evidence that competition does not fully prevail in that industry.

The authors have, with the one exception noted, formulated and developed more fully than has previously been done the important objective price tests of the existence of competition. The writer is convinced, however, that their application of these tests to the cement industry, instead of demonstrating the prevalence of competition, establishes a strong presumption that price competition, at least in the neighborhood of the important producing regions, is totally or virtually non-existent.

The Present Status and Future Prospects of Quantitative Economics (Discussion)*

ECONOMISTS HAVE NOT ordinarily appeared at their best when engaging in methodological discussion. Writers who in the ordinary course of events were mild, tolerant, catholic in their own practice, in a word "sensible," were in their methodological preaching exceedingly prone to be dogmatic, bigoted, exclusivist. If they were defenders of old techniques, they saw insuperable difficulties blocking the path to the successful employment of the new, and proved their point by challenging the new techniques to perform impossible tasks. If they were exponents of new techniques, their brief for the new often reduced itself, under careful scrutiny, to unsupported ex cathedra pronouncements to the effect that their particular technique was the only sound one; that the old techniques were obsolete; and that in the calculable future the new techniques would completely win the day.

As I read it, the history of method in economics shows that power of economic analysis and equipment of analytical tools grow only by painfully slow accretions of knowledge and technique; that never has there been a time in which a generation has made such vast strides that it could afford to discard or even to neglect the achievements of the preceding generations; that economics has never been demonstrably aided by methodological discussion, except when it was a phase of actual experimentation with method in connection with some actual and specific problem; that methodological enthusiasms, by distorting and throwing out of balance the curriculum of training for young economists, and by diverting the energies of able men from actual productive work to the drawing up of magnificent programs and manifestos, have done much harm

*Reprinted from *The American Economic Review, Supplement*, Vol. 18, March 1928, pp. 30-36, by the courtesy of the American Economic Association.

to economics by promoting methodological fanaticism; that san-
guine prophesying as to the sole method which will prevail in the
incalculable future has always failed to bring enduring comfort
to the prophet or even to the most devoutly credulous of his
disciples. To the extensive discussion of method in economic theory
conducted in recent years by American exponents of new methods,
including the quantitative method, much of the preceding criticism
seems to me to be applicable in a peculiarly high degree.

It seems to be true, as we are told so often by the exponents
of the quantitative method in economics, and as we could not have
well avoided knowing even if they had not spoken on the subject,
that in the physical sciences progress has consisted in the discovery
of quantitative differences underlying what first appeared to be
solely differences in kind, in the development of techniques for the
more or less accurate measurement of variations in these quantities,
and in the discovery of mutual dependencies between different
sets of these variations. But the varied character of its subject matter
and the wide range of diverse problems with which it deals make
of economics an ill-ordered and sprawling discipline, concerning
itself in one direction with metaphysical, ethical, and introspective
psychological issues, in another direction with mass behavior in
relation to price phenomena, and in still other directions with
problems of agricultural chemistry, of industrial technology, and
of the art of getting rich quick. Under the circumstances methodological analogies from physics should not be applied to economics
as a whole without the most serious qualifications and reservations.
In one direction at least the path of progress in economics will
approximate the direction which the physical sciences have taken.
No one, I believe, would question this. But there will always be, at
least in the calculable future, a metaphysical penumbra to the most
concrete of economic problems which will resist tenaciously exploration by the methods of the physical scientist. And for some time
into the future there will be problems of interest to the economist
which will be elusive of the application of the techniques of precise
measurement and which will have to be dealt with by methods of
inquiry which in the dogmatics of the laboratory scientist have lost
their respectability. It is true, however, even of the physical
sciences, or at least so I gather from the recent writings of the more
articulate physicists, that they are losing some of their late Nineteenth Century preference for naive as against sophisticated meta-

physics, and also that until they have devised quantitative methods of dealing with problems they proceed brazenly by means of inferior methods without much apparent injury to their self-esteem.

If the term "quantitative" be used, as it has often been used by economists, in its common sense or non-technical meaning as applying to analysis in terms of incipient measurement, in terms of "more or less" relationships, as well as to analysis in terms of arithmetically measured factors, most of the old deductive economics was, of course, quantitative. But it is the statisticians who have been the fanatic advocates of exclusively quantitative economics, and though they are rarely explicit, it would seem likely that they wish to employ the term in its strict technical sense of precisely measured quantities.

In this sense the traditional economics was rarely, if ever, quantitative. Its propositions were stated in terms of more or less, of increase or decrease, and not in terms of how much more or how much less. The adequately cautious neoclassical economist never laid claim to the possession of sufficient information about his curves to enable him to fit equations to them. The systematic development of supplies of factual information will undoubtedly promote the application of quantitative methods in economic analysis. In the absence of the possibility of crucial experiments except perhaps at the periphery of economics where it makes contact with agricultural chemistry, with technology, or with individual psychology, the quantitative method will undoubtedly be statistical in form, and if quantitative analysis ever produces any quantitative economic laws they will most typically be laws in statistical form summarizing the observed mass behavior of mankind in the world of price phenomena. This sounds like an important concession to the possibilities of quantitative analysis in economics, and it is so intended. But I would also make important reservations. I have already hazarded to predict that for many years at least there would be much within the traditional range of economic inquiry which will wholly resist quantitative inquiry, and that it will also be many years before economists discover how to apply quantitative analysis to a wide range of problems which do not seem by their inherent nature to be ill-adapted to such analysis. Moreover, in the absence of the capacity for actual isolation of those factors whose modes of operation are the particular objects of inquiry, this technique of statistical analysis will always have to lean heavily on the theory of probabilities. It will never produce in fact, though it may in appearance and in the belief of its practitioners, precise categorical solutions. Economic phenomena are always the product of a host of factors and should therefore apparently provide a fertile field for the application of probability theory. But though many forces combine to produce an economic phenomenon, frequently, if not generally, a comparatively few factors are dominant in the situation, and these change so rapidly and as yet so unpredictably in their intensity and their relative importance that the deductive application to a given situation of knowledge as to the usual operation of a few of these dominant forces will often render more service than the most subtle elaboration of probability theory if unguided by the possession of such knowledge.

Some exponents of what they call quantitative economics appear to identify the accumulation of statistics with quantitative analysis, and to assume that such things as the measurement of the national income, and of its distribution by class or by geographical area, or the compilation of index numbers of prices or of trade, are the stuff of which the quantitative economics of the near future is mainly to consist. There is an important distinction between statistical enumeration, classification, compilation, on the one hand, and economic analysis on the other. Economic theory and political arithmetic are not the same thing any more than barometric readings and meteorology are the same thing. As a layman I venture to suggest that a good grasp of economic theory would make of the political arithmetician a better craftsman, and I feel certain that economic data in statistical form will prove invaluable to the economic theorist of the near future. But that there should be a close alliance between the two is not sufficient reason for identifying the two or for absorbing the one in the other. The search for mutual dependencies, for covariations, in economic phenomena, is the sole task of economic theory, and index numbers, estimates of national income, and so forth, no matter how much genius and theory may have gone into their attainment, once achieved are by themselves merely edifying facts and serve no imaginable purpose except as the theorist uses them as means to the discovery of relationships between things or the statesman or business administrator finds therein evidence of things that require to be done if he is to attain his ends.

There is a type of what is properly enough quantitative analysis which in economics I feel convinced is not likely to be productive of acceptable results; namely, the merely mechanical search for mutual dependencies among data selected almost at random. Several years ago there was a sudden wave of enthusiasm among American pedagogues for the Pearsonian coefficient of correlation, and a plague of graduate students in education spread itself over the land and began correlating furiously and indiscriminately and with an inverse correlation between zeal and discretion which seems closely to have approached, if not quite to have attained, perfection. As might have been anticipated in a world full of nonsense correlations, the results were grotesque and brought about a quick reaction. There are ominous signs, however, that economics is becoming similarly infected. I am completely skeptical as to the value of any purely empirical results of statistical analysis in economics, especially when by the mechanical application of statistical devices laws of striking simplicity and of fundamental importance are discovered to be ruling the economic universe. Where the mind unaided by statistical analysis sees complexity everywhere, and statistical analysis unaided by the mind finds beautiful simplicity, I am reactionary enough to place my faith in the intelligence of my predecessors. I do not believe that there are many economic time series which forecast their own future trend with sufficient accuracy to be much superior to the random guess as to future trends. That there is a law of the growth of population, which can be expressed in a simple algebraic equation; that there is a law of the growth of capital, namely, that it grows at the rate of 3 per cent a year; that normal price bears such a relationship to cost of production that on the average price will equal or exceed the cost of production of 88.7 per cent of the output and will yield 12 per cent per annum net revenue to the capital invested; that the business cycle has a normal duration of thirty-seven months; that there is a fixed law governing the distribution of income which can be stated in arithmetical terms or shown graphically; such propositions, except as they are presented merely as approximately accurate statements of what has on the average occurred in the particular instances surveyed, seem to me to be purely fantastic. Even upon the assumption that with the improvement in its technique and the accumulation of data economics can attain the same degree of exactitude as the physical sciences, I can see no reason why we should anticipate even the future attainment of laws of this type, for I see little resemblance

between such "laws" as the above, which deal with the joint unanalyzed products of a complexity of unanalyzed forces, and the laws
of the physical sciences which rest on carefully dissected and
abstracted factors in controlled situations and leave nothing in the
situation unaccounted for unless the residual unanalyzed elements
appear to be relatively insignificant in their importance. In so far
as statistical analysis can bring us nearer to the physical sciences in
our approach to precision and measurement, it will not be through
such modes of analysis as have produced the aforementioned "laws,"
but through an approximation, by means of statistical abstraction
of factors, to the actual abstraction which the physical scientist performs in his laboratory or in his range of data sometimes finds
adequately existent in the world of crude uncontrolled data. It
seems to me that even at its best quantitative analysis in economics
will produce quantitative results only as history, not as a basis for
quantitative prediction; and whether as history or as basis for
prediction there will be no specific importance to the precise degree
of relationships discovered by such analysis, a correlation for
instance of 0.6 and 0.9 for most purposes serving equally well as
guidance to future action and as an aid to the understanding of
past events. I even find some difficulty in thinking of economic
problems in which qualitative results, assuming their adequate
plausibility, would not serve any conceivable purpose of understanding and action as well as precise quantitative results. Statisticians
have given us as illustrations of the importance of quantitative
results in economics problems of technology, of engineering, in
which value considerations were not dealt with, or else problems
of war administration where economic considerations were regarded
as negligible.

It is not at all my intention, however, to depreciate the real
potentialities of quantitative methods in economics. What concerns
me is lest in their enthusiasm for new methods the statisticians
unduly minimize the value of old methods, and hamper themselves
in their own work by placing excessive reliance upon the capacities
of too restricted a set of tools. There is no longer any need, in
American economic circles at least, of preaching the quantitative
faith. There is need of urging upon its devotees a more tolerant
attitude toward the merits and possibilities of the older methods.

Rhetorically, at least, statisticians have been relegating to the
junk pile not only the old methods, but also the old problems which

had been attacked by those methods. We have been told that the economist of the early future will not be interested in the questions for which the older economists sought answers, but will concern himself with new problems and with only such problems as can be investigated by the new quantitative techniques. We have also been told that for some time into the future the new economists, who will of course be quantitative economists, will be content to make detailed investigations narrowly confined in their range and to build up a mass of information as to the empirically-discovered relationships within narrow ranges of concrete phenomena. These are almost precisely identical, in their relation to what has gone before in economic inquiry, to the prophecies of the German historical school some sixty years ago, and it is this resemblance alone which causes me concern. To a very substantial degree the German prophecies were fulfilled in so far as German economics was concerned, and German economics is now obviously struggling to repair the resultant damage, and by regaining command of the technique of analysis, whether in its predominantly neoclassical, its mathematical, or its quantitative variants, to regain the exalted position which it occupied before the historical school won its costly and temporary victory. Without some capacity to fit isolated phenomena into some general system, there can be no sense of proportion, no guide as to the significance and the proper interpretation of the empirically-discovered relationships between small groups of detailed phenomena, no working dominance over the wilderness of single instances which the economic world must seem to be to the economist who does not believe in general theory, no effective machinery for that creation of new hypotheses which, I would think, even the most empirically-minded of statisticians would find essential as a stimulus to really creative quantitative work. Nor can I see any more wisdom in the relegation of the old problems to the antiquarian. As time passes, changing interests and circumstances do render some older problems obsolescent and do bring forward novel problems. But I see no evidence of any revolutionary change in this connection, and I do see much evidence, for example, that many economists are wisely seeking in the English literature of the first two decades of the Nineteenth Century for light on the post-war problems of the present time. One list of the "new" problems which I have seen happens to include just that range of problems with which the older economics of a century ago especially concerned itself.

To me the most hopeful prospect in American economics is the extent to which economists possessed of both the capacity and sympathy for theoretical analysis of the old-fashioned kind, on the one hand, and of a good command of the tools of statistical analysis, on the other, are applying both techniques in happy harmony to the investigation of important phases of the economic process. So far, I am afraid, they have raised more questions than they have answered, but this, I suppose, is what is to be expected at this stage of their work, and in economic theory the asking of important questions is itself an important contribution. In so far as the old theory is concerned, the new quantitative work has suggested refinements and corrections, but its contribution has so far been most modest in its proportions, and I have not encountered any products of statistical inquiry which need make any eighty-year-old economist who was really a good economist of the old type feel that he has wasted his life. It is not in the slightest my object to dissuade any economist from pursuing quantitative methods, and I am fully convinced that the time is very soon coming, if it has not already arrived, when those of us who have not got a fairly good command of statistical methods will not feel respectable.

In the calculable future the day may arrive when theoretical inquiry of the old non-statistical form, with its inferences from unsystematic and inexpert observation, and its deductions from old and inadequately verified generalizations, will be in the main an instrument for the construction of hypotheses, and statistical analysis will be relied upon to give them the stamp of credibility. But it will not be the political arithmeticians, or the empirical statisticians who seem to think that the economic problems of the future will be solved out of a handbook of empirical formulae, who will render this service.

I do not think that the old economics was excessively general in its pursuit of wide generalizations, and I believe that even when all economists have also become statisticians those of them who are philosophically minded will still endeavor to build up all-embracing systems. Even today American statisticians are in fact finding the neoclassical economics not general enough, and are accepting the criticism of the Lausanne school that it deals simultaneously with the variations in too few factors to give an adequate bird's-eye picture of the general system of economic interrelationships as a whole. The wider and more comprehensive generalizations of the continental mathematical school, on the other hand, make necessary such extreme abstraction that they have admittedly not been capable of application to concrete phenomena or of verification by observation even to the degree to which the neoclassical economics has already realized these possibilities. The great achievement of the future in general economic theory, and one which American statistical economists who are also masters of the old techniques seem to me most likely to attain, will be by lessening the generality of the mathematical economics and widening that of the neoclassical economics to bring these into a harmony of such a character as to make the new product susceptible in some degree of statistical verification and of concrete applications. It is an achievement which without statistical analysis could not be made, but which without the old non-statistical techniques and accomplishments could not even be dreamed of.

Cost Curves and Supply Curves*

IT IS THE PRIMARY PURPOSE of this article to develop a graphical exposition of the manner in which supply curves are dependent upon the different possible types of technological and pecuniary cost situations, under the usual assumptions of atomistic competition and of rational economic behavior on the part of the producers. No attempt is made here at realistic description of the actual types of relationship between costs and supply, and the purpose is the more modest one of presenting the formal types of relationship which can be conceived to exist under certain simplifying assumptions. Analysis of this kind derives obviously from the path-breaking contribution of Alfred Marshall in his *Principles of Economics*. Interest in this type of problem has been largely confined to the Anglo-Saxon countries, and in these countries there has been a tendency until recent years for economists to accept and reproduce the general lines of Marshall's analysis somewhat uncritically and without much further elaboration. I have no very serious fundamental criticism to make of Marshall's analysis of the supply side of the exchange value problem. But Marshall's treatment is highly elliptical. A striking illustration of his tendency to telescope his argument is his common practice in his graphs of labeling cost curves and supply curves alike with the symbols *ss*, conventionally used for supply curves, and thus diverting the attention of his readers, and perhaps also occasionally his own attention, from the necessity of selecting from among the many possible types of cost curve that one which in the given circumstances alone has claims to being considered as also a supply curve. Marshall, moreover, although he made valuable additions to the conceptual terminology necessary for analysis of this type, nevertheless worked with vocabulary lacking sufficient terms to distinguish clearly from

*Reprinted from *Zeitschrift für Nationalökonomie*, Vol. III, 1931-I, pp. 23-46, by the courtesy of Springer-Verlag.

each other all the significant types of cost phenomena, and here also the terminological poverty tended to lead to inadequate classification not only on the part of his followers but on his own part. Marshall's analysis was excessively simple even on the basis of his own simplifying assumptions, and inadequately precise in formulation, and his followers have standardized an even simpler type of exposition of the relationship of cost to price.

In recent years a number of English economists, notably Pigou, Sraffa, Shove, Harrod and Robertson, have presented in the *Economic Journal* a series of criticisms, elaborations, and refinements of the Marshallian analysis which, in my opinion, go a long way both towards bringing out clearly the contribution contained in its implications as well as in its explicit formulations, and towards completing and correcting it where that is necessary. The indebtedness of the present paper to their writings is considerable and is freely acknowledged. But I have been presenting charts such as those contained in this article to my students at the University of Chicago for a long period antedating the writings referred to above, and if in the course of years these charts have undergone substantial revision and, as I am convinced, correction, chief credit is due to the penetrating criticisms of my students.

The analysis which follows is based on the usual assumptions and presuppositions of the Marshallian type of economics. As compared to the Lausanne School type of analysis, it contents itself with examination of the conditions of a partial equilibrium of a special sort, and does not inquire into the repercussions of the postulated changes in cost or demand conditions on the general equilibrium situation. Like all partial equilibrium analysis, including the allegedly "general" equilibrium theories of the Lausanne School, it rests on assumptions of the *caeteris paribus* order which posit independence where in fact there is some degree of dependence. For such logically invalid assumptions there is the pragmatic defense that they permit of more detailed analysis of certain phases of economic interdependence than would be possible in their absence, and that to the extent that they are fictions uncompensated by counterbalancing fictions, it is reasonable to believe that the errors in the results obtained will be almost invariably quantitative rather than qualitative in character, and will generally be even quantitatively of minor importance. As compared to the Austrian School, there is, I believe, no need either for reconciliation or for apology. On the somewhat superficial level on which analysis of the present type is conducted the basic issue as between the English and the Austrian Schools does not enter explicitly into the picture, and in so far as it has any bearing on the conclusions, this bearing is again quantitative rather than qualitative in character. The Austrian School starts with the assumption, usually tacit, never emphasized, that the supplies of all the elementary factors of production are given and independent of their rates of remuneration. The English School emphasizes, perhaps overemphasizes, the dependence of the amounts of certain of the elementary factors, notably labor and waiting, on their rates of remuneration. The techniques of analysis of each school are in essentials identical, and each school, if it were to apply its techniques to the situation postulated by the other, would reach identical conclusions. The difference in the assumptions of the two schools has bearing on the quantitative but not on the qualitative behavior of the prices of the elementary factors and therefore also of the money costs of their products, as the demands for these factors and products change. The conflict between the two schools has greater significance for the theory of the value of the elementary factors of production, i.e., for the theory of distribution, than for the theory of particular commodity price determination. For the present analysis, where it is assumed either that the prices of the elementary factors remain unaltered or that they undergo changes of a kind consistent with the basic assumptions of either school, the differences between the two schools would not affect qualitatively the character of the findings. All of the propositions laid down in this paper should, I believe, be acceptable to, or else should be rejected by, both schools.

The procedure which will be followed will be to begin in each case with the mode of adjustment of a particular concern to the given market situation when the industry as a whole is supposed to be in stable equilibrium. This particular concern is not to be regarded as having any close relationship to Marshall's "representative firm." It will not be assumed to be necessarily typical of its industry with respect to its size, its efficiency, or the rates of slope of its various cost curves, but it will be assumed to be typical, or at least to represent the prevailing situation, with respect to the general qualitative behavior of its costs as it varies its own output or, in certain situations, as the industry of which it is part varies its output. All long-run differences in efficiency as between concerns will be assumed, however, to be compensated for by differential rates of compensation to the factors responsible for such differences, and these differential rates will be treated as parts of the ordinary long-run money costs of production of the different concerns. In the long-run, therefore, every concern will be assumed to have the same total costs per unit, except where explicit statement to the contrary is made. It will be assumed, further, that for any industry, under long-run equilibrium conditions, the same relationships must exist for every concern between its average costs, its marginal costs, and market price, as for the particular concern under special examination. But the reasoning of this paper would still hold if the realistic concession were made that in every industry there may be a few concerns which are not typical of their industry with respect to the qualitative behavior of their costs as output is varied either by themselves or by the industry as a whole, and which therefore do not wholly conform to these assumptions. It may be conceded, for instance, that in an industry in which for most producers expansion of their output means lower unit costs there should be a few producers for whom the reverse is true.

Short-Run Equilibrium for an Individual Concern

Chart I, which represents the behavior of money costs in the short-run for a single concern with a plant of a given scale, is the fundamental graph, and is incorporated in or underlies all the succeeding ones.[1] It is assumed that this concern is not of sufficient importance to bring about any change in the prices of the factors as a result of a change in its output. Since unit money costs of production are the sum of the products of the amounts of the factors used in the production of one unit multiplied by the prices of the factors, any change in unit money costs as output varies must

1. The charts were drawn for me by Y. K. Wong of the University of Chicago. Where in any chart one curve is derived from another or a combination of other curves presented in the same chart, it is drawn mathematically to scale. No attempt has been made, however, to maintain the same scales as between different charts. An attempt has been made to use mnemonic symbols for the various curves, *MC* for instance indicating marginal cost, *P* indicating price, and so forth. It is hoped that this will facilitate reading of the charts.

in this case be due, therefore, to changes in the amounts of the factors required for the production of one unit, or to use Walras' term, to changes in the "technological coefficients of production."

Short-Run Cost Curves

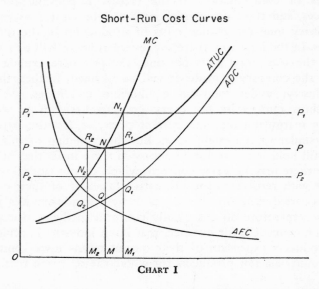

CHART I

The "short-run" is taken to be a period which is long enough to permit of any desired change of output technologically possible without altering the scale of plant, but which is not long enough to permit of any adjustment of scale of plant. It will be arbitrarily assumed that all of the factors can for the short-run be sharply classified into two groups, those which are necessarily fixed in amount, and those which are freely variable. "Scale of plant" will be used as synonymous with the size of the group of factors which are fixed in amount in the short-run, and each scale will be quantitatively indicated by the amount of output which can be produced at the lowest average cost possible at that scale. The costs associated with the fixed factors will be referred to as the "fixed costs" and those associated with the variable factors will be called the "direct costs." It is to be noted that the "fixed costs" are fixed only in their aggregate amounts and vary with output in their amount per unit, while the "direct costs" are variable in their aggregate amount as output varies, as well as, ordinarily at least, in their amount per unit. Amounts of output are in this as in all the succeeding charts measured along the horizontal axis from O, and money costs and prices along the vertical axis from O.

The curve AFC represents the trend of the average fixed costs per unit as output is increased. Since these are the costs associated with the parts of the working combination which, by hypothesis, are absolutely fixed in their aggregate amount, this curve must be a rectangular hyperbola.[2] The curve ADC represents the trend of average direct costs per unit as output is increased. Since the increase in output is the result of the application, to a constant amount of "fixed" factors, of increased amounts of the variable factors, the law of diminishing returns, if it is operating, should make the output per unit of the variable factor employed diminish, i.e., should make the "direct" technical coefficients of production increase, as total output increases. As the prices of the factors by assumption remain constant, the average direct costs must also increase as output increases, if the law of diminishing returns is operative. It is assumed, not, I believe, without justification, that within the useful range of observation the law of diminishing returns is operative, and the average direct cost curve is therefore drawn positively inclined throughout.[3] The curve $ATUC$ represents the trend of average total (i.e., fixed plus direct) unit costs as output is increased, and is, of course, the sum of the ordinates of the ADC and AFC curves. It is necessarily U-shaped for all industries having any substantial fixed costs, and is in this respect a universal short-run curve qualitatively descriptive of the short-run behavior of average costs of practically all concerns and all industries which cannot quickly and completely adjust the amounts of all the factors they use to variations in their rates of output. But the relative lengths and the relative rates of inclination of the negatively inclined and the positively inclined portions of the curve will differ from concern to concern and from industry to industry, depending upon the relative importance of the fixed to the total costs and upon the degree of sharpness with which the law of diminishing returns is operative for the variable factors. The curve MC represents the trend of marginal costs as output is

2. I.e., the equation to the curve will be of the form $xy = c$.

3. It is also drawn concave upward, to indicate the progressively sharper operation of the law of diminishing returns as the fixed factors are more intensively exploited.

increased. Any point on it represents the increase in aggregate costs as output at that point is increased by one unit.[4]

The marginal cost curve must cut the average cost curve at the lowest point of the latter. At the point of intersection, average cost and marginal cost are of course equal. But average cost is equal to marginal cost only when average cost is constant, i.e., when the average cost curve is a horizontal line.[5] The point of intersection of the marginal cost curve with the average cost curve when the latter is concave upwards must therefore be at the lowest point of the latter, where its tangent is a horizontal line.[6]

If this particular producer is an insignificant factor in his industry, i.e., if atomistic competition prevails, he may reasonably assume that no change in his output, and especially no change consistent with the maintenance of the scale of plant at its original level, will have any appreciable effect on the price of his product. Under these conditions, the partial demand curve for his product may be taken as a horizontal line whose ordinate from the base is equal to the prevailing price.[7] It will be to his interest to carry production to the point where marginal cost equals price, i.e., his short-run MC curve will also be his rational short-run supply curve. If price is MN, this will mean an output of OM and no extra profit or loss on his operations, i.e., the quasi-rent on his fixed investment per unit of output, NQ, would be equal to the fixed costs per unit. If price is P_1, output will be OM_1, and the quasi-rent per unit of

---

4. If y_a = average fixed cost per unit, y_b = average direct cost per unit, and x = output, then $ATUC = y_a + y_b$, and $MC = \dfrac{d[(y_a + y_b)x]}{dx}$. It is important to note that no consideration need be given to the fixed costs, if they really are absolutely fixed, in computing the marginal cost. Since $xy_a = c$, and $\dfrac{dc}{dx} = o, \ldots \dfrac{d[(y_a + y_b)x]}{dx} = \dfrac{d(xy_b)}{dx}$.

5. If x = output, and y = average cost, marginal cost $= \dfrac{d(xy)}{dx}$. If $y = c$, then $\dfrac{d(xy)}{dx} = y$. If y is an increasing function of x, then $\dfrac{d(xy)}{dx} > y$. If y is a decreasing function of x, then $\dfrac{d(xy)}{dx} < y$.

6. For a mathematical proof, see Henry Schultz, "Marginal Productivity and the General Pricing Process," *The Journal of Political Economy*, Vol. XXXVII (1929), p. 537, note 33.

7. This is equivalent to saying that the partial demand for his product has infinite elasticity.

output, N_1Q_1, will be in excess of the fixed costs per unit, R_1Q_1. If P_2 is the price, the output will be OM_2, and the quasi-rent per unit of output will be N_2Q_2, or less than the fixed costs per unit, R_2Q_2. All of these situations are consistent with short-run equilibrium, which, as far as individual producers are concerned, requires only that marginal cost equal price. The short-run supply curve for the industry as a whole is not shown in this chart, but is simply the sum of the abscissas of the individual short-run marginal cost (= individual supply) curves.[8]

Long-Run Equilibrium

The long-run is taken to be a period long enough to permit each producer to make such technologically possible changes in the scale of his plant as he desires, and thus to vary his output either by a more or less intensive utilization of existing plant, or by varying the scale of his plant, or by some combination of these methods. There will therefore be no costs which are technologically fixed in the long-run,[9] and if in fact the scale of plant is not altered as long-run output alters, it will be the result of voluntary choice and not of absolute technological compulsion. For an industry as a whole long-run variations in output can result from more or less intensive use of existing plants, or from changes in the scale of plants, or from changes in the number of plants, or from some combination of these. Under long-run equilibrium conditions changes in output, whether by an individual producer or by the industry as a whole, will be brought about by the economically optimum method from the point of view of the individual producers, so that each producer will have the optimum scale of plant for his long-run output. To simplify the analysis, it will be assumed that in each industry the optimum type of adjustment to a long-run variation in output for that industry as a whole will not only be alike for all producers but will involve only one of the three possible methods of adjustment listed above; namely, change in intensity of use of existing plants, change in scale of plants, and change

---

8. It is shown in Chart II.

9. This is, of course, not inconsistent with the proposition that at any moment within the long-run there will be costs which from the short-run point of view are fixed.

in number of plants. The theoretical static long-run, it should be noted, is a sort of "timeless" long-run throughout which nothing new happens except the full mutual adjustment to each other of the primary factors existing at the beginning of the long-run period. It is more correct, therefore, to speak of long-run equilibrium in terms of the conditions which will prevail *after* a long-run, rather than *during* a long-run. Long-run equilibrium, once established, will continue only for an instant of time if some change in the primary conditions should occur immediately after equilibrium in terms of the pre-existing conditions had been reached. The only significance of the equilibrium concept for realistic price theory is that it offers a basis for prediction of the direction of change when equilibrium is not established. Long before a static equilibrium has actually been established, some dynamic change in the fundamental factors will ordinarily occur which will make quantitative changes in the conditions of equilibrium. The ordinary economic situation is one of disequilibrium moving in the direction of equilibrium rather than of realized equilibrium.

For long-run equilibrium not only must marginal cost of output from existent plant equal price for each individual producer, but it must also equal average cost. If this were not the case, there would be either abnormal profits or losses, which would operate either to attract capital into the industry or to induce withdrawal of capital from the industry, and in either case would tend to bring about a change in output. For long-run equilibrium it is further necessary not only that each producer shall be producing his portion of the total output by what is for him, under existing conditions, the optimum method, but that no other producer, whether already in the industry or not, shall be in a position to provide an equivalent amount of output, in addition to what he may already be contributing, at a lower cost. The relations of costs to supply in the long-run will depend on the technological conditions under which output can be most economically varied, and the succeeding discussion will consist in large part of a classification and analysis of these conceivable types of technological conditions.

"Ricardian" Increasing Costs

Chart II illustrates a special case corresponding to the Ricardian rent theory in its strictest form. Let us suppose that a given industry is already utilizing all of the supply available at any price of a necessary factor of production, so that the output of the industry as a whole can be increased only by the more intensive

"Ricardian" Increasing Costs

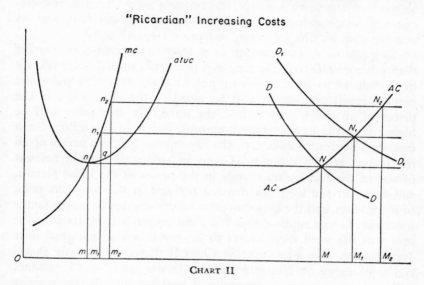

CHART II

utilization of the absolutely limited factor. Suppose also that no appreciable economies are to be derived, whatever the output of the industry as a whole, by a combination into larger productive units, or a subdivision into smaller productive units, of the existing concerns. In order further to simplify the analysis, it is assumed that the identical portions of the working-combination which in this case remain technologically fixed in amount whatever may be the short-run variations in output also remain economically fixed in amount whatever long-run variations in output may occur. If the particular concern whose costs are indicated in the left-hand portion of Chart II and the particular concern with which Chart I is concerned were identical, and if the two charts were drawn to the same scale, the *MC* curve in Chart I and the *mc* curve in Chart II would be identical, although the former represents the short-run trend and the latter represents the long-run trend of marginal costs as output is varied, i.e., for these assumptions, the short-run and the long-run marginal cost curves would be identical. The *atuc* curve in Chart II, continuing these assumptions, would simply represent

the short-run variations in average cost for this particular concern
as output was varied, *when long-run price was mn or MN*,[10] and
would be in all respects identical with the *ATUC* curve of Chart I.
When long-run price was *MN*, this concern would be in both short-
run and long-run equilibrium when its output was *Om*, and its
average cost, its marginal cost, and price were all equal.

Suppose now, that owing to a long-run increase of market
demand from *DD* to D_1D_1, long-run price rises to M_1N_1. It will pay
our producer to increase his output to Om_1, at which point the
new marginal cost, m_1n_1, will be equal to the new price. If the
prices of all the factors remain the same, the new price will be
higher than the new average cost m_1q. But it is impossible, for a
case such as this, to adhere to the assumption that the prices of all
the factors remain the same. Given an absolutely limited amount
of one of the factors, no change in the prices of the other factors,
and a rise in the long-run demand for and in the long-run price
of its product, and the long-run price of this absolutely scarce factor
must rise. Let us suppose that the fixed factor is land. Its price or
rent will rise until there ceases to be any excess of marginal over
average cost. The *atuc* curve in Chart II therefore has only short-
run significance. A long-run increase in the price of the product
will cause an increase in the price of land-use, and therefore a rise
in the entire *atuc* curve. The increase in land-rent, however, will
have no effect on marginal costs, and therefore on the long-run
mc curve, for it will be due to the increase in price of the product
and not to the increase in output of this particular concern. Even
if this producer maintained his output at *Om*, after long-run price
had risen to M_1N_1, the *atuc* curve would rise in the same manner
and degree. It would always shift upward in such a way, however,
that the *mc* curve would intersect it at its lowest point,[11] i.e., rent
for land would rise just sufficiently to make the new lowest average

---

10. The qualifying phrase in italics is important. Its significance is explained
in the next paragraph of the text.

11. Each successive short-run *atuc* curve of a particular producer, as the
long-run price of his product rises, consists of the ordinates of his former *atuc*
curve plus a new rent charge fixed in total amount regardless of his output,
and therefore of the form $xy = c$. As was pointed out in note 4, page 56, the
vertical addition of a rectangular hyperbola to an average cost curve does not
affect the marginal cost curve derivable from it. The same *mc* curve can,
therefore, continue to be the short-run marginal cost curve, even when the
short-run average cost curve is undergoing long-run changes consistently with
the conditions assumed in this case.

cost equal the new equilibrium marginal cost. When the long-run price was M_1N_1, therefore, average cost, marginal cost, and price would be equal for each producer under long-run equilibrium.

The AC curve in the right-hand portion of Chart II represents the long-run supply curve for the industry as a whole, and is simply the sum of the abscissas of the individual mc curves. It is also a long-run average cost curve for the industry as a whole inclusive of rent, and a long-run marginal cost curve for the industry as a whole exclusive of rent. For the individual producer, the changes in rent payments required as demand changes are due primarily to the changes in demand, secondarily to the changes in output of the industry as a whole, and only to an insignificant degree to his own changes in output. The individual producer will therefore not take the effect on his rent payments of increased output on his own part into account, and the supply curve for the industry as a whole will therefore be the marginal cost curve for the industry as a whole exclusive of rent.[12]

This appears to be the case usually designated in the textbooks as the case of "increasing costs." I have labeled it as "Ricardian increasing costs" to indicate its close relationship to the Ricardian rent theory. It is to be noted that as output increases the long-run average costs rise even if the increase of rents is disregarded and that there are increasing unit technological costs, therefore, whether the technical coefficients are weighted by the original or by the new prices of the factors. There are increasing marginal costs in every possible sense of the term costs.

If mc were the short-run marginal cost curve for a scale adapted to a long-run equilibrium output of Om, and if not all the factors which were technologically fixed in the short-run remained economically fixed in the long-run as output was increased, then, since there would be less scope for the operation of the law of diminishing returns, the long-run marginal cost curve for the particular

---

12. For the industry as a whole, however, the increase of output as demand increases will affect rent, on the one hand by influencing price and gross receipts, and on the other hand by influencing gross expenses. Depending upon the shift in position and the elasticity of the demand curve and upon the rate of slope of the industry marginal cost curve exclusive of rent, an increase of output when demand increases may make rent either greater or less than if output were kept constant. But under atomistic competition the possible results of keeping output constant when demand rises will play no part in the determination of output, of price, or of rent.

concern would be different from and less steeply inclined than the
mc curve, and the new short-run *atuc*$_1$ curve for a long-run equilibrium scale of output of, for example, Om_1 would have no simple
relationship to the *atuc* curve in Chart II. Similarly, the long-run
supply curve for the industry as a whole, since it is the sum of the
abscissas of the individual long-run marginal cost curves, would
then also be less steeply inclined than the *AC* curve in Chart II,
which would then be only a short-run supply curve for the industry
as a whole when the long-run equilibrium output of the industry
was *OM*.

Constant Costs

In the short-run, for industries which have any fixed costs whatsoever, constant marginal costs as output is varied are wholly
inconceivable if the law of diminishing returns is operative, and
constant average costs are inconceivable if there are increasing
marginal costs as required by the law of diminishing returns.[13]

In the long-run, however, constant costs are theoretically conceivable under two kinds of circumstances. The first case is when
each producer can vary his scale of production without affecting
his long-run average costs. The situation in this case for any individual concern will be as represented in Chart III. The curves
atuc$_1$ and *mc*$_1$ represent, respectively, the short-run trends of average and marginal costs as output is varied from a plant of scale
OA. The curves *atuc*$_2$ and *mc*$_2$, similarly represent, respectively,
the short-run trends of average and marginal costs as output is
varied from a plant of scale *OB*; and similarly, for scales *OC* and
OD. In the long-run any output would be produced from the
optimum scale for this output. The long-run average cost curve
would therefore be the horizontal line *AC*, which passes through
the lowest points of all the short-run *atuc* curves. Where average
costs are constant as output varies, average cost and marginal cost
are always identical.[14] This horizontal line would therefore also
be the individual producer's long-run supply curve.

---

13. Let x = output, y_a = average fixed costs per unit, y_b = average direct
costs per unit, and c and k be two different constants. Suppose that short-run
average costs are constant, i.e., that $y_a + y_b = k$. But $xy_a = c$. Then $xy_b =
kx - c$, and marginal cost, or $\dfrac{d(xy_b)}{dx} = \dfrac{d(kx - c)}{dx} = k$, which is inconsistent
with the law of diminishing returns.

14. See note 5, page 56.

This case presents certain difficulties when perfect competition prevails which make it impossible to indicate graphically the relationship between the long-run supply curves of the individual

Constant Costs

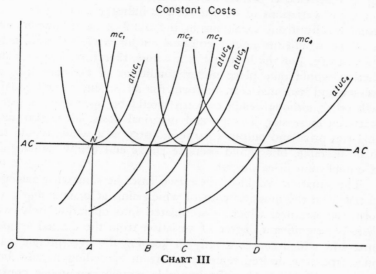

CHART III

concern and the industry as a whole. Read as an ordinary supply curve, the *AC* line indicates that in the long-run this concern would be unwilling to operate at any price under *AN*, would be willing to produce any amount at a price *AN*, and would be anxious to produce unlimited quantities at any price over *AN*. If the costs of different producers in the industry are not uniform, then the lowest cost concern would tend to monopolize the industry. If the costs of different producers are uniform, the supply curve for the industry would be indefinite, and in the long-run there would be a constant tendency toward overproduction, with consequent losses and a reaction toward underproduction. Actual long-run price and output would be unstable, but would oscillate above and below stable points of equilibrium price and equilibrium output.

The second conceivable case of long-run constant costs, not illustrated graphically here, would be presented by a situation in which all of the concerns within the industry and an indefinite number of potential members of the industry can operate at long-run minimum average costs uniform as between the different concerns, but with average costs increasing for each as its output increases. The long-run output of the industry would then consist of the sum of the outputs of all the member concerns, each operating at that scale at which its costs are at the minimum common to all, and variations of output for the industry as a whole would result wholly from variations in the number of producers, each of whom would maintain a constant output while he remained in the industry. For the industry as a whole, therefore, long-run production would take place under conditions of constant long-run average and marginal cost, uniform for all producers and equal to each other, although each concern would be operating subject to short-run increasing average and marginal costs. Here also actual long-run price and output for the industry as a whole would tend to be unstable, but would oscillate above and below stable points of equilibrium price output.

The situation would in these two cases be somewhat analogous to that of a thermostatic control which aims at maintaining a uniform temperature, which is stimulated into operation only when there is a significant degree of variation from the desired temperature, and which succeeds only in keeping the ever-present variations from the desired temperature from exceeding narrow limits in either direction. Completely stable equilibrium under constant cost conditions is only conceivable on the assumption of some departure from perfect competition, in consequence of which variations in output by individual producers, or entrance into the industry by new producers or withdrawal of old, are subject to some difficulty even in the long-run after the equilibrium price and output have once been momentarily established.

Net Internal Economies of Large-Scale Production

We owe to Marshall the important distinction between the "internal" and the "external" economies resulting from increased output. For present purposes we will use the term "net internal economies of large-scale production" to mean net reductions in costs to a particular concern resulting from a long-run expansion in its output when each output is produced from a plant of the optimum scale for that output. The word "net" is introduced to make it clear that increase in output may result at the same time in economies and in diseconomies and that it is only the excess of the former over the latter to which reference is made here. Internal economies of large-scale production are primarily a long-run phenomenon, dependent upon appropriate adjustment of scale of plant to each successive output. They should not be confused with the economies resulting from "spreading of overhead," which are a short-run phenomenon, represented by the negative inclination of the average fixed cost curve in Chart I. Internal economies of large-scale production need not be relatively greater for those particular costs which in the short-run are the fixed costs than for those particular costs which in the short-run are the direct costs. In the long-run, in any case, there are no technologically fixed or overhead costs, if the definitions here followed of "long-run" and of "fixed costs" are adhered to. Internal economies of large-scale production are independent of the size of output of the industry as a whole, and may be accruing to a particular concern whose output is increasing at the same time that the output of the industry as a whole is undergoing a decline. It is for this reason that Marshall gave them the name of internal, to distinguish them from the external economies which are dependent on something outside the particular concerns themselves, namely, the size of output of the industry as a whole.

Internal economies may be either technological or pecuniary, that is, they may consist either in reductions of the technological coefficients of production or in reductions in the prices paid for the factors as the result of increases in the amounts thereof purchased. Illustrations of technological internal economies would be savings in the labor, materials, or equipment requirements per unit of output resulting from improved organization or methods of production made possible by a larger scale of operations. Pecuniary internal economies, on the other hand, would consist of advantages in buying, such as "quantity discounts" or the ability to hire labor at lower rates, resulting from an increase in the scale of purchases.[15]

Chart IV illustrates the behavior of the cost curves for a particular concern which enjoys net internal economies of large-scale production. As in Chart III the *ac* curves and the *mc* curves repre-

---

15. Pecuniary internal economies are, theoretically, as likely to result from expansion of output from a given plant as from expansion of output brought about by increase of scale of plant. But it is only the latter form of expansion of output which is likely to be great enough to result in significant pecuniary internal economies.

sent the short-run variations in average and marginal costs respectively, as output is varied from plants of each indicated scale. The *AC* curve represents the long-run trend of average costs, that is, the trend of average costs when each output is produced from a plant of the optimum scale for that output, and is drawn so as to connect the points of lowest average cost for each scale of plant.[16] The *MC* curve is the long-run marginal curve for this particular concern

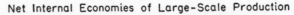

Net Internal Economies of Large-Scale Production

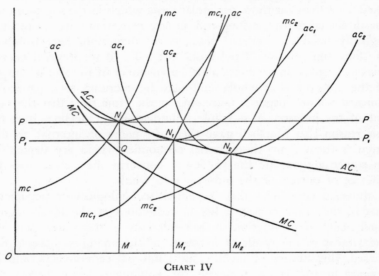

CHART IV

when the *AC* curve is interpreted as a continuous curve. It represents the increment in aggregate costs resulting from a unit increase

16. The *AC* curve would represent a continuous trend only if it is assumed that scale of plant can be modified by small increments. If the curve is interpreted as a discontinuous one, then only the points N, N_1, N_2,...on it are significant, and the significant long-run costs for the intervals between are the lowest short-run average costs available for the indicated outputs. It may be noticed that at certain points the short-run *ac* curves are drawn so as to sink below the long-run *AC* curve. If the *AC* curve is interpreted as having significance only at the N points, this is of no consequence. But if the *AC* curve is interpreted as a continuous curve, this is an error. My instructions to the draftsman were to draw the *AC* curve so as never to be above any portion of any *ac* curve. He is a mathematician, however, not an economist, and he saw some mathematical objection to this procedure which I could not succeed in understanding. I could not persuade him to disregard his scruples as a craftsman and to follow my instructions, absurd though they might be.

in output, when each output is produced from a plant of the optimum scale for that output. It is to be noted that while the short-run marginal cost curves are positively inclined, the long-run marginal cost curve is negatively inclined.[17]

The familiar proposition that net internal economies of large-scale production and long-run stable equilibrium are inconsistent under competitive conditions is clearly illustrated by this chart. When price is MN, this concern, if operating with the scale of plant represented by the short-run curves ac and mc, is in short-run equilibrium when its output is OM, for its short-run marginal cost is then equal to price. It will not be in long-run equilibrium, however, for its long-run marginal cost will then be only MQ, or less than price. Provided that no change in its output will affect market price, it will pay this concern to enlarge its plant whatever the price may be, and whatever its existing scale of plant may be. If thereby it grows so large that its operations exert a significant influence on price, we pass out of the realm of atomistic competition and approach that of partial monopoly. Even then, however, it would still be profitable for this concern to enlarge its plant and increase its output as long as long-run marginal cost was lower than long-run marginal revenue, or the increment in aggregate receipts resulting from a unit increment in output, after allowance for any reduction in price.[18]

---

17. If y, y_1, y_2, are the short-run average costs for scales of plant, OM, OM_1, and OM_2, respectively, as indicated by the ac curves; $Y =$ long-run average cost, as indicated by the AC curve; $x =$ output; mc, mc_1, and mc_2 indicate the short-run marginal costs as represented by the mc curves; and MC indicates the long-run marginal cost, as represented by the MC curve, then:

$$mc = \frac{d(xy)}{dx}; \quad mc_1 = \frac{d(xy_1)}{dx}; \quad mc_2 = \frac{d(xy_2)}{dx}; \text{ and } MC = \frac{d(xY)}{dx};$$

$$\text{and} \frac{d^2(xy)}{dx^2} > 0; \text{ and } \frac{d^2(xY)}{dx^2} < 0.$$

18. If $Y_p =$ long-run price, $X =$ long-run output, and $Y_c =$ long-run average cost, long-run marginal cost would be $\frac{d(XY_c)}{dX}$, long-run marginal revenue would be $\frac{d(XY_p)}{dX}$, and it would pay to carry production to the point where long-run marginal cost equalled long-run marginal revenue, or $\frac{d(XY_c)}{dX} = \frac{d(XY_p)}{dX}$. Under atomistic competition, $\frac{d(XY_p)}{dX} = Y_p$, which is independent of this particular concern's output. Whatever the price, therefore, this concern would always have an incentive to increase its long-run output as long as

For any particular concern operating under these conditions, and *a fortiori* for an industry as a whole consisting of such concerns, there is no definite long-run supply curve. At any price *MN* higher than the asymptote of the *AC* curve, this producer will be willing to produce any quantity not less than *OM*.

To negatively-inclined long-run cost curves such as the *AC* and *MC* curves in Chart IV, Marshall has denied the characteristic of "reversibility," i.e., of equal validity whether output is increasing or decreasing, on the ground that some of the economies accruing when the output of a concern, or of an industry as a whole, is increased will be retained if the output of the concern or of the industry returns to its original dimensions.[19] This reasoning appears to involve a confusion between static and dynamic cost curves. The reductions in costs as output is increased indicated by curves such as the *AC* and *MC* curves in Chart IV are purely functions of size of output when scale is adjusted to output and not of lapse of actual time during which improved processes may happen to be discovered. The economies associated with output *OM* are economies which are not available for any output less than *OM*. The only basis on which the irreversibility of these curves, as static curves, could logically be posited would be the existence of possible economies of a type adapted to any scale of output but discoverable only when output is great, where invention, but not its exploitation, was a function of scale of output.

Net Internal Diseconomies of Large-Scale Production

Cases are clearly conceivable where increase of scale of plant would involve less efficient operation and consequently higher unit costs. The prevailing opinion in the United States that for most types of agriculture the one-family farm is still the optimum mode of agricultural organization would indicate that in this coun-

---

long-run marginal cost remained less than that price. If partial monopoly resulted, however, marginal revenue, or $\dfrac{d(XY_p)}{dX}$, would become a function of market demand and of competitor's supply and would be smaller than Y_p, and a point of stable long-run equilibrium might exist, depending on how the other producers reacted to variations in output by this one. If complete monopoly resulted, there would probably be a definite point of stable equilibrium. These questions, however, are beyond the range of this paper.

19. *Principles of Economics*, 8th ed., 1922, p. 808.

try at least agriculture was subject to net internal diseconomies of large-scale production after an early stage in the size of the farm-unit had been reached. But when increase of output by means of the increase of scale of existing plants involves a substantial increase in unit costs, it will always be possible for the industry as a whole to avoid the net internal diseconomies of large-scale production by increasing its output through increase in number of plants without increase in their scale.[20] This case has no practical importance, therefore, except as it represents an economic barrier against increase in scale of plants, and it is not worth while to illustrate it graphically.

Net External Economies of Large Production

External economies are those which accrue to particular concerns as the result of the expansion of output by their industry as a whole, and which are independent of their own individual outputs. If an industry which enjoys net external economies of large production increases its output—presumably through increase in number of plants—the average costs of the member concerns of that industry will fall even though each concern maintains a constant scale of plant and a constant output. Like internal economies, external economies may be either technological or pecuniary. Illustrations of technological external economies are difficult to find, but a better organization of the labor and raw materials markets with respect to the availability of laborers and materials when needed by any particular plant, and improvement in productive technique resulting from "cross-fertilization," or the exchange of ideas among the different producers, appear to be possible sources of technological external economies resulting from the increase in size of the industry as a whole. Illustrations of pecuniary external economies would be reductions in the prices of services and materials resulting from the increase in the amounts of such services and materials purchased by the industry as a whole. Pecuniary external economies to industry A are likely to

20. Increase of scale should be distinguished from increase in output from the same scale of plant. In the former, all the factors are increased in about the same proportions; in the latter some factors remain fixed in amount. Whenever it is generally possible to increase all the factors in about the same proportion, i.e. to increase scale of plant, it is also possible, alternatively at least, to increase the number of plants.

be internal or external economies to some other industry B. If industry A purchases materials in greater quantity, their price may fall because industry B can then produce them at lower unit cost. But cases are theoretically conceivable where pecuniary external economies to industry A may not be economies to any other industry, as, for instance, if laborers should have a preference, rational or irrational, for working in an important rather than in a minor industry, and should therefore be willing to accept lower wages as the industry expands.

Chart V illustrates the case of net external economies of large production, irrespective of whether these economies are technological, or pecuniary, or both. As always, each concern will in the long-run tend to produce its output from the optimum scale

Net External Economies of Large Production

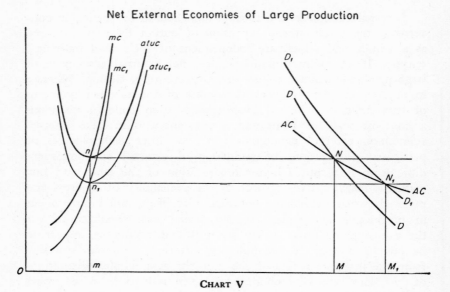

CHART V

for that output, and given that scale, to carry production to the point where its average and marginal costs are both equal to price. If *Om* represents the optimum scale of plant for the particular producer, i.e., the scale at which he can produce at the lowest average cost, if the long-run price is *mn* or *MN*, and if the long-run output for the industry as a whole is *OM*, this producer will be in long-run equilibrium when his output is *om*, and his average and his marginal cost are both *mn*. Suppose now that long-run demand rises from *DD* to D_1D_1, and that long-run output of the industry as a whole increases, as the result of increase in the number of producers, from *OM* to OM_1. Since, by assumption, this industry is subject to net external economies of large production, the short-run average and marginal cost curves of each particular concern will fall in the manner indicated in the left-hand portion of Chart V. This particular concern will be in long-run equilibrium with the new situation when its output is *om*, as before, but its long-run average and marginal costs will have fallen from *mn* to mn_1. The *AC* curve represents the trend of the individual average (and also marginal) costs as output of the industry as a whole changes by the amounts indicated on the horizontal axis. Any point on this curve represents the long-run average cost for every individual producer, and therefore for the industry as a whole, when the output of the industry as a whole is as indicated. It is theoretically the same as the supply curve for the industry as a whole. The long-run marginal cost curve for the industry as a whole is not shown on the chart. It would fall below the *AC* curve.[21] Its only relationship to the short-run marginal cost curves of the individual concerns would be that it was a function of the downward shifting of the lowest points on the individual short-run *atuc* and *mc* curves as the output of the entire industry increased. Under atomistic competition this marginal cost curve would have no influence on supply, since individual producers would not take it into account in deciding either upon their continuance in or their entrance into the industry or upon their scale of output when in the industry.[22]

---

21. If X = output of the industry as a whole, and Y_a = long-run average cost for the industry as a whole as represented by the *AC* curve, the *MC* curve for the industry as a whole would be $\dfrac{d(XY_a)}{dX}$, $< Y_a$. If average cost for a particular producer $= y_a$, then $y_a = f(X)$, and at long-run equilibrium, $y_a = Y_a$.

22. Employing terminology resembling that used by Pigou in his *The Economics of Welfare*, the marginal private net cost would exceed the marginal industry net cost. If the output of an additional producer be represented by ΔX, and the average cost of his output and of the outputs of the other producers by $y_a = f(X)$, then the marginal private net cost would be y_a, and the marginal industry net cost would be $\dfrac{\Delta(XY_a)}{\Delta X}$, $< y_a$.

Net External Diseconomies of Large Production

Although it has not ordinarily been given consideration, the case of net external diseconomies of large production is of indisputable practical importance. Pecuniary diseconomies of this kind will always tend to result from the expansion of output of an industry because the increased purchases of primary factors and materials which this entails must tend to raise their unit prices. In order that pecuniary diseconomies shall not result from the expansion of an industry's output, it is necessary, for both primary factors of production and materials, that the increase in demand by this industry shall be accompanied by a corresponding and simultaneous decrease in demand by other industries or increase in supply of the factors and materials themselves, or, failing this, that the materials, because of net external or internal economies in the industries producing them, should have negatively inclined supply curves.[23] These pecuniary external diseconomies, however, may be more than counterbalanced by technological external economies, and need not necessarily result therefore in net external diseconomies. External technological diseconomies, or increasing technical coefficients of production as output of the industry as a whole is increased, can be theoretically conceived, but it is hard to find convincing illustrations. One possible instance might be higher unit highway transportation costs when

---

23. It is worth pointing out that negative supply curves for the primary factors of production will not prevent an increased demand for them from a particular industry from resulting in an increase in their unit prices and therefore are not a barrier to pecuniary external diseconomies for that industry in so far as their primary factor costs are concerned. The negatively inclined supply curves of primary factors have a different meaning from the negatively inclined supply curves for commodities. If labor has a negatively inclined supply curve that means not that willingness to hire labor in greater quantities will result in a fall in the wage-rate, but, what is very different, that fewer units of labor will be offered for hire when a high rate of wages is offered than when a lower rate is offered. In the case of commodities, any point on a negatively inclined supply curve must be interpreted to mean that at the indicated price, the indicated quantity or more of the commodity can be purchased. In the case of labor, any point on a negatively inclined supply curve must be interpreted to mean that when the indicated wage-rate is obtainable, the indicated quantity of labor, but no more, will be available for hire. If the negatively inclined supply curve for labor has an elasticity of less than unity, as seems probable, it must be assumed that labor will prefer a high wage rate and partial employment to a low wage rate and fuller employment, and therefore will resist any movement toward the lower points on its supply curve.

an industry which provides its own transportation for materials and products expands its output and thereby brings about traffic congestion on the roads.

Chart VI illustrates the case of net external diseconomies of large production, whether technological or pecuniary. When the long-run equilibrium outputs of the industry as a whole are OM and OM_1, respectively, the *atuc* and *atuc₁* curves represent the

Net External Diseconomies of Large Production

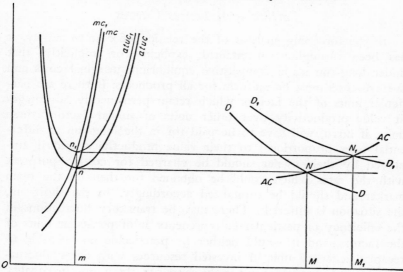

CHART VI

respective trends of short-run average costs, the *mc* and *mc₁* curves represent the trends of short-run marginal costs and *mn* and *mn₁* represent the long-run equilibrium average and marginal costs, for one individual producer. The reverse of the conditions when net external economies of large production are present, in this case the long-run equilibrium average and marginal costs of the individual concern rise as the output of the industry as a whole increases. The *AC* curve represents the trend of the individual average (and also marginal) long-run costs and therefore also of the industry long-run average cost as the industry as a whole varies its output. This is also the long-run supply curve for the industry as a whole. The long-run marginal cost curve for the industry as a whole is not shown on the chart. It would rise above the AC curve.[24] Since the individual producers will not concern themselves with the effect on the costs of other producers of their own withdrawal from or entrance into the industry, and since in this case it is assumed that variation in output takes place only through variation in number of producers, the marginal cost curve for the industry as a whole will, under competitive conditions, have no influence on output.[25]

Particular Expenses Curves

In the foregoing analysis of the relation of cost to supply, it has been throughout maintained, explicitly or implicitly, that under long-run static competitive equilibrium marginal costs and average costs must be uniform for all producers. If there are particular units of the factors which retain permanently advantages in value productivity over other units of similar factors, these units, if hired, will have to be paid for in the long-run at differential rates proportional to their value productivity, and if employed by their owner should be charged for costing purposes with the rates which could be obtained for them in the open market and should be capitalized accordingly. In the short-run, the situation is different. There may be transitory fluctuations in the efficiency of particular entrepreneurs or of particular units of the factors, and it would neither be practicable nor sensible to recapitalize every unit of invested resources with every fluctuation in its rate of yield. Even in the short-run, there must be equality as between the marginal costs of different producers under equilibrium conditions,[26] but there may be substantial variations as between

---

24. As for Chart V, if X = output of industry as a whole and Y_a = long-run average cost for industry as a whole, as represented by the AC curve, the marginal cost curve for the industry as a whole would be $\dfrac{d(XY_a)}{dX}$. If for the individual concern, y_a = average cost, then $y_a = f(X)$, and at long-run equilibrium $y_a = Y_a$.

25. In Pigou's terminology, the marginal industry net cost would exceed the marginal private net cost. If the output of an additional concern be represented by ΔX, and its average cost by $y_a = f(X)$, then the marginal private net cost would be y_a, and the marginal industry net cost would be $\dfrac{\Delta(XY_a)}{\Delta X}, > y_a$.

26. Since a time-interval is always present between the sale contract and at least some of the stages of hiring of factors and of actual production, there is

the average costs, and therefore as between the net rates of return on original investment, of different producers.

Statistical investigations of individual costs in the United States, based in the main on unrevised cost accounting records, have shown that the variations in average costs as between different producers in the same industry at the same time are very substantial, and that ordinarily a significant proportion of the total output of an industry appears to be produced at an average cost in excess of the prevailing price. To some extent these variations in cost can be explained away as due (1) to different and, from the point of view of economic theory unsatisfactory, methods of measuring costs, and especially the costs associated with the relatively fixed factors of production, (2) to regional differences in f.o.b. factory costs and in prices which, in an area as large as the United States, can be very substantial for bulky commodities without implying the absence of keen competition and (3), to the absence of atomistic competition. But even aside from such considerations, it should be obvious that such findings are in no way inconsistent with the propositions of equilibrium price theory as outlined above. Under short-run equilibrium the average costs, including the fixed costs, of any particular producer need bear no necessary relationship to price, except that the average direct costs must not exceed price. These statistical costs, moreover, are not the equilibrium costs of the theoretical short-run, but are the costs as they exist at an actual moment of time when short-run equilibrium with the fundamental conditions as they exist at the moment may not have been attained, and when these fundamental conditions are themselves liable to change at any moment.

It may be worth while, however, to show the relationship of the distribution of particular average costs within an industry at particular actual moments of time to the general supply conditions of the industry under assumptions of long-run equilibrium. To a curve representing the array of actual average costs of the dif-

---

opportunity under short-run equilibrium for some divergence between price and marginal cost, and therefore, between the marginal costs of different producers. It would be a more precise way of formulating the short-run theory to say that since all producers, if acting rationally, carry production to the point where anticipated marginal cost will equal anticipated price, and since price, in a perfect market, is uniform for all, marginal cost tends to be uniform for all producers, and variations as between different producers result only from errors in anticipation.

ferent producers in an industry when the total output of the
industry was a given amount, these individual costs being arranged
in increasing order of size from left to right, Marshall gave the
name of "particular expenses curve,"[27] and American economists
have called such curves, "bulk-line cost curves,"[28] "accountants'
cost curves," and "statistical cost curves." In Chart VII, the curves

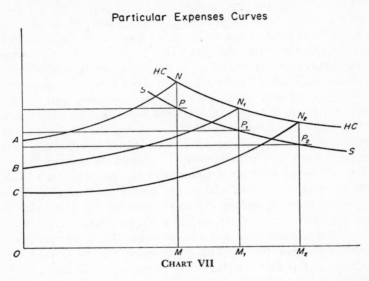

Particular Expenses Curves

CHART VII

AN, *BN*₁, and *CN*₂ are supposed to be the appropriate particular
expenses curves for an industry subject to net external economies
of large production, when the output of the industry as a whole
is *OM*, *OM*₁, and *OM*₂ respectively. Because the industry is subject to net external economies, the entire particular expenses curves
are made to shift downward as the output of the industry expands.

27. See *Principles*, 8th ed., Appendix *H*, pp. 810-811, footnote. It will be
noticed that his particular expenses curve, *SS*, is drawn so as to project somewhat beyond the point of total output for the industry as a whole, *A*. This is
an error, and no significance can be given to the part of the curve projecting
beyond the point of total output of the industry as a whole. If the output of
the industry were to increase up to the terminal point of this curve, the entire
curve would acquire a different locus.

28. "Bulk-line cost curves" because if a perpendicular is dropped to the
horizontal axis from the point of intersection of the price-line and the curve,
the greater part or the "bulk" of the output would be to the left of this "bulk-
line." See F. W. Taussig, "Price-Fixing as seen by a Price-Fixer," *The Quarterly
Journal of Economics*, Vol. XXXIII, February 1919, pp. 205-241.

(If the industry were subject to net external diseconomies of production, the particular expenses curves would shift upwards as the output of the industry expands. Corresponding modifications in the chart would have to be made as other assumptions with respect to the conditions under which the industry can expand its output were introduced.) It is to be understood also that no dynamic changes in prices of the factors or in average technological cost conditions for the industry as a whole are occurring except such as are associated with variations in output of the industry as a whole.

The *HC* curve is a curve connecting the points of highest-cost for each successive output. These highest-costs, though often so designated, are not marginal costs in the strict sense of the term, but are in each case simply the average costs of that producer whose average costs are the highest in the industry. If the statistical indications and also certain *a priori* considerations are to be followed, these highest average costs are likely to be, except in "boom years," distinctly higher than the true marginal costs,[29] and are so drawn in this graph. The P, P_1, P_2 lines represent price, and are drawn to intersect the particular expenses curves below their highest points, in conformity with the statistical findings. The curve *SS*, drawn through the P, P_1, P_2 points representing actual prices prevailing when the outputs are OM, OM_1 and OM_2, respectively, is a sort of actual semi-dynamic[30] supply curve.

What is the ordinary relationship between the *HC* curve and the *SS* curve under fully dynamic conditions cannot be postulated on *a priori* grounds, and only statistical investigation can throw much light on it. American investigators of particular expenses curves believe that they have already demonstrated stable and predictable relations between them and price, but a reasonable degree of scepticism still seems to be justified. One point, however, is clear on *a priori* even more than on inductive grounds. If the *SS*

29. If the AN, BN_1, and CN_2 curves were the actual particular expenses curves when the actual outputs of the industry as a whole were OM, OM_1 and OM_2 respectively, the actual marginal cost curve for the industry as a whole would be a curve representing the differences per unit increase of output between the aggregate costs represented by the successive areas, $AOMN$, BOM_1N_1, COM_2N_2, . . . as output was increased from OM to OM_1, to OM_2, to . . . . It would be negatively inclined, and would be much below the HC curve.

30. "Semi-dynamic" because certain types of dynamic changes have been assumed not to occur.

curve in Chart VII were not ordinarily below, and substantially
below, the *HC* curve, the familiar and continuously present phenomenon of bankruptcy would be inexplicable.

It is possible, moreover, to devise a theory of even long-run
static equilibrium which still leaves room for an excess of the *HC*
over the *SS* curves, and therefore for bankruptcy as a phenomenon consistent with long-run equilibrium. For such a theory,
however, long-run equilibrium would apply only to the industry
as a whole, and would be a sort of statistical equilibrium between
rate of output and rate of consumption. None of the individual
producers under this theory need be in long-run equilibrium at
any time. At any moment, some producers would be enjoying
exceptional profits, and others incurring heavy losses. The particular expenses curve could remain positive in its inclination and
fixed in its locus, but there would be necessarily a constant process
of shifting of their position on that curve on the part of the individual producers, and an equality in rate of withdrawal of producers from the industry through bankruptcy or otherwise, on
the one hand, and of entrance of new producers into the industry,
on the other hand. A theory of this sort would leave room for
pure profits even in a static state.

Supplementary Note to "Cost Curves and Supply Curves" (1950)*

I DO NOT TAKE ADVANTAGE of the opportunity to revise my 1931 article. Even the error in Chart IV (page 66) is left uncorrected, so that future teachers and students may share the pleasure of many of their predecessors of pointing out that if I had known what an "envelope" was I would not have given my excellent draftsman the technically impossible and economically inappropriate assignment of drawing an AC curve which would pass through the lowest cost points of all the ac curves and yet not rise above any ac curve at any point. It is left also to the reader to modify the general contour of the $ATUC$ curve of Chart I in conformity with the evidence which inductive studies seem to provide that the trough of this curve has a negative inclination throughout almost all of its possible course.

I feel it incumbent upon me, however, so as to avoid propagating serious error, to carry the analysis of costs a stage further in one respect by departing here from the traditional Marshallian pattern of assumptions to which the article adheres. The partial-equilibrium nature of the Marshallian assumptions leaves a wider range of possibilities to the long-run tendencies of costs for an expanding industry than is consistent with general-equilibrium analysis. I first saw this in 1938, and thereafter pointed it out to my students at the University of Chicago. But the first, and, to my knowledge, still the only, analysis in print similar to what I have in mind[1] is in Joan Robinson's excellent article, "Rising Supply Price," *Economica*, VIII, February, 1941, which has not attracted the attention which in my opinion

---

*Reprinted from R. V. Clemence, ed., *Readings in Economic Analysis*, Cambridge, Mass., Addison-Wesley Press, 1950, Vol. II, pp. 31-35, by the courtesy of the publisher.

1. I have since found the same doctrine expounded in an earlier article by R. F. Harrod, "Notes on Supply," *The Economic Journal*, Vol. XL (1930), pp. 232-241, especially pp. 240-241. [Note added in 1951.]

it eminently deserves. What follows is, I think, in substantial harmony with her argument, but is so presented as to provide a link with the analysis in my 1931 article.

The most significant long-run behavior of costs for many applications of value theory to concrete economic issues is the trend of unit costs, average or marginal, for a particular commodity (or group of commodities) as the total output of such commodity expands while the economy as a whole remains stable (or relatively stable), so that the expansion of output of this commodity is of necessity simultaneous with a corresponding contraction of output of all other commodities considered in the aggregate. Let us assume that in an otherwise stable economy a shift of wants occurs from other commodities to cloth, with a consequent expansion in the output of cloth. Except by coincidence, and even that conceivable only at a "point" rather than over a substantial range, the cloth industry will be using the various "factors" (or "ingredients," or "resources," or "input items") in proportions somewhat different from those in which the economy as a whole, and the contracting section of it, uses them. As the cloth industry expands, therefore, and bids for more factors, the contracting industries will not, at prevailing prices for the factors, be releasing factors in the same proportions in which the cloth industry is trying to acquire them; at prevailing prices for the factors, those which the woolen industry uses relatively heavily will be in short supply while those which it uses relatively lightly will be in excess supply. There will consequently occur a realignment of the prices of the factors, with those used relatively heavily by the cloth industry rising in price and those used relatively lightly by it falling in price.

Thus all industries must tend to be subject to "external net pecuniary diseconomies of large production" when they expand relative to the economy of which they are a part. The entrepreneurs in an expanding industry, to lessen the impact of these pecuniary diseconomies, will endeavour to reduce the ratio of their use of the factors which have risen in price to their use of the factors which have fallen in price. But the extent to which such change in the proportions in which the factors are combined is technically feasible and economically profitable is limited by the operation of the law of diminishing returns, i.e., increase in the relative use of the cheaper factors results in decreased ratios of output to input to these factors.

It is not possible therefore completely to escape the pecuniary diseconomies resulting from the relative changes in the prices of the factors by altering the proportions in which the factors are used, if it is assumed, as I do here, that the law of diminishing returns is operating in the long run.

There is presented on page 82 an arithmetical illustration of the conclusions derivable from this reasoning with respect to money costs per unit of product and allocation of resources as between different industries when in an economy of stable size a shift of wants of given extent in favor of cloth results in an expansion of the cloth industry. Case I represents what are for present purposes the essential characteristics of the assumed original equilibrium of the economy as a whole, and Case II represents a possible new equilibrium, consistent with all the assumptions made, after there has been full adjustment to the shift in wants. It is assumed in Case II that all the factors are fixed in amount, and also that the total national income remains at $320. There are in Case II as compared to Case I: an increase in the output of cloth; a rise in the price of factor B used relatively heavily by the cloth industry and decreases in the prices of other factors; a relative decrease in the use of factor B as compared to other factors for each industry (although not for all industry in the aggregate); a rise in the average cost and in the price of cloth (there would also be a rise in the marginal cost of cloth but this is not brought out explicitly in the illustration) and falls in the average costs and prices of all other commodities taken as a whole. The degrees of change from Case I indicated in the illustration are in every instance arbitrary, though consistent with equilibrium for the economy as a whole, but the directions of change are in every instance necessary ones.

The assumption that the factors are fixed in amount, i.e., that the amounts offered for hire are independent of their rates of remuneration, is an unnecessary one; though for fortuitous historical reasons it is a popular assumption in economic theory and even sometimes presented as dogma which it is not respectable to depart from, it is in fact wholly arbitrary and unrealistic. It is easy to modify the arithmetical illustration, however, to adapt it to other types of assumptions as to the character of the supply functions of the factors. I will not take the space required to do this here, but will confine myself to a summary account of the character of the

Factor	Rate of Remuneration Per Unit	By Cloth Industry	By Other Industries	By All Industries	Total Payments to Factors	Industry	Output: Units	A	B	C	Average Cost = Price
					Case I						
A	$4.00	1	29	30	$120	Cloth	4	$\frac{1}{4}$	$\frac{5}{4}$	$\frac{2}{4}$	$8.00
B	4.00	5	15	20	80	Other	36	$\frac{29}{36}$	$\frac{15}{36}$	$\frac{28}{36}$	8.00
C	4.00	2	28	30	120	All	40				8.00
				80	$320						
					Case II						
A	$3.40	6	24	30	$102	Cloth	8	$\frac{6}{8}$	$\frac{8}{8}$	$\frac{5}{8}$	$10.30
B	5.50	8	12	20	110	Other	30	$\frac{24}{30}$	$\frac{12}{30}$	$\frac{25}{30}$	7.92
C	3.60	5	25	30	108	All	38				8.42+
				80	$320						

Input per Unit of Output ("Technical Coefficients") comprises columns A, B, C.

necessary changes in the results which follow changes in the assumptions as to the supply functions of the factors, all other assumptions remaining as before.

Case III. Assume that each of the factors has a supply function such that the quantity offered for hire is an increasing function of the rate of remuneration. All price and cost changes as compared to Case I will be the same in direction as in Case II, but less in degree. The total quantity of factor B used by the economy as a whole will be greater and of factors B and C will be less than in Case I or Case II.

Case IV. Assume that factor B has a fixed supply, while the amounts offered of factors A and C are increasing functions of their rates of remuneration. The cost and price of cloth will rise more than in Cases II or III and the cost and prices of other commodities will fall less than in Cases II or III.

Case V. Assume that the quantity of factor B offered for hire is an increasing function of its rate of remuneration, while the supplies of factors A and C are fixed. The cost and price of cloth will rise, but less than in Cases II, III, or IV, while the prices of other commodities will fall more than in Cases II, III, or IV.

Case VI. Assume that the supply functions of all of the factors of production can be represented graphically by "rising-backward" curves, i.e., that as higher rates of remuneration are offered for them smaller quantities are supplied.[2] The rise in the cost and the price of cloth would be greater and the fall in the costs and prices of other commodities would also be greater than in any of the preceding Cases II to V.

In all these cases an increase in the long-run output of cloth can occur only at higher cost, and these or allied cases cover all the assumptions as to the supply functions of the factors which seem to me to be conceivable as realities if the possibility of migration of factors to or from the economy in question is excluded. If the reasoning here presented is valid, there is therefore a universal long-run "law" of increasing money costs as output changes in response

---

2. "Rising-backward" supply curves need to be interpreted differently from ordinary negatively-inclined Marshallian supply curves, even when they are geometrically identical. In the former case each point on the curve represents a maximum quantity; in the latter case each point on the curve represents a minimum quantity. Negatively-inclined supply curves of the second type for basic factors of production seem to me so improbable as to make analysis of their consequences pedantic.

to shifts in wants in an economy of constant national money income. The "law" will operate unambiguously, however, only after the expanding industry has reached the stage beyond which there are no net technological or efficiency advantages of increasing the scale of plants in order to increase output of the particular commodities concerned as compared to increasing the number of plants, i.e., where there are no "net technological economies of large-scale production." When this stage is ordinarily reached is a question of fact, but I know of no convincing evidence that the optimum-efficiency size, as measured by the ratio of optimum-plant-capacity to total output of the industry, is not quite moderate for any industry of appreciable size outside the fields of transportation and communication, where "plant" is difficult to define.

Mr. Keynes on the Causes
of Unemployment*

THE INDEBTEDNESS OF ECONOMISTS to Mr. Keynes has been greatly increased by this latest addition to his series of brilliant, original, and provocative books, whose contribution to our enlightenment will prove, I am sure, to have been even greater in the long than in the short run.[1] This book deals with almost everything, but the causes of and the future prospects of unemployment, cyclical and secular, are its central theme. It brings much new light, but its display of dialectical skill is so overwhelming that it will have probably more persuasive power than it deserves, and a concentration on the points where I think I can detect defects in the argument, though it would be unfair if presented as an appraisal of the merits of the book as a whole, may be more useful than would a catalogue—which would have to be long to be complete—of its points of outstanding intellectual achievement.

Written though it is by a stylist of the first order, the book is not easy to read, to master, or to appraise. An extremely wide range of problems, none of them simple ones, are dealt with in an unnecessarily small number of pages. Had the book been made longer, the time required for reading it with a fair degree of understanding would have been shorter, for the argument often proceeds at breakneck speed and repeated rereadings are necessary before it can be grasped. The book, moreover, breaks with traditional modes of approach to its problems at a number of points—at the greatest possible number of points, one suspects—and no old term for an old concept is used when a new one can be coined, and if old terms are used new meanings are generally assigned to them. The definitions

*Reprinted from *The Quarterly Journal of Economics*, Vol. 51, November 1936, pp. 147-167, by the courtesy of Harvard University Press. Copyright 1936 by the President and Fellows of Harvard College.

1. John Maynard Keynes, *The General Theory of Employment Interest and Money*, Macmillan and Co., London, 1936.

provided, moreover, are sometimes of unbelievable complexity. The old-fashioned economist must, therefore, struggle not only with new ideas and new methods of manipulating them, but also with a new language. There is ample reward, however, for the expenditure of time and attention necessary for even partial mastery of the argument.

1. "Involuntary" Unemployment

Mr. Keynes claims that the "classical"[2] economists recognized the possibility only of "frictional" and of "voluntary" unemployment, and that a vitally important chapter of economic theory remains to be written about a third class of unemployment, for which there was no place in the "classical" scheme of things, namely, "involuntary" unemployment. The concept of "frictional" unemployment relates to the inevitable loss of time between jobs, and presents no difficulties. "Voluntary" unemployment is defined as the unemployment "due to the refusal or inability of a unit of labor . . . to accept a reward corresponding to the value of the product attributable to its marginal productivity," but is used in such a manner as to require the addition to this definition of the proviso that the money wage offered must not be below what the laborer regards as a proper minimum rate of *money* wages. If laborers refuse available employment at a money rate below this minimum, or if employed laborers refuse to permit a prevailing money rate to be lowered and unemployment results for themselves or for others from this refusal, Keynes would apparently regard it as "involuntary" unemployment, but deny its possibility or probability. He defines "involuntary" unemployment as follows: "*Men are involuntarily unemployed if, in the event of a small rise in the price of wage-goods relatively to the money-wage, both the aggregate supply of labour willing to work for the current money-wage and the aggregate demand for it at that wage would be greater than the existing volume of employment.*" (Keynes' italics.) (p. 15). What he seems to mean by this is that any unemployment which would disappear if real wages were to be reduced by a rise in the prices of wage-goods, money wages remaining the same or rising in less

---

2. Used by him to mean the later economists, such as J. S. Mill, Marshall, Edgeworth, Pigou, who in the main were adherents of the Ricardian tradition; a usage which I shall follow here.

proportion, *but not falling,* would be involuntary. It is with "involuntary" unemployment so understood, its causes and its remedies, that Keynes' analysis of unemployment is primarily—and almost solely—concerned.

In Keynes' classification of unemployment by its causes, unemployment due to downward-rigidity of money-wages, which for the "classical" economists was the chief type of cyclical unemployment and the only important type of secular or persistent unemployment, therefore finds no place. As will be seen later, it is excluded on the ground that resistance to reductions in money wage-rates generally does not involve a reduction in the volume of employment and is, if anything, favorable to employment rather than the reverse. The omission charged against the "classical" economists is their failure to note the lesser resistance of labor to reductions in real wages if unassociated with reductions in money wages *per se,* and their failure to recognize the existence of a large volume of unemployment for which the former is an available and practicable remedy, but not the latter. Keynes' reasoning points obviously to the superiority of inflationary remedies for unemployment over money-wage reductions. In a world organized in accordance with Keynes' specifications there would be a constant race between the printing press and the business agents of the trade unions, with the problem of unemployment largely solved if the printing press could maintain a constant lead and if only volume of employment, irrespective of quality, is considered important.

The only clash here between Keynes' position and the orthodox one is in his denial that reduction of money wage rates is a remedy for unemployment. Keynes even follows the classical doctrine too closely when he concedes that "with a given organisation, equipment and technique, real wages and the volume of output (and hence of employment) are uniquely correlated, so that, in general, an increase in employment can only occur to the accompaniment of a decline in the rate of real wages" (p. 17). This conclusion results from too unqualified an application of law-of-diminishing-returns analysis, and needs to be modified for cyclical unemployment, as well as for the possibility that the prices of wage-goods and of other goods may have divergent movements. If a plant geared to work at say 80 per cent of rated capacity is being operated at say only 30 per cent, both the per capita and the marginal output of labor may well be lower at the low rate of operations than at the higher rate, the law of diminishing returns notwithstanding. There is the further empirical consideration that if employers operate in their wage policy in accordance with marginal cost analysis, it is done only imperfectly and unconsciously, and the level of wages they can be persuaded to establish is strongly influenced by the profitability of their operations as a whole, and not solely—if at all—by calculations of the marginal contributions of labor to output.

Keynes uses the term "full employment" to signify the absence of any involuntary unemployment (p. 16). He describes it also as the condition which would prevail "when output has risen to a level at which the marginal return from a representative unit of the factors of production has fallen to the minimum figure at which a quantity of the factors sufficient to produce this output is available" (p. 303). There are implied here several questionable propositions. The concept of diminishing marginal productivity is generally used in economics in a partial differential sense to indicate the diminishing increments of output which would result when some particular factor or group of factors was being increased, the remainder of the working combination being held constant. If all the factors are being increased simultaneously and in uniform proportions, it requires some such assumption as that of the general prevalence of external technical diseconomies from increased production if it is to be accepted that output and return per compound unit of the factors must be negatively correlated. There is also implied here the assumption that any increase in real wages (money wages remaining constant, or rising) will result in an increase in the amount of labor available. If, as widely-held opinion since the seventeenth century has maintained, and as Professor Paul Douglas' recent investigations for urban labor in the United States appear to confirm, the supply schedule of labor with respect to real wages is, for part of its range at least, negatively inclined, the volume of employment could conceivably be much greater when there was "involuntary" unemployment than when there was "full" employment, and Keynes' conditions of "full" employment might be met at an indefinite number of levels of employment.

"Full" employment rarely occurs, according to Keynes, and the main immediate responsibility for the persistence of "involuntary" unemployment lies with the persistence of interest rates at levels too high to induce employers to bid for all the labor available at the prevailing money rates of wages. An elaborate and strikingly novel analysis of the causes determining the level of interest rates leads to the conclusion that high "liquidity-preferences" of savers, an excessive disposition to save and a low marginal productivity of investment are responsible for the absence of such a relation between the rates at which savers are willing to lend and the rates at which entrepreneurs are willing to borrow for investment as would result in an approximation to "full" employment.

Mr. Keynes claims further: (1) that there can be "full' employment only when entrepreneurs make investments sufficient to absorb any excess of income paid-out by entrepreneurs over expenditures on consumption by income-recipients; (2) that the amount of investment entrepreneurs are prepared to make, or their "investment demand for capital," is governed by the relation of their anticipations as to the yield of additional investment, or what Keynes calls the "marginal efficiency of capital"[3] to the interest rates at which funds can be borrowed; (3) that the amount which income-recipients are willing to spend of their current income, or their "propensity to consume," a function primarily of the amount of their incomes,[4] determines the quantity of saving; and (4) the rate of interest is determined by (*a*) "liquidity preferences" and (*b*) the quantity of cash available to satisfy such preferences. The quantity of cash is generally assumed to be a constant. I accept most of this as valid in its general outlines, but I am unable to accept some of Keynes' account of how these "propensities" operate in practice or his appraisal of their relative strength.

2. *The Propensity to Hoard*

Keynes maintains that for centuries back the propensity to save has been so much stronger than the inducement to invest as to create a substantial barrier to "full" investment. He finds fault with the "classical" economists for their alleged neglect of the gulf between the desire to save and the desire to invest, i.e., for their neglect of "liquidity preferences." It was a shortcoming of the Ricardian wing of the classical school that in the face of strong

3. "*Anticipated* marginal efficiency of capital" would seem to me a more accurately descriptive label for the concept.

4. It is, in my opinion, probably dependent appreciably also on anticipations as to the prospective trend of income, and is surely affected significantly by amount of accumulated wealth at current valuations as well as by current income. See *infra*, §4, for further comments on this point.

criticism they steadfastly adhered to their position that hoarding was so abnormal a phenomenon as not to constitute a significant contributing factor to unemployment even during a period of severe deflation. In static equilibrium analysis, in which perfect price flexibility is assumed and monetary changes are abstracted from, there is no occasion for consideration of hoarding. In modern monetary theory it is generally dealt with, with results which in kind are substantially identical with Keynes', as a factor operating to reduce the "velocity" of money. There has been, I believe, common agreement among economists that when price-rigidities are important hoarding could present a serious and continuing problem, and that it is always a significant factor in the downward phase of a short business cycle. Keynes, however, attaches great importance to it as a barrier to "full" employment at almost all times, and apparently irrespective of the degree of flexibility of prices.

There are several reasons why "liquidity preferences" loom so large to Keynes as a source of trouble in the economic process. He takes it for granted that they are ordinarily so strong for the average person in control of liquid resources that a substantial interest rate is required to overcome them; and apparently that they cannot be overcome by *any* rate of interest if a still higher rate of interest is anticipated in the near future. He assigns to them the rôle of sole determinant (given the amount of cash available, which he treats ordinarily as a constant) of the rate of interest. He believes that the marginal productivity function of capital and therefore the investment demand for capital have little elasticity. Finally he assumes in general that nothing can satisfy liquidity preferences except that "cash" whose quantity is one of the determinants of the interest rate.

We have almost no reliable information about the strength of liquidity preferences under varying circumstances, and in the absence of statistical information of a genuinely relevant character discussion must be based largely on conjecture. Nevertheless I venture to present a series of considerations which, in the aggregate, seem to warrant the conclusion that Keynes has grossly exaggerated the extent to which liquidity preferences have operated in the past and are likely to operate in the future as a barrier to "full" employment.

(*a*) Keynes stresses the pressure which is exercised by the expectation of a rise in the interest rate on potential purchasers of securities, leading them to postpone their purchases in order to escape a capital loss. There are, however, in every country large numbers of investors who have been taught to buy gilt-edge securities on the basis of their yield to maturity and to disregard the fluctuations in their day-to-day market values. Even investors of a speculative type are ordinarily as anxious not to miss a "low" as not to buy too high. There are many opportunities for investment which are—or seem at the time to be—of the "now-or-never" type. There is a widely-prevalent aversion to the waste of "dead" cash.

(*b*) Keynes seems to exaggerate the actuarial valuation of post-ponement of investment during a period of anticipated rise in interest rates. Rising interest rates are frequently associated with periods of greater confidence in the security of the investment, as far as payment of principal and interest according to schedule are concerned; or in the case of equity securities, with periods of more favorable anticipations of long-run yields. Hence periods of rising interest rates are often associated with periods of rising rather than falling prices of securities, especially for equity securities. Keynes seems to be in error also when he asserts that, abstracting from the risk of default on principal or interest, it will be equally profitable to hoard as to invest at par in a long-term security paying 4 per cent if the market interest rate is rising by 0.16 per cent per annum. In the first place, hoarding and investment in a long-term security are not the only alternatives. Let it be provisionally granted that hoarding and the purchase at par of a 4 per cent long-term bond would prove equally profitable at the end of the first year if the interest rate during that year had risen by 0.16 per cent. The purchase at the beginning of the year of a one-year maturity security paying anything over 0.16 per cent would then have been more profitable even if it had to be exchanged for cash within six months, and even if the short-term interest rate were also gradually rising by as much as 0.16 per cent per annum. Secondly, even a purchaser of the long-term 4 per cent security would have been richer at the end of the first year than if he had hoarded his cash, unless the security were a *perpetual* bond.

(*c*) Even if it be granted that liquidity-preferences are as strong ordinarily as Keynes indicates, their operation as a barrier to investment would necessarily be important only if it be assumed (1) that liquidity-preferences can be satisfied solely by the holding of non-investment assets, and (2) that the quantity of such assets does not automatically respond to the demand for them. Keynes takes care of this second qualification by his assumption that the quantity of money—in the assumed absence of a positive central monetary control—is constant. Here, indeed, he concedes more than is necessary, for if liquidity preferences are assumed to be stronger during depressions than during periods of business expansion, then the quantity of money, under such monetary systems as have existed in the past, varies inversely with the strength of liquidity preferences. But he does not give adequate consideration to the first qualification.

The satisfaction of liquidity preference on the one hand and investment on the other are opposite phenomena only if the range of assets which can satisfy investment demand corresponds to the range of assets which can satisfy liquidity-preferences in such a manner that it shall be impossible to satisfy both by the same transaction. If liquidity-preferences can be satisfied by the holding of resources which are not identical with the "money" whose surrender is required to satisfy investment demand, the satisfaction of the former does not necessarily entail failure to satisfy the latter. Keynes explains liquidity-preference as a wish to retain one's resources in the form of money. There is no systematic examination of what is to be included as "money" for this purpose, but incidentally to his analysis of one particular form of surrender of liquidity, namely, exchange of money for a debt, he states:

> ... we can draw the line between "money" and "debts" at whatever point is most convenient for handling a particular problem. For example, we can treat as *money* any command over general purchasing power which the owner has not parted with for a period in excess of three months, and as *debt* what cannot be recovered for a longer period than this; or we can substitute for "three months" one month or three days or three hours or any other period; or we can exclude from *money* whatever is not legal tender on the spot. It is often convenient in practice to include in *money* time-deposits with banks and, occasionally, even such instruments as (e.g.) treasury bills. As a rule, I shall ... assume that money is co-extensive with bank deposits (p. 167, note).

If everything which satisfies liquidity-preference is to be included as money, then money must be broadly defined so as to include not only demand deposits and time deposits, but also short-term securities, any other assets which are readily marketable without serious risk of loss through depreciation of value, and even the command over credit from banks or others. But the conversion of newly-acquired cash into any other form of asset either involves investment directly or transfers the decision as between hoarding and investment to a banker or other intermediary between the original saver and the ultimate borrower for investment. If the banker permits his investments to remain constant while his cash reserves are increasing, or if he maintains the same cash reserves for idle as for active demand deposits, or for time deposits as for demand deposits, or for deposits as for banknotes in circulation, then the propensity to hoard which manifests itself in the maintenance of idle bank deposits does operate to check investment, but only with the connivance and support of the banking mechanism.

It may be objected that even if liquidity-preferences operate only, or in the main, to check purchases of long-term securities, they still operate as a check to investment; because the latter is and must be largely in durable goods, or in assets far removed from the stage of consumers' goods. But the relation between the period of investment intended by the saver and that intended, or in fact resulting, by the borrowing entrepreneur is not a simple one of necessary equality. It is highly flexible and approaches to free variability at the discretion of the borrower. Every money market has an elaborate machinery for transmuting short-term loans into long-term investments and long-term loans into short-term investments, to suit the convenience of original lenders and ultimate borrowers. The typical entrepreneur will shift from long-term to short-term borrowing, or vice versa, even though the time period involved in the particular operation is unchanged, or (as often) unknowable in advance. He may also be able to shift from long-term to short-term investment if the interest rate at which the latter can be financed is much lower than that at which he can conduct admittedly long-term borrowing. If savers have a 5 per cent per annum preference for cash over investment in 10-year bonds but only a ¼ per cent preference for cash over time-deposits or short-term securities, and if entrepreneurs want funds for 10 years and are unwilling to incur the sacrifice of their own liquidity which would be involved in the attempt to finance 10-year operations with say 3-month borrowings, middlemen will step in who are prepared to lend on long-term funds which they have borrowed on short-term. The modern money market is fortunately equipped to some extent with procedures for satisfying liquidity-preferences without providing genuine liquidity.

(*d*) The propensity to hoard exercises its influence as a restraint on investment through its tendency to raise interest rates. But in what seems to me the most vulnerable part of his analysis, his explanation of the determination of the rate of interest, Keynes assigns to the desire for cash for hoarding purposes a grossly exaggerated importance.

Keynes denies the validity of the "classical" doctrine that interest is the reward for saving and is directly determined by the supply schedule of savings with respect to the interest rate and the investment demand schedule for capital, and his exposition leaves the impression that the interest rate is not dependent to any important extent on these two factors. He denies that interest is the "reward" for saving on the ground that if a man hoards his savings in cash he earns no interest, though he saves just as much as before (p. 167), and claims that, on the contrary, it is the reward for surrender of liquidity. By analogous reasoning he could deny that wages are the reward for labor, or that profit is the reward for risk-taking, because labor is sometimes done without anticipation or realization of a return, and men who assume financial risks have been known to incur losses as a result instead of profits. Without saving there can be no liquidity to surrender. The saver who has no concern about liquidity gets the same reward as the person who saved with liquidity as his initial objective but is persuaded by the interest rate to lend; and the return is granted for loans irrespective of whether it is reluctance to postpone consumption or reluctance to surrender liquidity which keeps the supply of funds for investment down to the level at which borrowers are willing to pay the prevailing rate of interest for it. The rate of interest is the return for saving plus some surrender of liquidity.

Keynes explains the rate of interest as determined by the schedule of liquidity-preferences and the available quantity of money, the prevailing rate of interest being simply that price for the sacrifice of liquidity at which the desire to hold cash is equated with the quantity of available cash (p. 167). The rate of interest determines the amount of investment, given the investment demand for capital; but a change in the investment demand for capital will not affect the interest rate "if nothing has happened to the state of liquidity-preference and the quantity of money." (See especially the figure on p. 180, and the text on p. 181).

There have been previous attempts to discover a basis on which the interest rate could be held to be determined independently of the demand for capital, the level of wages, and other important elements in the economy, but the growing recognition of the basic interdependence of all the important economic variables has led to widespread scepticism that any such attempt could succeed. In Keynes' present attempt the fatal flaw is, to repeat, the exaggerated importance attributed to hoarding. In his discussion of liquidity-preferences Keynes distinguishes between the desire for cash for use in the current transaction of personal and business exchanges, and the desire for cash as a security against loss from unsuccessful investment. As I have already argued, the latter consideration should not operate as a barrier to short-term investment, and while it may induce a high long-term interest rate, it will be compensated for in part by a shift of borrowing to the short-term market. The pattern of behavior of the desire for transaction-liquidity is probably very largely the inverse of that of security-liquidity, or hoarding proper. As D. H. Robertson points out in his contribution to this symposium, the transactions-desire for cash is for cash to be used and not for cash to be held unused. It must therefore vary positively with the volume of investment, of income, and of expenditures for consumption. In so far as it consists of demand for cash from entrepreneurs for business uses, it is but a reflection of their investment demand for capital. In so far as it is a demand for cash from consumers who are living beyond their current income, it is the demand for consumption loans of older theory. Whatever its origin, demand for cash for transaction purposes is, dollar for dollar, of equal influence on the rate of interest as demand for cash for hoarding purposes. The demand for capital and the propensity to save (which is the reciprocal of the propensity to consume) are thus restored—though, I admit, in somewhat modified and improved fashion—to their traditional rôles as determinants of the rate of interest.

While (to repeat again) relevant statistical information is scarce, what we do know about the holders of cash balances in the United States points strongly to the importance of the transactions-motive for liquidity and to the relative insignificance in ordinary times of hoarding. It is the corporations, institutions, and governments that hold at all times the bulk of the cash balances, especially if savings deposits are excluded as constituting investments rather than cash. Moreover I suspect (I know of no data on the question) that at least in prosperous times the savers—those who add each

year to their estates—who are supposed by Keynes to be a source
of so much trouble because of their hoarding propensities, typically
hold in cash a smaller percentage of their incomes, let alone of
their total resources, than do the spenders. The former have investment habits, and abhor idle cash as nature abhors a vacuum. The
latter hold cash until the bills come in for settlement. It would at
least be interesting to know whether these are facts or fancies.

The importance of the transactions-demand for cash makes it
easy to explain a whole series of historical phenomena which do
not fit into Keynes' theory. Because the demand for cash for business use varies positively with the investment demand for capital,
and the demand for cash for personal use varies positively with the
level of income and of expenditures for consumption, there is no
need for treating as a perplexing puzzle the facts, that business is
active when interest rates are high and slack when interest rates are
low, and that the quantity of money and the interest rate are
historically correlated positively rather than negatively. There is
an important stabilizing influence, moreover, in these circumstances.
During a depression entrepreneurs and spenders release some of the
cash to supply the demand of hoarders for security, and during an
expansion of business the absorption of cash by business and by
spenders, serving as it does to raise the interest rate, keeps the
expansion from going beyond bounds; or, Keynes would say, from
even approaching reasonable bounds.

3. *Money-Wage Flexibility and Volume of Employment*

Keynes expresses sweeping dissent with the "classical" doctrine
that money-wage rigidity is a major cause both of cyclical and of
secular unemployment, although he freely grants that in general
increased employment must mean lower real wages. He maintains
that labor strongly resists money wage reductions but takes reductions in real wages much more calmly, and therefore that even if
money wage-reductions were logically a remedy for unemployment
they would not be a practicable one. His view is that a lowering
of money wage-rates, unless it proceeded simultaneously and
uniformly all along the line, would chiefly alter the relative rates of
wages of different labor groups. It would not be likely to increase
the aggregate volume of employment of labor, and on the balance
of probabilities would be more likely to reduce it. He does not

discuss the effects on employment which would result from pressure from labor for *increases* in money-wages, or from increases of money-wages made voluntarily on the part of employers, whether for humanitarian reasons or because of belief that high wages mean prosperity or in response to public opinion.

Keynes presents his own position mainly in terms of a criticism of a theory which he imputes to the "classical" economists, according to which a reduction of money wages *and a simultaneous corresponding reduction in prices* would increase employment because the same volume of monetary expenditures would purchase a greater physical output of commodities. He easily demolishes this by pointing out that, if money wages paid out were to fall in amount and investment by entrepreneurs (measured in wage-units) did not increase, the amount of money income available for expenditures would fall to an equivalent extent. His discussion of the effects of the wage-reduction on the volume of investment is mainly in terms of its influence on the expectations of entrepreneurs as to the future trend of wages, and he concedes that if entrepreneurs are led to expect further changes to be in an upward direction its effect will be favorable. He urges, however, that "it would be much better that wages should be rigidly fixed and deemed incapable of material changes, than that depressions should be accompanied by a gradual downward tendency of money-wages" (p. 265).

This does not meet the argument for wage-reduction—or rather money-cost reduction[5]—during a depression which I had understood to be the prevalent one in recent years. In this other doctrine, factor-prices are to be reduced, but not, or not in the same degree, the prices of consumers' goods. In Keynes' analysis perfect and active competition is assumed, and prices are supposed to fall immediately and in full proportion to the fall in marginal variable[6]

---

5. From the point of view of effect on *output*, the reduction of any part of variable costs is dollar for dollar of the same importance as the reduction of any other part of such costs, and it is only as against reduction of outstanding fixed costs, to the extent that they also do not consist of labor costs, that there is anything to be said for reduction of labor costs in preference to other costs. But from the point of view of the effect on the employment of *labor*, the reduction of labor cost is more favorable than the reduction to an equivalent amount of any other cost, because it will tend to lead to a substitution of labor for other factors, though it will not be as favorable as the reduction of both or *a fortiori* of all costs simultaneously and in the same proportions.

6. Keynes distinguishes between "factor costs" and "user costs," the two combined comprising "prime" costs. By user costs he means the amounts paid out

costs. If this occurred, and output remained the same, prices per unit would fall in greater absolute amount than would average variable costs,[7] and even more, if current labor cost were a negligible element in the fixed costs, than would average aggregate costs. The profit status of entrepreneurs would then be less favorable than before. What I understand to be the current doctrine is different. It looks to wage-reductions during a depression to restore profit-margins, thus to restore the investment-morale of entrepreneurs and to give them again a credit status which will enable them to finance any investment they may wish to make. It relies upon the occurrence of a lag between the reduction in wage-rates and a response in reduced volume of sales at the previous prices, during which interval entrepreneurs find prices to be higher than marginal costs and extensions of output therefore profitable, provided buyers can be found for the increased output. Increase in expenditures to restore depleted inventories and to replace inefficient equipment is relied upon to increase pay rolls sufficiently to provide the incomes with which the increased output can be bought, and the gain in employment—and in security of employment for those previously employed—is expected to release for expenditure the emergency reserves of the wage-earning class. On the assumption that a large part of an entrepreneur's expenditures are ordinarily of the postponable class in the sense that they can be deferred without forcing a reduction of the scheduled rate of current output, even though not without increasing the current cost of production; and on the further assumption that operations at a loss are conducive to the postponement of every expenditure not essential for current operation, the supporters of this doctrine maintain that recovery of

---

to other entrepreneurs for purchases from them and sacrifices incurred (extra wear and tear presumably) in employing equipment instead of leaving it idle. He claims that economists have generally equated supply price with marginal factor cost, ignoring user cost, whereas it should be equated with prime cost. I see no point in the distinction between purchases from entrepreneurs and direct purchases of the services of the factors. What is the point in distinguishing between the cost of coal to a steel mill according as it is bought from an outside mine or produced in its own collieries? Where is the line to be drawn between entrepreneurs and "factors"? I am sceptical as to whether any economists have, explicitly or by implication, excluded cost of purchased materials or depreciation of equipment through use from the costs supposed to determine supply price.

7. Because marginal costs would fall in the same proportion as average variable costs but would be greater in amount per unit than average variable costs.

a profit margin can lead for a time to an increase in entrepreneurs' expenditures many times the increase in their net income, or, alternatively, the reduction in their net loss. They do not contend that this is certain to occur, but on the ground that the chief factor in governing the action of entrepreneurs with respect to postponable expenditures is the current profit status of their operations as compared to their immediately preceding experience, they say that it is a reasonable probability. Where external pressure on prices in the face of rigid costs has been an important factor in the depression, they also expect a favorable influence on the volume of employment from the effect of a wage-reduction on profits and therefore on the volume of postponable expenditures, rather than from its effect on prices. While Keynes' analysis provides materials for strengthening this doctrine at a number of points, I cannot find in it any refutation of its general validity.

4. *Propensity to Consume*

Mr. Keynes himself tells us that the functional relationships of the various economic variables are more complex in fact than is formally recognized in his analysis. Simplification of this sort is inevitable, if analysis is to proceed at all. In the case, however, of Keynes' "propensity to consume" function, it seems to me that the simplification has been carried further than is necessary to prevent the analysis from becoming entangled in its own complexities, and further than is permissible if the concept is to be used fruitfully in the analysis of the short cycle.

Keynes explains the propensity to consume as a functional relationship between the amount of consumption measured in money-wage units and the amount of income similarly measured. On the assumption that income in terms of money wage-units corresponds substantially in its variations with the variations in level of employment, it is concluded that income, consumption, and level of employment are related to each other in a simple pattern. Writing C_w for amount of consumption in wage-units and Y_w for income in wage-units, and accepting as a close approximation that Y_w is a unique function of the level of employment, he states the propensity to consume function as: $C_w = \chi(Y_w)$ (p. 90).

Keynes lists a number of factors, (p. 96) "subjective" and

"objective," which might affect the value of χ, Y_w remaining constant, but he assumes in general that the "subjective" factors remain constant, at least over short periods, and that, given Y_w, χ depends only on changes in the "objective" factors, which in the aggregate he takes to be of minor importance as compared to changes in Y_w. Several "objective" factors which he does not appear to have taken into account seem important enough in the short cycle to be deserving at least of mention.

Keynes believes that, apart from the effect of a change in the wage-unit on the distribution of income between entrepreneurs and rentiers, who might have different propensities to consume, he has made adequate allowance in his formula for changes in expenditure resulting from changes in the wage-unit by measuring both consumption and income in wage-units. This disregards the possibility that, for short periods at least, the distinction which Keynes makes in his supply function of labor between the response of labor (1) to changes in real wages accompanied by corresponding changes in money wages, and (2) to changes in real wages resulting from changes in the prices of wage-goods, money wages remaining the same, may have a parallel in the propensity to consume function. The response of consumption to a reduction in real income may be, for a time, substantially different if the reduction takes the form of a decrease in money-income, prices remaining the same, from what it would be if money-income remained the same but prices increased.

Mr. Keynes claims that in general rich countries are worse off than poor countries with respect to avoidance of "involuntary" employment because of the lesser propensities to consume in the former than in the latter, and thus the greater potential importance of hoarding. Since I would contend that over long periods, given a flexible price system, the propensity to consume will affect the rate of capital accumulation rather than the volume of employment, I will confine myself to a consideration of the comparative situation of the rich and poor countries with respect to the short cycle. The possession of large accumulated resources should operate to level out the rate of consumption in the face of fluctuations in income, and therefore to check both the downward and the upward phases of the cycle. Corresponding to the charges against the entrepreneur's budget which are fixed in aggregate monetary amount regardless of current output, there are in the ordinary consumer's budget items of monetary expenditure which are fixed for a time, very much regardless of changes in his money income as far as reductions therein are concerned, and which tend to be increased only as the result of careful deliberation in response to anticipation of a change of some duration in the individual's economic status. Aside from the probability that such fixed charges are ordinarily a greater proportion of the expenditures of the rich than of the poor, the poor in times of severe depression have a partial means of escape from them, in the form of defaults, to which those with resources subject to levy cannot resort. What this amounts to is that C_w should be treated as a function not only of Y_w, but also of the amount of accumulated resources measured in wage units held by the individual. In so far as the possession of resources operates in the manner suggested here, wealth becomes a stabilizing rather than a disturbing factor. The explanation of the apparently indisputable fact that the cyclical disturbances are more severe in rich than in poor countries would then have to be sought elsewhere than in the differences between rich and poor in propensities to consume. My own guess is that it is to be sought largely in the differences between the cyclical behavior of rich and poor with respect to the disposition of the income which they do not spend. The rich hoard only during depressions and dishoard for investment during prosperity, whereas the poor hoard some of their emergency reserves during prosperity and dishoard during depression.

Mr. Keynes says that a fundamental psychological law, upon which we have a right to depend both on *a priori* grounds and on the basis of experience is that dC_w/dY_w is positive and less than unity; i.e., that in terms of wage-units consumption varies in the same direction as income, but in smaller absolute amount than income (p. 96). This seems altogether reasonable. It leaves unanswered, however, a question of some interest: does C_w ever, except perhaps under war conditions, exceed Y_w? Since the community excess of Y_w over C_w constitutes new investment, if C_w never exceeded Y_w there would be continuous, though fluctuating, accumulation of capital resources, even through the depths of depression. Mr. Keynes apparently must believe that for the world as a whole the C_w's must often and substantially exceed the Y_w's, for he holds that in spite of "several millenia of steady individual saving" the world is poor in accumulated capital assets.[8] But what evidence there is seems to indicate that, if any acceptable mode of measuring physical amount of capital could be found and applied, it would show that the western world has been getting wealthier fairly steadily during say the past century and a half, not only in terms of aggregate resources but per capita, in spite of a three-or-four-fold increase of population.

In connection with the propensity to consume concept, as with most of Keynes' concepts, the question arises in my mind how these concepts would have to be restated in order to provide specifications for the construction of statistical series by which his conclusions as to the nature and mode of behavior through time of the various functions could be inductively tested, and I regret that no suggestions of this sort are provided in this book. I am disposed to support Mr. Robertson in his claim that concepts expressed in more "monetary" terms, and expressions for the relationships between variables which make specific allowance for time-lags instead of assigning uniform time-units to all the variables, have for purposes of *a priori* analysis some points of superiority over Keynes' "propensity" concepts expressed in terms of a single time-unit. For purposes of inductive verification, assuming that the statistical data available will ever be in a form relevant to the answer of important questions, it seems obvious to me that the analysis would have to be extensively restated in terms of directions and degrees of time-lags.

8. "That the world after several millennia of steady individual saving, is so poor as it is in accumulated capital-assets, is to be explained, in my opinion, neither by the improvident propensities of mankind, nor even by the destruction of war, but by the high liquidity-premiums formerly attaching to the ownership of land and now attaching to money" (p. 242).

The Short View and the Long in Economic Policy*

ONCE UPON A TIME an academic economic theorist, by some freak of fate not likely to be often repeated, got himself slightly entangled in the machinery of formulation of government economic policy. What I plan to tell you tonight reflects largely, though not I hope too explicitly, what the process of policy-formulation did to his academic theorizing, and what his theorizing failed to do to the process of policy-formulation.

As an active participant in the policy-making process, the academic theorist suffers from a number of handicaps more or less peculiar to himself. For purposes of teaching, or of acceptable writing for his restricted audience of fellow-theorists, his conclusions are of little importance; and what matters above all is the rigor and elegance of his manner of reaching them. For policy, on the other hand, conclusions are vital, and often are all that is vital. For the purposes of academic theorizing, the premises the theorist starts from may without serious penalty be arbitrarily selected, narrowly restricted in range, and purely hypothetical in nature. But the selection of premises controls the conclusions reached, and for policy-determination it is therefore vital that all the important variables be covered by the analysis, and that the conclusions be not affected by the use of premises which are irrevelant for their purposes or less realistic than it is possible with the aid of available information to make them. To violate these rules in policy-making is to be guilty of the grossest irresponsibility. If he is not to be wholly in the way of the policy-maker, therefore,

*Presidential address delivered at the meetings of the American Economic Association, Dec. 27, 1939. Reprinted from *The American Economic Review*, Vol. 30, March 1940, pp. 1-15, by the courtesy of the American Economic Association.

the theorist must emerge from his ivory tower,—which is almost as hard as to return to it.

The theorist's habitual methods of analysis are such as to lead to "right" or "wrong" answers to manufactured problems, the premises and the criteria of rightness being so chosen as to make this not only possible but necessary. For the policy-maker, however, the problems are for the most part not of his own devising, but are presented to him by outside forces, in vague and ill-defined fashion, and what he asks of his advisers consists as much of help in determining what the problems are as of help in finding solutions for them. The theorist here is likely to find himself uninformed and unskilled.

The theorist's analysis is ordinarily couched in descriptive as distinguished from normative terms. If choices as between social values influence his thought, these choices are largely left implicit in his selection of premises, and are rarely, and then usually apologetically, expressly avowed. The policy-maker, however, is rarely satisfied with purely descriptive analysis. He insists that he be advised not only what will be the objective consequences of a specific line of action, but whether or not these are desirable consequences. While he has always some notions of his own with respect to the values which policy should serve, in my experience he always demands of his economists that they guide him also in the determination of what is socially desirable, and he expects the economist to acknowledge and to display some professional competence in giving such guidance.

There are always a number of different values to be considered, moreover, and satisfaction of one often involves disregard of the other. This makes necessary a sort of weighing process, in which the decision is presumably made partly on the strength of quantitative information as to the number of persons affected by alternative courses of action, their economic status and needs, and so forth, and partly on the basis of a qualitative ranking of values in terms of some sort of scale of worth. The theorist as such here also lacks experience. He is hampered, moreover, by his tendency to dissect the mental processes by which decision is reached in such matters, and he tends to feel and to give discomfort by his reluctance to express in definite and assured terms the conclusions which he knows he has reached only by vague and imperfectly communicable processes of thought.

The effect of the action on the subject is all that the theorist has been trained or conditioned to think about with respect to public policy. The official and the legislator, on the other hand, should, and in any case invariably do, think also of the effect of the action on the actor. The economist conditioned to the purity of abstract thought is liable to be unreasonable in his refusal to recognize that the official, in choosing his time for action and his manner and degree of action, must give regard to their impact on his relations with superiors, colleagues, Congress, and the public, and to their effect on the prestige of his agency and the morale of his staff. But the official must operate in this way if those with whom he has to deal from day to day are to give him that coöperation and good will which are essential not merely for his own personal success and comfort but for the satisfactory execution of his functions.

The higher officials in Washington, whether they be political appointees or career men, in my opinion, need make no apologies. for their standards even to college professors, elect of the elect though we be. As far as I have observed, the higher officials in Washington as a group work as hard, as disinterestedly, coöperate in common tasks as loyally, think as straight within their own special fields of competence, as does the ordinary run of college professor. They certainly do not live on the moral heights continuously, but they are called upon more often than academic men to rise to them, and, in my honest judgment, they respond to the call as often and as fully as in all probability we ourselves should under like circumstances.

In one respect in particular, of special interest to economists, I have observed them with ever-increasing admiration—namely, their patience and generosity in thir dealings with their economic advisers. In the course of expounding the economic verities, the economists repeatedly expose their divided counsels. They especially reveal that conflict within their ranks between ancient dogmas and resurrected or newly-invented heresies with which much of the remainder of my talk will deal. Those officials who come into frequent contact with squads of economists, as they note the repeated conflict of testimony, must feel at times like the English judge who remarked that he had for years been trying motoring cases in which two cars, each of them on the right side of the road and each of them stationary, had been involved in a head-on collision—or even like that magistrate in a native court in Ceylon who, disgusted by the flagrant contradictions in the evidence of the successive witnesses, said to the officer of the court: "Call the next liar." This failure of the economists to speak as with one voice is a severe trial for the officials. I suspect, however, that they would find us even more trying if, when unpalatable advice was offered by one economist, they could not feel that there was a good chance that with a little search another economist could be found happy to swear that the advice which had been given was incredibly bad economics, or even was "orthodox" or "sound" economics, which are now very forceful epithets indeed in some high quarters.

To proceed with my catalogue of the handicaps of the economic theorist as a policy-maker. The economists of my generation and earlier were trained to concentrate on so-called long-run analysis in their pure theorizing. When they ventured into the discussion of questions of public policy, they accordingly tended to be preoccupied with the long view, with the effects which a given action would have on the more distant future, and to disregard or to weigh lightly its more immediate effects. A good illustration of what I have in mind is the famous poor-law controversy in England in the 1830's. The leading economists of the time all emphasized the allegedly injurious effects on the productive capacity and the will to work and to save of the poor which would result from generous, long-sustained, and assured poor-relief to the able-bodied. They stressed even more the growth of population and the consequent impairment of the basic earning power of labor which they believed would ultimately result from any substantial liberation of the poor from dependence solely on their own efforts for the means of subsistence of themselves and their children. The extreme conservatives and the extreme radicals of the time—who, as so often in history, were on the same side on a specific issue—and also the humanitarians and clergy, stressed in opposition to the views of the economists the moral and political rights of the needy to be given food and shelter with a minimum of humiliation and of deliberate interference with their accustomed patterns of family and social life. In this instance, as in many others, it was possible plausibly to picture the clash between the long view and the short as a clash between the hard-hearted and the humane, although the economists of the time of course insisted that the policy they advocated, while immediately severe, would ultimately prove to be the kinder of the two to the poor.

Although it is obviously not without direct relevance to present-day problems, I am not concerned here with the merits of this ancient controversy. I have cited it only to help make clear the differing turn which may be given to public policy accordingly as the long view or the short is dominant, and to illustrate the characteristic approach of the orthodox economist, from that day to this, to policy questions.

Now this habit of taking the long view is not only characteristic of the orthodox economic theorist, but in the discussion of matters of economic policy it is often the principal characteristic by which he can be disintinguished from other professional economists or even from the intelligent layman.

In the day-to-day process of adapting public policy to meet felt needs, on the other hand, the problems always manifest themselves in the form of immediate pressures of one sort or another, and the legislator or official tends to look for correspondingly immediate solutions. This is "natural" behavior, in the sense both that it is what one should expect to occur, and that it has its socially useful aspects.

Legislators and officials are typically busy and harried men. Except under the special circumstances of major election campaigns, when the pattern of party debate may by chance turn on the relative merits of the long-run programs of the contending parties, and except for the occasional opportunity of the legislator or the official to divest himself of the cares of the moment and, assuming the rôle of the statesman, to give patient examination to the needs of the future, there is constant preoccupation with the problems which are immediately pressing, and little stimulus to take thought as to whether the proffered solutions are likely to prove lasting ones. There is especially little urge to go hunting for problems which are not yet felt as such but which may prove troublesome in the distant future.

It would be a mistake, however, to take for granted that the immediate solution, the quickly-working one, is of necessity a defective one. The immediate solution to a problem no doubt frequently serves also with tolerable satisfaction as a permanent one, and in some cases may well be identical with the optimum permanent solution. Many problems, moreover, are themselves temporary in nature, and require therefore only temporary solutions. The immediate solution may be the only one for which public acceptance is obtainable, so that there is really no choice. There are circumstances, moreover, under which even a benevolent dictator, with no need to give heed to public clamor, would be wise to adopt a partial and temporary, but quick-working, solution in preference to a more complete and more lasting one which would yield its benefits only after considerable delay. Mr. Keynes, speaking with at least a trace of the accent of revelation, has told us that in the long run we'll all be dead. What I presume he meant by this apparently crystal-clear dictum was that if we took the long view, we, including our otherwise potential posterity, would—or might—all be dead —or dead or unborn—before that view could justify itself. This warning is scarcely much needed either by the public official or by the ordinary legislator, but for the reasons I have stated and not only because in respectable communities the dead and the unborn cast no votes. But for the academic economist it is a sound warning, and perhaps even a needed one. In times of severe social strain there may be real menace of catastrophe if there is not resort, even at the cost of bad after-effects, to a quick-working remedy which tides the economy over the crisis. At such times, the patience of the orthodox theorist may be out of place. But in the past, at least, such times have come only rarely.

Closely related to the habit of the theorist of preoccupying himself with those effects of proposed legislation which are more distant in time is his habit of searching for the repercussions of legislation which are so-to-speak more distant in space. Politicians are experts in tracing one kind of repercussion, the *political*. But they are indisposed to take account of *economic* repercussions, as the history of tariff controversy abundantly demonstrates. This indisposition, I think, they share with the general lay public, to whom, in matters of economic analysis, one step at a time is enough, if not too much. And since what the public doesn't know can't hurt the legislator, he has at least no selfish motive for following the theorist in his unsteady and circuitous wanderings from the proximate to the secondary, to the tertiary effects, and is content to act in terms of the seen, with worry about the unseen left to the economic theorist as a sort of occupational psychosis.

I do not include in my list of the handicaps peculiar to the economic theorist as a participant in the policy-formulating process two items which would probably appear high on such a list if prepared by those with whom the economist works—namely, first, his ignorance as a rule of the legal framework and legal folklore to which legislative drafting and the administration of the laws must conform; and second, his lack of experience and insight with respect to what is and what is not administratively feasible. These are omitted, however, not because the ordinary economist does have command of these skills, and not because they are unimportant, for such is decidedly not the case in either instance. But barriers to effectiveness of this general type, instead of being peculiar to economic theorists, are common to all kinds of specialized participants in a coöperative enterprise such as policy-formulation which makes demands upon a wider range of skills than single individuals can reasonably be expected to possess. The lack of legal and administrative training on the part of the economic theorist may be regrettable, but it is not fatal as long as he is not permitted to decide policy questions all on his own.

In the ordinary course of events, policy is, of course, ultimately decided not by the technical experts as such, whether they be economists or engineers or political scientists or sociologists, but by the legislators and the responsible executives with the aid of advice by the experts. That excellent formula, "The expert *should be* on tap, not on top" would be almost equally valid if it went, "The expert *is* on tap, not on top." This applies no more and no less to the economist than to the other professions—except for the lawyer, who is on tap *and* on top, and omnipresent, omniscient, omnipotent, and omnivorous in addition. In the process of tapping the experts for their specialized knowledge and skills, the technical equipment of one profession provides the offset for the gaps in the capacities of the others. And for those many things which in a world not clearly designed for full comprehension by man are beyond human knowledge, the lawyer always stands ready to provide precise formulae acceptable to the Supreme Court as unambiguous expressions of legislative intent.

Even with these two items omitted, the list of handicaps of the academic economic theorist as a participant in the formulation of public policy which I have given is discouragingly long. Others, moreover, would probably think they could easily make it even longer and even more discouraging to the theorist. Let it be clear, however, that I am not identifying the few "academic economic

theorists" with economists in general, and that I recognize that
there are many other types of economists whose serviceability in
policy-formulation and in other activities of government has been
amply and unquestionably demonstrated.

The non-theoretical economist, in particular, or the economist
who disclaims any theoretical prejudices, is in fact much more
adaptable to public service than the economic theorist with some
body of theory to which he remains faithful, whatever its species.
The non-theorist can adjust himself quickly to the changing flow of
events and issues. He is not bound by any set mode of analysis.
His mind but lightly encumbered by doctrines, dogmas, preconceptions, or even in some cases thoughts, the fortunate man can
move freely in any direction, wherever the wind may list. If he
feels the need for guidance, there is always available today yester-
day's position of his official superiors and tomorrow the different
position they took today. In finding good-sounding reasons for what
has already been decided upon, he has a distinctive and useful function, both because the vitality of the democratic process is dependent upon our continuing to believe that it provides us with reasonably wise and beneficent government, and also because statesmen's
intuitions have often a genuine economic logic dimly in their background. He shares also with other types of economists the useful
rôle of finding good uses for bad laws, and thus contributes to the
most important function of the art of public administration: the
making of silk purses out of legislative sows' ears.

The handicaps of the academic theorist of the older dispensation
as a useful member of a policy-formulating staff are probably even
more clearly visible to other members of the *economic* profession
than to members of *other* professions. There is in fact a definite
cleavage between the habits of thought of this species of theorist and
those of other groups in the profession, including many of those who
help guide Leviathan in its daily gyrations. The continued depression has obviously made a deep impression on the latter, and made
them impatient of or even violently hostile to the traditional corpus
of economic theory, which they look upon as an instrument for
the exercise of the tyranny of the dead mind over the living. They
seem to believe increasingly that its rôle has been, even in the
long-past days of its almost unchallenged dominance, "to light fools
the way to dusty death." The world it approvingly describes of
atomistic competition, and the ethical approval which, as they read

it, it translates to the actual world by its failure clearly to contrast the ideal with the real, make it appear to them too far divorced from the present-day realities and values to warrant faith in its usefulness as an aid to the guidance of social policy. Instead of the economy of effective competition, of freedom of individual initiative, of equality of economic opportunity, of steady and full employment, pictured in the traditional theory, they see an economy dominated by giant corporations in almost every important field of industry outside agriculture, an economy marked by great concentration of wealth and economic power, and great disparity of income and of opportunity for betterment. They note the apparently unending flow of evidence from investigating committees and courts of the flagrant misuse of concentrated economic power. They observe with alarm the failure of our economy for ten successive years to give millions of men able to work and anxious to work the opportunity to earn their daily bread. And seeing the actual world so, they refuse to accept as useful for their purposes a type of economic theory which as they read it either ignores these evils or treats them as temporary, self-correcting aberrations or excrescences of what is basically a sound economic system. Having rejected the conventional picture of the system, they tend increasingly to adopt another one, rapidly approaching equal conventionalization, but following another pattern, in which the evils are inherent in the system and cannot be excised without its drastic reconstruction and its substantial operation by government.

Their account of the traditional economic theory is not wholly a caricature, but it is overdrawn and distorted. It deliberately disregards the failure of government to behave according to the rules laid down by the orthodox theory as necessary if its conclusions are to have practical validity, and it especially overlooks the long line of great men in the orthodox tradition, by no means already at an end, who by no stretch of the imagination can be charged with having exploited it to protect evils against reform. But this is in the present connection significant only as it prejudices these zealous reformers against utilizing for their own good purposes the aid the old doctrines can still furnish. Their picture of the evils of the present economic system may also be painted in too strident colors, but it is undoubtedly close enough to the truth to make complacency indefensible. Where in my opinion they are most gravely in error, however, is that in rejecting lock-stock-and-barrel the traditional economic theory, they are abandoning habits of mind and analytical tools which are still essential if evils are not only correctly to be identified but are to be ascribed to their proper causes, and if remedies are not to be advocated which may prove worse than the diseases they are prescribed for.

As a by-product of the breach with the older body of doctrine, the economic profession is tending to wipe out that line of cleavage which in this country has been so marked almost since the foundation of the Economic Association between the teachings of the professional economists, on the one hand, and the practices of government and the beliefs of the lay public, on the other hand. I, for one, would welcome this reconciliation if it resulted from our final conversion of the lay public. I think, however, that the reverse has happened to a substantial extent, and that economic doctrine is now following public opinion and government practice much more than it is influencing them. For obvious reasons which have no counterpart in this country, this is now of course the routine situation in totalitarian countries. Its occurrence in this country is not, I am certain, due to any significant extent to a new subservience of the profession to external opinion. Its explanation lies largely, I think, in the fact that under the impact of depression conditions the economists have in large numbers abandoned the traditional economic doctrines, with their emphasis on the long view, and have turned instead to the short view which government and the lay public have always tended to take. It is true that in adopting the short view many of the younger economists have not merely taken over the lay notions bodily. Some of them have, in fact, given them a theoretical elaboration which for subtlety, refinement, and elegance need make no apologies to the older economics, and which remains faithful to older theorizing in at least one respect, that the tradition of unintelligibility to the layman is scrupulously observed. It is the quality of the judgment displayed, and not the quality of the analytical skill, which I venture to question. No matter how refined and how elaborate the analysis, if it rests solely on the short view it will still be close to the layman's economics and still be a structure built on shifting sands.

My aim this evening is not to praise the old-fashioned economic theorist, but only to help protect him from premature burial. The strongest line of defense I find available is the argument that he is the special custodian for society of the long view in economic matters, and that even in troubled periods that view is entitled not to undisputed dominance but to a full hearing. Since its value with reference to any specific issue can be tested only empirically and therefore only after a substantial period of time has elapsed, I shall present my case for the long view forward by taking the long view back into history with respect to several of the doctrines in the orthodox tradition. Not to make it too easy for myself, I shall deal only with doctrines that have been so conventionalized through time that they seem to the short-viewers flagrant examples of the freezing of doctrine into dogmas whose venerability is their only claim to virtue.

An underlying characteristic of the orthodox Anglo-American economics during its entire period of dominance was its basically optimistic outlook on the prospective trend of events. As a cursory inspection of the files of presidential addresses before the American Economic Association and its English prototype would confirm, the economists of the time believed that, despite wars, mistakes in government policy, and cyclical disturbances, private initiative, technological progress, and the improvement and wider diffusion of education had resulted in and would continue to result in a slowly rising secular trend of per capita income, enjoyed by steadily-growing populations. Imbued with this moderately optimistic long view, the economists listened neither to the occasional prophets of impending and lasting woe nor to the more frequent peddlers of patented devices for antedating the millennium. For the period up to 1914 at least, they proved on the whole to have been right. In the flush days of the 1920's, however, we were told: that what was then would continue to be, forever and ever; that the problem of the cycle had been solved by the Federal Reserve Board; and that we had entered upon a new era of perpetual boom. The great bulk of the economic profession, taking the long view, refused to give credence to this blissful picture. How right they proved we are unfortunately only too well aware. The perpetual boom having come to its dramatic end, it later subsequently became increasingly apparent that all the days of the 1930's were to be black, or gray. Some economists, simulating too closely, I think, the technocrats' over-emphasis of the purely technological elements in economic process and under-emphasis of the compensating and stimulating functions of the price system, and responding too sympathetically to the prevailing depression, have announced a second new era, but this time an era of perpetual gloom, the advent of the stagnant economy. There is even developing among the preachers of the new pessimism impatience with talk in terms of the concepts of business-cycle analysis, as carrying the unnecessarily optimistic implication that what goes down may some day come up. I have no doubt myself that these economists have genuinely succeeded in finding historical trends in our economic structure and process which operate to make the attainment of full employment increasingly difficult. But that must always have been true, and the weight to be attached to such findings should not be decided until equally ardent search has been made for factors operating in the opposite direction. Here, I take it, is an instance where appeal to the long view may save us from accepting as an adequately historical approach what fuller appeal to history would suggest was rather a hysterical approach.

It has long been standard dogma that budgets must be annually balanced, and that public debts must not be allowed to grow indefinitely. Governments, of course, have frequently violated the dogma, and not only have such violations not invariably been followed by disaster, but it would be a difficult task to disprove the proposition that in a substantial number of instances they proved highly beneficial. But as I read the history of the budget-balancing dogma, it developed as a convenient rule-of-thumb protection against the defense of uncontrolled expenditure and continuous deficits by the plea that the appropriate time for budget balancing was not quite yet but just around the corner. I am even convinced that most of the distinguished advocates of budget balancing during the nineteenth century would have conceded, though no doubt grudgingly, that even a continuous growth of public debt, given a moderate and asymptotic pattern of growth, would not in fact necessarily lead to disaster. On this question of the menace of a growing debt that virtuoso of the long view, Adam Smith, maintained his usual balance. When, during the American Revolutionary War, a young friend, Sir John Sinclair, lamented to him the misfortunes, presumably financial, in which the war was involving Britain, and exclaimed, "If we go on at this rate, the nation must be ruined!", Adam Smith replied, "Be assured, my young friend, that there is a great deal of ruin in a nation."

But when for the old dogma that budgets should be annually

balanced there is substituted a new dogma that budget balancing is merely a fetish, that as long as there are unemployed resources, whatever the cause of the unemployment, governments should point with pride to their lusty and bouncing deficits, instead of apologizing for them or shamefacedly concealing them as if they were born out of wedlock, the long view tells me that while this may not be the road to ruin it at least blazes a trail to it. It must not be forgotten that spending in itself is for the spenders the supreme pleasure, is the politicians' delight, and that what temperance in resort to it has prevailed in the past has been wholly due to the belief that somebody, some day, would have to be taxed to pay the bills. Even if this belief were properly to be regarded as completely a myth, it would still be one of the large class of highly useful myths.

Two related theses of the liberal tradition in Anglo-American thought have been: first, that under a system of free individual enterprise a higher level of economic well-being was attainable than under any other form of economic organization; and second, that a society organized on this economic basis was the only one compatible with the maintenance of political democracy. These, of course, are dogmas, not axioms, one economic and the other political in nature. Now that political democracy is under attack, frankly from the fascist right and as menacingly though not as frankly from the communist left which, like the serpent, licks its victim over before it swallows it, the political dogma has become increasingly acceptable even to those who reject the economic dogma. My concern here, however, is only with the economic dogma, whose acceptability has been destroyed or seriously impaired even for many economists by ten years of sustained and severe depression.

There are perhaps some economists who would deny that an individualistic system is at all desirable economically. This view I will not discuss, since even if I were to reject a substantially individualistic system on economic grounds, I should still prefer it, on non-economic grounds, to what seems to me to be its only practicable alternative, a comprehensively-planned economy under which, as some one has said, "All our hairs would be numbered, and all gray." There are many, however, who hold the view that while a system of free individual enterprise would be ideal if attainable, it is no longer possible in these modern days of great concentration of ownership and control of productive facilities, where the economic units are to a large extent huge corporations and trade unions rather than the single individuals of traditional economic theory, and where such competition as persists tends increasingly to be competition between giants instead of the atomistic competition of orthodox theory, and therefore to be cost-raising rather than price-reducing.

When, some four or five generations ago, freedom of private initiative was first systematically advocated as the ideal basis for an economic system, the menace of monopoly to the proper working of a system so organized was clearly perceived. It was then widely believed, however, that, although business-men admittedly found abhorrent the impact upon themselves of other persons' competition and grasped every opportunity to escape it, monopolistic power could not come into being on a large scale, or at least could not long maintain itself, except with government aid and sanction. In justice to those who were of this view, it should be noted that the grant of a corporate charter was then universally regarded as the grant of a special privilege potentially dangerous to society, and it was therefore then assumed as a matter of course that such grants would be made only sparingly and would be jealously circumscribed, in each specific instance, by restrictions as to permitted size, nature and range of activities, and right of participation in the civil liberties enjoyed by genuine individuals.

Whether now, after several generations of unrestrained grant of corporate charters and of great development of mass-production requiring large economic units for its operation, it is still possible, through proper regulation and restriction by government of the activities of large corporations, to restore an essentially competitive price system, is a question to which I freely confess I do not see a clear answer, although I look forward eagerly for much-needed enlightenment to those sessions of this meeting where this question will be discussed by an exceptionally-qualified group who, I have reason to know, have been giving it very serious and disinterested consideration. The only point I wish to make now is that the old dogma, that monopoly power is basically the product of governmentally protected or sanctioned special privilege and will not survive on a large scale if such special privilege is withdrawn or kept to its practically minimal limits, still has sufficient plausibility to warrant further inquiry. It seems to me a reasonable hypothesis, one worth examination, for instance, that if much of the impressive array of governmental encouragements to monopoly could be removed, or, where removal was impracticable, if government regulation were directed to foster cyclical patterns of price-behavior following the competitive pattern, the chief evil product of monopoly, the price-inflexibility problem, would shrink to easily tolerable dimensions.

Consider for instance, some of the elements in the prevailing pattern of government relationship to monopoly and to price-inflexibility. Promiscuous issue of wide-open corporate charters by the states; until within the last year or two slack and faint-hearted enforcement of the anti-trust laws, already gutted by court sabotage; protection of monopolistic price-structures by the federal tariff; positive encouragement of monopolistic price-practices by such legislation as the N.R.A. act, the Webb-Pomerene act, the Guffey Coal act; so-called "fair-trade" laws which compel businessmen to act as if they were monopolists even if they wish not to; concealed protection of monopoly by doctored building and other ordinances; tacit encouragement to monopoly through acceptance in government contracts, systematically and without protest, of identical bids and of list prices higher than even the monopolists can obtain in what remains of the open market; approval, and even enforcement, for regulated industries such as railroads, of rate policies which make rates behave even more perversely, as far as cyclical flexibility is concerned, than the prices of unregulated monopolies; encouragement to and protection of labor monopolies; deliberate schooling of agriculture in the pleasures and profits of monopolistic behavior.

The record of government encouragement to monopoly, when looked at in conjunction with government's spasmodic efforts to enforce competition and its intermittent clamor against monopoly, reminds me, and justifiably so, of an old cartoon I once saw, depicting a political demonstration in the streets of London, in which the determined-looking marchers carried two banners, one of which bore the slogan, "NO MONOPOLY!" and the other the slogan, "NO COMPETITION!"

All that I suggest, therefore, with respect to the dogma that free competition can substantially survive if government gives it due protection and encouragement, is not that its validity under modern conditions is obvious, but that we have not the right definitely to reject it before it has been given an honest and thorough test.

As a final illustration of the possible survival of usefulness of old dogmas which were the product of the long view, I cite the proposition that the timidity of capital makes the maintenance of "business confidence" necessary if investment is to be maintained at the level required for sustained prosperity. According to this dogma, the capitalist will hoard his own money, or will send it abroad—be there any safe place to send it—and will refrain from borrowing other people's money for investment purposes, if even a faint shadow is cast on the political security of his investment. The spokesmen for capital have found this dogma very much to their liking, and have been claiming for some six years that a political shadow *has* been cast over the security of their investments, and that this has been responsible for the low rate of new invest-ment, and consequently for the persistence of depression. To rein-force their claims, they have done their trembling in public, with vocal accompaniments.

There is no specific invocation of old dogmas, I understand, which the economists of the new enlightenment regard as more absurd, more insubstantial and unsubstantiated, than the claim that the timidity of investment capital under the impact of political fears has been a significant factor in causing the low rate of new invest-ment of the past six years or so. The capitalist, they agree, is a timid beast, but they assert that it is only the risk of loss he is really timid about. He invests, they say, when he sees a clear chance of profit, and hoards when he doesn't, regardless of whether the gov-ernment of the day is stroking his fur or barking at him. They point out that the annual volume of new investment was even smaller in 1931 and 1932 than in any year since 1933, although if in these earlier years political shadows were being cast on the se-curity of investment they could not have been more than mere foreshadowings of prospective shadows. They cite also the sub-stantial recovery of the new investment level in 1936-37, when capital was still insisting that it was scared. They have even pro-duced a statistical proof that "confidence" has nothing to do with the volume of investment, which takes the form of a demonstra-tion that the rate of investment is so highly correlated with the rate of retail sales or of consumers' spending that no other factor need be invoked to explain its major fluctuations.

To my perhaps naïve mind, the dogma still carries some shreds of credibility, despite those weighty inductive refutations. As I understand it, the dogma is not that the degree of confidence in the intentions of government with respect to invested capital *alone* governs the rate of investment, but merely that some minimum degree of such confidence is a necessary condition of the continuance of investment at a high level. The correspondence of the rate of investment with the rate of retail sales seems at least as available to support the thesis that the rate of investment determines the level of national income, to which thesis even the most timid capitalist will happily subscribe, as to support the argument that the rate of spending of income governs the rate of investment. But the only practical lesson I care to draw from the possible validity of this dogma of the timidity of capital in the face of political threats is that, if government has any designs on capital, it would be wiser to bite before and bark afterwards, if bark it must.

I hope—but do not expect—that I shall not be misunderstood as holding that full and invariably appropriate guidance for government policy under present-day conditions can be found in the old dogmas or in what could until recently be called "accepted" economic doctrine. I know no economist who would take this position, and if one were to be found I should agree that he was trying to make a fool's paradise out of his private ivory tower. My claim is much more moderate and, I hope, much more sensible. What I contend is that for various reasons, but chiefly as a psychological reaction to the impact of continued and acute depression, some economists have been discarding too indiscriminately their inherited intellectual ballast, with the result that they sway too easily with each passing wind. With apologies to you for the form in which I state my claim, I contend merely that there is life in the old dogmas yet. I concede that new light is needed and all that I ask is that our minds be kept open to acceptance, strictly and only on their merits, of both the old lights and the new.

Nor do I ask for a sympathetic hearing for the old dogmas in the belief or desire that such a hearing would lead to a cessation or even slowing-up of the present endeavors to find remedies for prevailing evils through positive government action. Obedience to some of the old dogmas would in fact lead to an intensification of governmental action. As far as I am concerned, I have been much more impressed by the undue inertia of government in the face of acknowledged evils than by its rash venturesomeness in action, although I think I have seen both qualities displayed. It is not a middle way between action and inaction, therefore, which I urge. It has been said that throughout all the history of man Confucius alone succeeded in making the middle way either emotionally exciting or intellectually stimulating, and I have my doubts even about Confucius. As many persons who appeal to the middle way use the term, it really becomes a disguised plea that we should halt between the premises and their conclusions. That is not what I am pleading for. Let evils be dealt with, promptly and decisively. But in choosing the manner and direction of action, let us pay heed to the old as well as the new wisdom, and let us especially beware of old poisons in new bottles.

The Role of Costs in a System of Economic Liberalism*

I AM GOING TO SPEAK on the role of costs in a system of economic liberalism. I fear I am not going to give you neat solutions for the very serious and very difficult problems in the behavior of costs that I will discuss. I am not even sure after listening to the very interesting address that has just been given—perhaps I am even less sure than I was half an hour ago—that I am altogether clear as to what this system of economic liberalism is that I am to take as my frame of reference. I am, therefore, also going to attempt, both in self-defense and also to help you defend yourselves against me, to define the economic liberalism about which I am talking.

I like old-fashioned interpretations of old-fashioned terms. If we become convinced that some old institution, or some old set of attitudes, has become obsolete, or if we discover that it is evil instead of good, we had better continue to call it by its old name, and confess that our opinions have changed, rather than conceal the change in opinions by transferring the old name to the new ideas. In the same way, if something which was once looked upon as evil is now regarded as the proper goal of mankind, we should still give it its old name, even if that has acquired ugly connotations, and admit that our views as to whether it is evil or good have changed. Having been brought up and no doubt indoctrinated in what used to be called liberalism, I am going to stick through thick and thin to using "liberalism" to mean what it used to mean, regardless of whether I, or the rest of the world, have changed views as to its merits.

*Address delivered before the First 1947 Economic Institute of the Chamber of Commerce of the United States, Jan. 11, 1947, in Washington, D. C. Reprinted from *Economic Institute on Wage Determination and the Economics of Liberalism*, Washington, Chamber of Commerce of the United States, 1947, pp. 15-33, by the courtesy of the publishers.

In one sense, at least, I believe that I am in substantial agreement with the preceding speaker as to what the essence of liberalism is if we are to keep old-fashioned meanings for old-fashioned terms; that is, it is a requirement of liberalism that the individual cannot be coerced or pushed around by other single individuals or groups of which he is not an equal member; that in the political sphere the persons who exercise authority over him exercise it only as authority derived from the individuals over whom it is exercised, and who in the aggregate can remove those persons or punish them if they have misbehaved; and that so also in the economic field, the essence of economic liberalism is that the individual cannot be pushed around by other individuals or by groups of which he is not a part.

It doesn't mean that the individual can't be pushed around. In our world the individual gets pushed around. But if he gets pushed around only by impersonal forces, or by personal forces to whose character and constitution and permanence he, as an individual, makes at least an atomic contribution and whose strength and authority is wholly determined—or determinable—by the decisions and choices of ordinary individuals in the mass, that is still consistent with liberalism.

If freedom means freedom from coercion, freedom is not of this earth. But if the coercion is to be consistent with liberalism, it must come from natural forces or if it is exercised through particular persons or institutions wielding "authority," whether political or economic, that authority must be derived by what we would regard as democratic political processes from the individuals against whom it is to be exercised, must be subject to withdrawal by these individuals at their pleasure in the aggregate, and therefore has to be exercised within the limits and restraints imposed by this necessity of constantly obtaining popular approval or consent.

So far, I am not sure that there is any disagreement between the preceding speaker and myself. I don't know of any way of making a conclusive defense of such freedom by logical argument. I like a society in which the individual has that sort of freedom. I know of no way, even as an economist, of demonstrating that liberalism is necessarily superior in the volume of income it will produce for society than alternative systems. I would bet that it will produce more at least for vigorous and enterprising peoples, but I am for it even if it could be shown to be an economically inefficient system.

I like it; it is itself one of my values, and it fits well enough the rest of my system of values.

I assume that a good many of you, if not perhaps all of you, are old-fashioned enough to accept this freedom from personal coercion as a value and that we don't have to argue about that here.

There was one thing, however, that bothered me a little in the preceding talk as I listened to it. It seemed to me that it showed some concern about the illegitimate authority over individuals that trade unions might exercise and a great deal of concern about the authority over individuals that the state might exercise, leaving the impression that there is no legitimate authority that the state can exercise, that the state is little else but the enemy of freedom. There was no mention at all of another authority, an authority out of which, I believe, spring most of the evils (in any case, many of the evils) which are associated in your thinking and in my thinking with the defective operation of the modern state in western "liberal" society and with the evils of the modern trade union in western society. I refer to the evil of monopoly economic power, as wielded by either the giant trade union or the giant corporation.

In my old-fashioned liberalism, there are no inherent rights for trade unions, but there are also no inherent rights for corporations. The trade union and the corporation are aggregates of economic and political power with no true attributes of personality. As such, like the state, they are all suspect of the true liberal. It doesn't mean that they are not sources of more good than evil, or, whether in the net good or evil, that they are not inevitable, but it does mean that there are no general "rights" of trade unions or "rights" of corporations or "rights" even of the state in a truly liberal society. There are for them only franchises, delegated powers, granted to them by society, by a democratic society, and granted only as that society decides that the continued grant of such rights either confers net positive benefit upon the mass of individuals or is a lesser evil than any available alternative.

It is in that sense only that I am an economic liberal. It is also the sense, I believe, in which the founders of the liberal philosophy were economic liberals. I don't think that you will find a word of kindness for the corporation, say, in the writings of Adam Smith, or in the writings of the great American liberal, Thomas Jefferson. The corporation was treated in the eighteenth century as presumptively an evil, sometimes a necessary evil, but then to be specially

chartered, with whatever privileges it was to be permitted to exercise
to be specifically stated in the charter, to run only for a limited
time, and to be renewable at the pleasure of the elected representatives of the people.

I still feel the same way about corporations, and I feel the same
way about trade unions. I believe they are both necessary; I believe
that it is absurd to think that at least in our time we can do without
them. I believe they both can be made engines of great service
to mankind. But in the light of the particular issue which we are
discussing, the issue of economic liberalism, they are basically both
to be regarded as menaces as soon as they become large, menaces to
be disciplined and regulated by a democratically elected political
authority, the state.

To turn to my specific assignment, the particular role of costs
in the working of a system of economic liberalism. What we have
in fact is, of course, not a pure system of economic liberalism. I
may at times be discussing the role of costs in terms of what is
really a model, a construct, and not a reality, namely, a genuinely
complete system of economic liberalism. At other times, in the interest of realism, I may shift to a discussion of the expedient roles of
costs in the mixed and imperfect system we have today and will
continue—for some time—to have. I will try to make clear as I go
along in what sense I am talking. I warn you, however, that I may
not always succeed, for I am not at all sure that I have clarified
my own thinking sufficiently so that it is always clear even in my
own mind whether the behavior of costs I am recommending is
proper not only for an ideally competitive society but also for a
society like our own American society, in which authority, political
and economic, is applied in great doses, not only by the state (and
not only very often perversely and foolishly by the state) but also
by trade unions and by business corporations and by farm organizations (and by them, also, often perversely and foolishly).

The costs I am talking about are of two kinds. They are the
money costs, which are the prices paid for productive services and
materials by business, and they are also the "real" costs in the sense
of the utilization of the time of laboring men, the utilization and
exhaustion of natural resources and the utilization of accumulated
capital in the process of production.

I am going to talk about the role of costs, I repeat, in a society which is not by any means a completely and genuinely economically liberal society; it is a society in which decisions are made in accordance with the principles of power politics to a large degree; and as long as we accept as inevitable and even as necessary, as I do, both the large corporation and the large trade union, power politics in part it must be. And I don't believe that in this field, as in the actual international field of power politics, power conflicts can be settled or its problems resolved by formula. I believe it is a problem of *ad hoc* pushing here and pulling there, correcting here and moderating there, as its defective working becomes apparent and as public opinion becomes aware that something has to be done. And what has to be done today may prove five years from now to have been wrong, and may then have to be undone and even reversed.

For an economic theorist, like myself, who is fascinated by the inherent elegance, coherence, and simplicity of economic theorizing starting out from definite, explicit, and radically simplified premises, this is all very irritating. Because it does not lead to sharp conclusions, it possibly gives the impression of fuzziness of mind. It *need* not be the mind that is fuzzy, however. The system that the mind is trying to analyze is fuzzy, mixed, promiscuous, a product of centuries of largely fortuitous development, a product of the imperfections of man as a political animal. Our job as liberals is to make the best of it, trying to retain enough of what in this sphere is its great value, enough of that part of the social pattern which protects the individual against being pushed around by other individuals. Even though I am an economist—the Chairman has vouched for that—I place, at least for any civilization that is above the mere subsistence line, that value of individual freedom much above the value of a high level of material income.

In the perfect society that I dream about, or sometimes become nostalgic about on the assumption that it once existed—that there once was a golden age in this sense—costs have two major economic functions. First, they constitute the most important disciplinary force on business enterprise to make it strive for efficiency in the use of productive resources. Secondly, through the influence of the efforts of businessmen to minimize costs in their service-buying operations, costs, as service-prices, provide the major incentive to the owners of these services, to the laborer or the landlord or the

capitalist, to make these services as serviceable as possible to production and to make these services available for employment in the
optimum volume.

Costs exercise their disciplinary force on business enterprise
through comparison with product-prices. They thus guide business
in pursuit of profits to select what to produce, how much to produce, where and when to produce it, and by which of the available
processes to produce it. Through a comparison of costs and prices
with the productivity of the services hired, cost analysis coerces
and lures the businessman into experimentation, into observation,
into invention, with a view to finding out more economical ways of
producing the things he is going to produce and more profitable
things to produce.

Those are the economic functions, as I see them, of costs in a
system of liberalism. They are not very different, I think, under
any other system which regards waste as an evil, which tries to
rationalize the use of resources, although the political implications,
and especially the implications for freedom of the individual, can,
of course, be very different under different economic systems.

It so happens that what are costs to the buyers of services constitute income to the owners of the services. Out of this rise difficult
questions of economic theory which are even more important to
the public than they are to the economist, and on which, unfortunately, the economists are very badly divided.

In this sort of ideal system, self-interest is assumed to be the
major motive power, the strong drive relied upon to get owners
of productive services to put them into useful shape and to put
them usefully to work. Some people call it the profit system. Many
persons who so call it think it an invidious term; they think that it
exposes a weakness of a competitive society.

There are such things as illegitimate profits. To me, however,
legitimate profits are as proper as legitimate wages, and illegitimate
profits are invidious to me even when they are not illegal. It would,
moreover, be as appropriate to call the system I have described a
rent system or an interest system or a wages system as to call it
a profit system.

This system, however, is everywhere gone, or going, or surviving only in part and very much on the defensive, and I believe
that holds true even in the United States in spite of the recent election returns.

The weakness of this system's survival value is due in part to the fact that old-fashioned names for old good things, which names have earned an honorific status, have been applied to modern corruptions of the old good things. These modern corruptions are being defended by a logic and in terms which apply only to those old, and to some extent long-gone, conditions and practices.

I believe in free enterprise. The essence of liberalism is free enterprise; not, however, free enterprise for the United States Steel Corporation but free enterprise for the individual, for the small man. What freedom the United States Steel Corporation or the National Miners' Union should have should be a matter constantly under scrutiny and consideration by the democratically-elected representatives of the people, and by their masters, the people at large, and only such freedom should be given to them as, in the light of current conditions, is decided to be in the interest of the American individual, whether he be a common man or a highly uncommon one.

The reason why this old system is disappearing is in part because it was permitted to get corrupted. In its corrupted stage, it failed to deliver the goods during the great depression, and that great depression has had an effect, in many respects a psychotic effect, which will persist for many years. Its effect, I suppose, was as marked on the thinking of the economic profession as anywhere else. There are many economists who are still suffering from depression shock.

That system, in its corrupted form, and for some even in its pure form—even when it works smoothly and brings prosperity—fails to give moral satisfaction to many people, especially to people with a strong moral sense or a delicate social conscience. They don't like the inequality that comes with it. They don't like the involuntary idleness of deserving poor who want work and can't find it that appears to them to be associated with it. They think they see a good deal of reward without service to society or out of proportion to service to society, and a good deal of service to society, especially their own, without adequate reward. They dislike competition; they dislike the competitive spirit, both as means to an end, and irrespective of its fruits.

The competitive spirit is not repugnant to my perhaps imperfect social sense. The competitive spirit operates in an impersonal way to lead ordinary, unsaintly persons like most of us into emulation in the service of society in the interest of serving themselves. To my way of thinking, emulation in serving society through serving one-self is, both in its social consequences and of itself, irrespective of its consequences, not less creditable than are, in their everyday mani-festations, emulation in gaining votes or in gaining political power by other means, or emulation in getting status or medals, or even emulation in accumulating grace in heaven, which are the major alternatives to economic competition as social discipline. The con-crete and matter-of-fact service to society which profit-seeking com-petition renders in a pure system of economic liberalism gives it claims to virtue in my crass materialistic moral philosophy, according to which that man is a good man who well serves human beings of his own kind on this earth in the way they wish to be served, even if he serves them because he wants to serve himself. But its chief claim to virtue is that whether it serves society well or ill in the material field, it alone can serve individual freedom well.

This reliance upon the fact of cooperation without demanding much of its spirit is the intellectual strength at least and I believe for generations was the practical strength of this system of eco-nomic liberalism. It could make a good society out of men who were very, very far from being capable of sanctification. It brought about economic cooperation even without the will to cooperate and without much formal organization for cooperation. Even the saintly are liable to become wolves if they are pressed hard enough by hunger, and the system of economic liberalism for a time worked to avoid hunger for most people and certainly for more persons than escaped hunger under any other system known to human experi-ence.

I know of only one other kind of effective social cooperation. The preceding speaker referred to the rival system in very much the same terms I would have been happy to have used first. It is the system of the servile state, the state in which the individual is pushed around by authorities, by the dictates of personal power over which he has no effective control even in the aggregate. Whether, in its minor aspects, it is fascist or whether it is communist, or, making a substitution for the New Deal, the third member of the preceding speaker's unholy trinity, whether it is theocratic, should not, for the true liberal, be a matter of fundamental consequence.

I want to turn now more specifically to the imperfections and corruptions of this ideal system of economic liberalism in so far as they bear particularly on the question of costs and their operation. The system works badly on its cost side if the "real" costs, the amounts of the productive resources necessary for the production of a unit of product, are higher than they need be. The system also works badly on the cost side if the money costs, the money rewards for productive services, are too low to represent adequately and fairly the services rendered. The system also works badly from the point of view of costs if the money costs are too high or too low, relative to the prices of the products, to support continuous high-level employment.

I warn you to take notice that on the last point I am being evasive. Twenty years ago, perhaps even fifteen years ago, I am sure that I would have said, "if the money costs are too high," whereas I am now saying, "too high or too low," in deference to recent trends of economic thinking, about which I will have more to say later on. But I fear I will be evasive to the end on this particular issue.

What is meant by real costs being too high? Or, more important, how can imperfections of the system augment the real cost at which society gets its products and thus diminish the amount of product it yields? It means that there is too low a level of working efficiency in relation to possible levels. There are two main sources of remediable low levels of working efficiency in that sense. One is the result of the exercise of monopoly power, and the other is the result of the failure of individuals to develop their productive potentialities and the failure of the state (and I must confess I here see a useful and healthy positive role for the state) to help them to develop their productive potentialities.

First, as to monopoly power and its effects on costs. Monopoly power, I repeat—I probably will repeat it again later before I am through—is always an evil for those who genuinely believe in free enterprise. Freedom is a human value to be enjoyed by human beings. It yields its fruits of satisfaction, of dignity, of security, only to individuals as real persons.

Monopoly is sometimes a lesser evil than its working practical alternatives. Sometimes, therefore, it should be tolerated, but always, I insist, it should be put on the defensive. My concern here, however, is only with the effect of monopoly on costs. Monopoly raises real costs in a number of ways. First I will speak of labor monopolies, which is just another term for "strong" trade unions.

The closed union plus the closed shop, the two combined, assum-

ing that they use the power at their command, by excluding otherwise eligible workers from work in a particular occupation force
them into less productive fields, and thus lower the general level
of productivity of labor as a whole. That such practice occurs in
American trade unionism everybody knows. Just how important
it is, I don't know; and I don't know how I can find out. The
exclusions from work on account of race are, however, obviously
and shamefully important.

Labor monopolies, in creating an artificial scarcity of eligible
workers, also lower working efficiency of the productive resources
of a community by lessening the pressure on these workers to do
a good and a full day's work for a good and a full day's pay. This
removal of the pressure to do a good job can happen even without
the existence of a formal union, through tacit agreement among the
workers. I am not an expert in this field, but I suspect from my reading of old English material, even of the eighteenth century, that you
can have trade unionism without any trade unionists being aware
of it; that the mores and codes of trade unionism can develop without formal organization. Even in the days when trade unions were
not very strong, were loosely organized, and when only minorities
of the workers joined and paid dues, workers, whether members or
not, often operated in some respects as if they belonged to very
compact societies. With respect to at least some practices, the attitude of the law in this country today towards big business is very
much the same as the attitude of eighteenth-century law in England
was toward trade unionism, that is, it aims at the prevention of certain monopolistic practices involving conspiracy or collusion. But
business knows, and labor then knew, that there are some kinds
of collusion that have not yet been labeled as such by the judges,
that collusion is possible without conspiracy, and that, with proper
mental discipline, one can even practice collusion unconsciously
so that one can go on the witness stand and honestly affirm one's
innocence. The practice of labor monopoly, like the practice of
business monopoly, is in some degree possible without the deliberate
organization of monopoly.

When I speak of monopolistic "trade unionism," therefore, I
include any code of practices on the part of the workers that they
may have acquired or inherited as a natural reaction to their situation, provided it leads to the same concrete results, restriction of
access to an occupation and deliberate reduction of the amount of

output per worker per day. In this respect, the strong trade union, as compared to the weak trade union or to unorganized labor, can and usually does operate as an effective labor monopoly. As an effective labor monopoly, it adds to real costs by restriction of output through working rules, by the unreasonable shortening of the working week (as say in the American building trades at a time of acute scarcity of housing for what some of them would call their own class), by the prevention of the adoption of labor-saving methods of production, by interference with efficient management, by protecting the inefficient and the unfaithful worker against discharge, and, no doubt, by still other means.

I don't regard this as a case against trade unionism in general. In the present sort of world, I would want trade unions to survive and to be strong in spite of these evils, and even if I thought it impossible to reduce the importance of these evils, because I believe that the worker in the modern society needs protection against other aggregates of power, needs protection against overwork, against personal indignity, against job-insecurity and underpayment, and can get it effectively and adequately only through his trade union.

What the extent of these cost-raising practices is, I don't know, and I don't know how to find out. We had a few years ago a big TNEC investigation mainly of the evil practices of business; we need a TNEC to study the evil practices of organized labor. I would like it to be more objective and better-planned and administered than the TNEC was on the whole; I would like it to start out with clearer objectives as to what it was trying to do; whatever the reality might be, I would like it to avoid the appearance of witch-hunting which the TNEC investigation in part had. In general, I would like to see, let us say, rather than the TNEC, the type of old-fashioned English royal commission investigation—orderly, un-hysterical and unsensational, not wasteful of a great deal of money, avoiding blunderbuss methods of inquiry, and clear beforehand as to the purpose of the investigation. There is need for such an investigation. Even before TNEC we knew a good deal about the extent as well as the nature of monopolistic practices by business. We know very little quantitatively about the extent of restrictive practices by trade unions.

As to business monopoly, I have no doubt that my imagination has not enabled me to discover all the ways in which business monopoly leads to a raising of costs. But let me cite a few. Monopolistic organizations of business often (and perhaps almost always) tend to provide an umbrella for the weak and the inefficient concern. What I am now charging the monopolies with is that they are too kindhearted, rather than too hardhearted. It may, of course, be possible that this toleration of the weak rival results not from kindness of their hearts, but because the elimination of the inefficient requires resort to the practices of price competition, which are so abhorrent to big business, and might well turn out to be more costly to them than sharing the spoils with a few weaklings. It is one of the most important aspects of the cartel form of monopoly organization in particular that it provides an umbrella for the inefficient entrepreneur by guaranteeing him a share of the market.

Secondly, the monopolist practices socially costly ways of seeking to maximize his profits. I am not criticizing the aim of the monopolist in trying to maximize his profits. The businessman as businessman performs his social duties in seeking to maximize his profits. But I would aim at a system in which the pursuit of maximum profits operates generally in the interest of the community as a whole.

A truly competitive firm can seek to augment its profits along the following lines: by lowering its prices to get an increased volume of sales; by increasing the efficiency of its operations to get a lower cost per unit for its output; by devising new products or improvements of old products. All these three procedures are certainly by-and-large beneficial to the community. A monopolistic firm has all these avenues to profits available to it, but it has some additional ones not open to the genuinely competitive businessman. It can seek larger profits by raising prices, with the awareness that its market will not disappear in consequence; it can use its monopoly power as a buyer of services to force down the prices it pays for services; and (and possibly most important) it can augment its profits by cost-raising methods as distinguished from the cost-reducing and price-reducing methods which alone are available to the fully-competitive producer.

The cost-raising methods of increasing profits can take the form of increased sales effort, or of false differentiation of product, promoted by advertising which may contain no useful information and some misinformation and, as in one of its notorious manifestations, may contribute to the demoralization of modern capitalism by printing in large type and blaring over the radio day-after-day statements and testimonials which everybody knows are fakes.

Of course, this is not the whole story about monopoly as cost-raising. There are real and important economies of size which may require the number of firms to be below the number at which real price-competition is possible, although I don't think economies of size play a large part in the growth of giant firms. A firm which has monopoly power is not compelled to use it and may refrain from using it for one reason or another; one explanation of the tendency of monopolists not to exploit their monopoly power to the full—or not sometimes to over-exploit it—is that their cost account-ants give them bad advice from the point of view of maximization of profits. Also, the monopoly organization of one branch of industry may be necessary as a defense against the monopoly power of a related other branch, or as a defense against the monopoly power of trade unions.

It is arguable—at least it has been argued by economists whose status and reputation make it incumbent to assume that they argue only arguable things—that a measure of monopoly power—I would be inclined to agree if they said a chemical trace of monopoly power—scattered throughout industry is good. It lessens certain kinds of frictions and costs of excessive mobility; it gives a certain momen-tary sort of security of anticipations which promotes planning; it preserves incentives for leadership in innovating design, products, processes.

Therefore, here again, one of the very important things that we still need to know, in spite of the TNEC investigation, is what is the degree of monopoly power actually exercised by monopolistic business in the United States. Please note that when I say "monopo-listic business," I don't mean that these businessmen are not highly competitive; I don't mean that they could not go on the witness stand and honestly swear that they are anxiously and eagerly com-peting all the time and even that they are fearful of being crushed by competition. But the competition they are engaged in is largely of the cost-raising type that renders no good, certainly no net good, to society, as distinguished from the cost-reducing or price-reduc-ing type of full competition.

Certain other imperfections in the economic system whose prev-alence can be charged to inadequate activities of the state result likewise in failure of the system to develop its maximum potentialities for economic welfare. There are many types of urgently-needed economic activities which individuals do not find it to their profit to engage in, and which even large corporations are not likely to regard as suitable fields for their operation. These the state, either directly or indirectly, must provide for, or they will not be done. I refer to such activities as drainage over a wide area, irrigation over a wide area; protection against erosion in so far as the individual cannot take care of that by taking care of his own little piece of land; coordinated development of urban land. These are all cases where small-scale individual effort is inherently ineffective in meeting the social need, where concerted effort is needed, and where, at least often, concerted effort over a wide enough area cannot be expected in the absence of state participation.

There is another important field for government activity which was not stressed sufficiently, I believe, by the founders of economic liberalism, which is urgent even in the United States, and which for countries like China and India probably constitutes the most important single element in the planning of a sound liberal society; that is, to overcome the inertia of individuals where that inertia is the result of inadequate education, of bad health, of bad nutrition, of regional isolation, of bad traditions, and above all of the operation of that great vicious circle of modern society, poverty breeding poverty, bequeathing it to the children, and thus cutting-off their access to health, to knowledge, to reasonable education, and so forth.

It is the major positive economic function of the liberal state to discover the pockets (and they may be more than pockets; they may be great areas) of undeveloped productive capacity on the part of individuals and by non-coercive methods to raise their service-ability to themselves and to society. This calls for education, for health work, for guidance and subsidization of migration to regions with better natural endowment, and so forth.

Where the underprivileged are regionally concentrated, I would on the whole, I believe, aim remedial measures at the youth. Routine relief to prevent hunger and cold should, of course, be given regardless of age, and routine old-age pensions regardless of location of residence. But where there are large regional pockets of backward persons who are backward mainly because opportunity has not been available for them, I would work to cure that mainly by investing in opportunity for the young, on the ground that the return to society for its social investment is likely to be largest if it is so directed.

Let me now deal briefly with the second kind of imperfection with respect to costs as they operate today, where money costs, the rewards for services, are sometimes too low to represent adequately and equitably the services rendered. In general, it has been the farmers and labor who have complained about this. All I can say about it, if I am not to go beyond the limits of my knowledge, is: that it is theoretically quite possible that there shall be such inequities whenever there is monopoly power as a buyer on the part of any buyer of services or buyer of products; that there is every reason to suppose that the frequent complaints on this score are sometimes justified; and that in the days of the Granger Movement they were a staple of American political controversy. Buyers' monopolies seem always to be more explosive politically than seller's monopolies. They do not seem, however, to be a serious problem today, perhaps because farmers and workers, as sellers, are now themselves strongly enough organized to be secure against obvious exploitation by those to whom they sell.

The third kind of imperfection in the operation of costs is the deviation of money-costs from the level consistent with maintenance of high level of employment. All economists are agreed that cost-prices must be properly geared to product-prices if mass unemployment is not to occur. Where economists differ is as to whether the difficulty usually lies in money-costs that are too high or in money-costs that are too low. I will assume that nobody wants inflation, and that will simplify the discussion, although like most assumptions introduced to simplify a discussion it is contrary to the fact.

Leaving out the inflationists (and at least among economists there are not many of those), there are two main schools of thought on this issue. At one extreme are those who see money-costs only as direct barriers or obstacles to output and who believe that wage-reduction, interest-rate reduction, reduction in any other cost-prices, always promotes employment until the stage of absolutely full employment is reached. This school blames cost-rigidities for most of the unemployment that occurs, and it tends to blame labor for most of the cost-rigidity.

I generally am supposed to belong to this school, I believe. I have never attached any peculiar importance to wage rates in this connection beyond their importance in the total cost budget of business. Whenever I have spoken in this connection I have always insisted that tax rates, public utility rates, railway rates, retailers' mark-ups, landlords' rents, and any other costs that enter into the money-costs of production are, dollar for dollar, equally important with wage rates. If in fact they are of lesser importance, it is because more dollars are paid out for wages than for these other costs. If there are still survivors of the money-cost-reduction school of avoiding unemployment, then in fairness to the issue, to their own reputation for objectivity, and to the potential appeal of their argument, they ought to acknowledge explicitly that wage costs are not the only rigid costs that need to be broken down if unemployment threatens.

At the other extreme are those who see money-costs only as income, as "purchasing-power" so-called, and who stress the argument that production can go on only as there is purchasing-power to take the product off the market as produced. They tend to distinguish here between wages and other kinds of income on the ground that wages constitute income destined quickly to be spent, whereas they say or suggest that interest and rent and profits tend to go into hoards, uninvested and unspent in large degree.

The two schools would give diametrically opposite advice as to policy when unemployment prevails or is anticipated, and indeed they are giving diametrically opposite advice at this moment. One would lower wages by legislation, or by exhortation if they thought that were practicable. Since 1933, I suspect, not very many people think that state-sponsored wage reduction is a workable remedy politically in a democratic society no matter how sound it may be economically. The other school, instead of lowering wages, would raise them.

In the past as sharp difference of position as this has been highly unusual, even among economists. There is a natural temptation to explain some of the sharpness of difference on the basis of social bias. I do think, as I look around among economists, that the cost-reducing school tends to consist (aside from the reactionaries who don't believe in crossing bridges while they are still standing, and who are embarrassing company) of persons like myself who are only moderately enthusiastic about trade unions, who, in short, are moderate liberals, if you will accept the definition of a moderate liberal as a man with one foot firmly imbedded in the nineteenth century while the other one gropes in the air for Utopia. On the other hand, the wage-increasing school seems to include many who find in wage increases a specific against both inflation and deflation, and who tend never to find any virtue in an increase of rent, or interest, or profits. I believe, however, that the main source of the sharp difference in views is that a difficult theoretical as well as practical problem is involved, and that what renders it difficult and what has postponed its resolution (if it is resolvable, because not all economic problems are resolvable) is the scantiness of the evidence that this world, and particularly the economic parts of it, was created by Providence in such a manner as to be completely understandable by man. And it is a very foolhardy assumption on the part of the economist that he must now or even in the future undertake to answer every question put to him even if they all are of a kind proper to be put to economists.

That economists tend to react to the difficulties of the problem by reaching different views rather than by refraining from offering solutions is perhaps the result in part of the fact that modern economic society is more complex than it is convenient for economists fully to recognize, that therefore they select and simplify without full awareness of the extent of their simplification, and that the particular selections of elements to be considered are not identical as between different schools. When we start from different premises, it is not surprising that we reach different conclusions.

Wages, as we have seen, are both costs and incomes. As costs, they certainly are obstacles to employment; as income, they certainly are a stimulus to employment. They have that ambivalent role, and we must always remain aware of it. It seems to me, however, that discussion sometimes overlooks the distinction between wage rates per person per hour or per day and the size of the payroll. Any measure which guarantees an increase in the payroll at a time of unemployment is sure to promote either fuller employment or inflation or a mixture of both. But it doesn't necessarily follow (and I think many economists have taken that step without further argument) that any increase of wage rates will have the same consequences. An increase of wage rates may quite conceivably reduce the payroll, and the identification of the conditions and circumstances under which a rise in wage rates would decrease as compared to those under which it would increase the size of the total payroll is the real problem for the economist here. What should make him hesitant to reach definite conclusions is, it seems to me, that you can logically move to conclusions in either direction depending upon what sort of assumptions you are making, or information you have, as to the pattern of anticipations which general changes in the level of wages will give rise to in the minds of businessmen, of investors, of consumers, and of labor itself, with respect to the future trend of prices and employment and the profitability of new investment. I still believe that wage-reduction, if made across the board and once-for-all, would promote and not reduce employment during a depression. But I don't advocate it as strongly as I once did, since I no longer believe in its political practicality or desirability, and I don't believe in it at all if it is associated with a deflationary monetary policy as well.

In the absence of full competition, moreover, there is at least one element of truth, of almost indisputable truth, in the Robert Nathan argument, as I gather it from the newspapers—I have not seen his report—that wages, even at a time of inflationary pressure and even at a time of nearly full employment, can be raised without resulting in an increase in prices, even in the absence of official price controls. I present this case in order to bring my friend monopoly once more into the picture.

Suppose you have a large-scale monopolized industry in this country which sets fairly stable prices to the public and departs from them only at long intervals; suppose that it is a monopoly also in the hiring of services and particularly of labor. Labor in that industry is strongly organized and by collective bargaining, let us say, gets an increase of 25 per cent in the wage rate, at a time when the industry is operating below capacity but at a high rate of profit. There is nothing in the nature of a quasi-monopolistic economic system which justifies you in concluding that the monopolist will decide that it would be profitable for it either to raise its prices or to contract its output. Under certain conditions, improbable but theoretically conceivable, it may even decide that a larger output and a lower price will then be profitable. In such case, its payroll will rise, spendable income will increase, some of that payroll will flow to other industries, and the volume of employment for the economy as a whole will rise without increase of prices to consumers.

If the newspaper reports of Nathan's position do not do him an injustice, however, his argument rests primarily on simple and largely irrelevant arithmetic, and not on economic analysis, or, at least, not on economic analysis of this sort. In any case, this particular argument requires for its validity very special conditions which seem certain not to prevail over a wide range of industry.

I do not regard it as part of my assignment to propose a program of concrete action with respect to costs under existing circumstances. Were I to do so, it might well involve a detailed exposure of the wide range of my ignorance on some matters of very great current importance. I expect some of that ignorance to be dispelled by my colleagues on this program during the course of the day.

Tension between Government and Business*

THE TOPIC ASSIGNED TO ME is infinite in its scope, while my range of knowledge, and even of opinion, has very definite limits, and I am sure it would be inexpedient for me to assume that your patience and tolerance are unbounded. I will therefore confine myself to a few points of special interest or relevance at this time.

Since the onslaught of the great depression, American business has been very much on the defensive before American public opinion, and one of our great political parties has remained in power without a break since 1932 largely by virtue of reflecting or responding to, and at times perhaps even stimulating, this trend in public opinion. There have been previous periods in American history which offer a parallel. But never before, I believe, was there as much danger to private enterprise in the hostility to it, partial or sweeping, among large sections of the American people, as there is at present. Before World War I critics of private enterprise had no real alternative to offer beyond abstract speculations unsupported by actual experience and working models. Today the American economy is one of only a handful of national economies which is substantially a free enterprise economy, and even American businessmen, conscious of a variety of federal regulations and restrictions on their freedoms, probably become truly conscious of how free they still are only when they contemplate the state of affairs in England, in Sweden, in Australia, in Hindustan, or in American-occupied Western Germany and Japan—to say nothing of Soviet Russia and its satellites. There is now no scarcity of knowledge as to procedures and ways of regulating business so as to make it less free, or of liquidating private enterprise altogether.

---

*Address delivered at the 306th regular meeting of the National Industrial Conference Board, Inc., Sept. 22, 1949, in New York. (Printed in *The Commercial and Financial Chronicle*, Sept. 29, 1949, pp. 1252, 1273.)

It is not an adequate answer to proposals for such regulation or liquidation to say that they will lower the level of material prosperity. It is not an adequate answer partly because it is sometimes, perhaps often, difficult or impossible to demonstrate convincingly that it is a true answer. It is not a satisfactory answer partly because a good deal of mankind today, whether foolishly or wisely, demands of its national economies other merits over and above that they shall yield prosperity. If forced to make deliberate choice, many might prefer these other things to refrigerators, chromium-plated automobiles, and economic freedom, and many can easily be persuaded, even when such may not be the case, that it can have these other things and refrigerators and political freedom too, if only it is patient enough.

The American economy has demonstrated its capacity to deliver over the years high-level prosperity, as measured by previous American standards of living and, still more, as measured by current standards of living in other countries whether these operate under free enterprise or under other systems. It is my impression that an overwhelming proportion of the American public, including sections that are cold or hostile to American "business," are ready to assign to the inventiveness, venturesomeness, and administrative genius of the American captain of industry a substantial part of the credit for this prosperity. But more is asked today of an economy than that it produce prosperity.

What are these other things which men ask of economic systems of their country in addition to prosperity? In addition to a high average standard of living? They ask, and have learned or been taught to ask increasingly, that this prosperity shall prevail with a fair degree of stability, instead of accruing in a succession of hysterical booms and desperate depressions. They ask that this prosperity shall be distributed, as between employers and employees, the privileged and the underprivileged, the country and the city, north and south, not with arithmetical equality but without glaring departure from visible equity. They ask also that there shall be for those in modest economic circumstances some measure of organized security other than through humiliating charity against the buffeting of fate, against the economic hazards of old age and death, of sickness and disability, of undeserved unemployment. I believe that, above all these, they ask for status and dignity, for a place in the sun, for protection against being pushed around by other men not obviously superior to themselves except in possession of superior power derived from wealth, or class, or combination of strength. The racial minorities, of course, ask also for freedom from discrimination on account of complexion, creed, or racial origins. For these other things, men who regard them as lacking and have learned to want them, for economic security, equity, dignity of status, men in large numbers may be willing to pay a heavy price in prosperity and, alas, even in freedom. In increasing numbers they have become convinced that these other things are obtainable only from government, from government which imposes on private enterprise the pattern it shall follow, or from government which wholly takes over from private business—and from the labor unions —the conduct of the national economy.

Many of these critics of business are unfair, some of them deliberately and calculatingly so. Many of these critics do not know when they are well off. Many of these critics of private enterprise are Utopian in their demands of human society; they ask for better bread than can be made even from the best of the wheat that is available. Some of them may be maladjusted individuals who would complain even in heaven if only that the harps were not tuned to their liking. It is unreasonable to ask of any human institution that it attain perfection, and even perfection is not to all men's tastes. All of this is true, and no doubt relevant. But it settles no issues. The dissatisfaction with the economic *status quo* is too widespread, too deep, too varied in character, to be safely disregarded by businessmen, and others who are not businessmen are unwilling to disregard it even if they do not share it. In a democracy, if dissatisfaction with an institution is widespread, there will always be politicians—or statesmen—who will give heed to it, and who will do things to the institution.

The believer in free enterprise, in its moral virtues or at least respectability as well as in its superiority from a material point of view over any rival system as a working method of organizing society for production, should keep an ear open for these criticisms. Refusal to do so, whether because of inertia, or self-righteousness, or overoptimism, or defeatism, may well lead in time, in some period of strain and emergency, to free enterprise going here as it has gone elsewhere. Above all, the believer in free enterprise as it operates in this country should not be led by the fact that he finds nothing seriously disturbing to his peace of mind in the editorial columns of the great metropolitan dailies—or weeklies—to underestimate the prevalence of criticism, or its potential rate of growth in quantity and intensity if the economic barometer should drop. The businessman, per capita, profits most, and has, in this sense at least, most at stake in the survival of free enterprise. He should therefore find a special interest, if not a special responsibility, in striving wisely and skilfully to strengthen its appeal to the public mind, perhaps by increasing the extent to which it merits such appeal.

One method of pursuing this objective I certainly would not recommend. To search for "dangerous thoughts" in the printed page, in sermons from the pulpit, or in the classroom, and to attempt through influence, financial pressure, or legal coercion, to suppress the critic, is a procedure which, whatever its short-run success might indicate, in the long-run weakens the institution on whose behalf it is applied. If free enterprise is so fearful of frank, or even of prejudiced, appraisal that it resorts to suppression of freedom of thought to avoid it, it will be subjected to an even more prejudiced appraisal by means of a whispering-campaign of major proportions. The objective believer in it on its net merits as they are in fact, or as they might be made to be, will refuse to speak about what is good in it if he is not left free to speak or think of its possible deficiencies. There is bigotry in the criticisms of American free enterprise, but the best ways of coping with it do not include matching it with an opposite bigotry.

The American press is at the moment full of manifestations of the copywriters' art devoted to what seems to be a concerted program of "selling" the virtues of free enterprise to the American public. This is perfectly legitimate, and in principle it does not appear entirely inconceivable that it would have some significant effect beyond providing an increase not urgently necessary in the revenues of the large-circulation press and of the firms who sell salesmanship. Perhaps mine is not a typical reaction to it, but most of what I have seen of it seems to me clearly ineffective. It obviously lacks in frankness, in objectivity, in punch, and in reasoned argument. If it does not claim for free enterprise all the credit for the more favorable aspects of the American climate, by dogmatic assertion repeated *ad nauseam* it does try to persuade an audience which thinks it has personal experience to the contrary that there is not a cough in a carload and that only the best leaves are used, the others presumably being fed to the cows.

There is much of substance that could be said for free enterprise, even as it is as distinguished from what it might be made to
be, provided only that there was no pretence that it is without
remediable flaws. If this campaign were conducted to appeal to the
intelligence of the American public instead of to its supposed susceptibility to pointless slogans and to endless repetition of meaningless rhythms, the result, I believe, would be valuable education both
for audience and script writers. Not only would the hold of free
enterprise on the American public be strengthened on the basis of
its merits, but there would be an indirect by-product of value. Has
no one ever told the copywriters of the disarming effect of a little
frankness, especially when what is revealed was not really a secret
before? No one really demands that business be conducted by saints
in the intervals left between their long sessions at prayer and private good works. Everyone in fact knows that business is conducted
for the most part by corporations, and while we have some sort of
authority for the proposition that corporations are soulless, I think
that, with some mental application, the spokesmen for business
could develop a plausible case for the proposition that generosity
and public spirit come more easily to the corporation acting in its
corporate capacity than to the individuals who manage it and the
shareholders who get the thin bottom slice of the earnings as
dividends.

There has been since 1932 a definite and substantial element of
hostility in the relations between American business and American
Government. To some extent this may be inherent in the relations
between two contenders for power, and there may have been
even under the Harding, Coolidge, and Hoover regimes some sections of the business world who did not regard the grip government had on them as a friendly embrace. I can easily conceive of too
much unity between government and business for the good of the
country, whether this unity took the form of government acting
as the agent of business or of business, through bribes or coercion
or fear, submitting passively to every edict of government. I think,
however, that there has been a clearly artificial element in this
hostility, serving badly both the interests of good government and
the legitimate interests of business in its own prosperity. Politicians,
columnists, demagogues, and reactionaries all have to some extent
manufactured or encouraged this hostility in calculating fashion to
serve their private or ideological objectives. Others have simply and

irrationally found in it an outlet for the hyperactivity of their glandular apparatus. One consequence has been that the relations on the policy-making and pronouncement-making levels of government and business, upon whose character so much of the fate of the country depends, have at frequent intervals been either frigid—meaning *cold* war but *hot* exchange of epithets—or have resulted in far less mutually beneficial cooperation than would have been achievable if an atmosphere of emotional distrust and enmity had not been created. There is unlimited scope for beneficial mutual discussion and negotiation between government and business with respect to problems common to both. But I have seen a single strongly-phrased sentence—this happened to be in a solicited letter from a distinguished New York businessman to a very distinguished Washington politician—put an end to what had been a good resolution, reluctantly adopted, to substitute friendly diplomacy for open warfare, on a vital matter of public and of business policy.

So far my talk has been in general and rather abstract terms. Time limitations would prevent treatment of all the significant types of contact between government and business even if I had the necessary competence. I will select for special comment, therefore, three major fields in which government and business can cooperate, or can fight each other: the monopoly problem; economic stabilization; and the impact of the tax structure on the strength of the free enterprise system.

It may sound like a paradox to you if I state my belief that the greatest special service the Federal Government has ever rendered to the free enterprise system was in the passage and enforcement of anti-trust legislation. Practically all the support on economic and on ethical grounds which economic theory provides for the free enterprise system rests on the assumption that enterprise is not only private and free but that it is competitive. There are two major ways in which competition can be eliminated or narrowly restricted in a free enterprise system: through cartellization and through the development of giant firms, or "trusts." European experience clearly indicates that, of these two methods, cartellization impairs the working of a free enterprise system more seriously than does the trust movement, but may arouse less public hostility to the monopolists than does trustification of business. Cartels tend to protect the small firm, whether efficient or inefficient, and to stifle or deaden most of the incentives to efficiency.

The British trend toward socialism has been in large measure a reaction against the deadening effect on business enterprise of cartellization, and the British in the past and now, because of the absence of any serious equivalent to our anti-trust legislation, really have only Hobson's choice: between the inefficiency of central economic planning subject to dual control of government and trade unions, and the inefficiency of private enterprise when cartels make it unnecessary for the individual firm to be efficient to survive. What they now have in England is a combination of government economic planning and of government-sanctioned cartellization, probably the worst possible mixture that could be prescribed for a country in special need of enterprise, efficiency, and flexibility.

American anti-trust legislation has substantially prevented the development of domestic cartels in the American economy, although so-called Fair Trade legislation has made possible in the retail field a considerable approximation to the British situation, and authentic cartels are legal and in some important instances, as for example, the dairy industry and the California fruit-growing industry, are operative, in agriculture.

Where American anti-trust legislation has seriously failed is in preventing the growth of giant firms, with sufficient economic power to set the pattern of sales prices and of prices to suppliers. It is in general the efficient firm which finds it easiest to grow in size, but because efficiency is a cause of size it does not follow that size is a cause of efficiency. There is no convincing evidence that the giant firm, or the giant plant, is more efficient in production than the moderate-sized firm, or plant, and there are many incentives to growth in size of firm which have nothing to do with efficiency and some which make the power of size a working substitute for efficiency. An efficient small firm is often worth more to a giant firm in the same industry than it is worth to the owners of the small firm or to the national economy, and all who are acquainted with the history of American business know of cases where sick giants have absorbed healthy and flourishing moderate-sized rivals not to add to their productive efficiency but to add to their monopoly power as seller and as buyer.

Aside altogether from the efficiency aspects of the problem, the presence of giants in American industry fosters the widespread feeling that where there is great power there will inevitably be instances of its abuse, the belief that the mere existence of giants increases the economic hazards for the small firm and tends to substitute competitive sales effort which can choke off the most efficient small rivals for competition on the basis of price and quality of product. The price-leadership system has been American business's mode of adaptation of the inherent aspiration of business for monopoly to the existence of anti-monopoly legislation.

The present Administration in Washington and the present Supreme Court seem to be genuinely sympathetic with price-competition (outside the fields of agriculture and labor). If price-competition is to be restored in this country, the antitrust legislation will have to be strengthened so as to place limits or checks, direct or indirect, on growth of size of large firms where efficiency considerations do not make such growth urgent — which means in most cases. I think American business will make a serious mistake, both as to its own special interests and as to the consequences for the durability of free enterprise, if in the case of a contest between government and the giants as to what shall be the prevailing pattern of the American economy it unqualifiedly takes the side of the giants. I would even argue that it is in the long-run interest of the giants themselves to cooperate with government in finding non-disturbing and relatively painless ways of checking the intensification of industrial elephantiasis.

The next type of possible conflict between government and business on which I will comment arises out of differences of attitude as to how to deal with the peculiar instability of the American economy. Here I believe there has been serious error on both sides. Government has used the need for economic stabilization as a pretext for justifying extravagance and irresponsibility in expenditures, and has exploited times of unemployment to extend permanently the range of its activities where public approval of such extension could not have been obtained on its merits *per se*. Business, on the other hand, has for the most part insisted that an exact annual budgetary balance is a specific for all ills, good in boom times as in times of depression, and has tended also to take a hostile attitude to the use of monetary and credit policy as an instrument of stabilization. In some business quarters, any suggestion that it might be possible to take most of the sting out of the business cycle by some combination of flexible monetary and fiscal policy is sufficiently refuted by the charge that this is "Keynesian," as if Keynes was a peculiar sort of monster who was incapable even by inadvertence of making any proposals which would be at least worthy of objective consideration.

I will not expand on the urgency of stabilization. I will only point out to you, first what you already know, that in the outside world the belief in the inherent instability of the American type of private enterprise is the strongest propaganda weapon in the hands of those who want to do away with every vestige of free enterprise; and, second, what you may or may not know, that there is no other country in the world where even the most conservative of businessmen share the hostility of American business to experimentation in the use of credit policy and/or fiscal policy as instruments of economic stabilization. May I also call to your attention the lack of warrant for complacency as to the attitude of the American public, including the attitude of many businessmen, toward free enterprise if once again free-wheeling American enterprise and mass-unemployment get closely associated in the American mind.

I believe that ways can be worked out of applying monetary and fiscal policy to the stabilization of the American economy which do not appreciably lessen the pressures on government for economy and efficiency in its own operations, and which do not involve an extension of the range of government participation in industrial activity as a by-product. These ways are to increase the stress on monetary policy as distinguished from fiscal policy and, in the use of fiscal policy, to introduce the required anticyclical flexibility predominantly on the taxation side of the budget rather than on the expenditure side.

Finally, a word on the impact of the tax structure on the health and strength of the private enterprise system. If the contribution which business enterprise has the potentiality to make to an ever-rising American standard of living is to be realized, American business must have incentives to take calculated risks and must have access on reasonable terms to American savings to finance this risk-taking. If the structure of the tax system is such that the risk-taker must bear all the losses which occur but can hope to get only a thin slice of any profits before taxation, he will look for safety rather than for venturesome growth.

I believe that our present tax structure is inherently such as to act as a wet blanket on the risk-taker, and that under stable economic conditions all the dice are now loaded against the risk-taker. I cannot see that the consequences have as yet been serious, but this is because the deadening effect of the heavy impact of taxes on profit margins has been offset by the expansive effect which inflation has had on the size of profit margins. In fact, I think our tax structure as it has been since the war period has on the whole been well suited for an inflationary period. Given the severity of the tax load as a whole, however, its unbalanced impact on profit margins can have ominous consequences during a period of deflation or depression.

As particular aspects of the tax structure which could deepen a depression and retard the operation of the natural recuperative forces, so as to tend to make depression chronic once it has made its appearance, I cite without claims to completeness: first, the double taxation of income earned through the corporate form of enterprise; second, the preferential treatment of debt capital as compared to equity capital; third, the incomplete provision for averaging of income for tax purposes over a number of years, including carry-back provisions for losses; and finally, the arbitrary limitations on the time-allocation of tax allowances for depreciation and obsolescence.

I do not think that on these tax issues there is a sharp conflict of social attitudes, and the major obstacles to reform lie, I think, in normal government inertia and in the technical difficulties of tax reform which lead to lack of agreement among the experts as to the best form which tax revision should take. As long as prosperity is on a high level, the pressure for reform will be slack, but it is important that progress be made in tax revision along these lines in anticipation of the time when it will be urgently needed.

In this discussion of some of the sources of tension between government and business, I have tried to be objective, and to reach my conclusions on the basis of my passionate desire for the indefinite survival of a healthy, strong, and socially beneficial private enterprise system. I hope you will not find any parallel between my type of objectivity and that of the Irish judge who pledged himself to keep to the middle path between partiality and impartiality.

Full Employment at Whatever Cost*

I. Deficiency of "Effective Demand" as the Cause of Unemployment

THE DOCUMENT HERE UNDER REVIEW is a unanimous report on national and international measures for full employment prepared at the invitation of the Economic and Social Council of the United Nations by a group of economists appointed by the Secretary-General.[1] The economists involved are a distinguished lot: John Maurice Clark in association with Arthur Smithies, Nicholas Kaldor, Pierre Uri, and E. Ronald Walker.

The report, in its analysis and recommendations, is definite and concrete, and simple and forthright in exposition; and rarely does it permit the clarity of its diagnosis or the force of its recommendations to be obscured or weakened by plurality of objectives or by complexities of problems where they can be avoided by dogmatism or ellipsis. The report is presented not as an academic exercise, to be mulled over in leisurely debate among experts, but as a practical basis for a comprehensive program of substantially immediate and definitive action by governments, acting separately and through international conferences and agencies. No questions are posed without accompanying answers. There is a "concurring statement" by J. M. Clark appended to the report, which I will not take into account, since its precise significance and the significance of his note that "all members of the committee have expressed general agreement" with views expressed in the statement are not clear to me. Except for Clark's statement, there is not a hint that the group were not completely of one mind with respect to the analysis and recom-

*Reprinted from The Quarterly Journal of Economics, Vol. 64, August 1950, pp. 385-407, by the courtesy of Harvard University Press. Copyright 1950 by the President and Fellows of Harvard College.

1. National and International Measures for Full Employment. Report by a Group of Experts appointed by the Secretary-General (United Nations, Lake Success, New York, December 1949).

mendations contained in the report, although it covers a wide range of matter on which there is much division of opinion in both expert and lay circles. Economics is here an exact science challenging even the claims to being such of the physical sciences. This demonstration of the capacity of economists to reach agreed and unqualified conclusions should, I suppose, be the occasion for professional congratulations and rejoicing. Instead, it brings a slight shudder to my spine.

The analysis presented here of the causes of unemployment and the means by which governments can remove or prevent it is "Keynesian" in the simplest and most mechanical sense of that adjective. It is, I have no doubt, much more Keynesian than was at least the final Keynes himself, especially in its confidence in forecasts and targets and in formulae, and in its unqualified pursuit of a single social goal. All of the operative analysis—that part which supports, and is essential as providing premises for, the conclusions, or is supported by the conclusions—could, I am sure, be reduced to a small set of algebraic equations. Moreover, these could be interpreted as strictly mechanical equations or as statements of identities, and perhaps would have to be so interpreted, to make them lead necessarily to the authors' practical recommendations. Economic process is treated as simple and mechanical and completely responsive to political regulation, and political process is treated as consisting in the reaching of decisions by unified and sovereign authorities and of their subsequent execution, or enforcement by government officials.

The analysis can also be summarized verbally with great brevity without leaving out anything which the authors show that they regard as of great significance. The volume of employment is a function, a simple, stable, and unique function, of the level of effective demand, allowance being made for a small amount of genuinely frictional unemployment. Where the level of effective demand, private plus public, is too low to cause full employment, all that is necessary, in industrial countries, to remove the unemployment is to increase the public contribution to effective demand by the appropriate amount, which can be closely estimated in advance. A variety of ways of increasing effective demand is available, and no strong preferences are shown as between them, each country being left to make its choice between them in conformity with the idiosyncrasies of its political values and its economic and political institutions. But the obligation to remove nonfrictional unemployment by some means is treated as absolute and unqualified.

Although effective demand is the key concept of the entire analysis and I cannot see that much would remain if it were left out, there is not even a gesture in the direction of defining it. At many crucial points in the report "effective demand," to make sense, must be interpreted to mean demand effective in giving employment, and the ease and smoothness of flow of the argument does, I think, derive in large part from the use of "effective demand" to mean not more than this.

There are several points in the argument, however, where inadequacy of effective demand is not made solely responsible for the existence of unemployment and where it is acknowledged that increase of effective demand would not (could not?) be an effective remedy. In the case of "frictional" and "seasonal" unemployment, deficiency of effective demand is absolved from being the cause. As we shall see, however, even here increase of effective demand is held to be a substantial cure for most of what is ordinarily regarded as such unemployment, so that genuinely "frictional" and "seasonal" unemployment become merely the unemployment which increase of effective demand cannot cure, normally of very small dimensions. With respect also to "underdeveloped countries," lack of capital equipment instead of lack of effective demand is made the cause of "underemployment." Although there is no reference to it, I presume that the authors would also concede that the unemployment associated with strikes and unemployables is not caused by deficiency of effective demand.

Had the authors frankly defined "effective demand" as the quantity of labor which employers are ready to hire at prevailing wage rates and adhered rigorously and consistently to this definition, they could have reached their conclusions even more quickly and smoothly without surrendering any realism or relevance of much consequence to them, since the close connection approaching identity between level of effective demand and level of employment constitutes the heart of their doctrine, and anything else affecting volume of employment in industrial countries is either left unmentioned or rejected as of little or no significance.

There is in appearance at least a striking resemblance between the semantic and logical form of the authors' argument and the monetary inflation doctrine of Thomas Attwood and the Birmingham School of the early nineteenth century, with obvious progress confined to the substitution for the quantity of money (or M) as constituting effective demand of something more complex, perhaps the monetary level of expenditures (or MV) or the real level of expenditures (or MV/P). In any case, I regard the "effective demand" argument as so truistic in nature that, going slightly further in their own direction than the authors themselves, I concede that there is no unemployment of any consequence that a sufficient increase of "effective demand" cannot remove. But I regard this as a very meager contribution to the exposition or solution of the crucial issues connected with the problem of serious unemployment.

I grant that unemployment, even frictional and seasonal and capital-scarcity unemployment, and even unemployment associated with strikes, can be cured if the demand for labor by employers can be increased always to such a degree that they hire all laborers who offer themselves and yield to all demands of labor unions whose rejection would involve a strike. I grant also that governments, by direct action, coercion, labor camps, deficit financing, monetary inflation, and other means, can lead employers, including themselves as such, to increase their demand for labor sufficiently to eliminate involuntary unemployment and even a good deal of voluntary unemployment. There remain at least three vital issues, even for those who are genuinely anxious that unemployment be minimized: the issues of economic efficiency, or maximization of real income; of inflation; and of freedom. The first of these issues is not dealt with even by implication in the report, although it would be fantastic to suppose that the authors do not regard it as an issue of consequence; and I will not open it here for discussion, although the absence of emphasis on it is probably not to be regarded as fortuitous. I propose, however, to examine in some detail what the report has to say that bears on the two other issues.

II. Full Employment and Inflation

To many persons it is a matter of serious concern whether under modern conditions, even in a socialist country if it adheres to democratic political procedures, employment can always be maintained at a high level without recourse to inflation, overt or disguised, or if maintained whether it will not itself induce an inflationary wage

spiral through the operation of collective bargaining or other "structural" aspects of a modern economy.

The report speaks with appropriately righteous disapproval at
the appropriate points of *general* price inflation — though not of
suppressed inflation — and stability of prices is always treated as
desirable. But where there is the slightest question of paying a price
in less employment to avoid inflation, even open and general inflation, the answer is in the negative. "Our task here is ... to urge that
it would be inappropriate for any country to pursue policies having
the effect of raising unemployment above the level resulting from
seasonal-frictional causes, merely in order to restrain upward pressures on prices" (§88). The test of adequacy of "effective demand"
is always the level of employment without regard to the level of
prices, and especially without concern as to the extent of direct
controls that may be necessary to prevent the inflation from being
overt. "Under normal conditions, any unemployment exceeding the
amount which is due to the frictional and seasonal factors ... is a
clear indication of a deficiency in effective demand" (§24). "A rise
in prices provides no necessary evidence of a general excess of
demand" (§175; also §89). There is no suggestion of any circumstances under which the authors would not wish a "deficiency" in
effective demand to be corrected or would wish a demand not in
"general excess" to be reduced.

Passages taken out of their context are always liable to give a
distorted impression of their intended meaning. That the reader
may have at least a partial protection against this danger in the
present instance, I present here in full a paragraph of the Report
which contains one of the passages quoted above, which I treat as a
crucial one:

175. The government has, at all times, a variety of means at its disposal
to combat and check an upward movement in prices. Indeed, measures to
curb inflation are likely to be more effective in operation than measures
that have ordinarily been taken in the past to reverse deflationary trends.
It is essential, however, that governments should take positive action
appropriate to the particular situation which arises. While inflationary
pressures which result from a general excess in effective demand must be
counteracted by general measures to curb excessive demand, a rise in prices
provides no necessary evidence of a general excess of demand. And if
attempts were made to curb such price increases by restrictions of demand, they might only lead to reductions in employment and production

even without a reduction in prices. Price increases resulting from factors other than a general excess of demand require selective measures of a direct or indirect nature, rather than measures which are the inverse of measures taken to stimulate demand. They should take the form of qualitative or quantitative credit control (introduced in particular threatened sectors of the economy), direct controls over inventories and selective controls over prices.

I interpret this paragraph, and the report as a whole, as holding that "inflation" does not exist, or at least is not being "general," unless it is accompanied by (a) "general excess of effective demand," i.e., a state of no nonfrictional unemployment plus (b) general, or at least very widespread, inflationary pressure on prices. Unless general inflation so understood exists, no comprehensive anti-inflationary measures should be taken. If any anti-inflationary measures are to be taken, they should be "selective" measures, and the measures should be "direct," as I, though apparently not the authors of the report, interpret the term, i.e., they should have impact only on particular categories of prices, entrepreneurs, etc., instead of being general monetary or budgetary anti-inflationary procedures.

This means to me the statement of a preference, under most relevant inflationary situations, for suppression or disguise of inflation through direct controls in preference to general anti-inflationary measures of the "compensatory" variety. The report, it is true, advocates only "selective" controls, and presumably only a selection of selective controls, so that some sectors of the economy would still, in keeping with their program, be free from detailed regimentation, under conditions of inflationary pressure. But for "suppressed inflation" to exist, it is not necessary that the suppression be universal, and complete. Indeed, I know of no actual case, even in Russian experience, where, given marked monetary inflation, direct controls were comprehensive enough to suppress or disguise every manifestation of price inflation or even to prevent general price levels from rising substantially as measured by any species of price index. I must therefore interpret the report as advocating, as long as there is not full employment, resort to suppressed and disguised inflation, in preference either to generally open price inflation, or to "compensatory" general anti-inflation.

Even what appears to be frictional and seasonal unemployment, moreover, is to be attributed to a deficiency of effective demand if a dose of inflation, no matter how severe, can cure it.

There has undoubtedly been a tendency in the past to exaggerate the quantitative importance of the minor causes of unemployment, and to overlook the fact that the main reason why seasonal and other intermittent workers are not absorbed during the slack periods, and why workers displaced from their regular work remain unemployed, is the lack of alternative employment opportunities, which in turn is due to a deficiency of effective demand. This was proved by British experience during the war, when large-scale so-called 'structural' unemployment, which had previously been attributed mainly to lack of mobility of labour, melted away, leaving an acute labour shortage. Similarly, the large-scale 'transitional' unemployment that was expected in many countries after the war simply failed to materialize, because as people were displaced from war jobs they were immediately absorbed into other employment. (§25; cf. also §§76, 86.)

If this means anything in the context of this report, it means that the very severe wartime and postwar inflations, open and suppressed, in so far as they increased employment, were normal and healthy manifestations of a desirable increase of "effective demand," and that the percentage of unemployment which can appropriately be regarded as recalcitrant to treatment through increase of effective demand and must therefore either be tolerated or dealt with by other means is extremely small — in fact, practically negligible. The authors do, indeed, claim that the amount of inflation it took during the war and postwar periods to achieve full employment "is not really relevant from the point of view of the relationship of inflation to a peace-time full-employment policy," since there was then an abnormal amount of occupational transfer to be brought about (§86). Perhaps a stronger point in this regard could be made to the effect that the inflation was probably carried much farther than was necessary to achieve full employment. But it is clear that the authors are prepared to accept whatever degree of inflation is necessary to achieve full employment, and they cannot very consistently accept as relevant the employment achievements of postwar inflation while denying the relevance of the inflation by which they were accomplished.

The authors take general price inflation rather seriously, although they do not tell us why. Where price inflation results from the stimulation of "effective demand," however, their remedy, as long as there is not a "general excess of demand," that is, as long as there is not full employment, is to suppress and disguise the inflation by direct and selective controls, such as selective credit controls, direct controls over inventories, selective controls over prices, controls over capital issues, control and allocation of materials (§§69, 87, 157, 158, 175-179). Nothing of the familiar full program of suppressed inflation seems to be omitted, except consumer rationing and subsidization of the cost-of-living index, and these, I have a right to suppose, were omitted by inadvertence or for brevity and not from distaste for them.

That after all the experience and the debate of the past decade the preference for suppressed over open inflation can be so blandly presented without argument, without any discussion of the comparative evils of open inflation, on the one hand, and, on the other hand, of the absenteeism, the unpenalized inefficiencies, the padded personnel in plants, the upgrading for pricing and downgrading for quality and service, the queues, the bottlenecks, the misdirection of resources, the armies of controllers and regulators and inspectors, associated with suppressed inflation, is to say the least surprising, as is the failure to balance degrees of unemployment cured thereby against the costs of curing them.

The sixty-four-dollar question with respect to the relations between inflation and full-employment policy is what to do if a policy to guarantee full employment leads to chronic upward pressure on money wages through the operation of collective bargaining. The authors take a good look at the question — and run away.

If there is evidence of a continuous general upward pressure of money wages exceeding substantially the rate of increase of productivity and leading to offsetting price increases, the situation requires such action by the government, jointly with organized labour and employers' associations, as would ensure that any wage increases that may be granted will not result in a general price inflation. The character of the action to be taken would naturally depend on the conditions ruling in each country. (§176; cf. also §87.)

It would be nice to have this spelled out for any country this side of the Iron Curtain, but especially for the United States. It would be particularly interesting to have some concrete suggestions, even for Britain but especially for the United States, as to how the following suggestion could be carried out in practice:

A persistent upward pressure in the general level of wages could also result from continuing attempts to adjust *relative* wages to reflect differences in skill, in training, and in relative attractiveness of different occupations. . . . One remedy may be to improve existing systems of wage-bargaining, so that wages applicable in different trades and crafts and in different industries could be settled simultaneously. (§88.)

III. Full Employment and Economic and
Political Institutions

With respect to the issue of the compatibility of the authors' proposals with political and economic freedom, the authors say that "The measures recommended in the present report to sustain effective demand do not involve any basic change in the economic institutions of private enterprise countries. At the same time, it is clear that a full employment policy could not be pursued if the principles of any particular system were to be construed so rigidly as to rule out any and every kind of government action that might be required to achieve the desired goal" (§5). They also say that "The implementation of a full-employment policy along the lines of these recommendations does not require any alteration in the political system and institutions of any country" (§178). There is every evidence that the authors tried sincerely to adjust their proposals to the minimum requirements for economic freedom and for democratic processes of decision-making in countries committed to "free enterprise," and especially the United States. I think they have not succeeded, and that they have underestimated these minimum requirements even for a semi-socialistic country like Great Britain; and consequently have more seriously underestimated them for the United States.

Confining myself for the time being to their program of "domestic measures," disregarding minor points not clearly fundamental to their program as a whole, and points which seem to me to be reasonably arguable either way, I will comment only on two issues where I see sharp and substantial conflict between basic American economic and political institutions and their program.

First, the fiscal recommendations call in effect for a degree of centralization and concentration of control over budgetary planning and administration in the executive branch of the government such as Congress is wholly unlikely to consent to and may perhaps not have the constitutional right to consent to. They call also, incidentally, for a degree of coordination of fiscal planning within the executive branch which I regard as desirable and not inconsistent with basic American principles, but unfortunately not consistent with past American experience, and not existent now, except perhaps on paper. Compensatory budget policy is given a major stabilization role, rightly, I think, in the authors' program. During the fiscal year just ended the federal deficit was currently (we now know erroneously) estimated at five billion dollars. It was on the whole a prosperous year, and ended on what seems to me to be a distinctly inflationary note, although without "full employment." The Chairman of the President's Council of Economic Advisers is reported to have claimed that the administration planned the deficit that way in order to stave off a threatened recession, and the Secretary of the Treasury is reported to have replied that on the contrary the deficit was unplanned and was due to unforeseen circumstances. The President and the Bureau of the Budget may have still other views. The report calls for a degree of coordination in fiscal planning which this country does not now enjoy and will not enjoy unless important economic and political changes are made in our fiscal institutions and procedures.

Second, the recommendations of the report calling for rigid adherence to a full-employment formula and for a wide range of direct controls if necessary to prevent the full-employment measures from resulting in undesired open inflation involve a substantial extension of government intervention in the economic process and a substantial and, in peacetime at least, unprecedented abandonment of the free market.

IV. Domestic Measures to Prevent Unemployment

The report makes comprehensive and detailed, but for the most part familiar, recommendations with respect to domestic measures for the stabilization of employment. Much of this I find highly acceptable in general, though not often in detail. I welcome particularly the stress on flexibility of taxes as an alternative to flexibility of expenditure programs as a budgetary compensatory device. I miss, however, any exposition of the grounds on which such preference can in principle be strongly supported, especially where there is concern for the survival of the free enterprise system. I fear also that the technical problems of designing flexible taxes are formidable and have scarcely been explored as yet, and while I have a substantial degree of confidence — based mostly on hope — that they can be solved, I am sure that it will take years of study, debate, and experimentation before important use can be made of them as a counter cyclical device. A study of this problem made at my instigation as far back as 1934 at the United States Treasury resulted in quite negative conclusions on the part of the highly competent experts involved.

I have more confidence, however, than do the authors in the stabilizing efficacy of measures in the monetary field even with respect to the promotion of recovery from a depression. The historical experience to which the authors appeal, without specific particularization, as showing negative results in this connection does not appear to me to have much relevance: (a) because of the small amount of pertinent experience, and (b) because what little experience there is shows mainly that half-hearted attempts at maintaining liquidity are not of themselves sufficient to offset the depressive effects of other powerful factors, including perverse government measures, permitted to operate in the opposite direction. I believe it is historically true that there has never been in any important country a period of sustained mass unemployment during which serious illiquidity as measured by prosperity standards of liquidity was not permitted to prevail.

Less familiar, and more controversial, are the recommendations for commitments by governments to precisely formulated "targets" of maximum unemployment which if exceeded automatically bring into operation fiscal corrective measures estimated or forecast to be sufficient to bring unemployment down to or below the target level.

I favor automatic fiscal stabilizers as part of a program to prevent mass unemployment. The criticism I offer of the authors' specific plan, therefore, is a limited one, and fundamentally I think I am in substantial agreement with them. I question the preferability of use of volume of unemployment rather than of employment as the guide, partly because unemployment as a residual phenomenon is much more variable and much harder to define and identify for specific purposes than is employment. If volume of unemployment is made the criterion for the coming into action of the automatic stabilizers, it is not clear to me what operative function is performed in the authors' scheme by the range of unemployment (two to four per cent, or three to five per cent are suggested), as distinguished from the middle point of the range (i.e., three per cent, or four per cent). I cannot see why if allowance is to be made for part time employment it should not also be made for overtime, especially as circumstances are conceivable where recovery would show itself initially more in an increase of overtime than in the hiring of additional personnel. There is no explanation in the report of the procedures by which the automatic mechanism is to be suspended or reversed as the unemployment figures fall below the target level.

More important, I question the role assigned by the authors to the automatic measures to be brought into operation by the variation in the unemployment index. They propose that these measures be given a residual function to perform, with complete responsibility for bringing unemployment — immediately and by a single definitive application — down to the target level, in so far as all other measures past or current have failed to do so. This, I believe, exaggerates the mechanical character of the problem and exaggerates the degree of possibility of determining in advance how much compensatory action is needed to offset a given amount of unemployment, and leaves no place, at least in the authors' exposition, for supplementary or offsetting action if the automatic measures prove inadequate or excessive, and for adjustment to lags in the effects, or to anticipatory effects, of the automatic measures. Their proposal does have an apparent advantage in that it lends itself to the making of precisely-formulated commitments to other countries, but it has even here the disadvantage that precision in the commitments as to the steps to be taken will inevitably involve substantial uncertainty as to the economic consequences of these steps in relation to the fundamental objective of preventing serious unemployment and will probably result in unwillingness to set high goals.

More practicable, and more logical, I think, than the use of automatic stabilizers as a residual or final measure would be their use as a basic "built-in" stabilizer, not for any specific portion of the task, and expected to be supplemented or offset as circumstances call for it by improvised measures, by *ad hoc* legislative or administrative action, tailored to the special circumstances, the perceived lags and trends, of the moment. This would relieve us of any excuse for the pretension that we know how to design a completely effective employment thermostat, while leaving to the thermostat all the scope as a stabilizer that it has potentialities for fulfilling. Using the automatic stabilizer in this way would permit of automatic experimentation with stimulators or depressants applied initially in mild doses, with cumulative step-ups at say three-months intervals if there is further deterioration in employment, or recovery at less than some specified rate, so that some room is left for delayed effects of earlier doses or for self-recovery, and so that the extent of remedial intervention can be limited, or, if automatic, can be neutralized by *ad hoc* offsetting action, where there appears to be a probability that a deficiency or excess of economic activity is being caused by a factor of temporary character. Above all, the procedure I suggest would lessen our reliance upon our capacity to forecast either the course of employment or the effect of the stabilizers upon it. The authors recommend (§166) that we should go even further in their direction and make the automatic mechanism a hair-trigger one by using more "sensitive" but less relevant signals such as percentage of unemployment in the sensitive industries. I suspect that if this were done governments would be kept busy offsetting the unstabilizing effects of the automatic stabilizers — or repealing in disgust the stabilizing measures. But it would be a pretty toy to watch.

There is still another reason why I would not favor definite commitments to a precise employment or unemployment target. That is, on grounds already indicated, that the avoidance of unemployment and the avoidance of inflation are both important goals, and definite commitment to either may well be a formidable and even insuperable obstacle to substantial attainment of the other. It may be necessary, therefore, to balance degrees of the one against degrees of the other, and to surrender a little of one goal if the other is not wholly to be missed. Until there is clearer evidence that this is not the case, the freedom to balance one goal against the other should not be surrendered.

V. *International Disequilibrium*

The international analysis is directed towards finding remedies for two basic problems: (a) international transmission of unemployment through declines in imports and in capital exports; and (b) balance-of-payments disequilibrium. Since the chief long-run concern of the report in connection with the second problem is with the deflationary pressure exercised by the surplus balances of countries where there is deficiency of effective demand on countries maintaining full employment, the two problems merge into one.

Just as in its treatment of domestic aspects the report never defines the key concept "effective demand," so in its treatment of international aspects it never defines the key terms "disequilibrium," relating to problems to be solved, and "stabilization," relating to remedies or goals.

The discussion starts from the proposition that the world is now suffering from an "acute underlying disequilibrium," a "chronic imbalance," in which the United States plays a dominant role, and which must be cured by internationally planned action as a first step towards building stability into the international economic pattern.

The present *disequilibrium* in international economic relations has three main aspects. The first is the *inability* of western European countries to finance their imports by current earnings, and, in particular, to pay for their imports from the dollar area, which at present are only temporarily assured through the aid furnished by the United States under the European Recovery Program. The second is the large import surpluses of a number of underdeveloped countries in Latin America and in the Far and the Middle East, financed, in greater part, by the drawing down of balances accumulated during the war in western European countries and in the United States. The third is the large export surplus of the United States both in transactions with Europe and with other areas. The universal character of this export surplus makes it very *difficult* for any country to cover a deficit with the United States through surpluses earned in other countries. (§103); (italics mine).

That after the devastation and depletion of resources which World War II brought to Western Europe it should experience import surpluses is of itself a gratifying and hopeful fact, not demonstrating an undesirable "disequilibrium," and not a sign of disaster unless of past disaster being remedied by appropriate means. Even the magnitude of the "disequilibrium," which in real terms and relative to aggregate real incomes is not out of line with that which followed World War I, does not prove that there is a fundamentally unhealthy situation, or a "chronic" situation requiring major surgery for its cure, especially as in large part the Western European import surpluses are the free gifts of the United States and Canada and have been caused by them.

That Latin America and other non-European countries are spending their wartime accumulations of dollars and sterling on import surpluses is natural and healthy, provided the spending is reasonably well directed, since there is no better use to which surplus dollars and sterling can obviously be put.

The fact that with Europe and other areas each buying more from the United States than they sell to it, the United States has an export surplus with each area, is an arithmetical truism, not the statement and still less the description of a problem. Interpreted without stress on the three words, "disequilibrium," "inability," and "difficult," the statement tells us nothing which an appropriate arrangement of the balance-of-payments statistics would not tell us, and constitutes merely a most elementary exercise in double-entry bookkeeping.

The report, however, must be interpreted as endeavoring to say something genuinely significant, and the words I have italicized and other passages in its text reveal, not clearly or explicitly but sufficiently, what its authors must have in mind.

The following passage does not add much light: "Unless the deficit countries succeed in paying for their essential imports out of current earnings, their ability to import the raw materials essential for their industries will be seriously endangered." (§102.)

For this to be both true and relevant, it would be necessary that the "deficit countries" have no substantial monetary reserves and no credit abroad, that their imports be for the most part essentials, and that they need to continue in substantially the present volume and value. All of this may be true, but it is not compulsory to take their truth for granted in the absence of some sort of evidence, even if that is a common practice today. For the authors, however, these and similar passages serve as support for the proposition vital to their case for their remedial program in the international field, that, as they put it: "Without the restoration of over-all equilibrium in balances of payments, it will be impossible to achieve the kind of stable international framework within which full employment policies can succeed." (§102.)

In the standard vocabulary of the literature of advocacy of comprehensive economic planning on a national basis, "equilibrium in balances of payments" means a planned and contrived equality of current exports and current imports in each country, and often, though not necessarily, as between each pair of countries. From the point of view of "full-employment" policy, this is a rational goal. In order that any country shall be able to guarantee for itself full employment without substantial deviation, it is reasonable to believe that it will have to regulate its trade in such fashion as to make sure that imports shall never for any appreciable period exceed exports. To execute the policy governments are likely to find it necessary, or at least highly expedient, not only narrowly to restrict or completely to outlaw outward capital flows—including liquidation of old indebtedness — and to enforce rigid exchange controls, but tightly to control all foreign trade if not to take it over, and this may involve equalizing over short periods of time their balances with particular countries. This is a price for the blessings of a full-employment policy which enthusiastic central planners are willing to pay, and one which they tend to accept as not a heavy price. Except for a proposed rigid pattern of investment relations between advanced and underdeveloped countries, the authors of the report are to all appearances prepared to pay this price without tears, both for an interim period before their full program is brought into operation, and thereafter if unemployment still persists.

In the restoration of the world to a state of "over-all equilibrium in balances of payments," a major role is assigned to the United States chiefly because of its economic size. (§60.) But the economic size of the United States is pointlessly exaggerated, when it is measured by its share in world *industrial* production, where share in world production would be more significant, and by its share in world *exports* where share in world imports—or in world trade—would be more appropriate to the report's own line of reasoning.

The authors also attribute special importance to the United States as a destabilizing influence on the ground that its imports consist largely of commodities in which the bulk of the requirements is satisfied out of domestic production, and therefore have a peculiarly high cyclical flexibility in volume. I do not feel sure that the extent to which imports are a fractional supplement to corresponding domestic production is specially high in the United States. I would concede that there is high amplitude of cyclical variation in the *value* of American imports, and that this does bring us special responsibilities to the outside world. It is my guess, however, that this high variability of the value of our imports is mainly due not to the cause given in the report but to the greater amplitude of the cycle in modern times in the United States as the result largely of the higher level of prosperity in this country, as well as to the importance in our imports of raw materials and foodstuffs which have a high cyclical amplitude of variation in their prices.

In preparing the ground for the presentation of their program of regulation of international economic relations, the authors insist that "in the successful attainment of the twin goals of full employment and the creation of a relatively free multilateral trading system, the former must certainly take precedence over the latter." (§65; cf. also 6.) The latter is retained as an ultimate goal, but only for a drastically changed world as far as international economic relations are concerned. For the interim world, they reject multilateralism and praise bilateralism and trade barriers in general as promotive of employment, with no reference to the possibility that what is gained in employment through restriction in imports may be lost through the directly or indirectly associated decline in exports, and with only a single unemphasized concession that by its discrimination between different sources of imports, it "militates against the optimum allocation of the world's resources" (§64). Except for its full-employment pledge, all references to the ITO Charter are in terms so studiedly neutral that they do not preclude a deep hostility to its leading principles for which the present report was not an expedient medium of expression.

The authors place their main reliance for the achievement of international equilibrium on the stabilization of domestic economies, with their program of international measures designed to take care of the deficiencies or failures in the domestic full-employment programs, of failure of some countries to set up such programs, and of the special problems presented by "underdeveloped" countries. This seems to me a sound distribution of emphasis as between domestic and international measures, although an interesting essay could be written on the possibilities of international disequilibrium despite complete achievement of domestic stability. In the international field, the authors present a program of measures, all of which have the merit of being substantially novel and provocative of fresh thinking.

VI. Harmonization of Foreign Trade Targets

The first recommendation is for a meeting of governments under the auspices of the Economic and Social Council to develop a joint program for "a new structural equilibrium in world trading relationships." The new structure is to result primarily from an exchange and reconciliation of national foreign trade "targets." These targets are to be separately set up for the main constituent items of their balances of payments. "An analysis and comparison of these targets would reveal the nature of the inconsistencies in the policies and aspirations of the different countries and would provide a means for adjustment of these policies through consultation and negotiation between governments." (§187.)

If this proposal does not intend more than a repetition of the procedure of the OEEC in the first year of operation of that organization, the results of that experiment, which seemed ridiculous to many when it was first pressed upon the OEEC countries by the ECA, and seems even more ridiculous in retrospect, should not have been taken as encouragement to repeat it under less auspicious circumstances: more countries, less urgency, the absence of external coercion to reach agreement. If the proposal is intended to make it incumbent upon countries to convert their "aspirations" into plans, and to set up adequate controls to obtain execution of these plans, it is an ominous proposal for free enterprise economies.

I feel confident that one can say little more about the functioning of foreign trade "targets" than: (1) that in free or substantially free economies, they are not likely to be genuinely and authoritatively made operative as regulators of foreign trade; (2) that whatever their authoritativeness, they are unlikely to be hit or even near-missed and are unlikely to have even short-run stability; (3) that given rational "national" planning, national targets are certain to be internationally irreconcilable as targets; and (4) that if there is an external sanction for execution of targets, each country will have a strong incentive not to disclose its real aims and to resist their reconciliation with those of other countries. This is despite the significant achievements, though by fewer countries, in a more limited field, and on a *quid pro quo* basis, of bilateral bargaining on a multilateral basis with respect to trade barriers attained by GATT. If there were any serious prospect that this proposal would have any practical results, it would be interesting to contemplate what practical measures could be taken to implement it which would not present difficulties of reconciliation with the Havana Charter. The proposal in its initial form is so vague, however, that it is probably futile to speculate on what it might mean if actually carried into effect.

VII. Stabilization of International Investment

The second major proposal in the international field is for the stabilization of international investment. The primary concern of the authors is clearly with investment in "underdeveloped" countries, but no definition is offered of "underdeveloped country," and the concrete provisions of their scheme cover all foreign investment without distinction as to its location.

The authors claim that "it is only through the rapid growth of production and real income of the underdeveloped areas that the world economy as a whole can attain that steady rate of growth that would permit the needed structural adjustments to be brought about without a contraction of world trade." (§191.) This may be true. For growth of production in the underdeveloped countries to be rapid they assert that the flow of capital to them must be "both adequate and stable." There can be no argument about the need for adequacy, but the need for "stability," especially as used here to mean a constant annual volume, is at least questionable. The capacity usefully to absorb capital presumably would vary with circumstances from year to year, and there is no particular virtue in a horizontal longer-run trend that I can see. Of the rival itches to which central planners are liable, the itch to freeze seems to me even more dangerous than the itch to manipulate.

The authors state as a further condition for the proper flow of capital that the bulk of it should be channelled through an appropriate international organization: "in order to satisfy both the legitimate desires of the borrowing countries to limit the extent of foreign influence in their territories, and the legitimate requirements of the lending countries to obtain adequate security and a reasonable return on their loans." (§191.)

Debtor countries do seem to prefer government loans to private direct investment, and loans by international agencies to loans by single governments, but the reasons are various and are not confined to considerations of foreign influence. It may also be true that loans through an international agency may be more secure for the original lenders than direct intergovernment loans. There is little experience that is genuinely relevant to go on, however, and what the repayment record will be for international lending agencies is a matter on which there is scarcely any visible basis even for conjecture. But if there is to be a substantial international flow of capital in the future, it seems unlikely to me that it will be predominantly through international agencies even if the borrowing countries would prefer it that way. The authors declare a preference for public over private investment, but as they give no reasons for their preference there would be no point in exploring this issue here beyond pointing out its conflict with the American preference, official and unofficial.

To achieve their objective of a stable international flow of capital, the authors propose that the lending countries should commit themselves to total annual foreign investments net of repayments and liquidations (and, I presume, although this is not stated, net of inward flows of foreign capital) at a planned level for five-year periods, and that to the extent to which such levels are not reached otherwise the amounts in deficit should be put by these governments at the disposal of the International Bank for Reconstruction. These levels of lending, I gather, are to be maximum as well as minimum levels.

The IBR would be authorized by a revision of its charter to set up a new department to lend the funds so placed at its disposal. The loans would be to governments only (why?), and for general developmental purposes only. Other details are given, which need not detain us, but nothing is said as to what happens in case of non-compliance by a debtor with the conditions of the loan contract. In the case of losses by the department of the Bank, these losses would be borne proportionately by the lenders to the Bank.

If the lending standards of this department of the Bank are intended to be less rigorous than the present standards of the Bank, or than ordinary banking standards—this is not stated or implied in the report—it might be a good idea, and it would certainly make lending to the Bank more attractive, to have the risks borne by a wider range of countries than the few lenders—or perhaps the single lender. It might be good discipline under the new dispensation, where lending is becoming morally obligatory for richer countries while the creditor's status is steadily deteriorating, if the costs of disregard of debt obligations were not all borne by the lenders.

I see some merit in minimum commitments to lend, but not in commitments as rigid as these, and no merit at all in maximum limits. (That the levels of lending are intended as maxima as well as minima seems inferable from §202, footnote 2.) That the world should ever let itself be regimented into such a degree of rigidity that precisely planned levels of lending by individual countries would be a logical part of an over-all world pattern seems to me a fearsome prospect, but is, I hope, a highly implausible one.

The merits I see in the proposal reduce themselves to three points, but these are of some weight: (1) the Bank should by some means be endowed with larger resources, so that it could widen the range of its lending activities; (2) the limitation by its charter of the

Bank's operations, "except in special circumstances," to loans "for
the purpose of specific projects of reconstruction or development"
should be removed; and (3) all direct relationship between the
countries providing the funds lent and the specific loans made by
the Bank should be terminated. If the Bank is to serve as a "stabilizing" agency, it would seem to me to be preferable that it should
have a mandate to use the additional resources as far as practicable
on an anticyclical basis than that it should have to lend according to
a rigid formula set in advance.

At the present time the Bank complains not of its scarcity of
resources but of the absence of appropriate projects for loans. As to
what countries under existing circumstances would conceivably be
willing to commit themselves to minimum levels of foreign lending,
not substantially lower than their actual present or expected levels,
and as to whether, if the commitments were substantial, suitable
borrowers would bid for the use of the funds on the terms suggested
by the authors, I make no conjectures. The accounting requirements
which the report proposes for debtors seem to me, indeed, to go
beyond reasonably conservative banking requirements, and to be
both impracticable and illogical.

VIII. Stabilization of International Trade

The third and final major international proposal of the report
is a plan for stabilizing the flow of international trade, "whereby the
international propagation of deflationary pressures and the consequent tendency towards a cumulative contraction of world trade
may be effectively prevented." (§199.)

Whenever the imports of a country participating in the plan
decline as the result of a "general decline in effective demand"
within its economy, such country is to be required to deposit with
the International Monetary Fund an amount of its own currency
equal to the fall in the value of its imports less the fall, if any, in
the value of its exports, as compared to a "reference year" or
earlier year of high level of employment. Any other participating
country will be entitled to purchase this currency with its own
currency to the extent of the fall in value of its exports to, less the
fall, if any, in value of its imports from, the depositor country, as
compared to the depositor country's reference year. The currency
of a purchasing country received by the IMF is to stand to the

credit of the depositor country concerned and to be made available to it for the finance of its current transactions in any subsequent period to the extent of the diminution in its monetary reserves during the preceding unit period.

The authors characterize their plan as one which would "operate on principles that are simple, clear and definite so as to make the operation of the scheme as smooth and predictable as possible." (§203.) This is pardonable pride of authorship, but these matters do not with the best of skills of draftsmanship lend themselves to simple, clear and definite solutions. Under their plan it would be left to some authority, the original negotiators, the participating countries, or the IMF, to solve the following problems:

(1) Lags between the events which create rights to purchase currency and the establishment of these rights because of the inevitable delay in recording the events in a manner appropriate for action; (2) reconciliation of balance-of-payments statistics as between pairs of countries in the face of all the notorious difficulties resulting from incomplete recording, errors, and differences as between countries in methods of valuation for statistical purposes of commodity and service imports and exports; (3) identification of source and destination of commodities moving in transit, entrepôt, and processing trade; (4) the treatment of consignment shipments, shipments to branch plants, unpaid shipments, goods travelling with owner, etc.; (5) the assignment of trade to a unit period when there is a lag between physical arrival and formal entry for customs; (6) the measure of the "volume" of trade (required under the plan to make allowances for price changes under certain circumstances); (7) selection of an appropriate "reference year"; (8) determination whether a decline in imports is the result of "a general decline in effective demand" within the importing country or is due to other causes.

All of these difficulties are "soluble," no doubt, in the sense that an international authority with power to do so could find answers of a sort for them, in advance by general rule or *ad hoc*, and countries with tight and comprehensive exchange controls could find answers with comparative ease for most of them. But the plan is directed largely to the United States. Who would find the answers to these questions for the United States, and how?

The authors say of their plan that it "provides a powerful and flexible weapon for offsetting the effects of fluctuations in economic activity and employment in any one country upon other countries which are themselves maintaining full employment." (§140.) Let us see:

(1) The relief provided would be limited by the extent to which countries participated in the scheme.

(2) Unless periodic changes were made in "reference years," general economic growth would result in a progressive attrition of the economic significance of the scheme, since the volume of imports of a later depression year would in time exceed the volume of imports of the reference year.

(3) The willingness of countries to use their rights to purchase the currency of a depository country cannot be taken for granted. (a) The purchase of dollars by England, for example, would under this plan be a close equivalent to the increase in frozen sterling balances, with the important difference that the right to draw upon these balances would depend not on the will of the United Kingdom but on a decline in the external reserves of the United States regardless of the circumstances in which England found herself at the time. (b) If the dollar deposits were being made at a time when England also was undergoing a severe depression, there might not be a desire in England to import beyond the level of current earnings. (c) England might have abundant reserves and therefore not be interested in the opportunity to purchase dollars, even though her dollar exports had declined.

(4) Under partial participation in the scheme, depository countries might not be the chief countries with which other participating countries had experienced a decline in exports, so that obligations to deposit would greatly exceed rights to purchase.

(5) Even with complete participation, obligations to deposit and rights to purchase might not match, because a depositary country, A, may be an importer from B, while C is an importer from A, and an exporter to B. Country B which has a right to purchase A's currency is not interested in it, while country C is interested in acquiring A's currency but has no right to do so and is not interested in using the right it has to purchase B's currency.

(6) Unless all participating countries participated also in the investment stabilization plan and unless the agreed "levels" of investment under that plan were maximum as well as minimum levels, there would be no relief under the plan for B if its scarcity of A's currency were due to a decline in A's lending below a previous

actual level though above the agreed level. Even if the investment stabilization scheme provided for maximum as well as minimum levels and even if A were a participant in it, there might still be no relief to B if its difficulties were due to a diversion of A's loans from B to C, with A shifting its loans because it is eager for exports and can promote them more effectively by lending to C than to B.

(7) B acquires a right to purchase A's currency only if A has had a *general* decline in imports as the result of a "decline in effective demand" as well as a decline in imports from B. To B it will ordinarily make no difference what the cause of the decline in A's imports in general was. In any case B can have no assurance that a decline in A's imports from it will give it a right to purchase A's currency until A has conceded, or the IMF has found, that the over-all decline in A's imports was due to a decline in effective demand in A, and B would have only a few months leeway in which to use A's currency after its right to purchase had been determined.

(8) The scheme would make no provision—it makes no claims to doing so—for a scarcity of A's currency which could be attributed to a relatively slower rate of inflation in A than in most of the rest of the world, if unaccompanied by unemployment in A. In the postwar period it has been the slower rate of inflation in the United States rather than deflation in the United States which has caused dollar scarcity, and it is quite possible that if "dollar scarcity" really becomes "chronic" this will continue to be a major factor. If the authors had made their plan to conform with the IMF charter provisions as closely as they indicated, they would have protected participating countries from losing any privileges because of their practice of inflation in conformity with "social or political policies." This is the only point in the entire report where I feel called upon to commend it for its moderation.

How much would be left of the scheme despite all of these possible leaks I make no attempt to surmise, although something of consequence would be left if the United States were a participant. I would look, however, for a less mechanical and potentially more powerful method of promoting the authors' objective, one not tied up as this is with limitations made necessary by the assumption of indefinite continuance of inconvertibility of currencies, of comprehensive exchange controls, of bilateralism, and of rigidly-planned foreign trade. This is not the place to expound the alternatives I would suggest, especially as I do not regard them as practicable or desirable until *after* convertibility, retreat from national economic planning, and multilateralism had made substantial progress. Their main features, however, may be indicated if only to contrast them with the inflexibilities of the authors' proposals. (a) I would add to the resources of the IMF and give it increased *discretionary* power to provide liquidity for commercial purposes for countries under balance-of-payments difficulties. (b) I would have a new agency set up to do countercyclical lending on a longer-term basis on a *discretionary* rather than formula basis, but with a mandate to lend when it was urgent that lending should be done and to press for repayment when counterinflationary action was in order.

IX. *Final Comments*

I am fully and regretfully conscious of how unsympathetic my account of the report has been. I would like to find concluding words which would soften the impact of what I have said above. Such words, however, would be empty or insincere. I have found myself in conflict with the values, the goals, as well as with the technical analysis in the report. Those who share the affection for or tolerance of a closely regulated society which I have found in the report will rightly find much of my criticism of no weight or even perverse. I should say also, in all fairness, that from the recommendations made by the authors even more ardent individualists than I am can salvage a substantial number of ideas useful for the building of even their kind of a better world, and I have tried to take note of these as I went along. But there are many costs I would not be prepared to pay for "full employment" even if the alternative were failure to attain it by a significant margin—although I would have the unemployed generously taken care of. *Mass* unemployment *is* intolerable, but I believe it will be found possible to provide solid guarantees against its occurrence, on an international as well as on a domestic basis, by means which serve to strengthen rather than to undermine the foundations of what remains of a free market, free trade, free enterprise world.

PART II

History of Economic Thought

The Utility Concept in Value
Theory and its Critics*

THE UTILITY THEORY OF VALUE is primarily an attempt to explain price-determination in psychological terms. Some traces of the recognition of the existence of psychological determinants of price can be found throughout the history of value theory. But for our immediate purpose, it will suffice to begin with the English classical school. The classical economists borrowed from the language of common sense the term "utility," and gave to it the technical meaning of the capacity of a good to satisfy desire. They claimed that the existence of utility was pre-essential to the existence of exchange value. It was in costs of production, however, that they found the ultimate[1] determinants of exchange values, and they used ambiguously both psychological (labor pain, abstinence) and objective (money expenditures, hours of labor) concepts of cost. Under the influence of Jevons, Walras, and the Austrians, writing in the seventies and eighties, but with predecessors ignored by their contemporaries,[2] the emphasis was shifted to demand, and demand was derived from the utility of the classical school, but with the latter concept now elaborated into a psychological law of diminishing utility and with special emphasis on marginal utility, or the utility of terminal units in the order of acquisition or consumption, as the ultimate determinant of exchange value. Jevons and the Austrians, however, failed to distinguish clearly between utility schedules and individual demand schedules, and by expressing utility schedules in monetary terms, they practically identified them with demand schedules, with the consequence that they reasoned from equivalence

*Reprinted from *The Journal of Political Economy*, Vol. 33, August 1925, pp. 369-387, September 1925, pp. 638-659, by the courtesy of the University of Chicago Press.

1. Ultimate, that is, in so far as concerned the scope of their analysis.
2. Notably, W. F. Lloyd in England, 1834; Dupuit in France, 1843; Gossen in Germany, 1854.

of price-offers by different persons to equivalence of utility for these persons. In this respect, their predecessors, Lloyd[3] and Gossen,[4] but not Dupuit,[5] were more acute in their analysis. This error was, however, soon discovered and corrected, especially by the mathematical economists of the utility school.[6] Recognition of and allowance for the difference between the psychological utility schedule and the objective individual schedule of price-offers is now to be found in the writings of all the competent contemporary exponents of the utility theory.[7] Jevons, Walras, and the Austrians either explicitly rejected or ignored the claims of disutility or "pain costs" as an independent determinant of price and explained money costs as a derivative of demand, leaving marginal utility as the sole ultimate determinant. But with few exceptions,[8] the present-day exponents of the utility theory accept disutility as a co-ordinate factor with utility in the determination of price.[9] Under the leadership of Marshall, there later became evident a tendency to shift

---

3. W. F. Lloyd, *A Lecture on the Notion of Value* (London, 1834, p. 28.

4. H. H. Gossen, *Entwickelung der Gesetze des menschlichen Werkehrs* (reprint of 1889), pp. 82, 83.

5. Vide Léon Walras, *Éléments d'Économie Politique Pure* (4th ed., Lausanne, 1900), pp. 446, 447.

6. Cf., for example, Alfred and Mary Paley Marshall, *Economics of Industry* (2d ed.; London, 1881), pp. 69-70 (the first edition was not available for examination); P. H. Wicksteed, *Alphabet of Economic Science* (London, 1888), pp. 68 ff. Walras apparently had been in possession of the correct doctrine in 1873, when he published his first work (see the Preface to his *Éléments d'Économie Politique Pure*, 2d ed., Lausanne, 1889).

7. Cf., however, B. M. Anderson, *Social Value* (Boston, 1911), chap. v and *passim*, who attributes to the Austrian school and its followers a constant confusion between demand curves and utility curves. In his anxiety to make an impressive list of the utility theorists who have gone astray in this manner, he even includes Marshall and Davenport, who have been particularly expert in avoiding the error. Some glaring and notorious examples of the error have, however, escaped him.

8. For England, Wicksteed, and for the United States, Alvin Johnson (and Fetter?) appear to be the sole important surviving upholders of the original Austrian position.

9. Bohm-Bawerk himself, in reply to critics of his doctrine, disclaimed that he had ever rejected disutility as an independent determinant of price, but explained that he had merely ignored it as not being in controversy at the time. He conceded that it was a theoretically co-ordinate factor with utility, though practically of minor importance, in determining price ("The Ultimate Standard of Value," *Annals of the American Academy* [Sept., 1894], pp. 23 ff.; "One Word More on the Ultimate Standard of Value," *Economic Journal* [Dec., 1894], pp. 720, 721). His concessions were inadequate, however, to satisfy his critics, and are hard to reconcile with many passages in his earlier writings.

emphasis from marginal utilities to utility schedules as a whole as factors in the determination of price.

The utility theory, upon the completion of these stages in its development, appeared to have attained its final form, and it has undergone no modification of importance in the last thirty years or so. In its developed form it is to be found sympathetically treated and playing a prominent rôle in the exposition of value theory in most of the current authoritative treatises on economic theory by American, English, Austrian, and Italian writers.[10]

In the scientific periodicals, however, in contrast with the standard treatises, sympathetic expositions of the utility theory of value have become somewhat rare. In their stead are found an unintermittent series of slashing criticisms of the utility economics. Its psychology, it is alleged, is obsolete; its logic faulty; its analysis and conclusions tainted with class bias; its service to economic enlightenment nil. The critics vie with one another in finding terms sufficiently vigorous to express to the full their dissatisfaction with it. To cite some characteristic examples: "The hocus-pocus of marginal utility does not explain price";[11] the utility theory is enmeshed in a vicious maze of circular reasoning;[12] serious injury has been wrought in economic theory by "the pernicious concept of utility dragged into economics by Jevons and the Austrians," which "adds nothing to that of value and should be abandoned";[13] "Marginal-utility economics . . . has not contributed and it cannot contribute to the elucidation of any practical problem."[14] The critics are not in doubt as to the damaging effect of their criticisms. As one of them says:[15] "The descriptive powers of some newcomers

---

10. In France and Germany the developed utility theory has many exponents, but has never attained the position of the dominant value theory.

11. R. G. Tugwell, "Human Nature in Economic Theory," *Journal of Political Economy* (June, 1922), p. 330.

12. Anderson, *op. cit., passim;* O. F. Boucke, "A Unique Situation in Economic Theory," *American Economic Review* (Dec., 1922), p. 603.

13. F. H. Knight, "Normal Price in Value and Distribution," *Quarterly Journal of Economics* (Nov., 1917), pp. 67 and 70 n. Knight has subsequently recanted somewhat, however. Cf. *ibid.* (Nov., 1921), p. 146.

14. E. H. Downey, "The Futility of Marginal Utility," *Journal of Political Economy* (April, 1910), p. 268.

15. Tugwell, *op. cit.,* p. 319. A critic of an older generation can be cited whose "descriptive powers"—more explicitly, his command of the vocabulary of derogation—surpassed even that of these "newcomers," and who was even more outspoken in his expression of contempt for the intellectual caliber of the utility economics. Cf. H. M. Hyndman, *The Economics of Socialism* (London, 1896), chap. vii, "The Final Futility of Final Utility."

in the theoretical field have been brought to bear on accepted doctrine with devastating consequences. The results might almost be called an exposé."

On some points the critics could be set off against one another, some crediting to the utility economics, as its only contributions, what others attack as its chief errors. But on one point the critics are in unison, in the refrain if not always in the pitch, and that is that the utility theory rests on an unsound psychology. The heart of the utility economics is the law of diminishing utility, which maintains that any person acquiring or consuming successive units of a good without important intermission of time will derive from each successive unit less "utility," or "pleasure," or "gratification," or "satisfaction," or "benefit," or "ophelimity," or "capacity to satisfy desire," than he derived from the preceding one.[16] To use this law in the explanation of the mode of determination of particular exchange values or prices, it is necessary to establish a causal sequence between it and price. The utility theorist commonly does this in elliptical fashion and by resort to the assumption or argument, generally implicit, that the intensity of desire for objects is governed by and is quantitatively a more or less accurate reflection of the utility or satisfaction-yielding power of the objects. It is this leap from utility to desire that involves the psychological reasoning which the critics allege to be hedonistic and rationalistic. The causal sequence, fully expressed, is, according to the utility theorists, from (1) a potential or future schedule of diminishing utility of successive units of a good to (2) a more or less accurate and conscious anticipation of this utility schedule, to (3) a corresponding desire schedule, to (4) a comparison, unit by unit, with the desire for what must be given in exchange for this good if it is to be obtained, which gives (5) an individual demand schedule in terms of the price-good, which compounded with the demand schedules of other persons gives (6) the market demand schedule, which is a determinant of (7) price.

The critics deny the reality of this alleged sequence. The hedonism and rationalism which it implies, they assert, are either wholly absent from human behavior or are not dominant characteristics of it. They point out that men commonly seek, not utilities

---

16. Utility theorists have used all of the terms listed above, and few of them have consistently used one term only. For our present purposes, we may take them as substantially synonymous.

nor pleasure, but objects, and that they do not commonly engage in deliberative and careful comparisons and calculations of the units of pleasure which successive units of the same good, or units of different goods, or units at different stages of removal from the present, will yield to them. They ridicule the notion that man's desires are held in leash and spring into action only after completion of fine actuarial comparisons of the hedonic potentialities of different commodities.

Modern psychology is clearly on the side of the critics. Men do not ordinarily have pleasure, or even pleasures, as the conscious object of their desires. Human behavior, in general, and presumably, therefore, also in the market place, is not under the constant and detailed guidance of careful and accurate hedonic calculations, but is the product of an unstable and unrational complex of reflex actions, impulses, instincts, habits, customs, fashions, and mob hysteria. In the light of modern psychology, "Let reason be your guide" is apparently a counsel of unapproachable perfection.[17] The utility economics, as ordinarily formulated, is bad psychology. But what of it? How vital is its dependence upon its erroneous psychology? How extensive would be the changes required in its mode of analysis and its conclusions if all of its psychological elements which were in conflict with the current fashions in psychological doctrine were either brought into accordance with it or ruthlessly excised? The critics, of course, have said that the utility economics stands or falls with its psychology, but have they made their case?

Part I. The Utility Concept in Price-Economics

Many of the utility theorists in the main confined their value theory within the limits of price-economics; that is, they made it their chief, if not their sole, concern to explain the mechanism of price-determination, without appraising that mechanism from an economic welfare or other ethical or quasi-ethical standpoint. They probed into the psychological background of objective market

---

17. Though utility economists have pointed out that too fine and constant calculation as to the comparative desirability of alternatives would itself be ill advised from a rational point of view because of the mental wear-and-tear which would result. Cf. Wicksteed, *Alphabet of Economic Science*, p. 129; H. J. Davenport, *Economics of Enterprise*, p. 101 n.

demand because they desired more light on the character and the origin of demand and not because they were interested in the consumer's psychology per se. This can, at least, be inferred from the fact that the earliest systematic exponents of the developed utility theory, notably Gossen, Jevons, Walras, Böhm-Bawerk, and Wicksteed, used the law of diminishing utility and the concept of marginal utility only or mainly as a means of introducing and finding a causal background for negatively sloping demand schedules and market-price equilibria,[18] and to explain why, in the terms of the current conventional graphics, the market demand schedule always (or as a rule) "slopes downward and to the right." In so far as concerns the main stream of doctrinal development, the clear notion of demand schedules appears to have been the contribution of the utility theorists and to have been suggested by the prior concept of diminishing utility schedules.[19] As has already been pointed out, some of the earlier utility theorists did not distinguish clearly between utility curves and pecuniary demand schedules.

I can find no evidence in the writings of the early utility theorists to support the thesis of many of the critics that they found their utility doctrines ready to hand in the contemporary psychology and that they used these psychological doctrines as major premises from which to derive a priori their price-theories. Their writings do not show any special acquaintance with the psychological speculations current at the time. The references in the earlier literature to psychological sources are very few in number, and not otherwise important. The critics have at times taken for granted that the economists derived their law of diminishing utility from the Weber-Fechner law of the psychologists and have assumed that if they demonstrated, as could readily be done, that psychologists as a rule apply the law to the sensations only, and not to feelings, they had removed from under the utility theory of value the foundation

---

18. In this connection, confirmation is offered by Pareto's development of a theory of price-determination, on the basis of Edgeworth's "indifference curves" or series of equilibria of individual preference as between combinations of different commodities, which carries the analysis of the mechanism of price-determination behind pecuniary demand schedules without using or reaching utility schedules (Vilfredo Pareto, *Manuel d'Économie Politique* [Paris, 1909], pp. 168 ff.).

19. Cournot, of course, had given clear mathematical expression to the schedule concept of demand without relating it to utility, but the early utility theorists were not acquainted with his work.

upon which it rested.[20] I can find little evidence that the early utility theorists had ever heard of this law.[21] The resemblance between the Weber-Fechner law and the law of diminishing utility, such as it is, seems to be due to similar but independent processes of observation or to coincidence, but not to direct derivation of the latter from the former. The law of diminishing utility, whether sound or not, has been developed by the economists as a product of their own observation and has not been borrowed from psychology.[22]

Wherever the utility economists may have obtained their psychology, however, it cannot be gainsaid that it is faulty. But for the price-economist who wishes merely to make a first contact between objective price and human psychology, much of the theorizing with respect to utilities, and certainly all the hedonistic and rationalistic elements therein, are irrelevant to his purpose. If there be substituted for the law of diminishing utility a law of diminishing desire—or if utility be defined and used to signify desire—if all references to gratification, satisfaction, benefit, pleasure, pleasantness, pain, irksomeness, and unpleasantness be eliminated, there will remain sufficient to supply an immediate psychological background for the concept of the negatively inclined pecuniary demand schedule, and therefore for the explanation of the mode of determination of market price. Diminishing desire need be referred to only to explain diminishing price-offers as quantity available increases.[23]

---

20. For a recent example, see A. J. Snow, "Psychology in Economic Theory," *Journal of Political Economy* (Aug., 1924), pp. 493 ff., who refers to Dickinson's appeal to the Weber-Fechner law as if it were a typical example.

21. The only citation to the Weber-Fechner law that I have encountered in the early literature of the utility theory is by F. Y. Edgeworth in his *Mathematical Psychics* (London, 1881), p. 62. His reference to the law, however, is only by way of analogy, and he plainly recognizes that acceptance of the Weber-Fechner law does not necessarily lead to acceptance of the law of diminishing utility. The only recent instances I can find of economists in the utility tradition who appeal to this law for support of their value doctrines are F. A. Fetter (*Economic Principles* [1915], p. 40), G. P. Watkins (*Welfare as an Economic Quantity* [1915], p. 26), and Z. C. Dickinson (*Economic Motives* [1922], pp. 233, 234).

22. I do not intend to deny that the utility theorists inherited the hedonic element in their theory, the postulate that utility and desire were quantitative correlatives, from the psychologists.

23. Cf. Z. C. Dickinson, "The Relations of Recent Psychological Developments to Economic Theory," *Quarterly Journal of Economics* (May, 1919), p. 384: "The law of diminishing utility, a purely psychological postulate, giving

The variations between the demand schedules for a given commodity of different persons can be explained as due either to differences in the intensity of their respective desires or to differences in
the intensity of their aversions to surrendering the price-commodity
or to both. It is not necessary, moreover, for any purpose proper to
price-economics, to insist upon either the comparability of desire as
between different persons or the general prevalence of deliberate
and reasoned calculation on the part of individuals of the relative
intensity of their desires for different units of the same or different
goods, or to impute to the desires of any person, even hypotheti-
cally, any quantitative relationship inter se beyond that which can be
expressed through the primary function of numbers of indicating
order. All that the price-economist need assume with respect to an
individual's desires is that they vary in intensity and that the desire
for a further unit of a good diminishes with the increase in the
number of units already acquired.

This avenue of escape from the pitfalls of rationalistic hedonism
has long been clear to many utility economists. Gide, as long ago as
1883, suggested "desirability"[24] and Wicksteed, in 1888, proposed
"desiredness"[25] as a substitute for utility. These terms are perhaps
objectionable because they unnecessarily objectify desire, but they
are otherwise in the spirit of the argument presented here. The
critics, it is true, have expressed impatience with such attempts as
the foregoing, which they have characterized as unsuccessful endeavors to cover up the unsound psychological presuppositions of
their theories by minor and deceptive changes in terminology. In
so far as price-economics is concerned, however, the critics have
relied on vigorous assertion to demonstrate that a recasting of the
utility theory in the manner indicated will not suffice to render it

---

greater precision to the tendency of exchange value of a commodity to decrease
as the supply of the commodity is increased, has rendered very great service in
economic analysis." This particular service can be as fully rendered, and with
the advantage of freedom from disputatious psychological matter, if there be
substituted a law of diminishing desire for the law of diminishing utility.

24. Cf. *Cours d'Économie Politique* (4th ed.; Paris, 1894), p. 55 n.

25. *Alphabet of Economic Science*, p. 8. Cf., also, H. J. Davenport, "Proposed Modifications in Austrian Theory and Terminology," *Quarterly Journal
of Economics* (May, 1902), p. 361. The position taken in the text as to the irrele-
vance to the price-economics of the utility theorists of their hedonistic and rationalistic doctrines is essentially that of Davenport in his *Value and Distribution*
(1908), pp. 303-10.

free from hedonistic taint without lessening its serviceability as an explanation of the mechanism of price-determination.

I have assumed, of course, that there is a law of diminishing desire. Certain apparent exceptions to the law can be cited, but it is not difficult to explain them in terms consistent with it. The collector, for instance, who seeks a complete set of coins, or stamps, or first editions, would ordinarily desire the last unit necessary to complete his set as intensely as, if not more intensely than, the first unit. The matcher of pearls may well have a mounting desire for successive pearls which match with those already acquired, until he has enough for a complete chain. The intensity of desire for the second glove of a pair may well be greater than for the first in the absence of the second. In all of these instances, however, a complete set is the proper unit to take to observe the operation of the law, and the law may be expected to manifest itself as between successive sets. The perfect miser's attitude toward gold coins is probably not in accordance with a law of diminishing desire, but the miser presents a psychopathic rather than a normal case. He is a collector whose initial set is never complete.

According to the utility theory, as presented above, the market demand curve derives its negative slope from the downward inclinations of the desire curves of the individuals in the market. If instances should be found, therefore, where market demand curves for particular goods were positive in their inclination, it might seem to imply that many if not all of the purchasers of such goods had positive desire curves for them. Cunynghame has suggested as an instance of a class of commodities for which there might be a positive demand curve a particular edition of a hymnbook which is useful in direct proportion as it is widely used.[26] Goods such as metric measuring instruments or interchangeable parts, or say a telephone, whose direct or instrumental serviceability is dependent to a large degree upon their wide use, belong to this class. So also do fashion and style commodities,[27] as distinguished especially from commodities whose virtue lies wholly in their rarity. But this is not a true instance of a positive demand curve in the static sense, and

---

26. Henry Cunynghame, "Exchange Value, Monopoly and Rent," *Economic Journal* (March, 1892), p. 39.

27. Fashion commodities, of course, may lose their value if their use becomes too widespread.

does not at all imply positive desire schedules. A person's desire for successive units of such goods will vary directly with the generality of their use, but inversely, as for other goods, with the number of units he already possesses. The demand of each individual may rise as the use of the good spreads, but at any given moment, given the extent of its use, he will take fewer units at a high than at a low price.[28]

But instances are conceivable of the existence of true, positively inclined demand curves. Commodities which have prestige value derived mainly from their expensiveness may have demands which for part of their range are positive in inclination, as may also commodities whose quality is judged by purchasers mainly from their price. In both these instances, however, the positive inclination of the demand schedule will be due to the fact that at any given price, x, purchasers will desire any nth unit more than they would have desired an nth unit at a lower price, y. It does not follow that the desire curves will also be positive in their inclination, i.e., that at any given price, or irrespective of price, purchasers will desire second and third units more than first units. The failure in these instances of the demand schedule to follow the desire schedules in its inclination is due to the fact that for such commodities the desire schedules are functions of actual price as well as being variables of it.

Another possible instance of a positively inclined demand schedule may be cited. Assume that wheat is the cheapest food in terms of calories, and that a householder needs $2x$ calories in the course of a year. Assume, further, that he has \$200.00 annually to spend on food and that when wheat is \$1.00 a bushel he can secure the $2x$ calories as follows: \$100.00 for 100 bushels of wheat, giving $1\frac{1}{2}x$ calories, and \$100.00 for other less economical foodstuffs, giving $\frac{1}{2}x$ calories. If wheat rises in price above \$1.00 per bushel, the necessary amount of calories can be obtained only by increasing the number of bushels of wheat purchased, and decreasing the quantities of other foodstuffs purchased.[29] Here is an instance where quantity purchased will increase as price rises, even though price itself does not contribute to the appeal of the good. But even this case can be explained consistently with the existence of negatively inclined

---

28. If extent of use and price are closely related, it will, however, be difficult to separate the influence of price from the influence of extent of use on the amount which buyers will take.

29. Cf. Alfred Marshall, *Principles of Economics* (6th ed.), p. 132.

desire curves, if reference is had to J. B. Clark's reasoning that the desire for a commodity is really a composite of desires for the various qualities of the article.[30] In this simplified case, what the consumer desires is calories and variety, and the desire for calories is urgent and provision must be made for its satiation before the desire for variety can be satisfied. But once the $2x$ calories are obtained, there may be no further desire at all for calories, and the remaining funds will be devoted wholly to the securing of variety. Both the desire for calories and the desire for variety, however, will be negative in their inclination.

It should be clear, also, that the utility theory does not posit a direct relationship between consumers' desire curves and the market demand schedules of professional operators in middlemen's markets, though critics of the utility theory have sometimes failed to see this.[31] The removal of middlemen's demand schedules from consumers' desire schedules, both as to time and as to stages in the process from the beginning of production to final consumption, results in certain differences of behavior as between them.[32] A middleman's demand is governed largely by his opinion as to the prospective demand of consumers—or more immediately, as to the prospective trend of price—and all sorts of influences may contribute to the formation of that opinion, some of them intimately connected with the trading process itself. Where buyers are influenced by the behavior of other operators, whether consciously or not, especially in highly speculative markets, price-rises resulting from eager bidding on the part of some operators are likely to induce like eager bidding on the part of others and to result in still further increases in price.[33] Under such circumstances volume of sales is for a time likely to show a positive, instead of a negative,

---

30. Cf. *Distribution of Wealth*, pp. 214 ff. It can also be explained by reference to the existence of very steeply inclined curves of utility of or desire for money.

31. Cf., especially, E. H. Downey, "The Futility of Marginal Utility," *Journal of Political Economy* (April, 1910), pp. 265 ff.

32. Cf. Alfred Marshall, *Principles*, p. 100 n: "... The demand for a commodity on the part of dealers who buy it only with the purpose of selling it again, though governed by the demand of the ultimate consumers in the background, has some peculiarities of its own."

33. For an early reference to the tendency in speculative middlemen's markets of price-increases to lead to increased eagerness to buy, see Eugene Schwiedland, "Étude sur les Rapports existant entre les Prix en Gros et en Détail," *Revue d'Économie Politique* (1890), pp. 48 ff.

correlation with price. But such instances neither necessitate any qualification to the universality of the law of diminishing desire, nor do they serve to discredit the proposition that even middlemen's demand schedules are ultimately dependent upon consumers' desire schedules.

It has been objected against the validity of the use of a concept of diminishing desire in value theory that we have no evidence of diminishing desire except as inferred from diminishing price-offers, and that to explain the negative slope of the demand curve by the existence of a law of diminishing desire and in turn to infer the existence of such a law from the negative slope of the demand curve is to indulge in circular reasoning.[34]

But the negative slope of the demand curve is a direct inference from experience, and the law of diminishing desire is a working hypothesis serving to explain the general recurrence of that phenomenon. Until it is demonstrated to be contrary to established fact, or until a better hypothesis is available, the law of diminishing desire can stand on this fact alone. But the evidence from introspection, for whatever it may be worth, and from the observation of human behavior in other fields than the economic market, lends further confirmation to the hypothesis. As Lloyd pointed out over ninety years ago,[35] our situation with respect to desire is closely comparable with the state of our knowledge with respect to heat prior to the discovery of the thermometer. The existence of different degrees of heat was then a hypothesis supported only by the fact that it was the only available explanation of other resultant phenomena and by introspection with respect to sensations. Nevertheless, the lack of means of direct measurement of heat did not put it out of the realm of scientific discussion even for those most exacting of scientists, the physicists. Even with the thermometer,

---

34. Cf., for example, O. F. Boucke, "A Unique Situation in Economic Theory," *American Economic Review* (Dec., 1922), p. 603.

35. *A Lecture on the Notion of Value*, pp. 29-30: "It would indeed be difficult to discover any accurate test by which to measure either the absolute utility of a single object or the exact ratio of the comparative utilities of different objects. Still it does not follow that the notion of utility has no foundation in the nature of things. It does not follow that because a thing is incapable of measurement, therefore it has no real existence. The existence of heat was no less undeniable before thermometers were invented than at present." For later instances of appeal to heat for a parallel with desire, cf. Wicksteed, *Alphabet of Economic Science*, p. 15; Edgeworth, "Professor J. S. Nicholson on 'Consumers' Rent,'" *Economic Journal* (March, 1894), p. 155.

temperature is arbitrarily defined and is measured only indirectly by its effect on the height of a column of mercury. The parallel would continue to be close if the accepted rule that each equal unit of increase of temperature will bring about an equal rise in the mercury column were a hypothesis no more susceptible of proof than the economic theory of the relationship between diminishing desire and diminishing pecuniary demand.

Some of the critics of the utility economics have not confined themselves, however, to attacks on the validity of its psychological presuppositions, but have claimed to demonstrate that even if its psychology were conceded to be valid it was guilty of various logical errors in making its inferences therefrom. The main conclusion in the field of price-economics resulting from the utility analysis is that for each purchaser of a series of commodities the purchase prices measure the relative marginal utilities of these commodities. For the "marginal utility" concept of the utility theorists, marginal desire may likewise be substituted and will serve equally well the only legitimate function of the concept in price-economics, namely, as a logical device for expressing with greater precision the subjective relationships between small, final increments of different goods. Substituting marginal desire for marginal utility, this proposition may be expressed as follows: The market prices of a series of commodities (if purchasable in small units) measure for each purchaser his relative marginal desires for all of the commodities actually purchased by him. As has already been pointed out, some utility theorists have gone beyond this and in their confusion of utility curves and demand schedules, and especially because of the dangerous practice of expressing utility schedules in pecuniary terms, have spoken of price as measuring the marginal utilities of the same goods to different persons and of different goods to society as a whole. Criticism of this error is fully justified, but it should not be directed against the utility school as a whole.[36]

---

36. The character and the source of the error can be clearly brought out by a quotation from Böhm-Bawerk (*Positive Theory of Capital*, p. 161): "First, since the relations of Wants and Provision among individuals are extremely various, one and the same good may possess an entirely distinct subjective value [=marginal utility] for different persons . . . without which, indeed, it is difficult to see how there could be any exchanging at all."

To the economist who distinguished utility schedules from individual demand schedules, it would be obvious, especially if he refrained from expressing utility schedules in pecuniary terms, that what was necessary to a profitable exchange between two persons was not that to A good *x* have a higher and good *y*

On the other hand, there is no merit in the argument of those critics who contend that the attempt to demonstrate a causal sequence from utility schedules to price must necessarily fail once it is admitted that price is not a satisfactory measure of utility as between individuals.[37] The price of a particular commodity is determined in part by the market demand for it, and the market demand is a compound of the individual demands. The individual demands are, in turn, resultants of the contact, for each individual, of his desire to acquire that particular commodity with his desire to retain, or to make other use of, what must be surrendered to obtain it. In this way individual desire schedules are an ultimate determinant of market price and have "market significance."

The utility theory of value has also been charged with the vicious circle of explaining exchange value by exchange value, because it maintains that value is determined, not merely by desire, but by desire backed up by purchasing power, i.e., value.[38] But this is a charge which can be made with equal force against the simple demand-and-supply explanation of value determination, since it maintains that demand is a determinant of value and defines demand in terms of purchasing power. This alleged circular reasoning, however, is merely the perception on the part of the utility economists of the mutuality of relationship between exchange values. The utility theory rightly represents values as being mutually related, each value being an item in a system of interdependent values. In its fullest development it would explain how with a given set of desire (and aversion) schedules and a given distribution of accumulated wealth and of capacities for labor, saving, etc., a certain set of prices or exchange values would result. But this task has not been found feasible, even in the abstract, and the utility theorist confines himself to explaining selected and minute phases of the

---

have a lower marginal utility than to B, or vice versa, but that to A the ratio between the marginal utilities of goods x and y be different from the corresponding ratio to B. If good x and good y each had for A double the marginal utility that they had for B, there would be no basis for an exchange.

37. Cf., for example, W. H. Hamilton, in his review of Henderson's *Supply and Demand, American Economic Review* (March, 1923), p. 93: "His [i.e., Henderson's] admission of differences in income as affecting the amounts which purchasers are willing to pay for an article makes his 'laws,' that 'the marginal utility of a commodity to anyone diminishes with every increase in the amount he has,' applicable only to individual economy and robs it of market significance."

38. B. M. Anderson, *Social Value*, chap. vi.

process of price-determination under hypothetical conditions of stability of the surrounding situation. Of no stage in his reasoning is it accurate to say that it explains value by value, though it is true—and logically irreproachable—that it makes the value of commodity w a function of the values of commodities x, y, and z. If this be a vicious circle, there is no merit in avoiding them.[39]

Some defects of Böhm-Bawerk's exposition of the utility theory, which were unfortunately imitated by some later writers but which many utility theorists, and especially those using the mathematical method, avoided, have given the critics some openings for well-merited criticism. Böhm-Bawerk at first did not have an adequate notion of either utility schedules or demand schedules. He built up a continuous demand schedule, which he described in subjective terms but expressed in objective terms, from a series of discontinuous, individual demand schedules, for each of which only one point was given. In his exposition, in consequence, the famous "marginal pairs" of buyers and of sellers were singled out for excessive attention, and to "the marginal buyer" was attributed the rôle in price-determination which, were it not more logical to attribute it alike to every unit of the demand, belonged to the marginal purchases of every purchaser. This served to obscure for Böhm-Bawerk himself for a time, and for his readers, the true character of the relationship between diminishing utility and price. On the basis of Böhm-Bawerk's exposition, many "points" can be made against the utility theory which could not be made if the exposition of other representatives of the school, such as Edgeworth, Wicksteed, or Alfred

---

39. Anderson first makes an unqualified charge against the Austrians of circular reasoning and then proceeds to take most of the sting out of his arraignment by the following anticlimax: "If the Austrian analysis attempt nothing more than the determination of particular prices, one at a time, on the assumption that the transactions are, in each particular case, so small as not to disturb the marginal utility of money for each buyer and seller, and on the assumption that the values and prices of all the goods owned by buyers and sellers are already determined and known, except that of the good immediately in question, it is clear that it but plays over the surface of things. If it attempt more it is involved in a circle" (*op. cit.*, p. 48). Though some mathematical economists have succeeded in relaxing somewhat the severity of these assumptions without becoming involved in circular reasoning, this is a fair enough description of what the utility theory, in the field of price-economics, has aimed to accomplish. Whether or not this is but playing on the surface depends on what is surface and what undersoil, and on how deep one must probe before one has penetrated the surface. On these matters there is room for much inconclusive and barren debate.

Marshall, Davenport or Fisher, Walras or Pareto, were taken as the basis for attack.[40]

The common criticism of the utility theory, that it is an inadequate because incomplete theory of value,[41] is really a criticism of the range of activity of the theorists who have accepted the utility theory rather than of the theory itself. The criticism comes from those who want a theory of value which will not limit itself to a static or instantaneous flashlight analysis of the value-determination process, but which will delve into the origin and growth of the wants and desires which lead to the existence of exchange values. To subdue their impatience, it might be pointed out to them that there are not, and cannot be, such things as "complete theories," and that Mill's dictum to the contrary notwithstanding, there will always continue to be some neglected phases of the value problem. When they suggest that a static theory is of no service, because the consumer becomes a different person, with a new set of values, every time he buys a cigar or a meal, they exaggerate the instability of human behavior, and they contradict their own assertions about the importance of habit and custom. When they ask for the development out of value theory of a theory of consumption they often lay down specifications which call for a theory of life.[42] But when they demand that there be added to, or substituted for, the hypotheses and the observations from crude and limited observation a body of fresh and fertile data derived from systematic and comprehensive observation of human behavior, and when they charge that utility theorists have unduly limited themselves in the range of their investigations, there is force in their remarks. There does not appear to be much promise that efforts further to refine or elaborate

40. For criticisms of the utility theory resting for their validity on the discontinuity of Böhm-Bawerk's individual demand schedules, see Anderson, *op. cit.*, pp. 29 ff.; Downey, *op. cit.*, pp. 260 ff. For criticism of Böhm-Bawerk's use of discontinuous schedules, cf. F. Y. Edgeworth, "The Theory of Distribution," *Quarterly Journal of Economics* (February, 1904), pp. 189 ff. For concessions by Böhm-Bawerk to his critics, see *Kapital und Kapitalzins* (3d ed., 1912), p. 388 n.

41. Cf., especially, Thorstein Veblen, "The Limitations of Marginal Utility," in *The Place of Science in Modern Civilisation* (New York, 1919), pp. 231 ff.

42. It is to be regretted that utility theorists have often called their utility analysis a theory of consumption. It cannot be claimed for the utility theory that it does more than open a pathway to the development of such a theory, and I see no particular reason for belief that this is the most serviceable avenue of approach, even of those already available.

upon the utility theory will be productive of results commensurate with the effort involved. It may even be true that the theory has already been overrefined and overelaborated for all theoretical and practical purposes. If the flood of criticism of the utility theory results in diverting effort from its further development to the pursuit of research in fresher fields, it will have an important accomplishment to its credit. But if the utility theorists have expended too much effort on the subtleties of utility analysis, the critics have expended too much effort—and venom, also—on criticism thereof. With the need for research in new directions so urgent, and the promised harvest therefrom so rich, it is somewhat surprising that they could have devoted themselves so patiently, persistently, and repetitiously to the elucidation of the allegedly palpable errors and inadequacies of the older doctrines!

There must not be denied to the utility analysis, nevertheless, some positive contributions to knowledge in the field of price-economics. It has, for the first time, afforded a satisfactory explanation of the disparity between value in use and value in exchange which so puzzled the classical economists. It provides a hypothesis, in harmony with what is known of human nature, which adequately explains the downward slope of the demand schedule and which is as yet alone in the field. It throws some light on the causes and the types of interrelationship which exist between the prices of different goods. It bridges the gap, partially at least, between the price or exchange-value theory of economics and the psychological "general theory of value" of the philosophers. Whether or not these contributions are "important" is a matter of individual definition of terms, or of individual judgment, or interest. In Part II I propose to examine the significance of the utility analysis in the field of "welfare economics."

PART II. THE UTILITY CONCEPT IN WELFARE ECONOMICS

The Legitimacy of Welfare Economics

In the recent literature on economic methodology, of which an outstanding characteristic has been the demonstration on a priori grounds of the lack of validity of the a priori method, protests recur, resting also on a priori grounds, against the conduct of economic analysis in welfare terms. One basis for such protests is that welfare is an ethical concept, involving the making of ethical evaluations, and that such evaluations are repugnant to the inherent nature of uncorrupted scientific analysis. There does not seem to be any essential conflict between this dogma of the laboratory and the use of the utility concept, not only in price-economics, but even in analysis intended to provide a basis for the making of welfare judgments.

Let us assume for the present that welfare consists of a flow of utility and that utility means satisfaction. Economists can accept satisfaction as a quantity, without committing themselves to any position with respect to its ethical quality. If they be welfare economists, they can consider the bearing of economic institutions and processes on "maximum satisfaction," but if they refrain from taking any position with respect to the goodness or the evil of these satisfaction consequences they will have succeeded in keeping their analysis free from ethical taint. Economics suffers, however, from the fact that it shares its terminology with other disciplines and with the language of common sense. The term "utility" suggests a particular school of ethics, while "welfare" is hard to distinguish from the *summum bonum* of most humanist schools of ethical doctrine. But economics can conceivably employ these concepts without giving them ethical meaning within the proper limits of its own range of inquiry. If economics wishes to make its findings helpful in the making of ethical appraisals, which is surely not an illegitimate aim, it may well apply itself to the study of the consequences, for whatever is the ethical *bonum*, of economic structure and process. By the selection of the data which he investigates the economist may suggest by implication what in his judgment is the proper basis for ethical judgment, but provided he does not defend his selection on ethical grounds it is at least not obvious that he has offended the scientific proprieties.

That utility and welfare have been used in economics as ethical concepts may be conceded, but it does not follow that their use necessarily involves ethical judgment. When Knight cites the use of utility by economists in the justification of progressive taxation as illustrating the ethical nature of the concept,[43] he merely points

---

43. F. H. Knight, *American Economic Review Supplement* (March, 1921), p. 145.

out that it has been used for ethical purposes. It is not the acceptance of utility as an *economic datum*, but the acceptance of maximum satisfaction as the *summum bonum*, or as an important element therein, which serves some economists as the justification for progressive taxation. If there are utility theorists who hold with Knight that "men who know what they do want—and who have not sapped their vitality by unnatural living or too much of a certain kind of thinking—[do not] want their wants satisfied"[44] they might come to the same conclusion as other utility theorists with respect to the contribution of progressive taxation to maximum satisfaction of wants, but would use this conclusion as the basis for an ethical condemnation of progressive taxation. Whatever ethical implications the conclusions of the economist with respect to utilities may carry with them, these implications are for the ethicist or for the economist only in other than his professional capacity to act upon.

In any case, most welfare economists carefully disclaim any intention of pronouncing final ethical judgments.[45] For most of them, it is true, there is no difference in kind between the economic welfare with which they attempt to deal and total or general welfare, but merely the limitation in the range of welfare problems considered and in the comprehensiveness of their analysis thereof which professional division of labor enforces upon them.[46] They are always ready to admit, however, the possibility of serious conflict between the economic and the non-economic utilities. They ordinarily go no farther toward ethical judgment than to claim the existence of a strong presumption that an increase in economic satisfactions or in economic welfare will contribute to total welfare.[47] If their welfare economics is in any degree an encroachment upon the field of ethics it is so as a casuistry in a partial and tentative ethics which admittedly does not take into account all the elements necessary for final ethical judgment.

---

44. F. H. Knight, "Ethics and the Economic Interpretation," *Quarterly Journal of Economics* (May, 1922), p. 470.

45. Fetter, however, asserts that it is necessary for welfare economics to distinguish between the "good" and the "bad" in acts of individual choice ("Value and the Larger Economics. II," *Journal of Political Economy* [December, 1923], p. 792).

46. Cf. A. C. Pigou, *The Economics of Welfare* (London, 1924), pp. 10 ff.

47. Cf., for example, Henry Sidgwick, *Principles of Political Economy* (London, 1883), pp. 518 ff.; Pigou, *op. cit.*, p. 20.

Utility as a Welfare Concept

The welfare economist, if he is of the utility school, generally defines and measures welfare in subjective terms of utility. But there pervades the utility economics a threefold ambiguity in the use of the term "utility," whose persistence is facilitated by the lingering traces of psychological hedonism in its analysis and by the lack of clearly-defined dividing lines in its organization between price problems and welfare problems. Utility is sometimes used to signify satisfaction, pleasure, happiness, or whatever the stuff of welfare is thought to be;[48] at other times to signify the capacity of goods to contribute to welfare, or to yield satisfactions.[49] In recent years there has been a tendency to confine its meaning to "capacity to satisfy desire" or "desiredness," and then to abandon it, because of its ambiguity, for the latter term.[50] The time seems to be approaching when there will be a utility economics which carefully avoids employing the term which originally gave it its name!

Among welfare economists of the utility school it has been the general tendency to take satisfaction (in some cases, pleasure) as the unit of welfare. If the function of welfare economics is to contribute data which will serve the social philosopher or the statesman in the making of ultimate welfare judgments, this tendency leads, perhaps, to a hedonistic ethics. It is not necessarily entangled, however, in a hedonistic psychology, since if it avoids using price as a measure of satisfaction it need not commit itself to the existence of any close relationship between desire and satisfaction. The day seems definitely to have passed, however, when the philosophically-minded and the psychologically-sophisticated would give their support to an ethics written in terms of a pleasure element alone, or of any other single element. To say nothing of transcendentalists engaged in the pursuit of absolute values which derive their sanctions from other sources than current human desires and satisfactions, there are many who would place greater stress on the importance of the process of desire-fulfilment itself than on the gratifi-

---

48. Cf. Alfred Marshall, *Principles of Economics*, 6th ed., p. 93: "The *total utility* of a thing to anyone (that is, the total pleasure or other benefit it yields him). . . ."

49. Cf. F. A. Fetter, *Economic Principles* (New York, 1915), pp. 25, 509.

50. Cf. Pigou, *op. cit.*, p. 23. For this meaning of the word "utility," "capacity to excite or induce desire" would be preferable, as less ambiguous, than "capacity to satisfy desire."

cations or other states of consciousness which result from such fulfilment. Some emphasize the absence of unfulfilled desires, therefore, as more conducive to welfare than a great flow of satisfactions which still leaves their recipient discontented. The economist, whether naïvely or as a *modus operandi* while awaiting the solution by other disciplines of their own problems, has given scant attention to these difficulties.[51] Directly or indirectly influenced by the utilitarian tradition which has been so powerful and persistent in economics, he has seemed content to make his analyses in satisfaction terms, without evidencing much fear that a new revelation in philosophy or psychology, or old knowledge newly applied, would expose a lack of relevance of his analyses or his conclusions to human welfare. He is quite possibly wrong, but in the absence of clearer light he can but hope that there is a sufficient element of truth in

51. Exception must be made for F. H. Knight, who has probed these problems to their epistemological depths with a zeal, and with a capacity, for the subtleties of metaphysical inquiry each of which is surely unsurpassed among contemporary economists. His writings cannot be disregarded by anyone who wishes to cope seriously with the problem of the nature of the fundamental concepts of economics as a welfare discipline. At first inclined to limit economic inquiry to investigation of data external to man and of human behavior in its strictly objective manifestations, he later found this position untenable, and has reached the conclusion that economics, like even the physical sciences, though in greater degree, must deal with the metaphysical entities which lie behind the objective regularities which can be observed in the external world. He now not only concedes the legitimacy of economic investigation in terms of desire or of satisfaction, but he characterizes this as an intermediate or tentative stage preparing the way for an inquiry into the origin of the judgments upon which man builds a hierarchy of good-and-bad, higher-and-lower values, by which he subjects desires to an evaluation more fundamental than the merely quantitative standard of more-or-less satisfaction, or pleasure. I am disposed to accept his reasoning up to a certain point. Whether or no there is a hierarchy of absolute values which overlays the evaluation in terms of more-or-less satisfaction, we must for pragmatic reasons proceed as if for our purposes quantity of satisfaction were an adequate basis for welfare judgments. Knight would set us a task with which few of us are adequately equipped to grapple. We still have so far to go before we will have attained adequate control of the technique of the satisfaction-calculus that it seems unwise to attempt an even more difficult and more elusive type of subjective mensuration.

The progressive development of Knight's thinking on these and allied problems can be traced in the following of his writings: *Risk, Uncertainty, and Profit* (Boston, 1921), chap. iii; "Ethics and the Economic Interpretation," *Quarterly Journal of Economics*, May, 1922; "The Ethics of Competition," *ibid.*, August, 1923; "Relation between Economics and Ethics," *American Economic Review Supplement*, March, 1922; "Economic Psychology and the Value Problem," *Quarterly Journal of Economics*, May, 1925; "Fact and Metaphysics in Economic Psychology," *American Economic Review*, June, 1925.

his premises to give enough validity to his conclusions to justify—in a utilitarian sense—the effort expended in reaching them.

Objective Indicia of Welfare

Whatever may be the content of welfare, it is a matter of general agreement that it is subjective, internal, rather than objective, external, to man. But the difficulty, if not the complete impossibility, of measuring subjective quantities directly (and the doubt on the part of some whether qualitative differences between desires or between satisfactions do not so completely overlay quantitative differences as to make futile, even for the purposes of abstract speculation, the idea of a subjective calculus of welfare) has led to attempts to find objective indicia of welfare. Most notable has been the attempt to use price or exchange-value as the measure, or as an element in the measure, of welfare. Perhaps the chief contribution of the utility school to welfare economics has been the negative one of demonstrating the inadequacy at their best of such measures of welfare, because in many respects they conceal or are inapplicable to the very problems for whose solution they are intended to serve as instruments.

The inadequacies of price as a measure of welfare may be illustrated in connection with the problem of tracing the changes in welfare from one period in time to another for a given community.

1. If money income be proposed as a measure of the trend of welfare, there is the obvious objection that the monetary unit, from the point of view of the thing it specifically measures, objective exchange-value, is a yardstick which varies arbitrarily in its own length from time to time. If allowance is made, by reference to a perfect index number, for the year-to-year fluctuations in the exchange-value of the monetary unit, there is left virtually "real" or objective income, the flow of goods and services, as the measure of welfare. This is still inadequate, if for no other reasons than those adduced below.

2. The summation of miscellaneous goods and services must necessarily be accomplished in terms of relative price. Granting that a satisfactory method is devised to make provision for the constant shifting in relative values, prices measure the relative marginal significance for purchasers of the different goods, and welfare is a matter of total utilities (or total satisfactions), not marginal ones.

This can readily be demonstrated by reference to the paradox of value that aggregate exchange value may diminish as total utility approaches its maximum.

3. Even if an objective measure were devised which would make allowance in terms of a common objective denominator for shifts in the relative total significance of different goods, this would still leave unsolved the problem presented by absolute changes throughout the range of goods in their total significance for the individuals comprising the community. If all prices remained the same, and every person's real income were doubled, an objective measure would indicate a doubling of welfare. But the diminishing-utility principle would establish a presumption that a doubling of objective income would less than double welfare.[52] Moreover, more goods may be needed if new evils are to be warded off[53] while maintaining the same flow of positive satisfactions. Or changes may occur in the total attitude of individuals to material income, a trend toward the simple life, or a greater appreciation of leisure, or, through the progress of education and physical well-being, an increase in the zest with which the material goods of life are enjoyed. A measure of welfare in terms of objective income will not reflect such changes in the slightest degree.

4. Changes in the relative distribution of income as between different classes will bring about changes in the amount of welfare, even though the aggregate real income of the community remains the same.[54] This is so generally accepted a corollary of the law of diminishing utility that further elaboration is unnecessary here.

5. Real income as a measure of welfare breaks down completely in the case of the transfer of commodities from the "free goods" class to the "economic goods" class in consequence of greater

---

52. Thus Ricardo, lacking full possession of this principle, stated that if a man gets two sacks of corn where formerly he had gotten only one, "he gets, indeed, double the quantity of riches—double the quantity of utility—double the quantity of what Adam Smith calls value in use" (*Principles of Political Economy*, chap. xx, p. 265, in Gonner's edition).

53. E.g., transportation costs resulting from greater distances between places of employment and available residential sites; medical expenses, because of greater prevalence of disease.

54. Cf. Henry Sidgwick, *Principles of Political Economy*, p. 76: "If wealth were measured by its utility, 'amount of wealth' would partly be determined by the manner in which the wealth is distributed; and we could not say how much wealth there was in a country till we knew how it was shared among its inhabitants."

scarcity of the commodities in question, and is in the same degree ill-adapted to indicate changes in welfare resulting from such increases in the available amounts of commodities as take them out of the class of "economic goods" and put them into the class of "free goods." An adequate welfare calculus must take into consideration the importance for welfare of free goods, and no calculus in terms of price can do this.

6. Real income as a measure of welfare is ill-adapted to deal with public goods, an increasingly important element in welfare. Estimates of the trend of real income either ignore the services rendered gratuitously to individuals by the government or, measuring them through the inclusion in the community income of the amounts paid as taxes, include them at their money costs, which may grossly exaggerate or grossly underestimate their welfare significance as compared to commodities measured in terms of their market values.

7. A calculus of welfare in terms of real income would reflect only the flow of welfare on the consumption side, and would leave out of the picture the satisfactions and the disutilities accruing from the process of production itself. An increase in real income resulting from an increase in the length of the working day may mean a decrease, rather than an increase, in human welfare. A constant flow of real income, if accompanied by a progressive diminution in the fatigues and pains of production and by an increase in the amount of satisfaction derived from the productive effort itself, as distinguished from its material products, will be consistent with a steady upward trend in welfare.

8. Even if price, or real income measured in terms of price, could be used as a measure of subjective quantities, what it would reflect would be the extent of desire for goods, and not the amount of satisfaction derived from their acquisition and consumption. A measure of desire can serve the purpose of a measure of satisfaction only if the two are quantitatively closely related, and there is abundant ground for scepticism in this regard.[55] If welfare is a quantity of satisfaction, price, therefore, would not be an acceptable measure even if it did measure desire accurately.

The important contribution of the utility theory to welfare economics seems, up to the present, to have consisted in just such demonstrations of the inadequacy of price, and of all objective

---

55. See *infra*.

measures formulated in terms of price, as measures of welfare, and in exposition of the qualifications which must accordingly be made in conclusions with respect to welfare based on a price-calculus thereof.[56] The utility theorists, however, have often concentrated their attention on the single factor of inequality in the distribution of wealth, to the neglect of the other factors which militate against the acceptance of price as an adequate measure of welfare. In several notable instances economists who have formally accepted the utility analysis but were not well disposed toward a calculus in subjective terms have found irksome its questioning of the validity of objective measurement of welfare, and by minimizing, on one pretext or another, the degree of conflict between analysis in utility terms and analysis in objective terms, or by selecting for consideration only those problems in which the conflict is least sharp, or perhaps least apparent, have succeeded in reverting to measurement of welfare in terms of price, while retaining the language and the superficial appearance of subjective measurement.

The chief offender in this respect was Alfred Marshall. He disposed very neatly of inequality in the distribution of income as an objection to the measurement of welfare in price terms. "On the whole however," says Marshall, "it happens that by far the greater number of the events with which economics deals, affect in about equal proportions all the different classes of society; so that if the money measures of the happiness caused by two events are equal, there is not in general any very great difference between the amounts of the happiness in the two cases."[57] This has been justly characterized as a "cavalier dismissal of the effect of 'differences of wealth' and 'differences in sensibility.' "[58]

---

56. For early analyses in utility terms of the inadequacy of price as a measure of welfare, see especially F. Y. Edgeworth, *Mathematical Psychics* (London, 1881), *passim;* Henry Sidgwick, *Principles of Political Economy* (London, 1883), chap. iii; Philip H. Wicksteed, *Alphabet of Economic Science* (London, 1888), pp. 75 ff., 86 ff. Reference should be made also to two recent articles by F. Y. Edgeworth in which, with characteristic penetration and finesse of technique, he discusses the problem of objective indicia of welfare ("The Plurality of Index Numbers," *Economic Journal*, September, 1925, and "The Element of Probability in Index Numbers," *Journal of the Royal Statistical Society*, July, 1925).

57. *Principles of Economics*, 6th, ed., p. 131. For the same argument, in very much the same language, see Z. C. Dickinson, "The Relations of Recent Psychological Developments to Economic Theory," *Quarterly Journal of Economics* (May, 1919), p. 407.

58. C. E. Persons, "Marginal Utility and Marginal Disutility as Ultimate Standards of Value," *Quarterly Journal of Economics* (August, 1913), p. 548.

Granted that there are some problems in connection with which the existence of inequality in incomes may be safely disregarded, it is nevertheless difficult to overestimate the extent to which the problem of inequality pervades and underlies the important problems to which economics has traditionally applied itself. It is necessary only to mention taxation, government expenditures, poor relief, immigration, land policy, and above all, the problem of inequality itself to make clear that a calculus of welfare which abstracts from inequalities in the distribution of wealth and income is a *Hamlet* with Hamlet omitted from the cast.

The problems raised for welfare economics by the possibility of disparity between desire and satisfaction have been quite generally evaded by utility theorists in very much the same manner as Marshall evaded the problem of inequality. As has already been pointed out, utility theorists as a rule take welfare to mean satisfaction. Now price, if it measures any subjective quantity, measures desire, and is a measure of satisfaction only to the degree in which desire is an accurate reflection of satisfaction. But if there exists a welfare economics it is as an unsystematic and very much incidental appendage to price analysis, very imperfectly differentiated in technique and in objectives. A welfare economist who accepts satisfaction as the content of welfare cannot, therefore, accept price as a measure of welfare unless he accepts desire as an accurate, or at least approximate, measure of satisfaction; but rejection of price as the measure of welfare involves an arduous reconstruction and reorganization of his thinking and of his economic "system." If appeal could be made to the hedonistic psychology, there would be no problem. Desire could be taken as a fairly accurate reflection of the satisfaction which would result from its fulfilment, and whatever was acceptable as a measure of desire would therefore be acceptable also as a measure of satisfaction. But the modern utility theorist disavows faith in the hedonistic psychology and in the complete rationality of human behavior. He nevertheless finds ingenious ways of proceeding with the discussion of desire quantities as if they were satisfaction quantities, while maintaining the appearance of logical consistency.

Pigou, for instance, concedes that the possibility of disparity between desire and satisfaction "obviously has great theoretical importance," but denies that it has great practical importance because "it is fair to suppose that most commodities, especially those of wide consumption that are required, as articles of food and clothing are, for direct personal use, will be wanted as a means to satisfaction and will, consequently, be desired with intensities proportioned to the satisfactions they are expected to yield."[59] This need be conceded only if expectations are never grossly mistaken, if the desires for "food and clothing" *are* simply desires for instruments for the satisfaction of primary physical needs whose serviceability for the purpose in view can be accurately judged by the ordinary purchaser,[60] and if desires, even if originating in a careful calculation of the satisfaction-potentialities of commodities, may not persist after a change in circumstances has deprived them of their rational basis[61]—a rather formidable series of qualifications. And Marshall, after citing impulse, habit, morbidity, self-abnegation, mistaken expectations, and other possible causes of disparity between desire and satisfaction, concludes that as direct measurement of neither desire nor satisfaction is possible, it is necessary to fall back on price and make it serve, "with all its faults, *both* for the desires which prompt activities and for the satisfactions that result from them."[62] So also Dickinson cites, with apparent approval, Böhm-Bawerk's justification of the assumption of general harmony between desire and satisfaction on the ground that the causes of disparity "are usually such as cannot be reduced to any general principles, and the undue emphasis of them simply leads to agnosticism."[63]

To assume the lack of disparity between desire and satisfaction

59. *Economics of Welfare*, p. 24. Cf. also, to much the same effect, Vilfredo Pareto, *Manuel d'Économie Politique*, Paris, 1909, pp. 250-251: "Quant à la substitution de la sensation de la consommation possible à la sensation de la consommation effective, si on considère des actions qui se répètent, et c'est ce que fait l'économie politique, ces deux sensations, en somme, se trouvent dans un rapport constant et tel que, sans erreur grave, la première peut remplacer la seconde."

60. Cf. F. H. Knight, "Ethics and the Economic Interpretation," *Quarterly Journal of Economics* (May, 1922), pp. 463 ff. for an interpretation of desires for food, shelter, and clothing as desires for a whole set of cultural values rather than desires for mere nourishment, protection from the elements, etc.

61. Even as pronounced a hedonist as J. S Mill saw the necessity of this qualification. Cf. his *System of Logic*, 8th ed., Bk. VI, chap. ii, p. 4: "As we proceed in the formation of habits and become accustomed to will a particular act or a particular course of conduct because it is pleasurable, we at last continue to will it without any reference to its being pleasurable. Although, from some change in us or in our circumstances, we have ceased to find any pleasure in the action, or perhaps to anticipate any pleasure as the consequence of it, we still continue to desire the action, and consequently to do it. In this manner it is that habits of hurtful excess continue to be practiced although they have ceased to be pleasurable."

62. *Principles of Economics*, p. 92 n.

63. Z. C. Dickinson, *op. cit.*, p. 401.

is arbitrarily and unwisely to limit the scope of welfare economics. The effects of ignorance on the part of the buyers of the degree of suitability of commodities offered for sale for their intended purposes, the practice of fraud, cunning, misrepresentation on the part of sellers—in fact, the whole problem of unfair methods in trade in so far as the unfairness is to the buyers—these are current evils which would not exist if the assumptions of Pigou and of Marshall were in accordance with the facts. There is a range of problems here, not to be dismissed without investigation as unimportant, and, without effort to find uniformities, as unsusceptible to scientific generalization. Is it not probable, for instance, that the modern development of aggressive salesmanship is tending to increase the disparity between desire and satisfaction, and that commodities pushed by intensive methods of selling are overdesired in comparison to the satisfactions they will yield, and play a disproportionate part in the ordinary consumer's budget as compared to the few commodities which are still permitted to make their own appeal? Is it not possible that there is a common underestimate of the contribution which governmental services make to individual welfare, resulting from the favorable advertising which private enterprise provides for its own products—and to the unfavorable advertising which it often spreads with respect to the products of government activity?

In one respect, however, the utility school has made systematic allowance for the disparity between desire and satisfaction, namely, where a substantial interval of time elapses between the experience of the desire and its satisfaction. With the exception of Pantaleoni, who, to preserve inviolate the purity of his hedonic economics, here maintains an elegant consistency,[64] the utility school uniformly recognizes a definite bias in favor of present satisfactions as against satisfactions distant in time. They make this bias, in conjunction with the actuarial allowances for the uncertain duration of life, the risk of changes in wants, and the chances of augmented income in the future, an integral part of their interest theory, as explaining the preference for present over future consumption.[65] The same procedure, if extended to other phases of disparity between desire and

---

64. *Pure Economics* (London, 1898), pp. 86 ff. Cf. also Wieser, *Natural Value* (London, 1893), pp. 16 ff.

65. Pigou also makes some important applications of it to welfare problems, as establishing presumptions in favor of government measures for the conservation of exhaustible resources and against taxation which tends to fall heavily on capital (*op. cit.*, pp. 24 ff.).

satisfaction, would quite conceivably afford a basis for equally serviceable generalizations.

Though we should conclude, in spite of the tendency even of utility theorists to revert to price as a measure of welfare, that price is not an adequate measure, it might be argued that we should, nevertheless, abandon the fruitless search for a practicable subjective measure and resort to some objective measure other than price. Such, for instance, seems to be the position of Wesley Mitchell: "In becoming consciously a science of human behavior, economics will lay less stress upon wealth and more stress upon welfare. . . . At present welfare thus conceived is rather vague, but it is capable of being made objective and definite in reference to such matters as food, clothing, shelter, sanitation, education, fatigue, leisure."[66] True enough, if taken one at a time, and for one individual at a time, and at a particular moment of time, which, for most practical purposes, means not true at all. What if more or better shelter involves more fatigue? Or what if more food for Jones involves less food for Smith? Or what if more food for Jones now involves less food for Jones next year? An objective criterion of welfare cannot handle problems involving such conflicts of interest without equating them in terms of price. If this is done we are back to wealth as the measure of welfare. And the important and difficult problems of welfare are important and difficult precisely because they arise out of just such conflicts of interest.

Welfare as a Long-Run Concept

A common shortcoming of the welfare economics of the utility school, and one, moreover, from which their classical predecessors were in large part free,[67] is their typically short-run approach to the problems of economic welfare. It is especially true of the Austrian school that they have restricted their discussion of the realization of utilities from the consumption of transitory goods to the immediately realizable utilities, to the neglect of the consequences for future welfare resulting from such consumption. This preoccupation with the immediate effects of consumption could not be explained

---

66. "The Prospects of Economics" in *The Trend of Economics* (R. G. Tugwell, editor), New York, 1924, p. 31.

67. Cf., for example, the classical treatment of the effects of high standards of consumption on future population and wages.

away by reference to the assumption of an omniscient economic man, competent adequately to take into account the entire flow of utilities, immediate and prospective, positive and negative, which would result from a given act of consumption, for, as has been shown, even the economic man was not presumed to give adequate weight to future utilities. The explanation probably is to be found in the adequacy for price-economics of a utility concept which expresses only immediate desires, and in the fear of the ethical entanglements which would apparently result from any departure from immediate intensity of desire as an all-sufficient test from the economic point of view of the comparative worth of goods.

The utility concept, however, if given so narrow an interpretation, cannot adequately serve the needs of a welfare calculus. Consider, for example, this explanation of the meaning of utility from a widely-used text:

> *Anything that is capable of satisfying a human want is a good, and possesses utility.* We need here to guard against a misunderstanding which the word "utility" might suggest. Utility is the power to satisfy wants, not the power to confer benefits. Cigars are as "useful" in the economic sense as bread or books, for all three satisfy wants. Economic wants may be serious, frivolous, or even positively pernicious, but the objects of these wants all alike possess utility in the economic sense.[68]

If the immediate satisfaction to an individual from the consumption of a given quantity of whiskey and a given quantity of ennobling literature be the same, but if the consumption of whiskey would result in future pains and frustrations for its consumer, whereas the acquisition and study of the good literature would contribute to a happy old age, the economist must, for welfare-calculus purposes, attribute greater utility or greater importance to the books than to the whiskey.[69]

---

68. R. T. Ely, *Outlines of Economics* (1920), p. 105. Compare with Marshall's definition: "The total utility of a thing to anyone (that is, the total pleasure *or other benefit* it yields him) . . ." (*Principles*, p. 93. Italics mine.)

69. Fetter distinguishes between welfare "in an immediate or narrow sense," as an important factor in the determination of exchange values, and welfare "in a broader and truer sense . . . the abiding condition of well-being" as the important quantity with which welfare economics must concern itself (*Economic Principles* (1915), p. 509). So also McGoun's distinction between "higher" and "lower" desires ultimately rests on comparisons of the satisfactions derived *in the long run* from their realization (A. F. McGoun, "Higher and Lower Desires," *Quarterly Journal of Economics* (February, 1923), pp. 291 ff.).

Individualistic vs. Group Measurement of Utility

Most utility theorists may also justly be charged with failure to distinguish between an individualistic and a group concept of welfare, and to make adequate use of the latter. The "individualistic" concept of welfare may be taken to be that which bases its measurements of welfare solely in terms of the additions to, or the subtractions from, the welfare of the particular individuals, taken one at a time, who are directly affected by the institution or activity under investigation at the moment. A group concept of welfare, on the other hand, would endeavor to take into account the totality of influence, favorable or unfavorable, of such institution or activity on all who are affected thereby, directly or indirectly. It would thus take into account in connection with any particular price-transaction not merely those utilities which influence the determination of that price, but also those utilities, or disutilities, which accrue therefrom to persons who played no direct part in the transaction.

The laissez faire philosophy, with its fundamental assumption of an essential harmony between individual and group interests, covered up the need for a distinction between individual and group welfare, and was itself reinforced by the failure to test actual institutions in terms of such a distinction. But just as there have been few economists who were unqualified exponents of the laissez faire philosophy, so also there have been few economists who have concerned themselves with welfare problems as such without at times applying the group standard in their welfare appraisals. With but rare exceptions, however, welfare economists of the utility school confined their use of the group standard to problems which affected groups of persons *en masse* and could not possibly be handled in terms of solitary individuals. The entire range of economic activities which were wholly or mainly under the governance of the price system and of the principle of free contract, such as buying and selling, hiring and firing, saving and spending, assumption and avoidance of risk, they appraised solely in terms of an individualistic analysis. They took it for granted that every freely contracted purchase-and-sale transaction brought gain to each of the two active participants, not only disregarding, as we have seen, the effects of ignorance and fraud on the part of one or the other of these participants, but overlooking the possibility that economic transactions may have vital bearing on the welfare of persons not directly concerned therewith, and failing to perceive that mere disparity in bargaining power might lead to exploitation of one party to a "free" contract by the other, even though both were honest, equally intelligent, and equally well-informed.[70]

Nevertheless, even when the utility theorists used an individualistic test of welfare, there was throughout their discussion the implication, either clearly expressed or readily to be inferred, that it was the welfare of the group which was important, and the welfare of individuals as comprising in their aggregate the group. And in dealing with matters of governmental policy, and especially in their support of specific departures from the laissez faire policy and in their treatment of the problems of government finance, they wholly abandoned the individualistic standard. These problems could not be handled at all in terms of the welfare of individuals taken singly, either because it was too obvious to be overlooked that an activity which would bring profit to some might injure others, or because these problems concerned benefits of an intangible and indivisible sort, accruing to the community as a whole and not imputable in measurable proportions to particular individuals. They here used a group standard of welfare, though there is little evidence in their writings that they were conscious of their change in standards as they proceeded from the discussion of problems of free contract to the treatment of the relationship between government and its citizens.[71]

---

70. Recognition of the importance of disparity in bargaining power as affecting the terms of the wage contract, and consequently the expediency of adherence to a policy of strict laissez faire, is lacking in even so late a work as W. S. Jevons, *The State in Relation to Labor*, London, 1887. See p. 42: "*Laisser faire* policy might still be maintained [i.e., wisely and justly] if everybody understood his interests." But even during the period of undisputed sway of the classical economics among the learned there was a current tendency in the business and political world even to exaggerate the extent to which superiority of financial resources could determine the outcome of commercial competition, to the disregard of community interests and of genuine advantages in productive efficiency (cf. my *Dumping: A Problem in International Trade*, p. 46).

71. Cf., however, F. von Wieser, *Natural Value* (London, 1893), pp. 228-42, for a discussion of the differences in standards actually operative as between the realm of free contract and the sphere of government activity, and for further elaboration of these differences, his "Theorie der gesellschaftlichen Wirtschaft," in *Grundriss der Sozialökonomik* (2d ed., Tubingen, 1924), Vol. I, Part II, pp. 292-302.

Utility Analysis as Capitalistic Apologetics

In its early stages of development the utility analysis was made use of to explode the Marxian surplus-value theory. It was, consequently, charged by the Socialists with being merely a retreat by orthodox economics to a new line of defense made necessary by the successful Marxian attack on the classical argument for laissez faire.[72] In recent years it has again been attacked, and by learned economists who are themselves fully equipped with the traditions and the technique of the orthodox doctrines, as by its nature necessarily leading to a capitalistic apologetics. The grounds upon which this modern attack is based can be adequately indicated by citations from two of the foremost critics. "Political economy," writes J. M. Clark, "does not defend the existing system, but it selects for explanation the elements of co-operation in it, which are the elements that everybody approves of. The Austrian theory . . . is relevant to these good elements in the existing system, and it is not *positively and constructively* relevant to any other side of the case."[73] "The study of utility seems to be oriented by the question: 'To what is value equal?' rather than by the broader question: 'How does value function in relation to human wants?'"[74] "When theory has studied the meaning of value in terms of utility, its very attitude and inquiry have presupposed an equilibrium between utilities and thus have been oriented by a static point of view and static assumptions. The emancipated counterpart of this equilibrium inquiry is a study of the entire process of economic guidance, in which the utility theory appears as an interpretation of one phase only of guidance by one agency only, viz., the static or the hedonistic phase of guidance by individual initiative. For this is the only phase of guidance which falls within the requirements of a theory of equilibrium."[75] "That economic theorist," says Hamilton, "is indeed an ex-

---

72. Cf. H. M. Hyndman, *The Economics of Socialism* (London, 1896), chap. vii.

73. "Economic Theory in an Era of Social Readjustment," *American Economic Review Supplement* (March, 1919), p. 284. Italics his.

74. "Economic Theory in an Era of Social Readjustment," *American Economic Review Supplement* (March, 1919), p. 289. This contrasts with Knight's complaint that utility tends to become an ethical concept, and to take us "from the realm of fact to that of what ought to be" ("Normal Price in Value and Distribution," *Quarterly Journal of Economics*, November, 1917, p. 67).

75. "Economics and Modern Psychology," *Journal of Political Economy* (January, 1918), pp. 3-4. Cf. Wieser, "Value in the Economy of the State," *Natural Value*, Bk. VI.

pert at logomachy who can use a nomenclature of 'utility,' 'dis-utility,' and 'productivity,' and yet hedge the words about in such a way that he escapes the implication of making the system of prices as a whole represent such a use of limited resources in satis-fying wants as to insure to society the greatest surplus of utility over disutility."[76]

Clark is obviously making a tacit assumption that utility analysis has been strictly confined within the limits of price economics, and he attributes to the utility school as a whole and as a logically in-evitable outcome of its mode of analysis a restricted scope of inquiry and a type of conclusion therefrom which fairly characterizes only some of its exponents. Hamilton's assertion that only by word-juggling can utility analysis avoid leading to a defense of the status quo puts the cart before the horse, for it is only by word-juggling that utility theorists have avoided facing the serious questioning of the status quo which the utility analysis logically leads to. The utility analysis yields different products to different men. Most of its exponents may probably be rightly classed as conservative in their outlook on economic problems, and some of them have un-questionably used the utility theory to support their faith in the goodness of things as they are. Others of its exponents have been radicals, and have found the utility analysis a serviceable weapon in their assaults upon private property and the capitalistic organization of society.[77] It is altogether questionable that the utility school as a group has been more ardent in its defense of things as they are than its classical predecessors, and it seems apparent that utility analysis, if applied in the field of welfare economics, makes defense of laissez faire and eulogy of the capitalistic system more, rather than less, difficult than it would be to an economics written wholly in pe-cuniary terms.

I have already argued that much of what passes for utility theory is really objective price-theory presented in the purloined terminol-ogy of subjective analysis, and that it was by reversion in fact to price-calculus, while maintaining the semblance of subjective calcu-lus, that many utility theorists managed to avoid dealing with the less

---

76. W. H. Hamilton, "The Place of Value Theory in Economics II," *Journal of Political Economy* (April, 1918), p. 392.

77. Cf. especially Adolphe Landry's *L'Utilité Sociale de la Propriété Individu-elle*, Paris, 1901, where a vigorous attack on private property by means of price analysis is intensified in the second half of the book by the application of the utility analysis.

pleasing aspects of private property and the unrestrained operation of the profit motive. But in spite of the generally conservative tendencies of the utility economists and the selective discrimination with which they chose the problems to be subjected to the utility analysis,[78] the utility theory seems on the whole to have shaken, rather than strengthened, their belief in the virtues of the existing economic organization.[79] It was not wholly without basis that J. S. Nicholson, in 1893, in his presidential address before the economics section of the British Association for the Advancement of Science, warned his audience that the new-fangled diminishing utility and maximum satisfaction doctrines were leading economists to socialism and away from the rock-ribbed individualism of the classical economics.[80] The utility theory is a mode of analysis, not a set of conclusions, and what conclusions will be reached by it will depend on the character and the fullness of the data to which it is applied and the skill and honesty with which it is used.[81] It would be trite, were it not for the extent to which the principle *Maledicti sunt qui ante nos nostra dixerunt* seems to pervade certain phases of recent American economic theorizing, to suggest the possibility that some, at least, of the older utility theorists applied the analysis honestly, and that intellectual curiosity occasionally got the best of social bias with the others.

Practicability of a Subjective Calculus

The advocate of a subjective calculus of welfare encounters the objection that it is not possible to measure subjective quantities, whether they be desires, satisfactions, pleasures, or pains, except through their objective manifestations in price offers or other types of behavior. I believe the answer lies in the fact that we all do repeatedly measure desires and satisfactions as such, our own and those of other persons, and that much of our family relations, our

78. Rather than, as Clark puts it, the selective character of the technique itself.
79. Compare, for example, Edgeworth's *Mathematical Psychics,* or the concluding chapter of Wieser's *Natural Value,* or, in this country, Fetter's or Davenport's writings, with the typical surviving expositions of pre-utility economics.
80. *Report of Sixty-third Meeting* (London, 1894), pp. 843 ff.
81. Cf. W. C. Mitchell "Wieser's Theory of Social Economics," *Political Science Quarterly* (March, 1917), p. 111: "[The utility theory] has been . . . adopted as a substitute for Marxism by one set of socialists, and decried as a covert defence of the established order by another set."

contacts with our friends and neighbors, and the relations of government with its citizens are actually guided, whether well or ill, by such calculations. Such calculations of subjective quantities may never be exact, and may often be grossly inaccurate, but they can, and often must, be made in the absence of means to more precise measurement. Moreover, no one asks that economics abandon the pecuniary calculus and substitute therefor a purely subjective one. For many purposes the pecuniary calculus serves all needs. In any case, it is an institutional fact, an important force in human behavior and in the guidance of economic activity, and must be fully reckoned with by the economist. But for many purposes the pecuniary calculus is a grossly imperfect instrument whose results require modification by calculations of subjective quantities before they can serve as an acceptable guide to action or to understanding.

The subjective type of measurement cannot, at least not as yet, yield absolute quantities as its product. The most it can attain is the discovery of more-and-less relationships, and even that with a very small degree of reliability. But there is a wide range of human activity in which only imperfect instruments are available with which to guide conduct toward perfection. Those who insist that welfare economics confine itself to measurement in terms of prices, because prices are data for statistical investigation, whereas the subjective conditions reflected by prices are not, have succumbed to an all-too-prevalent methodological fanaticism which prefers the accurate but superficial to the approximate but fundamental, and which makes adaptability to its special technique of investigation, rather than importance, the standard for the selection of problems and the delimitation of the scope of inquiry. Statistics is a tool, not an end. The imperfect measurement of variations in welfare may serve as a better guide to action than the perfect measurement of something which has something to do with welfare.

Adam Smith and Laissez Faire[*][1]

1. The Harmonious Order of Nature

AN ENDEAVOR to make a just appraisal of Adam Smith's original contributions to economic doctrine would even today be a task of extraordinary difficulty. On the one hand, what was serviceable in his doctrines has become so thoroughly incorporated in our modern thinking that we discover it upon the slightest provocation in whatever we may read that was written before his day, and we are especially prone to make a virtue of obscurity in his predecessors by taking it for granted that it conceals premature insight rather than unduly prolonged lack of it. On the other hand, there is always great danger lest what we credit to a writer as priority of doctrine may not in reality be merely an indecent exposure of our own ignorance concerning his predecessors. There is much weight of authority and of evidence, however, that Smith's major claim to originality, in English economic thought at least, was his detailed and elaborate application to the wilderness of economic phenomena of the unifying concept of a co-ordinated and mutually interdependent system of cause and effect relationships which philosophers and theologians had already applied to the world in general. Smith's doctrine that economic phenomena were manifestations of an underlying order in nature, governed by natural forces, gave to English economics for the first time a definite trend toward logically consistent synthesis of economic relationships, toward "system-

*Lecture delivered at the University of Chicago on Jan. 21, 1927, in a series commemorative of the one-hundred and fiftieth anniversary of the publication of the *Wealth of Nations*. Reprinted from *The Journal of Political Economy*, Vol. 35, April 1927, pp. 198-232, by the courtesy of the University of Chicago Press.

1. References to Adam Smith's writings are to the following editions: *History of Ancient Physics*, and *Theory of Moral Sentiments*, in "Essays Philosophical and Literary by Adam Smith" (Ward, Lock & Co., London, n.d.); *Wealth of Nations*, Cannan edition; *Lectures*, Cannan, editor.

building." Smith's further doctrine that this underlying natural order required, for its most beneficent operation, a system of natural
liberty, and that in the main public regulation and private monopoly
were corruptions of that natural order, at once gave to economics a
bond of union with the prevailing philosophy and theology, and
to economists and statesmen a program of practical reform.

Smith was *the* great eclectic. He drew upon all previous knowledge in developing his doctrine of a harmonious order in nature
manifesting itself through the instincts of the individual man. The
oldest source in which he expressly finds an approach to his own
views is in the science of the classical philosophers: "In the first
ages of the world . . . the idea of an universal mind, of a God of
all, who originally formed the whole, and who governs the whole
by general laws, directed to the conservation and prosperity of the
whole, without regard to that of any private individual, was a notion to which [the Ancients] were utterly strangers . . . [but] as
ignorance begot superstition, science gave birth to the first theism
that arose among those nations, who were not enlightened by divine
Revelation."[2]

The Roman *jus naturale*, through Grotius and Pufendorf,
strongly influenced Smith's thinking. The Renaissance emphasis on
the individual, the naturalistic philosophy of Shaftesbury, Locke,
Hume, Hutcheson, the optimistic theism of the Scotch philosophers,
the empiricism of Montesquieu, were more immediate and more
powerful influences. Science, philosophy, theology, psychology, history, contemporary observation of facts—all of them were made to
produce, under Smith's capable management, an abundance of evidence of the existence of an order in nature in which beneficent
intentions toward mankind could be discerned. If Smith at times
showed more catholicity than scientific discrimination in what he
accepted as supporting evidence, if some of this evidence appeared
upon close scrutiny to be conjectural, contradictory, irrelevant, or
inconclusive, the richness of argument, the power of his exposition,
the attractiveness of his conclusions served to overwhelm the captious critic and to postpone closer scrutiny to a later day.

Smith's major claim to fame, as I have said, seems to rest on his
elaborate and detailed application to the economic world of the
concept of a unified natural order, operating according to natural

2. *History of Ancient Physics*, pp. 391, 392.

law, and if left to its own course producing results beneficial to mankind. On every detail, taken by itself, Smith appears to have had predecessors in plenty. On few details was Smith as penetrating as the best of his predecessors. There had been earlier pleas for freedom of internal trade, freedom of foreign trade, free trade in land, free choice of occupations, free choice of place of residence. Some philosophers, notably Shaftesbury and Smith's own teacher, Hutcheson, had already extended to economic phenomena, though sketchily, the concept of an underlying natural order manifesting itself through the operation of physical forces and individual psychology. But Smith made an original forward step when he seriously applied himself to the task of analyzing the whole range of economic process with the purpose of discovering the nature of the order which underlay its surface chaos. Claims have been made for the Physiocrats, but the evidence indicates that Smith had already formulated his central doctrine before he came into contact with them or their writings. As early as 1755 Smith had publicly asserted his claim to priority, as against some unnamed rival, in applying to the economic order the system of natural liberty. In doing so, he cited a lecture, delivered in 1749, which even in the fragment which has survived contains the essence of his fully developed doctrine, as expounded in the *Wealth of Nations*. It even uses an English equivalent of the very phrase "laissez faire," which the Physiocrats were soon to make the war cry of the system of natural liberty.

Projectors disturb nature in the course of her operations on human affairs, and it requires no more than to *leave her alone* and give her fair play in the pursuit of her ends that she may establish her own designs. . . . Little else is required to carry a state to the highest degree of affluence from the lowest barbarism but peace, easy taxes, and a tolerable administration of justice; all the rest being brought about by the natural course of things. All governments which thwart this natural course, which force things into another channel, or which endeavour to arrest the progress of society at a particular point, are unnatural, and, to support themselves, are obliged to be oppressive and tyrannical.[3]

In his *Theory of Moral Sentiments*, Smith develops his system of ethics on the basis of a doctrine of a harmonious order in nature guided by God, and in an incidental manner applies his general doctrine with strict consistency to the economic order. In his later

---

3. John Rae, *Life of Adam Smith*, London, Macmillan & Co., 1895, pp. 62-63. Italics mine.

work, the *Wealth of Nations*, Smith devotes himself to a specialized inquiry into the nature of the economic order. It is a commonplace among the authorities on Adam Smith that it is impossible fully to understand the *Wealth of Nations* without recourse to the *Theory of Moral Sentiments*. The vast bulk of economists, however, who have read the *Wealth of Nations* without reading the *Theory of Moral Sentiments*, have not regarded Smith's masterpiece as an obscure book, as one especially hard to understand. On the other hand, the very authorities who are most emphatic in asserting the need of reference to the *Theory of Moral Sentiments* to understand the *Wealth of Nations*, once they embark upon their self-imposed task of interpreting the latter in the light of the former, become immersed in difficult problems of interpretation for which scarcely any two writers offer the same solution. The system of individual liberty is much in evidence among the interpreters of Smith, but that natural harmony which should also result is strikingly lacking. The Germans, who, it seems, in their methodical manner commonly read both the *Theory of Moral Sentiments* and the *Wealth of Nations*, have coined a pretty term, *Das Adam Smith Problem*, to denote the failure to understand either which results from the attempt to use the one in the interpretation of the other. I will endeavor to show that the difficulties of the authorities result mainly from their determination to find a basis for complete concordance of the two books, and that there are divergences between them which are impossible of reconciliation even by such heroic means as one writer has adopted of appeal to the existence in Smith's thought of a Kantian dualism. I will further endeavor to show that the *Wealth of Nations* was a better book because of its partial breach with the *Theory of Moral Sentiments*, and that it could not have remained, as it has, a living book were it not that in its methods of analysis, its basic assumptions, and its conclusions it abandoned the absolutism, the rigidity, the romanticism which characterize the earlier book.

II. The "Theory of Moral Sentiments"

In the *Theory of Moral Sentiments*, Smith develops the doctrine of a beneficent order in nature, manifesting itself through the operation of the forces of external nature and the innate propensities implanted in man by nature. The moral sentiments, self-interest, regulated by natural justice and tempered by sympathy and benevolence, operate in conjunction with the physical forces of nature to achieve the beneficent purposes of Nature. Underlying the matter-of-fact phenomena of human and physical nature is benign Nature, a guiding providence, which is concerned that natural processes shall operate to produce the "happiness and perfection of the species." Smith is unfortunately far from explicit as to just how Nature makes certain that nature shall not betray the former's intentions, though he does say that Nature dictates to man the laws which he shall follow.[4] It seems, however, that the essence of Smith's doctrine is that Providence has so fashioned the constitution of external nature as to make its processes favorable to man, and has implanted *ab initio* in human nature such sentiments as would bring about, through their ordinary working, the happiness and welfare of mankind. The many titles by which this beneficent Nature is designated must have taxed severely the terminological resources of the Scotch optimistic theism. Among them are: "the great Director of nature."[5] "the final cause,"[6] "the Author of nature,"[7] "the great Judge of hearts,"[8] "an invisible hand,"[9] "Providence,"[10] "the divine Being,"[11] and, in rare instances, "God."[12] Smith definitely commits himself to the theism of his time. The harmony and beneficence to be perceived in the matter-of-fact processes of nature are the results of the design and intervention of a benevolent God.

The idea of that divine Being, whose benevolence and wisdom have, from all eternity, contrived and conducted the immense machine of the universe, so as at all times to produce the greatest possible quantity of happiness, is certainly of all the objects of human contemplation by far the most sublime. . . . The administration of the great system of the universe, . . . the care of the universal happiness of all rational and sensible beings, is the business of God and not of man. To man is allotted a much humbler department, but one much more suitable to the weakness of his powers,

---

4. *Theory of Moral Sentiments*, p. 75.
5. *Ibid.*, p. 71 n.
6. *Ibid.*, p. 80.
7. *Ibid.*, p. 96.
8. *Ibid.*
9. *Ibid.*, p. 163.
10. *Ibid.*, p. 163.
11. *Ibid.*, p. 210.
12. *Ibid.*, pp. 80, 97.

and to the narrowness of his comprehension; the care of his own happiness, of that of his family, his friends, his country.[13]

Thus self-preservation, and the propagation of the species, are the great end which Nature seems to have proposed in the formation of all animals. . . . But though we are . . . endowed with a very strong desire of those ends, it has not been intrusted to the slow and uncertain determinations of our reason to find out the proper means of bringing them about. Nature has directed us to the greater part of these by original and immediate instincts. Hunger, thirst, the passion which unites the two sexes, the love of pleasure, and the dread of pain, prompt us to apply those means for their own sakes, and without any consideration of their tendency to those beneficent ends which the great Director of nature intended to produce by them.[14]

Society can get along tolerably well even though beneficence is absent and self-interest and justice alone operate. "Society may subsist among different men, as among different merchants, from a sense of its utility, without any mutual love or affection; and though no man in it should owe any obligation, or be bound in gratitude to any other, it may still be upheld by a mercenary exchange of good offices according to an agreed valuation." Beneficence "is the ornament which embellishes, not the foundation which supports, the building. . . . Justice, on the contrary, is the main pillar that upholds the whole edifice." "Society may subsist, though not in the most comfortable state, without beneficence; but the prevalence of injustice must utterly destroy it."[15]

There are no serious flaws in the harmonious operation of natural forces, even in the economic order, where self-interest, which is ordinarily a virtue, but if not regulated by justice may degenerate into vice, is the most powerful of the impulses to action:

If we consider the general rules by which external prosperity and adversity are commonly distributed in this life, we shall find, that notwithstanding the disorder in which all things appear to be in this world, yet even here every virtue naturally meets with its proper reward, with the recompense which is most fit to encourage and promote it; and this too so surely, that it requires a very extraordinary concurrence of circumstances entirely to disappoint it. What is the reward most proper for encouraging industry, prudence, and circumspection? Success in every sort of business. And is it possible that in the whole of life these virtues should fail of attaining it? Wealth and external honours are their proper recompense, and the recompense which they can seldom fail of acquiring.[16]

---

13. *Ibid.*, p. 210.
14. *Ibid.*, p. 71 n.
15. *Ibid.*, p. 79.
16. *Ibid.*, p. 146.

The poorer classes have little if any ground for complaint as to their lot in life, and no reason to seek to improve it except by methods which contribute to the general welfare of society. "In the middling and inferior stations of life, the road to virtue and that to fortune . . . are, happily, in most cases, very nearly the same. . . . The good old proverb, therefore, that honesty is the best policy, holds, in such situations, almost always perfectly true."[17] Beneficent Nature so operates the machinery behind the scenes that even inequality in the distribution of happiness is more apparent than real:

[The rich] are led by an invisible hand to make nearly the same distribution of the necessaries of life, which would have been made, had the earth been divided into equal portions among all its inhabitants, and thus without intending it, without knowing it, advance the interest of the society, and afford means to the multiplication of the species. When Providence divided the earth among a few lordly masters, it neither forgot nor abandoned those who seemed to have been left out in the partition. These last, too, enjoy their share of all that it produces. In what constitutes the real happiness of human life, they are in no respect inferior to those who would seem so much above them. In ease of the body and peace of the mind, all the different ranks of life are nearly upon a level, and the beggar, who suns himself by the side of the highway, possesses that security which kings are fighting for.[18]

Smith concedes that the processes of nature operate at times with what, by man's standards, are results so unjust that they arouse our indignation:

Fraud, falsehood, brutality, and violence, . . . excite in every human breast such scorn and abhorrence, that our indignation rouses to see them possess those advantages which they may in some sense be said to have merited, by the diligence and industry with which they are sometimes attended. The industrious knave cultivates the soil, the indolent good man leaves it uncultivated. Who ought to reap the harvest? Who starve, and who live in plenty? The natural course of things decides it in favour of the knave; the natural sentiments of mankind in favour of the man of virtue.[19]

This is a familiar dilemma of the optimistic theology, but Smith is precluded from adopting the familiar solution that "the ways of the Lord are inscrutable" by the fact that he is at the moment engaged in the task of formulating with great precision and assurance just what the ways of the Lord are. A contemporary economist of

17. *Ibid.*, 58.
18. *Ibid.*, p. 163.
19. *Ibid.*, pp. 147-148.

Adam Smith, Josiah Tucker, who was also by the necessity of his
profession a theologian, when faced with an apparent conflict between the processes of nature and the "fundamental Principle of
Universal Benevolence" found an ingenious solution in the conclusion a priori that there must be something wrong in the appearance
of things: "I conclude *a priori*, that there must be some flaw or
other in the preceding Arguments, plausible as they seem, and
great as they are upon the foot of human Authority. For though
the Appearance of Things at first Sight makes for this Conclusion
. . . the Fact itself cannot be so."[20] Smith also succeeded in keeping
his theory alive when the force of conflicting fact seemed to
threaten to destroy it, but his method was more gentle to the facts.
Man has been given by nature one standard by which to judge it,
but nature has retained another and different standard for itself.
"Both are calculated to promote the same great end, the order of
the world, and the perfection and happiness of human nature."[21]
Only an inordinately exacting critic would suggest that this solution is not wholly satisfactory, since Smith can have logically
reached it only by applying to nature its own standard, which it
was not appropriate for man to use. But if this solution does not
satisfy, Smith has another one. If we despair of finding any force
upon earth which can check the triumph of injustice, we "naturally
appeal to heaven, and hope that the great Author of our nature
will himself execute hereafter what all the principles which he has
given us for the direction of our conduct prompt us to attempt even
here; that he will complete the plan which he himself has thus
taught us to begin; and will, in a life to come, render to every one
according to the works which he has performed in this world."[22]
If, judged by men's standards, the order of nature does not result
in perfect justice on earth, we apparently have two alternative explanations: either that man's standards are an inadequate basis for
appraisal, or that there is opportunity in a future state for redress of
the injustices of the present one.

What we have, therefore, in the *Theory of Moral Sentiments*
is an unqualified doctrine of a harmonious order of nature, under
divine guidance, which promotes the welfare of man through the
operation of his individual propensities. Of these, self-interest is the

---

20. *Four Tracts* (Glocester, 1774), p. 12.
21. *Theory of Moral Sentiments*, p. 148.
22. *Ibid.*, p. 149.

most important one, in so far as economic life is concerned, though it is subject to the regulations of natural justice, to which it must conform. "In the race for wealth, for honours, and preferments, he may run as hard as he can, and strain every nerve and every muscle, in order to outstrip all his competitors. But if he should jostle, or throw down any of them, the indulgence of the spectators is entirely at an end. It is a violation of fair play, which they cannot admit of."[23] In economic matters, benevolence plays but a minor rôle. There is no express formulation of a principle of laissez faire, and no explicit condemnation of governmental interference with individual initiative; but it is quite clearly implied that self-interest, if regulated by justice, which may be natural justice, but is likely to be more effective if it is administered by a magistrate, is sufficient to attain the ends of Nature in the economic world. There is convincing evidence from other sources that Smith was already an exponent of the system of natural liberty.

III. *The System of Natural Liberty in the "Wealth of Nations"*

Traces of the general doctrine expounded in the *Theory of Moral Sentiments*, that there is a beneficent order in nature which, if left to take its own course, will bring to mankind maximum happiness and prosperity, are undoubtedly to be discovered in the *Wealth of Nations*. Traces of every conceivable sort of doctrine are to be found in that most catholic book, and an economist must have peculiar theories indeed who cannot quote from the *Wealth of Nations* to support his special purposes. But it can be convincingly demonstrated, I believe, that on the points at which they come into contact there is a substantial measure of irreconcilable divergence between the *Theory of Moral Sentiments* and the *Wealth of Nations*, with respect to the character of the natural order.

In the first case, the emphasis in the *Theory of Moral Sentiments* upon a benevolent deity as the author and guide of nature is almost, though not quite, completely absent in the *Wealth of Nations*. There are only a few minor passages in the later work which can be adduced as supporting evidence of the survival in Smith's thought of the concept of a divinity who has so shaped economic

23. *Ibid.*, p. 76.

process that it operates necessarily to promote human welfare: an incidental allusion to "the wisdom of nature";[24] a remark that with respect to smuggling the laws of the country had "made that a crime which nature never meant to be so";[25] and a more famous passage, the main reliance of those who would completely reconcile the doctrines expounded in the two works, in which Smith repeats the phrase "the invisible hand" which he had used in the *Theory of Moral Sentiments*.[26] The only explicit reference to God is one which could have given but scant comfort to the natural theology of his time: "Superstition first attempted to satisfy this curiosity [about natural phenomena], by referring all those wonderful appearances to the immediate agency of the gods. Philosophy afterward endeavoured to account for them from more familiar causes, or from such as mankind were better acquainted with, than the agency of the gods."[27] To the extent that Smith in the *Wealth of Nations* does expound a doctrine of a harmonious order in nature, he accounts for it, as a rule, and perhaps even invariably, by reference to "more familiar causes [and] to such as mankind were better acquainted with, than the agency of the gods." The significance for our purposes of this virtual disappearance from the *Wealth of Nations* of the doctrine of an order of nature designed and guided by a benevolent God is that it leaves Smith free to find defects in the order of nature without casting reflections on the workmanship of its Author.

To some extent Smith makes use of this freedom. In both works he finds an inherent harmony in the order of nature, whereby man, in following his own interests, at the same time and without necessarily intending it serves also the general interests of mankind. In the *Theory of Moral Sentiments*, this harmony, as I have shown, is represented as universal and perfect. In the *Wealth of Nations*, this harmony is represented as not extending to all elements of the economic order, and often as partial and imperfect where it does extend. Where harmony does prevail, it is as a rule a sort of average or statistical harmony, revealing itself only in the general mass of phenomena and leaving scope for the possibility that natural processes whose general effect is beneficial may work disadvantageously

---

24. *Wealth of Nations*, II, 172.
25. *Ibid.*, II, 381.
26. *Ibid.*, I, 421.
27. *Ibid.*, II, 256.

in individual cases or at particular moments of time. As a rule, though not invariably, Smith qualifies his assertions of harmony by such phrases as "in most cases," "the majority," "in general," "frequently." For example, the exercise of common prudence is a prerequisite if the system of natural liberty is to operate harmoniously, and "though the principles of common prudence do not always govern the conduct of every individual, they always influence that of *the majority* of every class or order."[28] "It is advantageous to the great body of workmen . . . that all these trades should be free, though this freedom may be abused in all of them, and is more likely to be so, perhaps, in some than in others."[29] Drawbacks "tend not to destroy, but to preserve, what it is *in most cases* advantageous to preserve, the natural division and distribution of labour in the society."[30]

There are a number of well-known passages in the *Wealth of Nations* in which Smith asserts the existence of a more-or-less complete harmony between the general interests of society and the particular interests of individuals.

It is not from the benevolence of the butcher, the brewer, or the baker, that we expect our dinner, but from their regard to their own interest. We address ourselves, not to their humanity but to their self-love, and never talk to them of our own necessities but of their advantages. . . .[31] Every individual is continually exerting himself to find out the most advantageous employment for whatever capital he can command. It is his own advantage, indeed, and not that of the society, which he has in view. But the study of his own advantage naturally, or rather necessarily leads him to prefer that employment which is most advantageous to the society. . . .[32] As every individual, therefore, endeavours as much as he can both to employ his capital in the support of domestic industry, and so to direct that industry that its produce may be of the greatest value; every individual necessarily labours to render the annual revenue of the society as great as he can. He generally, indeed, neither intends to promote the public interest, nor knows how much he is promoting it. By preferring the support of domestic to that of foreign industry he intends only his own security; and by directing that industry in such a manner as its produce may be of the greatest value, he intends only his own gain, and he is in this, as in many other cases, led by an invisible hand to promote an end which was no part of his intention. . . .[33] The natural effort of every indi-

28. *Ibid.*, I, 278. Italics mine.
29. *Ibid.*, I, 456.
30. *Ibid.*, II, 1-2. Italics mine.
31. *Ibid.*, I, 16.
32. *Ibid.*, I, 419.
33. *Ibid.*, I, 421.

vidual to better his own condition, when suffered to exert itself with freedom and security, is so powerful a principle, that it is alone, and without
any assistance, not only capable of carrying on the society to wealth and
prosperity, but of surmounting a hundred impertinent obstructions with
which the folly of human laws too often incumbers its operations; though
the effect of these obstructions is always more or less either to encroach
upon its freedom, or to diminish its security.[34]

But whereas in the *Theory of Moral Sentiments* such general
statements as these comprise the main substance of the doctrine of
a harmonious order in the economic world, in the *Wealth of Nations* they play a much more modest rôle. Though Smith in the
Wealth of Nations frequently makes general statements intended
apparently to apply to the entire universe, he has always before him
for consideration some concrete problem, or some finite section of
the universe. In no instance does Smith rely heavily upon his
assertions as to the existence of harmony in the natural order at
large to establish his immediate point that such harmony exists
within the specific range of economic phenomena which he is at the
moment examining. Such demonstration he accomplishes primarily
by means of reference to the nature of these specific phenomena,
by appeal to some self-evident principles of human psychology, by
citation of historical object lessons, or by inference from contemporary experience. The general statements, though they may, as
has been asserted, reveal the secret basis of Smith's conclusions, are
given the appearance of mere obiter dicta, thrown in as supernu-
merary reinforcements to an argument already sufficiently fortified
by more specific and immediate data. Smith's argument for the existence of a natural harmony in the economic order, to be preserved
by following the system of natural liberty, is, in form at least, built
up by detailed inference from specific data and by examination of
specific problems, and is not deduced from wide-sweeping generalizations concerning the universe in general. What were the secret
mental processes of Adam Smith whereby he really reached his conclusions it seems at this late date somewhat difficult to talk about
with any degree of assurance.

Nowhere in the *Wealth of Nations* does Smith place any reliance for the proper working of the economic order upon the operation of benevolence and sympathy, the emphasis upon (the latter
of)* which was the novel feature in the account of human nature

---

34. *Ibid.*, II, 43.
*The words in parentheses are needed as a clarification of the original text. J. V.

presented in the *Theory of Moral Sentiments*. In the *Wealth of Nations*, benevolence is not merely as a rule left out of the picture of the economic order; when mentioned, it is with the implication that it is a weak reed upon which to depend. "By pursuing his own interest he frequently promotes that of the society more effectually than when he really intends to promote it. I have never known much good done by those who affected to trade for the public good. It is an affectation, indeed, not very common among merchants, and very few words need be employed in dissuading them from it."[35] The only other instance in which Smith concedes the possible operation of benevolence in the economic world he also does not take too seriously:

> Whatever part of the produce . . . is over and above this share, he [i.e., the landlord] naturally endeavours to reserve to himself as the rent of his land, which is evidently the highest the tenant can afford to pay in the actual circumstances of the land. Sometimes, indeed, the liberality, more frequently the ignorance, of the landlord, makes him accept of somewhat less than this portion. . . . This portion, however, may still be considered as the natural rent of land, or the rent for which it is naturally meant that land should for the most part be let.[36]

The consequences of the intervention of liberality apparently are not "natural," are not in accordance with the intent of nature! Smith shows little faith in the prevalence of benevolence in the economic sphere. "Man has almost constant occasion for the help of his brethren, and it is in vain for him to expect it from their benevolence only. . . . It is not from the benevolence of the butcher, the brewer, or the baker, that we expect our dinner, but from their regard to their own interest."[37] "The late resolution of the Quakers in Pennsylvania to set at liberty all their negro slaves, may satisfy us that their number cannot be very great. Had they made any considerable part of their property, such a resolution could never have been agreed to."[38] Even the college professor cannot be expected to expend much energy in teaching effectively, cannot even be depended upon to teach at all, if it is not made to his interest to do so.[39] In the case of the clergy, the situation seems even more desperate. If they are endowed, they become indolent, and their

---

35. *Ibid.*, I, 421.
36. *Ibid.*, I, 145.
37. *Ibid.*, I, 16.
38. *Ibid.*, I, 365.
39. *Ibid.*, II, 250 ff.

zeal and industry become impaired. If, on the other hand, they are dependent upon voluntary contributions for their support, they become too zealous. He quotes from his skeptical friend Hume:

> . . . This interested diligence of the clergy is what every wise legislator will study to prevent; because, in every religion except the true, it is highly pernicious. . . . Each ghostly practitioner, in order to render himself more precious and sacred in the eyes of his retainers, will inspire them with the most violent abhorrence of all other sects, and continually endeavour, by some novelty, to excite the languid devotion of his audience. No regard will be paid to truth, morals, or decency in the doctrines inculcated. Every tenet will be adopted that best suits the disorderly affections of the human frame. Customers will be drawn to each conventicle by new industry and address in practising on the passions and credulity of the populace.[40]

Smith laid little stress even in the *Theory of Moral Sentiments* upon the importance of benevolence in the economic order. But writers who have labored under a sense of obligation to find a basis for reconciliation of the *Wealth of Nations* with the *Theory of Moral Sentiments* have nevertheless discovered a problem in the insignificant rôle assigned to benevolence in the *Wealth of Nations*. Buckle's solution of the problem was that in the *Wealth of Nations* Smith was deliberately abstracting from all principles of human nature except self-interest, whereas in the *Theory of Moral Sentiments* he aimed at a complete picture of human nature. Not a trace of evidence is discoverable, however, that Smith in the *Wealth of Nations* was aware that he was abstracting selected elements from the totality of human nature. It awaited a later and knener mind, Ricardo, to discover the possibilities of the technique of deliberate abstraction in the field of economics. A more ingenious attempt at reconciliation rests, in part, on the identification of self-interest as used in the *Wealth of Nations* with rational pecuniary interest, with a desire for more wealth, and by demonstrating that Smith takes into account other motives than the rational desire for more wealth, claims to demonstrate that Smith did not exclude all principles but self-interest from the economic sphere. But self-interest meant to Smith not only the desire for wealth, but self-love in all its possible manifestations. "It is the interest of every man to live as much at his ease as he can."[41] "Avarice and ambition in the rich, in the poor

---

40. *Ibid.*, II, 276.
41. *Ibid.*, II, 250.

the hatred of labour and the love of present ease and enjoyment," envy, malice and resentment,[42] all of these are manifestations of self-interest; the agreeableness, the ease or hardship, the cleanliness or dirtiness, the honorableness or dishonorableness, of the different employments are all factors affecting the attractiveness to labor of different occupations, as well as the wages paid: "Honour makes a great part of the reward of all honourable professions."[43] Smith distinguishes also between what a man is interested in and what is to his interest. Man is sometimes ignorant of the latter. "But though the interest of the labourer is strictly connected with that of the society, he is incapable either of comprehending that interest, or of understanding its connexion with his own."[44] It is what a man regards as his interest, even though mistakenly, that controls his actions. But every possible impulse and motive to action is included under self-interest except a deliberate intention to promote the welfare of others than one's self.

From his examination of the operation of self-interest in specific phases of the economic order and of the consequences of government interference with the free operation of self-interest, Smith arrives at an extensive program for the extension of the system of natural liberty through the abolition of existing systems of governmental regulation, though he nowhere brings the several items in that program together. Four main reforms are advocated. Free choice of occupations is to be established through the abolition of the apprenticeship regulations and settlement laws; free trade in land, through the repeal of laws establishing entails, primogenitures, and other restrictions on the free transfer of land by gift, devise, or sale; internal free trade, where such does not already prevail, by the abolition of local customs taxes; and most important of all, free trade in foreign commerce, through the abolition of the duties, bounties, and prohibitions of the mercantilistic régime and the trading monopolies of the chartered companies. These various restrictions and regulations are objectionable either because they operate to keep commerce, labor, or capital from following the channels in which they would otherwise go, or because they attract to a particular species of industry a greater share of the factors than

---

42. *Ibid.*, II, 203.
43. *Ibid.*, I, 102.
44. *Ibid.*, I, 249.

would ordinarily be employed in it. In all of these cases there is close harmony, under the system of natural liberty, between the interests of individuals and the public interest, and interference by government, instead of promoting, hinders, though it does not necessarily prevent, the attainment of prosperity.

In England all of this program has been achieved, and in so far as such things can be traced to their source, the influence of the *Wealth of Nations* was an important factor in bringing about the reforms. That they were genuine reforms most economists will admit, though even in England there is no longer the unanimity there once was on these matters. It is a somewhat ironical coincidence that the least important plank in Smith's program, the reform of the English law of property, should be in process of final achievement only as the permanence of the greatest of his victories, the establishment of free trade in foreign commerce, faces its first serious threat in sixty years.

IV. Flaws in the Natural Order

The foregoing is familiar matter. What is not so familiar, however, is the extent to which Smith acknowledged exceptions to the doctrine of a natural harmony in the economic order even when left to take its natural course. Smith, himself, never brought these together; but if this is done, they make a surprisingly comprehensive list and they demonstrate beyond dispute the existence of a wide divergence between the perfectly harmonious, completely beneficent natural order of the *Theory of Moral Sentiments* and the partial and limited harmony in the economic order of the *Wealth of Nations*. Masters and workmen have a conflict of interest with respect to wages, and the weakness in bargaining power of the latter ordinarily gives the advantage in any dispute to the former.[45] Masters, traders, and apprentices, on the one hand, and the public on the other, have divergent interests with respect to apprenticeship rules.[46] The interest of merchants and manufacturers is in high profits, which are disadvantageous to the public.[47] Merchants and manufacturers have interests opposed to those of the

---

45. *Ibid.*, I, 68-69.
46. *Ibid.*, I, 125.
47. *Ibid.*, I, 100; II, 112 ff.

farmers and landlords,[48] and of the general public.[49] "People of the same trade seldom meet together, even for merriment and diversion, but the conversation ends in a conspiracy against the public, or in some contrivance to raise prices. It is impossible indeed to prevent such meetings, by any law which either could be executed, or would be consistent with liberty and justice."[50] The corn-dealer, on the whole, performs a useful service, but because of his "excess of avarice" he does not perform it perfectly.[51] The merchant exporter sometimes finds it to his interest, when dearth prevails both at home and abroad, "very much [to] aggravate the calamities of the dearth" at home by exporting corn.[52] Men commonly overestimate their chances of success in risky ventures, with the consequence that too great a share of the nation's stock of capital goes into such ventures.[53] It being the custom to pay attorneys and clerks according to the number of pages they had occasion to write, their self-interest led them "to multiply words beyond all necessity, to the corruption of the law language of, I believe, every court of justice in Europe."[54] Private initiative cannot be trusted to take proper care of the roads.[55] Division of labor operates to impair the intelligence, enterprise, martial courage, and moral character of the laborers,[56] though division of labor is itself "the necessary, though very slow and gradual, consequence of a certain propensity in human nature . . . the propensity to truck, barter, and exchange one thing for another."[57] In old countries, "rent and profit eat up wages, and the two superior orders of people oppress the inferior one."[58] This is only a partial list of the defects in the natural order, even when left to take its own course, which Smith points out, though it would suffice to provide ammunition for several socialist orations. This is a far cry from the account given in the *Theory of Moral Sentiments* of a perfectly harmonious order

---

48. *Ibid.*, I, 129.
49. *Ibid.*, I, 250.
50. *Ibid.*, I, 130.
51. *Ibid.*, II, 26.
52. *Ibid.*, II, 40.
53. *Ibid.*, II, 64-65.
54. *Ibid.*, II, 213.
55. *Ibid.*, II, 217.
56. *Ibid.*, II, 267.
57. *Ibid.*, I, 15.
58. *Ibid.*, II, 67.

of nature, operating under divine guidance, to promote its "great end, the order of the world, and the perfection and happiness of human nature."

In the *Theory of Moral Sentiments* Smith started out with a few general propositions about the nature of the universe which any educated Scotchman of his day would have vouched for as self-evident truths; and following them wherever they led him, he picked up en route a few more self-evident truths about the nature of human nature, and finally reached conclusions of the sort we have examined. Failing to compare his conclusions with the facts, he saw no necessity for qualifying them, and no reason for re-examining his premises. Unfortunately, these premises were in special need of careful scrutiny, for they were all drawn from a peculiar class of axioms which urgently require, but are incapable of, proof. In his earlier work Smith was a purely speculative philosopher, reasoning from notions masquerading as self-evident verities. In the *Wealth of Nations* Smith made use of a rich harvest of facts gathered by personal observation at home and abroad, by conversation and correspondence with many keen and intelligent observers of the current scene, by wide reading in a miscellany of sources, from law books to travelers' tales. With this factual material Smith kept close contact, and he never departed from it for long. He still, it is true, retained his flair for resounding generalizations of heroic range. There is a long-standing feud between sweeping generalization and run-of-the-mill factual data, and when Smith brought them together he did not always succeed in inducing altogether harmonious relations. But Smith's strength lay in other directions than exactly logical thinking, and he displayed a fine tolerance for a generous measure of inconsistency. It is to his credit that when there was sharp conflict between his generalization and his data, he usually abandoned his generalization.

There would be little ground for insistence upon reconciliation between the *Theory of Moral Sentiments* and the *Wealth of Nations* if it were simply a case of comparing one book written in 1757 with another written in 1776. It may not be as common as it should be for a man in his full maturity to advance beyond the level of his first book; but it surely is not a rare phenomenon requiring to be explained out of existence. In every respect which is of concern to the economist as such, with the possible exception of his treatment of benevolence, the apparent discrepancies between the *Theory of Moral Sentiments* and the *Wealth of Nations* mark distinct advances of the latter over the former in realism and in application of the saving grace of common sense. But in the last year of his life Smith made extensive revisions of and additions to the *Theory of Moral Sentiments,* without diminishing in any particular the points of conflict between the two books. This would make it seem that in Smith's mind, at least, there was to the last no consciousness of any difference in the doctrines expounded in the two books. Though we grant this, however, are we obliged to accept his judgment and to strain interpretations in order to find consistency prevailing where inconsistency appeareth to reign supreme? I think not. There persisted within the *Wealth of Nations,* through five successive editions, many, and to later eyes obvious, inconsistencies. When Smith revised his *Theory of Moral Sentiments* he was elderly and unwell. It is not altogether unreasonable to suppose that he had lost the capacity to make drastic changes in his philosophy, but had retained his capacity to overlook the absence of complete co-ordination and unity in that philosophy.

V. The Functions of Government

Adam Smith, as has been shown, recognized that the economic order, when left to its natural course, was marked by serious conflicts between private interests and the interests of the general public. This would seem to suggest that there was an important sphere in which government interference with private interests might promote the general welfare. In his one deliberate and comprehensive generalization dealing with the proper functions of the state, Smith made it clear, however, that he would narrowly restrict the activities of government. "According to the system of natural liberty, the sovereign has only three duties to attend to; . . . first, the duty of protecting the society from the violence and invasion of other independent societies; secondly, . . . the duty of establishing an exact administration of justice; and, thirdly, the duty of erecting and maintaining certain public works and certain public institutions."[59] Even here, however, he grants to government a somewhat more extensive range of proper activities than in many scattered dicta throughout the remainder of the book, where he was pri-

59. *Ibid.,* II, 184-185.

marily condemning some specific governmental activity and was not really giving serious consideration to the wider problem of the proper range of governmental activity. Smith had himself undermined what is ordinarily regarded as his principal argument for laissez faire, by demonstrating that the natural order, when left to take its own course, in many respects works against, instead of for, the general welfare. How can his adherence, notwithstanding, to a policy of narrow limitation of the functions of government be explained?

The *Wealth of Nations*, though it was from one point of view only a segment of a larger and systematic treatise on social philosophy, was at the same time a tract for the times, a specific attack on certain types of government activity which Smith was convinced, on both a priori and empirical grounds, operated against national prosperity, namely, bounties, duties, and prohibitions in foreign trade; apprenticeship and settlement laws; legal monopolies; laws of succession hindering free trade in land. Smith's primary objective was to secure the termination of *these* activities of government. His wider generalizations were invoked to support the attack on *these* political institutions. Everything else was to a large degree secondary. Smith made many exceptions to his general argument for laissez faire. But his interest as a reformer and a propagandist was not in these exceptions. He nowhere gathered together in orderly fashion the exceptions which he would have made to his general restriction of government activity to protection, justice, and the maintenance of a few types of public works and public institutions. When considering in general terms the proper functions of government, he forgot all about these exceptions. If he had been brought face to face with a complete list of the modifications to the principle of laissez faire to which he at one place or another had granted his approval, I have no doubt that he would have been astounded at his own moderation. I once heard a president of a state bankers' association at the afternoon session of its annual convention make the theme of his presidential address the unmitigated iniquity of government interference with business and the necessity of more business men in government in order that they should see to it that there was less government in business. In the evening of the same day he introduced to the audience the state commissioner of banking as one to whom the bankers were deeply indebted, because by promoting the enactment of sound regulations governing the entrance into the banking field and the practice of banking he had secured the suppression of irresponsible and fraudulent banking, to the benefit of the solid and respectable bankers there assembled and of the general public. He was as sincere in the evening as he had been that afternoon. Not only was Smith fully capable of this type of inconsistency, but there is in the *Wealth of Nations* an almost exact parallel of this modern instance.[60]

There is no possible room for doubt, however, that Smith in general believed that there was, to say the least, a strong presumption against government activity beyond its fundamental duties of protection against its foreign foes and maintenance of justice. In his *Lectures,* Smith had said: "Till there be property, there can be no government, the very end of which is to secure wealth [i.e., to make wealth secure], and to defend the rich from the poor,"[61] following closely Locke's dictum that "Government has no other end but the preservation of property." In the *Wealth of Nations* he was more guarded: "Civil government, so far as it is instituted for the security of property, is in reality instituted for the defence of the rich against the poor, or of those who have some property against those who have none at all."[62] What were the considerations which brought Smith to his laissez faire conclusions? His philosophical speculations about a harmonious order in nature undoubtedly made it easier for him to reach a laissez faire policy, though I believe that the significance of the natural order in Smith's economic doctrines has been grossly exaggerated. But was not government itself a part of the order of nature, and its activities as "natural" as those of the individuals whom it governed? Smith is obscure on this point, and an adequate answer to this question, if possible at all, would require a detailed examination of Smith's position in the evolution of political theory, especially with respect to the origin of government and the character of the state of nature in the absence of government. It is clear, however, that to Smith the activities of government in the maintenance of justice are an essential part of the order of nature in its full development, and that such activities are not interferences with the system of natural liberty.

In the *Theory of Moral Sentiments* there is a vague passage which seems to suggest that government itself is an agency of the

---

60. Cf. *ibid.,* II, 307.
61. *Lectures,* p. 15.
62. *Wealth of Nations,* II, 207.

order of nature, and to imply that all of its activities may, therefore, be as "natural" as those of individuals.[63] In the *Wealth of Nations,* Smith is a little more precise. He draws a definite line between those activities of government which are, and those which are not, in accord with the natural order, on the basis of empirical data. Government activity is natural and therefore good where it promotes the general welfare, and is an interference with nature and therefore bad when it injures the general interests of society. Whether in particular circumstances it works well or ill is to be determined only by examination of the character of those circumstances, though in most cases such examination may be expected a priori to reveal that it works badly.

This general presumption against government intervention in the affairs of mankind was itself largely the product of direct inference from experience. Against those particular activities of government which he subjected to special attack, viz., mercantilistic regulations, settlement and apprenticeship laws, legal monopolies, Smith thought he had specific objections, drawn from the results of their operation, sufficient to condemn them. Aside from protection and justice, these were the important activities of the governments of his day. In condemning them he was not far from condemning all the main types of government activity, aside from justice and protection, which were prominently in the public view. To justify these activities, it was necessary, Smith believed, to credit government with better knowledge of what was to a man's interest than the ordinary man himself was endowed with. This Smith could not concede. The standards of honesty and competence of the governments of his day with which Smith was acquainted were unbelievably low, moreover, not only in comparison with what they are today in England, Germany, and the Scandinavian countries, but apparently even in comparison with earlier periods in English political history. Smith had encountered few instances in which government was rendering intelligent and efficient service to the public welfare outside of the fields of protection and justice. The English government of his day was in the hands of an aristocratic clique, the place-jobbing, corrupt, cynical, and class-biased flower of the British gentry, who clung to the traditional mercantilism not so much because of a strong faith that it met the problems of a growing trade struggling to burst its fetters, but because they did not know anything else to

63. *Theory of Moral Sentiments*, pp. 163-64

do. Even when Smith was prepared to admit that the system of natural liberty would not serve the public welfare with optimum effectiveness, he did not feel driven necessarily to the conclusion that government intervention was preferable to laissez faire. The evils of unrestrained selfishness might be better than the evils of incompetent and corrupt government.

In this connection, Smith has, indeed, a lesson to teach the "new economics" of the present day, which is peddling antique nostrums under new trademarks, and which has substituted for the answer to all economic problems of the classically trained parrot, "demand and supply," the equally magical phrase, "social control." If the standards of public administration are low, progress from a life regulated by the law of demand and supply to a life under the realm of social control may be progress from the discomforts of the frying-pan to the agonies of the fire.

It is the highest impertinence and presumption, therefore, in kings and ministers, to pretend to watch over the œconomy of private people, and to restrain their expence, either by sumptuary laws, or by prohibiting the importation of foreign luxuries. They are themselves always, and without any exception, the greatest spendthrifts in the society. Let them look well after their own expence, and they may safely trust private people with theirs. If their own extravagance does not ruin the state, that of their subjects never will.[64] . . . The violence and injustice of the rulers of mankind is an ancient evil, for which, I am afraid, the nature of human affairs can scarce admit of a remedy.[65]

Where, by exception, good government made its appearance, Smith was ready to grant it a wider range of activities.

The orderly, vigilant, and parsimonious administration of such aristocracies as those of Venice and Amsterdam, is extremely proper, it appears from experience, for the management of a mercantile project of this kind. But whether such a government as that of England; which, whatever may be its virtues, has never been famous for good œconomy; which, in time of peace, has generally conducted itself with the slothful and negligent profusion that is perhaps natural to monarchies; and in time of war has constantly acted with all the thoughtless extravagance that democracies are apt to fall into; could be safely trusted with the management of such a project, must at least be a good deal more doubtful.[66]

Smith believed, moreover, that there were evils involved in the economic order which it was beyond the competence of even good

64. *Wealth of Nations,* I, 328.
65. *Ibid.,* I, 457.
66. *Ibid.,* II, 303.

government to remedy. To repeat a useful quotation: "People of the same trade seldom meet together, even for merriment and diversion, but the conversation ends in a conspiracy against the public, or in some contrivance to raise prices. It is impossible indeed to prevent such meetings, by any law which either could be executed, or would be consistent with liberty and justice."[67] We have tried, in this country, to abolish Gary dinners by law. Whether we have succeeded seems still to be open to argument.

So much for the negative aspects of Smith's theory of the functions of the state. Let us examine now what concessions he made to the possibilities of the promotion of human welfare through governmental action. Smith conceded that it was the duty of the government to provide protection against external foes, and on the ground of their necessity for defense, he approved of commercial regulations which on purely economic grounds he would condemn. "The act of navigation is not favourable to foreign commerce, or to the growth of that opulence which can arise from it. . . . As defence, however, is of much more importance than opulence, the act of navigation is, perhaps, the wisest of all the commercial regulations of England."[68] In the same spirit, Smith mildly supported bounties on manufactures necessary for defense, which would not otherwise be produced at home.[69]

Smith assigned to government also "the duty of establishing an exact administration of justice."[70] Unfortunately, Smith never succeeded in carrying out his original plan of writing a treatise on jurisprudence, and the scattered materials in the *Wealth of Nations* and the meager outline in the *Lectures* are insufficient to give us a trustworthy judgment as to what he would include under "justice." His own definition in the *Wealth of Nations*, "the duty of protecting, as far as possible, every member of the society from the injustice or oppression of every other member of it," if broadly interpreted, would assign to government the task of a major reconstruction of the economic order, since Smith, as has been shown, recited many phases of it in which injustice and oppression prevailed. It seems clear, however, that Smith, like later and more doctrinaire exponents of laissez faire, took for granted the inevitability of private property and class conflict, and understood by

67. *Ibid.*, I, 130.
68. *Ibid.*, I, 429.
69. *Ibid.*, II, 23.
70. *Ibid.*, II, 185.

justice the whole legal and customary code of his time dealing with individual rights, privileges, and obligations under that system of economic organization. It is also likely that Smith failed to see how far acceptance of even the prevailing code of justice carried him from a simple order of nature in which natural justice automatically emerges from the harmony of individual interests, independently of governmental machinery and sanctions. Punishment and enforcement of redress after the act in case of dishonesty, violence, fraud, clearly would be included under the "administration of justice." Smith would, perhaps, include as a proper phase of this function such preventive measures as would tend to give security against the perpetration of dishonesty, extortion, and violence. In any case, he does not oppose such regulations, though his *Lectures* indicate that he would include them under "police" rather than "justice."[71] "The institution of long apprenticeships can give no security that insufficient workmanship shall not frequently be exposed to public sale. When this is done it is generally the effect of fraud, and not of inability; and the longest apprenticeship can give no security against fraud. Quite different regulations are necessary to prevent this abuse. The sterling mark upon plate, and the stamps upon linen and woollen cloth, give the purchaser much greater security than any statute of apprenticeship."[72] Unqualified adherence to the principle of *caveat emptor* was apparently not a necessary implication of Smith's laissez faire doctrines. Enforcement of contracts is specified as an important function of government,[73] and a law obliging masters to pay wages in money rather than in kind is justifiable as a protection to the workers against fraud. "It imposes no real hardship upon the masters. It only obliges them to pay that value in money, which they pretended to pay, but did not always really pay, in goods."[74] "Where there is an exclusive corporation, it may perhaps be proper to regulate the price of the first necessary of life."[75] Protection of slaves against violence by their masters is approved of both as in accord with common humanity and as promoting the productivity of slave labor.[76] Smith recognized the existence of a higher social justice, which may override the "natural liberty" of

71. *Lectures,* 154, ff.
72. *Wealth of Nations,* I, 123-124.
73. *Ibid.,* I, 97.
74. *Ibid.,* I, 143.
75. *Ibid.,* I, 144.
76. *Ibid.,* II, 88.

the individual, but he would invoke it sparingly. Regulations of paper money banking "may, no doubt, be considered as in some respect a violation of natural liberty. But those exertions of the natural liberty of a few individuals, which might endanger the security of the whole society, are, and ought to be, restrained by the laws of all governments; of the most free, as well as of the most despotical. The obligation of building party walls, in order to prevent the communication of fire, is a violation of natural liberty, exactly of the same kind with the regulations of the banking trade which are here proposed."[77] But "To hinder . . . the farmer from sending his goods at all times to the best market, is evidently to sacrifice the ordinary laws of justice to an idea of public utility, to a sort of reasons of state; an act of legislative authority which ought to be exercised only, which can be pardoned only in cases of the most urgent necessity."[78] We have here, perhaps, the germ of that later maxim of convenient vagueness, that every individual should be protected in his natural rights, but only to the extent to which they do not interfere with the natural rights of others. There is no evidence that Smith would include as a proper phase of the administration of justice any drastic revision of the content of these rights.

There remains to be considered the third government function: "erecting and maintaining certain public works and certain public institutions, which it can never be for the interest of any individual, or small number of individuals, to erect and maintain; because the profit could never repay the expense to any individual or small number of individuals, though it may frequently do much more than repay it to a great society."[79] Smith here clearly assigns to the government a duty of promoting the general welfare other than in connection with protection and justice, if the means to do so are within the power of the government, but not within the power of individuals. What the relationship of this function is to the natural order Smith does not discuss in the *Wealth of Nations*. The attention given to it by Smith has been attributed to the influence of the Physiocrats. In the *Theory of Moral Sentiments* there is one passage which appears to praise such institutions, but may have been intended in a satirical sense:

77. *Ibid.*, I, 307.
78. *Ibid.*, II, 41-42.
79. *Ibid.*, II, 185.

The same principle, the same love of system, the same regard to the beauty of order, of art and contrivance, frequently serves to recommend those institutions which tend to promote the public welfare. . . . It is not commonly from a fellow-feeling with carriers and waggoners that a public-spirited man encourages the mending of high roads. When the legislature establishes premiums and other encouragements to advance the linen or woollen manufactures, its conduct seldom proceeds from pure sympathy with the wearer of cheap or fine cloth, and much less from that with the manufacturer or merchant. The perfection of police, the extension of trade and manufactures, are noble and magnificent objects. . . . They make part of the great system of government, and the wheels of the political machine seem to move with more harmony and ease by means of them. . . . All constitutions of government, however, are [ought to be?] valued only in proportion as they tend to promote the happiness of those who live under them.[80]

In the *Lectures*, the only relevant passage is a passing reference under the general heading of "Police" to what may be regarded as a detailed phase of this function of government, the promotion of cleanliness, presumably of the streets.[81]

In the *Wealth of Nations* the discussion lacks somewhat in breadth, perhaps because it is merely incidental to Smith's discussion of the financial aspects of government. The public works and public institutions in this class, says Smith, "are chiefly those for facilitating the commerce of the society, and those for promoting the instruction of the people."[82] He nowhere purports to give a complete list of the public works proper to government, but he mentions highways, bridges, canals, and harbors. In discussing the propriety of particular projects, however, he completely ignores the criterion he had laid down at the beginning of his discussion, namely, the impossibility of their being conducted profitably as private enterprises. The only reason he gives for his approval of government maintenance of the highways is that private management would not have a sufficient incentive to maintain them properly, and therefore could not be trusted to do so.[83] He apparently approves of government operation of canals, though he grants that they can be left safely in private hands,[84] and that they can be profitably managed by joint-stock companies.[85]

80. *Theory of Moral Sentiments*, pp. 163-64.
81. *Lectures*, p. 154.
82. *Wealth of Nations*, II, 214.
83. *Ibid.*, II, 217.
84. *Ibid.*, II, 216-217.
85. *Ibid.*, II, 247.

The modern issue of the propriety of government participation in commerce and industry is dealt with by Adam Smith almost solely from the viewpoint: Can the government make a net revenue out of it? He takes coinage for granted as a government function without considering any possible alternative. He apparently approves of government operation of the post-office, but if so, the only ground given is the ability of the government to manage it with successful financial results.[86] He in general disapproves of government ventures into business, but solely on the ground that the government is a poor trader and a poor manager. The public domain, except what may be needed for parks, should be disposed of, because the sovereign is a poor farmer and forester. Smith apparently could not read German, and makes no references to German literature. Knowledge of the success of some of the German principalities in managing the public domain, and in other phases of public administration, would perhaps have lessened Smith's opposition to government ventures into industry. The modern advocate of laissez faire who objects to government participation in business on the ground that it is an encroachment upon a field reserved by nature for private enterprise cannot find support for this argument in the *Wealth of Nations.*

Of government "institutions," other than public works, intended to facilitate commerce, Smith opposes legal monopolies in general, though he concedes the validity of a temporary monopoly when a trading company undertakes, at its own risk and expense, to establish a new trade with some remote and barbarous nation, and he indicates that he approves for the same reason of the institutions of patent and copyright.[87]

Smith supports the participation of the government in the general education of the people, because it will help prepare them for industry, will makes them better citizens and better soldiers, and happier and healthier men in mind and body. Public education is made necessary to check as far as may be the evil effects on the standards, mentality, and character of the working classes of the division of labor and the inequality in the distribution of wealth.[88] Here once more Smith draws a picture of the economic order under the system of natural liberty which is quite different from that

86. *Ibid.*, II, 303.
87. *Ibid.*, II, 245.
88. *Ibid.*, II, 267 ff.

beatific state which he dreamed about in the *Theory of Moral Sentiments.*

It is quite probable that Smith overlooked some current activities of government to which he would have given his approval if they had been called to his attention. The absence, for instance, in the *Wealth of Nations* of any discussion of poor relief as a public function has often been commented upon, and is generally regarded as having been due to oversight. But we have not yet revealed the full extent to which Smith showed himself prepared to depart from a rigid policy of laissez faire. The one personal characteristic which all of his biographers agree in attributing to him is absent-mindedness, and his general principle of natural liberty seems to have been one of the things he was most absent-minded about. We have already seen that in his more systematic discussion of the functions of government, Smith made important concessions to the possibility of government promotion of the general welfare through public works and institutions. In stray but frequent moments of intimate contact with facts apparently hostile to the principle of natural liberty, Smith conveniently forgot the principle and went beyond the limits set in his formal discussion to the proper activities of government. In arguing for the duty of government to support educational institutions which promote the martial spirit of the people, Smith incidentally concedes that "it would deserve its most serious attention to prevent leprosy or any other loathsome and offensive disease, though neither mortal nor dangerous, from spreading itself among them,"[89] from which it may reasonably be inferred that he would even more strongly support public action taken to prevent the spread of dangerous diseases, and thus would include public hygiene among the proper functions of government. In many instances Smith supported government restrictions on private initiative where neither justice nor defense was involved, and where the sole aim was to improve upon the direction which private initiative gave to the investment of capital, the course of commerce, and the employment of labor. He supported the compulsory registration of mortgages,[90] and he wrote approvingly of colonial laws which promoted agricultural progress by checking the engrossing of land.[91]

---

89. *Ibid.,* II, 272.
90. *Ibid,* II, 347.
91. *Ibid.,* II, 73.

To the great indignation of Jeremy Bentham, he approved of the prevailing restriction of the maximum rate of interest to 5 per cent, on the ground that if a higher rate were current, "the greater part of the money which was to be lent, would be lent to prodigals and projectors, who alone would be willing to give this high interest. . . . A great part of the capital of the country would thus be kept out of the hands which were most likely to make a profitable and advantageous use of it, and thrown into those which were most likely to waste and destroy it."[92] We may be inclined to agree with Bentham that this is an inadequate defense of the usury laws, but what makes it significant for our purposes is that it involves an admission on Smith's part that the majority of investors could not be relied upon to invest their funds prudently and safely, and that government regulation was a good corrective for individual stupidity.

Smith also makes several concessions to the mercantilistic policy of regulation of the foreign trade. He admits that there are circumstances under which export restrictions on corn may be warranted;[93] he approves of a moderate export tax on wool on the ground that it would produce revenue for the government and at the same time would afford an advantage over their foreign competitors to the British manufacturer of woolens;[94] he favors moderate taxes on foreign manufactures, which would still give to domestic workmen "a considerable advantage in the home market."[95]

Smith recommended that rents in kind should be taxed more heavily than money rents, because "such rents are always more hurtful to the tenant than beneficial to the landlord."[96] He would tax rent from leases which prescribe to the tenant a certain mode of cultivation more heavily than other rent, in order to discourage the practice of making such leases, "which is generally a foolish one."[97] He would tax at more favorable rates the landlord who cultivates a part of his own land, because it is of importance that the

92. *Ibid.*, I, 338.
93. *Ibid.*, II, 41.
94. *Ibid.*, II, 152.
95. *Ibid.*, II, 367. Smith may, however, have supported such taxes as an alternative to the existing higher taxes and prohibitions of import, and not as preferable to free import.
96. *Ibid.*, II, 316.
97. *Ibid.*

landlord, with his greater command of capital and his greater willingness and capacity to try experiments, should be encouraged to take an active part in agriculture.[98] He would penalize by heavier taxation the landlord who capitalizes a part of the future rent, because this is usually the expedient of a spendthrift, is frequently hurtful to landlord and tenant, is always hurtful to the community.[99] Shortly thereafter, however, Smith returns to laissez faire: "The principal attention of the sovereign ought to be to encourage, by every means in his power, the attention both of the landlord and of the farmer; by allowing both to pursue their own interest in their own way, and according to their own judgment; . . ."[100]

Smith gives a little support to the use of the taxing power as what would now be called "an instrument of social reform." He approves of a tax on the retail sale of liquor so adjusted as to discourage the multiplication of little alehouses,[101] and of a heavy tax on distilleries as a sumptuary measure against spirituous liquors, especially if accompanied by a reduction in the tax on "the wholesome and invigorating liquors of beer and ale."[102] He supports heavier highway tolls upon luxury carriages than upon freight wagons, in order that "the indolence and vanity of the rich [be] made to contribute in a very easy manner to the relief of the poor."[103] He asserts that "the gains of monopolists, whenever they can be come at [are] certainly of all subjects the most proper for taxation.[104] The modern single-taxer finds support for his cause in Smith's argument for the special taxation of land values. "Ground-rents, so far as they exceed the ordinary rent of land, are altogether owing to the good government of the sovereign. . . . Nothing can be more reasonable than that a fund which owes its existence to the good government of the state, should be taxed peculiarly, or should contribute something more than the greater part of other funds, towards the support of the government."[105] He lends mild support to the principle of progressive taxation: "It is not very unreasonable that the rich

98. *Ibid.*
99. *Ibid.*, II, 315.
100. *Ibid.*, II, 318.
101. *Ibid.*, II, 337.
102. *Ibid.*, II, 375.
103. *Ibid.*, II, 216.
104. *Ibid.*, II, 377.
105. *Ibid.*, II, 329.

should contribute to the public expence, not only in proportion to their revenue, but something more than in that proportion."[106]

Though there is nowhere in Smith's writings a general discussion of the possibilities of voluntary co-operation, he makes clear that he did not hope for much good from it. Making a reasonable inference from past experience, but a bad forecast of the subsequent trend, he saw in the joint-stock company very limited promise even for money-making purposes.[107] It was his verdict that the corporate guilds had failed to promote good workmanship.[108] Exception being made for the Scottish Presbyterian church, he saw even in religious associations much to blame.[109] About the only types of voluntary association in which Smith saw a high degree of effectiveness in accomplishing their purposes were associations of merchants and manufacturers to exploit the consumer and of masters to exploit the worker.

Adam Smith was not a doctrinaire advocate of laissez faire. He saw a wide and elastic range of activity for government, and he was prepared to extend it even farther if government, by improving its standards of competence, honesty, and public spirit, showed itself entitled to wider responsibilities. He attributed great capacity to serve the general welfare to individual initiative applied in competitive ways to promote individual ends. He devoted more effort to the presentation of his case for individual freedom than to exploring the possibilities of service through government. He helped greatly to free England from the bonds of a set of regulatory measures which had always been ill advised and based on fallacious economic notions, but he did not foresee that England would soon need a new set of regulations to protect her laboring masses against new, and to them dangerous, methods of industrial organization and industrial technique. Smith was endowed with more than the ordinary allotment of common sense, but he was not a prophet. But even in his own day, when it was not so easy to see, Smith saw that self-interest and competition were sometimes treacherous to the public interest they were supposed to serve, and he was prepared to have government exercise some measure of control over them where the need could be shown and the competence of

---

106. *Ibid.*, II, 327.
107. *Ibid.*, II, 246.
108. *Ibid.*, I, 131.
109. *Ibid.*, II, 273 ff.

government for the task demonstrated. His sympathy with the humble and the lowly, with the farmer and the laborer, was made plain for all to see. He had not succeeded in completely freeing himself from mercantilistic delusions, and he had his own peculiar doctrinal and class prejudices. But his prejudices, such as they were, were against the powerful and the grasping, and it was the interests of the general masses that he wished above all to promote, in an age when even philosophers rarely condescended to deal sympathetically with their needs. He had little trust in the competence or good faith of government. He knew who controlled it, and whose purposes they tried to serve, though against the local magistrate his indictment was probably unduly harsh. He saw, nevertheless, that it was necessary, in the absence of a better instrument, to rely upon government for the performance of many tasks which individuals as such would not do, or could not do, or could do only badly. He did not believe that laissez faire was always good, or always bad. It depended on circumstances; and as best he could, Adam Smith took into account all of the circumstances he could find. In these days of contending schools, each of them with the deep, though momentary, conviction that it, and it alone, knows the one and only path to economic truth, how refreshing it is to return to the *Wealth of Nations* with its eclecticism, its good temper, its common sense, and its willingness to grant that those who saw things differently from itself were only partly wrong.

Marshall's Economics, in Relation to the Man and to His Times[*]

MALTHUS ONCE SAID, with reference to Senior's lectures on population, that "it was among the disadvantages of public lectures, that the lecturer sometimes thought he was called upon to say something new, where there was nothing new to be said." Malthus, it may be ventured, would have been willing to concede that he had contributed substantially to placing Senior in that position by having himself previously said most of what was worth saying about population. Asked to speak to the Association on Marshall as part of the celebration of the fiftieth anniversary of the publication of his *Principles*, I find myself very much in the position Malthus thought Senior was in.

My own plight I attribute mainly to four factors: First, so much of what knowledge I may have about Marshall has been gained through the years from the late Dr. Taussig's writings, teaching, and conversation that I can no longer separate what I have learned for myself from what I have derived from him. Secondly, the fifty years and more of published commentary on Marshall's *Principles* have made it difficult to find fresh cause for praise or complaint. Third, the admirable *Memorials of Alfred Marshall*, 1925, edited by Pigou, and containing penetrating and enlightening contributions by Keynes, Edgeworth, and Pigou on the relation of Marshall's personality and social philosophy to his economics, has so thoroughly exploited the biographical data available even to insiders that not much scope is left to those who had never seen nor heard Marshall in the flesh nor had an opportunity to draw on the rich fund of oral Cambridge tradition. What would be ordinarily a substitute, published letters, are also unavailable except for the few published in

[*]A paper presented at the meetings of the American Economic Association, Dec. 29, 1940. Reprinted from *The American Economic Review*, Vol. 31, June 1941, pp. 223-235, by the courtesy of the American Economic Association.

the *Memorials*. Finally, Mr. Schumpeter has kindly made available to me in advance a generous-sized abstract of his paper on the pure theory aspects of Marshall's *Principles*, with the consequence that I cannot easily, without resort to plagiarism, fill out what I can find to say within my own assignment by encroachment on his.

If, then, what I say should sound unduly familiar and commonplace, solace must be sought in the also familiar and commonplace reflection that on the subject of Marshall what is new is highly unlikely at this late date also to be both true and significant. I will deal in turn with the influence on Marshall's economics of his political views, of his moral philosophy, and of some of his methodological predilections.

I

Marshall was in many respects a highly representative late Victorian intellectual. He was a Victorian "liberal" in his general orientation toward social problems, as probably also in the narrower partisan sense. English economics was throughout the nineteenth century intimately bound up with English politics, and throughout the century English economists had, probably without any important exception, political affiliations or preferences which influenced and were influenced by their economic doctrines. It is possible to ascertain with some degree of assurance the political affiliations of the earlier economists from their economic writings, but this requires an examination of their position with respect to issues which, though of minor importance for economics, sharply divided the various political groupings. On the major economic issues of the nineteenth century which were also important political issues, notably, foreign trade policy, the treatment of the poor, and the economic rôle of the state, there was much overlapping of position as between the political parties, at least during the first half of the century. By the middle of the century all the political parties as parties had accepted, or had ceased to contest, the free trade doctrine which stemmed from Adam Smith and which all the major economists except Malthus enthusiastically supported. By the late 1830's there was opposition only from one wing of the Tories and from the extreme radicals to the principle of confining relief to the able-bodied poor on the

basis of "less eligibility"; that is, of granting it only in such unattrac-
tive form that the incentives to industry, thrift, and prudential
control of the birth-rate should not be undermined, a principle
developed with almost complete agreement by the classical economists on the strength of Smithian individualism, Benthamite-
Malthusian population theory, and the Malthusian-Ricardian law of
diminishing returns, plus in all probability a large dose of unconscious puritanism. The period from 1800 to 1850 was, whatever
party was in power, fairly consistently a period of piecemeal legislative repeal, item by item, of the mass of legislation restrictive of
domestic freedom of enterprise which had survived on the statute
books from the mercantilist period, and this trend also was aided and
abetted by all the classical economists from the Benthamites, at one
extreme, to the most conservative Whigs, like Malthus and Senior,
at the other. On the major political issues of the first half of the
century, therefore, while there might be a question as to whether
the classical economists were determining the historical trend, or
merely riding it, it is clear that they were not fighting it. It can
now be seen, if it was not then possible to do so, that what conflict there then was between legislators and economists turned for
the most part on the pace, and not on the general direction, of the
legislative activity.

Even the Tory party, whose basic political philosophy seemed
to be that all institutions were evil when new and irreproachable
when aged, was moving, though slowly, reluctantly, and with
misgivings and internal dissension, on the paths mapped out for it
by the anti-Tory economists. It is in fact a paradox in the history
of the relations of economics and politics in early nineteenth century
England that the one political movement of importance which the
historians most unitedly ascribe to the influence of the economists,
the advocacy of extreme *laissez-faire* by the Manchester School,
was the only one which the leading economists felt impelled expressly to denounce as going counter to, or at least beyond, the
teachings of political economy. In so far as the dogmatic *laissez-faire*
position of the Manchester School found in its own day, aside from
the tariff question, any adherents among the ranks of economists,
these were Continental or American economists. John Stuart Mill,
Senior, Cairnes, McCulloch, Torrens, Longfield, the only English
economists of note of the period, all sharply dissociated themselves
from some at least of the doctrines of the Manchester School and

denied its pretensions to support from the "principles of political economy." The classical economists did espouse *laissez-faire*, but a *laissez-faire* avowedly subject to qualification and requiring specific justification in each case of potential application.

The Manchester School, in any case, had but a brief period of power. The growing information—and exaggeration—about working and living conditions in the factory towns, the steadily increasing political power of the working classes even under the restricted suffrage of the Reform Act of 1832, and the widespread humanitarian reaction against the doctrine of governmental impotence to remedy unmerited distress, made support of governmental inaction as a policy increasingly dangerous politically to any party which committed itself too strongly to it. With the establishment by the second Reform Act of 1867 of very nearly complete adult male suffrage, it became necessary for both the aristocratic Conservative or Tory party and the by-now predominantly middle-class Liberal party, if either were to gain or retain power as against the other, and if a third and "subversive" working-class party, as strong as or stronger than they, was not to come into being, to woo the working classes by support of a policy of wider governmental activity in relief of distress and poverty. Social reform through legislation thereafter became respectable political doctrine for both parties, and reform legislation in fact obtained active support alternately or simultaneously from both major parties during the remainder of the century.

During the period of Marshall's youth, John Stuart Mill was the only economist of great public eminence, and Mill, who in his own youth had been one of the original Benthamites, had in his intellectual development absorbed something from almost every major humanitarian and utopian current of his time while managing substantially to retain most of the form and much of the substance of the sterner doctrines of the Bentham-James Mill-Ricardo circle under whose discipline he had been brought up to a too-precocious maturity. With his too-catholic blending of the dour individualism and the unrelenting *a priori* political democracy of the classical school, the utopianism of the Owenites and the St. Simonians, the patriarchal humanitarianism of Wordsworth and Coleridge, and the new misgivings as to the workings of political democracy and social equalitarianism in actual practice as revealed in the United States, John Stuart Mill was the connecting link with respect to political presuppositions for Marshall, as for many later economists in England (and also in the United States), between the classical school of the 1820's and the late-Victorian neoclassical economics. It is substantially true that from the 1870's on all English economic *theorists* of any note were, although with varying degrees of certitude and enthusiasm, political liberals of the John Stuart Mill type. It incidentally seems also to be substantially true that all the English economic *historians* of note were conservative, imperialist, anti-democratic, in their political tendencies, or else went far beyond the liberals in their advocacy of radical social and economic reforms.

The data available on Marshall's political opinions are scanty and scattered. They suffice, however, to support the following summary of the substance and content of his political liberalism as being probably correct as far as it goes:

(1) Marshall was a believer in political democracy, meaning by it essentially universal (male) suffrage, decisions reached by free discussion and by majority vote, and an electorate educated at public expense. In the Benthamite tradition, he held these beliefs not on natural rights grounds, but on the utilitarian ground that they were essential for good government.

(2) Marshall was an individualist in most of the many senses of the term. His ultimate criterion for appraising the social value of any policy was the nature of its probable impact upon the character and well-being of *individuals*. His appraisals of policies and trends were always in terms of what they did for individuals, singly or in groups, and never in terms of their contribution to the prestige or power of an idealized "state" distinguishable from its people. His hope for social progress rested primarily on the capacity for industry, thrift, enterprise, voluntary coöperation, and "economic chivalry," of enlightened individuals, and he had limited, though some, faith in the possibilities of betterment through restrictive or coercive legislation or through the direct exercise of governmental enterprise in the economic field.

(3) Marshall also was essentially a political equalitarian in the Bentham-J. S. Mill sense. He not only wished every (male) adult to count as one and only as one in the machinery of political democracy, but he believed, with the English classical school, that in so far as there were significant differences in the capacities and the economic status of the different social classes these class differences were for the most part not due to biological differences in innate

capacity or character as between individuals but were due instead to environmental differences, to inequality of opportunity: "the poverty of the poor [was] the chief cause of that weakness and inefficiency which are the cause of their poverty."[1]

(4) Basically, Marshall's political doctrines carried the hallmark also of Victorian complacency and gentility. While he recognized the problem of poverty as a major one, he never revealed any doubt that it could be substantially resolved within the limits of British parliamentary democracy and of a free enterprise economy. He was impatient alike with theories of economic history which treated economic and social progress as if it was in any sense inevitable or automatic, and with pessimistic theories which treated it as impossible, or as impossible without revolutionary political changes. He was confident that if only there were sufficient goodwill ("economic chivalry") and economic understanding substantial progress would in fact occur, and he evidently had faith in the effectiveness of sound moral preaching to produce the goodwill and of sound Cambridge economics to produce the understanding. The progress he sought, moreover, was not to be merely a matter of more goods, but of access to and liking for a more leisurely and more refined life for *all* the people, so that even hod-carriers could be gentlemen. The stamp of these political doctrines is perceptible throughout his economic writings.

II

Marshall is said by his biographers to have come to economics from ethics. But his early interest in ethics arose out of his search for a guide to his conscience rather than from an intellectual interest in the metaphysical aspects of moral philosophy. In his younger days at Cambridge as student and teacher the conflict waged hot between utilitarian and idealistic theories of ethics, but there is no evidence that Marshall ever took real interest in this controversy or believed that it had immediate significance for his economics. It would be more accurate, I think, on the basis of the available evidence, to say that Marshall came to economics from his morals, from his zeal to make a contribution to the social betterment of man. Of the many passages in his writings which reveal Marshall's

---

1. "The Present Position of Economics" (1885), in A. C. Pigou, ed., *Memorials of Alfred Marshall* (London, Macmillan, 1925), p. 155.

conviction that it is the duty of educated men to strive for the
improvement of social conditions, and that a sound and moralized
economics is a valuable instrument to this end, and his self-dedica-
tion to economics in this spirit, the following are representative:

Is there not a great fund of conscientiousness and unselfishness latent
in the breasts of men, both rich and poor, which could be called out if the
problems of life were set before them in the right way, and which would
cause misery and poverty rapidly to diminish?[2]

It will be my most cherished ambition, my highest endeavour, to do
what with my poor ability and my limited strength I may, to increase the
numbers of those, whom Cambridge, the great mother of strong men,
sends out into the world with cool heads but warm hearts, willing to give
some at least of their best powers to grappling with the social suffering
around them; resolved not to rest content till they have done what in
them lies to discover how far it is possible to open up to all the material
means of a refined and noble life.[3]

... I have devoted myself for the last twenty-five years to the problem
of poverty, and ... very little of my work has been devoted to any inquiry
which does not bear on that.[4]

I see no grounds for questioning either Marshall's complete
sincerity in this connection, or the conformity of his life as a whole
—which of course does not mean the whole of his life in every detail
—to his announced principles. The moral earnestness with which
Marshall regarded the rôle of economics and his own rôle as an
economist was thoroughly Victorian, was altogether in keeping
with the spirit of his times in liberal educated circles. If, in so far
as simple formulae ever have validity when applied to the thought
of a generation, late eighteenth century thought can be said to
have reflected enlightenment without zeal, light without warmth,
and our present-day world to exhibit zeal without enlightenment,
heat without light, then it may be remembered that the late Victorian age in which Marshall reached maturity was the age of "sweet-
ness *and* light," of reason tempered—some would say alloyed—by
pity.

There are genuine differences in tone here between the Benthamite economists of the 1820's and Marshall. In one of the passages

2. Lecture by Marshall (1883) quoted in "In Memoriam: Alfred Marshall," by
Pigou, *op. cit.*, p. 83.
3. "The Present Position of Economics" (1885), *ibid.*, p. 174.
4. Alfred Marshall, "Minutes of Evidence taken before the Royal Commission
on the Aged Poor, June 5, 1893," *Official Papers* (London, Macmillan for the
Royal Economic Society, 1926), p. 205.

I have cited, Marshall spoke of the need for "cool heads but warm hearts." Bentham and his followers laid more stress on the dangers than on the benefits which might result from warmheartedness. The Benthamites had, as much as Marshall, dedicated their lives to the betterment of the conditions of the mass of mankind, and Marshall, like the Benthamites, believed that charity and goodwill unguided and unrestrained by "sound" general principles could do more harm than good. But Bentham's circle believed that acquaintance with sound principles was more urgently needed than goodwill. In Marshall's case this does not seem to be true, for Marshall seems on the whole to have been more fearful of too little stress on the heart than of too little exercise of the mind. There is a passage in Marshall's writings which is interesting not only because of its bearing on this point but also because it is the only passage in all of Marshall's writings in which I have been able to detect the slightest taint of humor—and even here it may well have been unconscious:

> G. Possibilities of Discrimination
> [between worthy and unworthy]
> . . . .
> 9. Patience in bearing other people's
> sufferings is as clear a duty as patience
> in bearing one's own, but it may be
> carried too far.[5]

John Stuart Mill was here again the connecting link between the Benthamites and Marshall. Under the influence largely of Wordsworth, he had reacted against his father's and Bentham's social philosophy as unduly cold and hard, and as lacking the moderating element obtainable from giving a larger rôle to "feeling." Mill introduced into the main line of English economic thought the sentimentality, the heart-throbbing, which Bentham, James Mill, Ricardo, McCulloch, Malthus, and Senior had carefully avoided. John Stuart Mill had thus made it more difficult for the humanitarians and the tear-evoking novelists to accuse the economists of having made it possible to freeze one's heart and yet live at peace with one's conscience. When Bagehot wrote, in a not wholly facetious vein, that "no real Englishman in his secret soul was ever sorry for the

---

5. "Royal Commission on the Aged Poor (1893). Memorandum and Evidence offered to the Commissioners by Professor Alfred Marshall. (i) Preliminary Memorandum. A. Preliminary Statement." *Ibid.*, pp. 202-3.

death of a political economist; he is much more likely to be sorry
for his life," it was not economists like J. S. Mill or Marshall whom
he had in mind. In any case, once Marshall had become the leading
British economist it ceased to be a common charge against economics that "it dries up the hearts and the imaginations of the most
who meddle with it" (Miss Lucy Aikin), or that all that it asked of
men "is that they should harden their hearts" (Robert Southey);
and the question whether humane men could be devotees of the
dismal science had ceased to be a live one.

While it could be argued that these were more largely differences
in mode of expression as between the Benthamites and Marshall,
corresponding merely to changes in verbal style, than differences in
substance, it seems clear that Marshall's lesser willingness to be
patient about the immediate woes of the poor led him actively to
seek means of reconciliation between advocacy of relief of distress
on humanitarian grounds and adherence to the Benthamite principle
that it was urgent to preserve unimpaired by excessive charity the
capacity for and the will to practice self-help on the part of the
poor. To take one instance: the classical economists, in appraising
the claims of the aged poor to generous relief, held that, as old age
was a foreseeable contingency, in general provision for it should be
regarded as an individual responsibility. They drew no distinction
between absence of reserves for old age due to expenditures on gin,
on the one hand, and to expenditures on the education, nutrition
and health of children, on the other. Marshall expressly refused to
follow them on this point:

> Too much stress is often laid both from the ethical and from the eco-
> nomical point of view on those forms of thrift which result in material
> provision for sickness and old age, in comparison with those forms which
> benefit the coming generation.
> This is greatly due to the influence exerted on the administrators of
> poor-relief and charity by the economic and social philosophy of the early
> years of this century.[6]

When Marshall spoke of the task of economics to search for
methods of opening up to all "the material means of a refined and
noble life," he again used language which the Benthamites would
not have found to their taste. Bentham would have spoken instead
in terms of making available greater provision for the poor, without setting limits as to the amount to be desired of such increase

---

6. *Ibid.*, p. 202.

in provision or inquiring as to its contribution to the refinement or ennobling of the life of the poor, provided only it contributed to their happiness. To Bentham, or so he claimed at least, "pushpin was equal to poetry" if they produced equal quantities of happiness, and he and his followers carefully avoided resort to any criterion for appraisal of the use which men made of their resources except its effect on their own, or their neighbors', or their children's happiness.

Here again John Stuart Mill was the connecting link between the strict utilitarianism of the early classical school, on the one hand, and the Victorian stress on refinement and nobility of Marshall, on the other hand; for Mill had diluted the Benthamite doctrine by insisting that over and above the purely quantitative differences between utilities there was a hierarchy of higher-and-lower, nobler-and-less-noble utilities which should be taken into account. Whatever may be the merits of this issue, and it is one on which there still seems to be as much room for inconclusive debate as there was when it was first raised, for Marshall the choice in favor of Mill as against Bentham was a convenient one. It not only put him in accord with the dominant ethical thought in the Cambridge of his time, but it also enabled him to retain an evangelistical note in his economics even after he had on intellectual grounds eliminated it from his theology.

Marshall, however, never explicitly discussed these ethical issues, and in fact sought deliberately to avoid being entrapped into open discussion thereof and into formal statement of his position by using as colorless and irenic terms as were available to express the ethical implications and presuppositions of his economics. Without surrendering or completely concealing his position, he thus succeeded fairly well in escaping the necessity of ever having to defend it.

III

Marshall came to economics also from mathematics. Educated at Cambridge, noted for its emphasis on the educational and disciplinary value of rigorous training in mathematics, he attained high distinction in that field as a student. He taught mathematics before he taught economics. He had not only distinct aptitude but also great liking for mathematical forms of reasoning. It is clear, however, that he had grave mistrust of the consequences of unrestrained employment of formal mathematics in economic analysis. One factor in this distrust was probably a lurking puritan suspicion of the morality of any highly pleasurable activity: the formulation and solution of economic problems in mathematical, and especially graphical, terms yielded him so much intellectual and aesthetic delight that it for that reason alone became somewhat suspect to him as a worthy occupation. Mathematics, and especially graphs, were Marshall's fleshpots, and if he frequently succumbed to their lure it was not without struggle with his conscience. It can also be said for Marshall that when he did succumb he not only frequently warned his readers not to take his mathematical adventures too seriously but shielded them from the young and the susceptible by confining them to footnotes and appendices where, as he rightly anticipated, only the hardened sinners already beyond further corruption would prolongedly gaze. Marshall also was anxious for a wide audience, and the fact that the bulk of his potential readers were both unable and unwilling to read economics in mathematical form no doubt was an additional consideration.

But Marshall had other and presumably better reasons for misgivings as to the effect on economics of the extensive use of mathematics. First, the mathematical approach required rigorous abstraction, whereas Marshall thought that the economist must strive to account for the concrete. Secondly, although this may not be wholly a different consideration, Marshall believed that economics must become more complicated and more biological in character, whereas mathematical economics tended toward excessive simplification and sought its prototype rather in mechanics than in biology.

Marshall from the first had a live sense of the complexity and variability of the interrelations between economic phenomena, and of the biological rather than mechanical nature of these interrelations. During his early years at Cambridge, as student and as teacher, the influence of Darwin and of Huxley was strong. Cambridge was becoming a center for distinguished work in the biological sciences, challenging in intellectual prestige to some extent the traditional academic aristocracies of theology, philosophy, the classics, and mathematics and the physical sciences. While I know of no evidence that Marshall was ever a serious student of biology, and I have been unable to find that there was any personal intimacy between Marshall and the distinguished Cambridge biologists, physiologists, pathologists, psychologists, and so forth of his time, biological ideas were then very much in the air, and could be absorbed without special effort. In any case, Marshall saw in bioligical rather than in mechanical modes of thought the most suitable instruments of economic analysis. ". . . in the later stages of economics, when we are approaching nearly to the conditions of life, biological analogies are to be preferred to mechanical, other things being equal. . . . The Mecca of the economist is economic biology rather than economic dynamics."[7]

The biological sciences have in fact proved least tractable of all the natural sciences to abstract mathematical analysis, for largely the same reasons, I suppose, which in all probability led Marshall, and others, to see but a limited scope for the fruitful use of mathematics in economic theory: (1) great complexity of the problems; (2) significant variables too great in number for their separate analysis and yet not great enough in number to make reliance upon technical probability theory without specific analysis of particular variables a safe procedure; (3) the absence of reversibility in the interactions of variables; (4) the restricted scope for completely controlled experiment; (5) the absence of that complete indifference of the investigator to the material with which he is working and to the nature of his results which is the only reliable guarantee of scientific objectivity which we can have.

Devotees of the mathematical approach to economic problems frequently claim for that approach that the alternative non-symbolic method, or the "literary method" as they too generously put it, is too imprecise and clumsy a tool for the exposition in all their complexity of the relationships between economic variables, with the implication that it is the complexity of economic problems, rather than their simplicity, which establishes a necessary and fruitful field for the use of mathematics. Marshall, both in his formal writings and in his letters of warning to his disciples against overindulgence in mathematics, seems to me to have taken exactly the reverse view, although not in so many words; namely: that non-symbolic language and simple statistical methods alone had the elasticity to deal with the infinite detail and variability of concrete economic phenomena; that resort to mathematics, unless confined to a preliminary stage of economic investigation, involved a greater degree of surrender of this elasticity than it was wise to accept; and that only

7. "Distribution and Exchange" (1898), *Memorials*, pp. 317-18.

the relatively simple propositions in economics could be expressed in mathematical form, and even then only at the cost of artificial and often serious further simplification. It must have been the complexities of the biological as distinguished from the mechanical aspects of economic problems which Marshall had in mind, for I cannot see how he could have intended to deny that, whatever the degree of complexity of the mechanical type economic problems may involve, they can be handled better with than without the aid of mathematics.

There was still another element leading Marshall to cry down the value of the mathematical method. Marshall, at least in his frequent moralizing moods, placed no high value on economic analysis as a good in itself, as a cultural pursuit or a substitute for chess. Writing to Edgeworth in 1902, he said:

> In my view "Theory" is essential. No one gets any real grip of economic problems unless he will work at it. But I conceive no more calamitous notion than that abstract, or general, or "theoretical" economics was "economics" proper. It seems to me an essential but a very small part of economics proper: and by itself sometimes even—well, not a very good occupation of time.[8]

From this and other passages it can be inferred that Marshall, believing as he did that it was "pure theory" which lent itself most fully to mathematical exposition, that for economics to be a serviceable instrument of human betterment it must be extended to include consideration of the concrete detail not readily or at all amenable to abstract mathematical treatment, and that the attraction of mathematics led some economists to neglect the concrete detail and to confine themselves to pure theorizing, minimized the usefulness of mathematics to economics in order to check the tendency toward what he regarded as undue abstraction.[9]

I am no mathematician myself, and I try always to remember and to profit from Edgeworth's merited reproof to an Italian economist who had had the temerity to question the usefulness of

---

8. Letter by Marshall to Professor F. Y. Edgeworth (1902), *ibid.*, p. 437.
9. *Cf.* J. M. Keynes, "Alfred Marshall, 1842-1924," *ibid.*, p. 37: ". . . Marshall was too anxious to do good. He had an inclination to undervalue those intellectual parts of the subject which were not *directly* connected with human well-being or the condition of the working classes or the like, although *indirectly* they might be of the utmost importance, and to feel that when he was pursuing them he was not occupying himself with the Highest. . . . When his intellect chased diagrams and Foreign Trade and Money, there was an evangelical moraliser of an imp somewhere inside him, that was so ill-advised as to disapprove."

Edgeworth's application of the mathematical method to taxation problems: "The withers of the mathematician are not wrung by these commonplaces. The use of the method is not necessarily attended with an exaggeration of its importance. The inability to use it is not a qualification for appreciating its usefulness." Professional mathematicians have assured me, moreover, that the uninitiated can have no conception of the feats which can be performed by the aid of the elastic, the precise, the versatile, and the delicate apparatus of the modern higher mathematics. Although they have also upon occasion suggested to me that economists are pressing it to perform false miracles, I venture no disclaimer, therefore, of whatever general or specific claims for their method mathematical economists may make, provided they are confined to mathematical claims beyond my understanding or ability to test. But non-mathematical economists with an inferiority-complex—which today includes, I feel certain, very nearly all non-mathematical economists —may be pardoned, perhaps, if they derive a modest measure of unsanctified joy from the spectacle of the great Marshall, a pioneer in mathematical economics himself, disparaging the use of mathematics in economics, and counting as wasted effort the mastery of any other economist's mathematical symbols. If, as seems doubtful, Marshall's warnings served to dissuade any budding Cambridge economic geniuses with aptitude for mathematics from acquiring an abundant command of its techniques, they no doubt served economics ill rather than well. But if they helped to check the descent of economics to the status of an unwanted foundling on mathematics' doorstep, they did render a useful service.

If Marshall's puritan conscience led him to disparage the method from which he undoubtedly derived the greatest intellectual excitement and joy, even that over-scrupulous conscience occasionally took a holiday. Marshall recognized that the instruments for a general ethical calculus were lacking, but he claimed that the institution of money provided an adequate basis for calculations of *economic* satisfaction and sacrifice: "The pure science of Ethics halts for lack of a system of measurement of efforts, sacrifices, desires, etc., fit for her wide purposes. But the pure science of Political Economy has found a system that will subserve her narrower aims."[10]

Marshall was well aware and repeatedly acknowledged that the

10. "Mr. Mill's Theory of Value" (1876), *ibid.*, p. 126.

monetary unit represented substantially different quantities of satisfaction and of sacrifice for rich and for poor, respectively. It would seem that this was an insuperable barrier to the use of market prices as a measurement of such satisfaction and sacrifice as between different persons, and that, with his acceptance of the problem of poverty as the major problem for economics, Marshall would have felt obliged to recognize that even for a calculus of economic happiness no satisfactory instruments of measurement were available. His zeal for quasi-quantitative analysis and for reaching value-judgments overcame, however, his other scruples, and he adopted an analytical procedure which operated to distract attention from the necessity of making full allowance for the inequality in the distribution of wealth and income in reaching such value-judgments. In a passage in his *Principles* which has not escaped unfavorable notice by others, Marshall offered what must be regarded as a glaringly weak defense of this procedure:

On the whole, . . . it happens that by far the greater number of the events with which economics deals, affect in about equal proportions all the different classes of society; so that if the money measures of the happiness caused by two events are equal, there is not in general any very great difference between the amounts of the happiness in the two cases.[11]

Marshall was here setting up a screen between himself and his readers, on the one hand, and the problem of poverty on the other, in order to be free to engage, without too sharp pangs of conscience, in what was for himself a delectable intellectual activity. This was not Marshall at his best, however, nor even the normal Marshall, and there have been few of us who have made conscience be our guide as to subjects of investigation and methods of analysis as steadily and as consistently as did Marshall.

I do not regard it as part of my function to render a definite appraisal of Marshall as man or as economist. In any case, those aspects of Marshall's work with which I have dealt are not really matters for appraisal, and narration and description are all that is called for. That Marshall was a great figure, one of the greatest, of our discipline, and that without being by any means flawless he nevertheless fully earned his status, I would strongly argue if I

---

11. Alfred Marshall, *Principles of Economics,* 6th ed., p. 131.

knew of sufficient dissent from significant quarters and on significant grounds to give any point to such argument.

But Marshall is now long dead, and the rule "De mortuis non nisi bonum" is a required rule of morals or of good manners only for men very recently dead. There would be no point therefore in treating Marshall, whether the man or his work, with special tenderness or reserve. He had, beyond doubt, his weaknesses on both counts, including some with which he may have infected his followers, so that we regard them as points of strength. I am sure also that even his virtues are not to be admired by us to the point of slavish imitation. Each generation should—and will—work out its own economics, borrowing from, reacting from, improving upon, retrograding from, that of the preceding generation. Marshall's economics is now distinctly that of a generation which is past, and is increasingly *not* that of our own. For one thing, it is essentially the economics of a society assumed to be free and to have its economic affairs conducted by free individuals. Freedom, whether of the economic system as such, or of individuals, has over a large part of the earth's surface either never existed or been suppressed. The appropriate economics of the day is, moreover, the economics of war and preparation for or against war, *Wehrwirtschaft*, and Marshall here has only very limited guidance to offer.

It was a characteristic of Victorian, including Marshallian, public utterances that they typically ended on a double note, of assurance, on the one hand, of continuance into the future of all the well-established institutions and cherished values of the Victorian Age, and of promise, on the other hand, of continued betterment of the social conditions of mankind. Both the Victorian complacency with respect to the present and the Victorian optimism with respect to future progress are now utterly inappropriate. As a social philosopher, Marshall is not yet merely a period piece. If he should become so in the near future, it would properly be a matter for concern, but not for surprise.

Clapham on the Bank of England*

Sir John Clapham wrote this history of the Bank of England[1] at the invitation of the Bank, as part of its celebration of its 250th anniversary. This is not, however, one of those ceremonial histories of banks with which we are only too familiar in which the excess of uncritical praise is matched only by the deficiency of significant information. This is a thoroughly scholarly account, heavily packed with relevant detail, of the record of the Bank through rough times and quiet years, in its relations with the Government, the money market, its customers, and its shareholders. All the records of the Bank were thrown open to Sir John, and he was left perfectly free to write as he saw fit. While the result is in my opinion somewhat too generous to the Bank, the occasion called for a reasonable display of human kindness, and at no time does the work descend to eulogy, while at some points the comments have a sharp enough sting. Except for a brief "Epilogue," the history ends with 1914. All comments made in this review on the record of the Bank are likewise without reference to the years since 1914.

Everyone is agreed that the Bank of England has been a remarkable institution, and this history makes it clearer in what respects it has been remarkable. Perhaps the most unusual aspect of the Bank's record has been its longevity. No other bank except the Bank of St. George, Genoa, as far as I know had anything like as long an unbroken history, and an earlier start than most of its rivals is not a sufficient explanation, since it had predecessors and since it has seen many other institutions rise, have their comparatively brief day in the sun, and then vanish—usually with a bang. Except for the Bank of England, it does not seem to be in the nature

*Reprinted from *Economica*, New Series, Vol. 12, May 1945, pp. 61-68, by the courtesy of the London School of Economics and Political Science.

1. Sir John Clapham, *The Bank of England*, Vol. I, *1694-1797*; Vol. II, *1797-1914*. The Cambridge University Press, Cambridge, *1944*, ix, 305 pp.; vii, 460 pp. 48s.

of banking institutions to last forever, or forever to deserve to last. The nearest rivalry in durability that can be claimed for any lending agency, public or private, that I know anything about is that of the Amsterdam private banking-house of the Gebroeders Neufville, which collapsed during the international crisis of 1763 after something like two centuries of active operations, and survival seems to have been more difficult for financial institutions in the late eighteenth and the nineteenth than in the seventeenth and early eighteenth centuries. The Bank of England had one or two narrow squeaks, and it had its due share of good luck. But its durability, financial and political, must be attributed mostly to the conservatism of its management and to the moderation, at least since 1689, of English politics.

The continued, and for the most part steadily-growing, prestige of the Bank is also a remarkable feature of its history, especially if it is considered that its resources were never great, its range of activities unspectacular for the most part, its directorate on the whole a very moderately distinguished lot either in the financial field or otherwise, and its facilities for winning public favor by well-designed publicity as to its achievements practically non-existent. Not much contribution to an explanation of the continued prestige of the Bank, as far as I can see, is made by this study of its history. It may be that the public did not like the long succession of critics by whom the Bank has been tormented, for these critics while often able and well-informed were also often partisan and sharp-tongued. It may also be that the longevity of the Bank largely explains its prestige—and the prestige of the Bank its longevity—especially since it operated in a country which has had the gift of endowing even its raw vintages with savor if it poured them from ancient enough decanters, and has had the sense not to smash its old bottles.

Remarkable also was the constitution of the Bank, if it be regarded as primarily a central bank, with major responsibilities for regulating, in the national interest, the national currency and keeping the national money market in good order. The authority for managing the Bank's affairs rested throughout its history with a small inner group of its directors, selected from the ranks of its shareholders. Anyone who wished to could buy shares in the open market, which were almost always a good investment and sometimes a good speculation, and except at the foundation of the Bank apparently no one ever bought the shares, or was asked to buy them, otherwise than on the basis of their financial attractions. The directors, moreover, were further limited to London merchants and merchant bankers, could rise to the highest Bank offices largely by seniority and financial respectability, without need of other more intellectual qualifications, and as directors were not expected to suspend any of their other business activities, even when these were such—as they often were—as to bring into direct conflict their personal interests and the interests and responsibilities of the Bank as central bank. No one, I am sure, would today even dream of setting up a new central bank on such a pattern. It is a tribute to the basic integrity and sense of social responsibility of the London businessman, and to the benevolent disposition toward England of a watchful Providence, that throughout its history the Bank escaped all but minor scandals and never suffered from worse than moderately bad management.

Sir John Clapham's history of this remarkable institution is a notable achievement, a splendid addition to his long record of productive scholarship in the field of economic history. To have accomplished it in the midst of the strains and stresses, physical and psychological, of a beleaguered England makes it all the more noteworthy. If the reviewer, nevertheless, asks for more at some points than the author has given, or asks for a different way of handling the available factual material, this is not intended to suggest that Sir John was under any obligation to write a different kind of a book. It is in the nature of economic historians to write historical narrative, as of economic theorists to expound hypotheses unsupported by historical investigation, and there is no reason to expect the twain to meet. Sir John, in particular, has made clear that he is not fond of the empty economic boxes of the theorists and has not made evident any great urge to fill them with the product of his own historical researches. His detailed account of the history of the Bank, if supplemented in several directions, should, however, make possible a more searching analysis of the rôle of the Bank in relation to the British national economy and to the international gold standard than has hitherto been practicable. It is predominantly with a view to suggesting some of the possibilities in this direction that I later venture to point out some of the aspects of the Bank's history on which we still are left knowing less than it would be good for us to know.

Meanwhile, I must pay tribute to the merits of Sir John's English, which I find admirably suited to his purposes. The book before us is marked throughout by rigorous economy of verbiage, precision of expression, unadorned but none the less graceful simplicity of exposition. The severity of the style is engagingly softened here and there by skilful turns of phrase which reveal a sense of humor kept under strict control. There is a welcome interest in the personalities of the important actors, and a notable capacity to sketch them revealingly in a few deftly-chosen words.

We are told much that was not known before, or not known clearly and authoritatively, about the operations and the fortunes of the Bank, its leading spirits, and the sources of its income. This is especially true with respect to the eighteenth century, and if sometimes what we are given suffices only to whet but not to satisfy our appetites, it is usually the meagerness of the Bank's records and not any shortcoming on Sir John's part which is responsible.

We are told a good deal about the operations of the Bank as, in effect, accountant and paymaster of the National Debt, and we get a glimpse of the hard bargaining which periodically recurred as to the terms on which the Bank should perform this administrative task for the Government. That this routine governmental function should ever have been entrusted to the Bank and, once so entrusted, that it should have been left there and indeed increasingly lodged there, without ever, apparently, giving rise to any demand from any quarter that it be recaptured, seems to me, however, to call for some explanation. In the days of *laissez faire* and civil service, it could no doubt be explained as a reflection of the Government's aversion to administrative burdens untempered by any realizable ambitions for the fruits of patronage. But what about the eighteenth century, when *laissez faire* was perhaps already practice but not yet principle, and when even grossly corrupt patronage was thoroughly respectable in the highest of circles? It would be interesting to know whether any other government, even within the British Empire, has ever made a similar delegation of its routine administrative obligations with respect to its internal debt. For the Bank, the importance of its management of debt-service seems to have been confined to its constituting a substantial, and needed, source of revenue.

On the most important aspect of the Bank's history from the national point of view, its rôle as regulator of the national money market, something, but not very much, is added to what was known before, and little if any revision is called for of the previous accounts with respect either to the general sequence of events or to the appraisal of the quality of the Bank's functioning. It seems clear that as a rule in times of crisis the Bank kept its head and did as much as it knew how to do—which at times was not much—occasionally at heavy cost and with rather serious financial risk to itself. But in quiet times and in times of prosperity it pursued with ful vigor the maximization of its profits, and it is not clear how its pattern of behavior at such times differed from what it would have been if there had been absolutely no question of its having any special public responsibilities or any obligations not equally shared by all other respectable banking institutions. By no means always, but occasionally, Sir John himself seems to take rather lightly these special responsibilities of the Bank, and to accept its own mediocre standards of proper behavior. For instance, with reference to an increase in dividend payments by the Bank in the crisis year, 1847, he comments: "A year of heavy discounts always provided funds for good dividends, and the Court is not to be blamed much for proposing them, nor proprietors for accepting" (II, 204). Or again, with reference to 1907: "Reserves might be too small, as everyone had been saying for thirty years and more, but they were handled and thrown into the fight with effect. And if that could be counted on, the British economy in reserve keeping could be defended. There is no call for bigger strategic reserves than will win your battles" (II, 389). True perhaps. But it was only the Bank's battles which these reserves sufficed to win completely. *England's* battles were on such occasions always lost, partially at least.

It is a commonplace that England was during the nineteenth century the efficient manager of the international gold standard, and that the Bank of England was the agency through which this management was applied. It is extraordinary, however, how little systematic study of the workings of the pre-1914 gold standard has ever been engaged in, and how little concrete evidence has been available as to the extent or the quality of its management. Except for the contribution to the prestige and the durability of the standard which England—and the Bank—made by maintaining unquestioned convertibility of "sterling" into gold throughout almost a century and by maintaining during the same period an absolutely free gold market, this history of the Bank reveals little or nothing to confirm the belief that the Bank, or any other English institution, deliberately or otherwise "managed" the gold standard.

Management of the gold standard could have taken a number of forms. By accumulation of excess gold reserves in good times and their release in times of strain, the Bank, or England, could have exerted a stabilizing influence on world price levels, counteracting both inflationary and deflationary tendencies as they manifested themselves. But the outstanding feature of English gold reserves during the nineteenth century was their inadequacy not only for this global task but even to preserve convertibility of sterling without frequent recourse to otherwise wholly undesirable deflationary pressure by the Bank on the English national economy. It may be that the need of the Bank for income for dividend-paying purposes was an adequate justification for the Bank's failure to accumulate larger gold reserves from its own capital resources. But there were many ways in which the Government could have made it possible for the Bank to acquire adequate gold reserves without depletion of its revenues. As far as England as a whole was concerned, it managed to operate its part of the international gold standard throughout the nineteenth century on an investment in gold stocks pitiably small in relation to the benefits which would have accrued to it and to the world if there had been less parsimony in this connection. The Banque de France and the Reichsbank seem to have had a better record in this respect.

There can be no doubt that London in the nineteenth century provided a wholly efficient and economical clearing-house for the exchange-business of the world. Until the 1880's, in fact, practically all overseas financial transactions were cleared in London and in terms of sterling. But this was profitable business for the London houses engaged in it, and if London had provided poorer facilities or charged higher commissions other money markets would gladly have replaced it. I know of no evidence as to the extent to which London was "banker" as well as "clearer." To the extent that sterling balances were serviceable abroad as monetary reserves, London, by granting credit abroad more freely in times of strain and contracting it in times of dangerous expansion, could have exercised a stabilizing rôle *vis-à-vis* the international gold standard despite the exiguous character of her gold reserves. But I know of no evidence that London played such a rôle, and as far as available information goes it may even be possible that London typically reduced her credits to abroad when it was most urgent that she should expand them and expanded them when contraction would have been more beneficial. It seems clear that as far as long-term loans were concerned England accentuated the cyclical fluctuations in the level of world activity rather than damped them down, and this for all we know may have been true also of her short-term transactions.

There were also important possibilities in international collaboration between central banks in dealing with local or general financial strains. But the Bank of England never showed any interest in developing connections with other central banks and in systematically planning in advance for collaboration in case of need. Instances of such collaboration were not rare in the nineteenth century, but they were always hastily extemporized at the critical moment, and in so far as the Bank of England was a participant it was as recipient rather than as giver of aid except for at the most two or three occasions.

In this field, the Bank of England was completely unenterprising and unimaginative. It contented itself with looking after convertibility of its notes, and left it to other countries to keep their monetary affairs in order in the same narrow sense. If there developed strains on its gold reserves more severe than it could confidently cope with, it was not too proud to accept help from outside when offered to it, and perhaps even upon occasion to solicit it. But as far as the international aspect of the gold standard was concerned, there is nothing in the record of the Bank as related in the work before us, or as previously known, which gives any support to the claim that the Bank "managed" the gold standard. Sir John quotes a former Bank official, Sir Ernest Harvey, as making even a harsher appraisal than this for the period before 1918: "the Bank was amazingly detached from international affairs; heard from no one; saw no one; only watched the gold and took the necessary steps semi-automatically" (II, 401).[2] The meager capital

---

2. An earlier Bank officer, John William Birch, once gave a more flattering account of the Bank's policy and procedures in this connection. In view of the scarcity of informative policy statements emanating from the Bank itself, it is worth quoting *in extenso:* "When I entered the Bank I remember in our discussions as to raising or lowering the Bank rate we were always talking about the balance of trade and trade returns. We know now that the balance of trade has

resources of the Bank, the absence of legislation which would force the large commercial banks to provide the central bank with the monetary resources necessary for effective control of the money market both in its internal and its international aspects, and the restricted view the Bank took of its responsibilities, may have had as a fortunate by-product that the Bank was not likely to involve England in serious economic difficulties through foolish positive action on its part. But they also prevented the Bank from even approaching full realization of its possibilities for service to the national economy and to the world economy.

Sir John, in this and other connections, never disregards the major issues in the record of the Bank about which controversy has been waged for over a century, never lapses into unwarranted praise of the Bank or into treatment of its shortcomings as if they were virtues, and occasionally makes adverse criticisms which are not less effective for being made calmly and regretfully. His general procedure, however, with its emphasis on the year-to-year sequence of events and its disemphasis on systematic appraisal, operates on the whole to give a more favorable impression of the quality of the Bank's administration of affairs than would have resulted from a more analytical examination of the record.

Sir John provides us with some useful statistical data, drawn from the books of the Bank, but more of such material would have been welcome, and there will be extensive scope for comparison by later workers in the field of the data he does provide with other statistical series bearing on the internal and international status of England. The data which he presents with respect to the Bank's loans and discounts in the nineteenth century are given in terms of the revenue they produced for the Bank instead of in the much more significant terms of the fluctuations in their absolute amounts, but this is presumably to be attributed not to undue interest in the

very little to do with our international balancing. The great thing which governs us is the enormous transactions on the Stock Exchange, in France, in Germany, and in the United States. These are the operations we have to follow most carefully. We have to observe the course of the foreign exchanges, and they are more carefully watched than they used to be. We have also to follow the movements of gold, and within the Bank we are not contented with simply working *le jour pour le jour,* but we try to look ahead and forecast what is likely to result from the negotiation of public loans, not only in this country but on the Continent. For instance, if a loan is contracted in Germany for the Argentine Republic it is more than probable that if gold is required, it will be taken not from Germany, but from England." *Journal of the Institute of Bankers,* viii (1887), 509-10. Birch was a director of the Bank from 1860 to 1897 and Governor in 1879–1881.

effect of the Bank's operations on its own financial fortunes but to
the manner in which the Bank kept its accounts. It would be useful
to know, with a view to the facilitation of further study, the full
extent of the records of the Bank available in or convertible into
statistical form for the period, say, from 1832 to 1914.

There follow some minor queries or emendations or elaborations
on details of Sir John's account of the history of the Bank.

A Court Vote of November, 1696, is referred to which gives
depositors "liberty to transfer any Sume from one Account to
another *not* under £5" as probably not starting a policy of permit-
ting inter-depositor transfers by check but only sanctioning and
regulating one "that had grown up to meet daily needs during those
years," *i.e.*, 1694 to 1696 (I, 141, italics mine). But there was an
earlier vote, in May, 1696, publicly advertised, which extended the
same privilege to transfers of "any sum under £5" as a temporary
measure to meet the shortage of means of payment while the recoinage was under way. Is it not as likely that it was the recoinage
which first gave rise to the practice as that, as suggested by Clapham, the Bank had "permitted it from the start"? (I, 142).

Sephardic Jews are referred to, as late as the early eighteenth
century, as having "Portuguese" and "Peninsular" connections in
the trade in bills of exchange and bullion (I, 127 and I, 134-35). This
was no doubt true of the Sephardic Jews in the first half of the
seventeenth century, but had not all their ties with Portugal and
Spain ended before the end of the century?

We are given, for the first time, a consecutive account of the
interesting "Subscription for the Circulation" established in 1711
and continuing until 1759 (I, 67-72). The Bank each year contracted
with the Government to "circulate," or give to holders cash upon
demand for, a specified amount of Exchequer Bills, and each year
took subscriptions from the market, of an underwriting character,
for corresponding amounts. Of these subscriptions, 10 to 20 per
cent were immediately payable in cash, and the remainder upon
demand from the Bank, with forfeiture of the cash already paid
in case of failure to meet the call. Interest was paid on the cash
subscriptions and a "premium" on the amount uncalled, with the
total payments working out at a very generous rate of interest on
the actual amount of cash subscribed. Calls for payment were infrequent, and seem to have been made only when the Bank was

being subjected to a run. This device gave the Bank a call on the money market in case of need and provided a more-or-less assured basis in advance for "borrowing from the market" to replenish its reserves when necessary. Some additional details of the history of the Subscription which I have run across recently may be of interest.

It seems probable that it is to Charles Davenant that the Bank— or the Government—owed the idea of the Subscription. He proposed in 1710 a scheme for financing the Government through issue of exchequer bills whose circulation was to be assured by a method identical with that adopted in the following year, except for one significant detail. Davenant, as a Tory, was hostile to the Bank, and under his scheme it was the Government and not the Bank which was to take subscriptions for circulating the exchequer bills (*New Dialogues*, Vol. II, 1710, pp. 164 ff. For Davenant's authorship of this tract—as well as of several others of the period credited by Sir John Clapham to others—see A. P. Usher's Introduction to *Two Manuscripts by Charles Davenant*, The Johns Hopkins Press, Baltimore, 1942.)

The Subscription was nominally open to the public, but it was so profitable to subscribers—if no call was made—that it was in practice reserved for Bank insiders. A printed copy of what appears to be a subscription blank for the Subscription of 1747 indicates the probable procedure for keeping the general public out. Subscriptions are declared to be acceptable from "all persons," with the proviso, however, of the "Subscribers being Persons with whose Abilities the said Governor and Company are well satisfied." (*A Preamble to the Books for taking a Subscription for Eighteen Hundred Thousand Pounds, for Support of the Credit of the Bank of England, and for circulating Exchequer Bills,* 1747, No. 37. In Kress Library, Harvard University.)

Sir John relates that there were two 20 per cent calls on subscribers in 1714, without further explanation (I, 69). The account given in a later tract throws some light on how the Subscription worked. In January, 1714, a rumor was about of an impending French invasion: "Now though this was entirely a Fiction, yet the Dread of its Reality so affected the Nation, that in an Instant the Public Securities fell, and a prodigious Run was made upon the Bank, who call'd in forty *per* Cent. from the Subscribers to the circulating of the *Exchequer* Bills, and deputed four of their Directors to wait upon the Treasurer in this Exigency to represent the Danger they were under ... (*A Letter from a Bystander to a Member of Parliament,* 1741/2, p. 10).

The account given here (I, 85-90) of the abortive negotiations for assistance by the Bank to the South Sea Company during the crisis in 1720-21 in the latter's affairs mentions Robert Walpole only in connection with the later settlement by arbitration of the claims of the Company against the Bank. A pamphlet written by or on behalf of Walpole which makes use of the original records of the negotiations (*Some Considerations concerning the Publick Funds,* 1735, pp. 85-91) reveals that he had an important rôle in these negotiations from the start, and indicates also that it was only under strong pressure from the Government that the Bank entered into the negotiations at all.

The statement *re* the Act of May 10, 1774, that " the decision of Government to deal with the gold [recoinage] and leave the silver in its existing state—and that could not have been much worse—was in effect the introduction of a gold standard " (I, 176) gives, I think, a misleading impression of the significance of the Act. Before 1774, both gold and silver coin were unlimited legal tender, but silver, at 5/2 per ounce, was undervalued, and gold was already the effective standard. Under the Act of 1774 silver coin was limited as legal tender by tale to £25, but beyond that sum it was still unlimited legal tender by weight at 5/2 per ounce. At that price full-weight silver coin would not have stayed in circulation before or after the Act, and the failure to recoin the silver had the effect, probably intended, of keeping it in circulation rather than of driving it out.

The Phineas Bond " of Philadelphia " cited as an *American* holder of Bank stock in 1801 (I, 289) was British Consul-General at Philadelphia. He had much to say on the damage to British interests allegedly resulting from the flow of British capital to the United States. (Cf. *Annual Report American Historical Association for 1897*, 1898, pp. 536-37.)

We are told that " The relation of the Scottish banking organisation to the English was peculiar, indirect, but important " in the eighteenth century and that " This power [of the Scotch banks] of drawing, directly or indirectly, *on the Bank's gold* for Scottish use was only important in difficult times " (I, 167, 168, italics mine). But Scotland was really on a *de facto* sterling exchange standard in the eighteenth—and nineteenth—century, very much as Canada was on a *de facto* U.S. dollar exchange standard before 1914. To the Scotch banks their power to draw on London to meet adverse balances in England was probably much more important than their power to draw *gold* from England to Scotland, where there would be little call for it even in difficult times.

The reference to Sir John Sinclair as "the reputed inventor of the Exchequer Bill cure for the evils of a crisis," *i.e.*, the special issue of exchequer bills against merchandise or other collateral to relieve a credit crisis (II, 34), is no doubt correct, but I can find no evidence of any such proposal by Sinclair prior to 1784, and the device seems to have been resorted to at least as early as 1782. This use of exchequer bills has theoretical as well as historical interest and someone should investigate its history.

In connection with the suspension of cash payments by the Bank during the Napoleonic Wars, the Bank is said to have gone on "buying gold as it could, at most unremunerative prices" in 1811-1812 (II, 30). Did not the Bank, however, sell the gold, through its bullion department, at the remunerative market prices? There has been some question about the nature of the gold dealings of the Bank during the suspension, and it would have been interesting to know what light the Bank's records throw on this question. I doubt whether it is correct to speak of Francis Horner as a "friend" of Ricardo as early as 1810 (II, 23). "For their stupidities [*i.e.*, those of Vansittart's Resolutions of 1811] the Bank was not responsible" (II, 28). Perhaps not, but the Bank matched them.

"His [Ricardo's] critics have pointed out that as a stock-jobber, with natural 'bear' leanings, Ricardo was interested in anything that would bring down the funds, as a curtailment of Bank issues or a return to convertibility most certainly would" (II, 23). The implication here, of course, was that Ricardo's opposition to the Bank was in part at least to be explained by his selfish profit interests. Silberling, it is true, did "point out" this blemish on Ricardo's record, as did also Angell on the basis of Silberling's data. But the only evidence presented by Silberling was derived from an anonymous pamphlet. (*The Bank—The Stock Exchange—The Bankers . . . An Exposé*, 1821.) Clapham elsewere in this work is very deprecatory of pamphlets as historical sources, especially if they are anonymous and especially if they are unfriendly to the

Bank. Even a cursory examination of this particular pamphlet would reveal that it was the product of a disordered mind. In it the routine business of the stock market is pictured as an elaborate succession of wild plots and conspiracies. Ricardo ("the great David") is described as openly carrying on bear-operations against the Funds. I know of no other evidence to this effect, and if the charge is true I cannot understand why more was not made of it at the time by the defenders of the Bank and the Government, who needed every available argument to offset the effect of Ricardo's criticism, but who nevertheless always referred to Ricardo as if he were a most respectable and upright person. Moreover, it is not clear to me why, since Ricardo was also a loan-contractor and a large fundholder on his own account, it would not have been as "natural" for him to have "bull" leanings. Nor would convertibility "certainly" bring down the funds. The usual effect of an appreciation of a currency is in fact to raise the value of gilt-edge fixed-income securities.

The Bank's records, it is made apparent by Sir John, are very scanty and unrevealing with respect to negotiations and discussions between the Government and the Bank. A thorough study of the relations between the two will not be possible unless there exist manuscript records in the Treasury archives or in the private papers of statesmen and former Bank officials. It may be that for reasons of convenience or better to preserve secrecy much of the discussion was carried on orally. It is more probable, however, that negotiations were usually in writing, but were kept semi-private in character, and that the records thereof were kept as private papers by the participants. In any case, Sir John did not find much in the Bank's records bearing on the negotiations between the Bank and the Government in the nineteenth century. For example, he found nothing in the records of the Bank to support the statement which I had made (without citation of my authority, I regret to say) that early in 1822 the Bank had refused to accede to a request from the Government to lower its discount rate. A statement to this effect was made by Lord Liverpool in the House of Lords on February 26, 1822 (*Hansard*, New Series, VI [1822], 715-16).

Robert Lowe, in June, 1873, introduced a Bill to authorize temporary increases in certain contingencies of the amount of Bank of England notes which could be issued in exchange for securities.

We are told that " no opinions from the Bank on Lowe's proposals have survived " (II, 289). It may be prudent to read this as " have survived in the records of the Bank itself." James Pennington for many years acted as an adviser to the Chancellor of the Exchequer on currency and banking matters. In the University of Chicago Library there are some fragmentary copies of correspondence between Pennington, on the one hand, and Arbuthnot, Trevelyan, and Goulburn, all associated in one connection or another with the Treasury, on the other, dealing with Bank of England matters. This correspondence shows that a proposal with some resemblance to Lowe's had been made by William Cotton, the then Governor of the Bank, to Goulburn in 1845, and was again under consideration in 1855. One item in this correspondence helps incidentally to explain the poverty of the Bank's records. Goulburn, in transmitting Cotton's letter to Pennington, writes : " I make this communication in perfect confidence,—the letter of the Governor to me, being more in the character of a private than an official letter."

Section 9 of the Bank Act of 1844 provided that if the Bank took over the note issues of other banks, it was to make additional payments to the Treasury " equal in amount to the net profit derived in the said issue department . . . from such additional issues after deducting the amount of the Expenses occasioned by the additional issue." This correspondence reveals that the interpretation of this provision gave rise to rather sharp discussions between the Treasury and the Bank. The Bank insisted that the deduction for expense should be on the basis of the cost, presumably the average cost, of issue through the Branches, where the cost was higher than at the Head Office. The Bank also asked for a guarantee against any risk of loss at the expiration of the Charter from a fall in the price of the securities held as cover for the additional issues. Goulburn, on the other hand, at least at first, held that the revenues and costs connected with the additional issues should be computed on what was in effect a marginal revenue and a marginal cost basis, and insisted that the chance of loss with respect to the securities be treated as " a banking risk " and as " part of the price paid by the Bank of England for its privileges." It would be interesting to know the dénouement of this controversy, which raises a nice issue in cost-accounting, and also reflects both the characteristic parsimony of the Treasury in its relations with the Bank and the constant and anxious concern of the Bank with respect to its revenues.

On these and other matters, we can safely take for granted that not much more could have been done on the basis of the Bank's own records than the work under review has done. For further light on these aspects of the pre-1914 history of the Bank, we must await the discovery and exploitation of relevant material in the papers of the Treasury and in the private papers of Bank and Government officials.

Power versus Plenty as Objectives of Foreign Policy in the Seventeenth and Eighteenth Centuries*

IN THE SEVENTEENTH AND EIGHTEENTH CENTURIES economic thought and practice were predominantly carried on within the framework of that body of ideas which was later to be called "mercantilism." Although there has been almost no systematic investigation of the relationship in mercantilist thought between economic and political objectives or ends in the field of foreign policy, certain stereotypes have become so prevalent that few scholars have seriously questioned or examined their validity. One of these stereotypes is that mercantilism was a "system of power," that is, that "power" was for mercantilists the sole or overwhelmingly preponderant end of foreign policy, and that wealth, or "plenty," was valued solely or mainly as a necessary means to attaining or retaining or exercising power. It is the purpose of this paper to examine in the light of the available evidence the validity of this interpretation of mercantilist thought and practice. Tracing the history of ideas, however, always runs to many words, and limitations of space force me to confine myself, even with respect to bibliographical references, to samples of the various types of relevant evidence. That the samples are fair ones I can only attest by my readiness in most cases to expand them indefinitely.

The pioneer historians of mercantilism were nineteenth-century German scholars, predominantly Prussians sympathetic to its economic and political philosophy, and especially to its emphasis on state interests as opposed to the private interests of citizens. The interpretation of mercantilism by Schmoller as primarily a system of state-building is familiar, and commonly accepted by

*Reprinted from *World Politics*, Vol. 1, October 1948, pp. 1-29, by the courtesy of Princeton University Press.

economic historians.[1]   A similar stress on the political aspects of
mercantilist commercial policy is common in the German writings.
The proposition that the mercantilists sought a favorable balance
of trade, wealth, and the indefinite accumulation of the precious
metals solely as means to power seems first to have been launched
by Baron von Heyking, who indeed claims priority for his interpretation.[2] Schmoller similarly interpreted the uncorrupted mercantilism of Prussia and of the non-maritime countries in general, but
he maintained that the "imperialism" of the maritime powers was
a debased mercantilism, characterized by an unscrupulous use of
military power to promote ultimate commercial ends, and half-
condemned it on that ground.[3]

     This   distinction   between   "pure"   mercantilism,   a   "Staats-
merkantilismus," which can obtain its full development only in an
absolute monarchy, and the mercantilism of countries where the
commercial classes are influential and the state has to serve and to
reconcile private economic interests, is also made much of by a
later German writer, Georg Herzog zu Mecklenburg Graf von
Carlow. For "pure" mercantilism, the ruling principle is not
economic but the promotion of the power of the state.[4] In general,
however, the historians have not distinguished between the

---

1. I suspect, nevertheless, that it is highly questionable. The economic unification of the nation-state appears mostly to have occurred before the advent of
mercantilism, as in England, or after its decay, as in France, Spain, Russia, Switzer-
land, Italy, the United States, or the British Dominions, if the national unification
of tariffs or other significant criteria are applied. Even Colbert promoted regional
as well as national self-sufficiency. As Moritz Bonn has commented (*Journal of
Political Economy*, LIV [1946], 474), "A parochialist like Gustav Schmoller
naturally deduced his impressions of mercantilism from the policies of primitive
Prussia."

2. *Zur Geschichte der Handelsbilanztheorie,* Berlin, 1880, Ch. 2, "Die Beziehungen der Theorie der Handelsbilanz zur Theorie des politischen Gleichge-
wichtes." The claim for priority is on p. 43. This chapter is a pioneer and valid
demonstration of the existence of a close relationship between mercantilist
balance-of-trade and balance-of-power theorizing and policy, but there is not a
trace of valid demonstration in it that wealth considerations were made wholly
subservient to power considerations.

3. See his *Umrisse und Untersuchungen,* Leipzig, 1898, especially Ch. I, "Das
Merkantilsystem in seiner historischen Bedeutung," pp. 42-60; see also "Die
englische Handelspolitik des 17. und 18. Jahrhunderts," in *Jahrbuch für Gesetz-
gebrung, Verwaltung, und Volkswirtschaft,* XX (1899), 1211-1241. F. Brie, *Impe-
rialistische Strömungen in der Englischen Literatur,* 2nd ed., Halle, 1928, p. 68,
characterizes English mercantilism of the eighteenth century, along Schmollerian
lines, as "kaufmännisch gefärbte Imperialismus."

4. *Richelieu als merkantilistischer Wirtschaftspolitiker und der Begriff des
Staatsmerkantilismus,* Jena, 1929, pp. 198ff.

mercantilism of the absolute and the constitutional states, and where they have dealt at all with the questions of the ultimate aims of mercantilism they have almost invariably asserted that these were solely or preponderantly political, although only too often with ambiguity or even outright self-contradiction, and almost invariably without presentation of substantial evidence.

A case in point is William Cunningham, the English economic historian. His predominant interpretation of English mercantilism was that it sought power rather than or much more than plenty, and that it valued plenty solely or mainly as an instrument or support of power, although he easily slipped, in this as in other analytical issues, into ambiguity if not hopeless contradiction.[5] An English economic historian sympathetic to mercantilism, W. A. S. Hewins, regarded this interpretation as unfair to the mercantilists, and offered the following rendition of Cunningham's position to indicate its inacceptability :

... one might almost imagine him [i.e., Cunningham] saying: "The mercantile system is concerned with man solely as a being who pursues national power, and who is capable of judging the comparative efficacy of means to that end. It makes entire abstraction of every other human passion or motive, except those which may be regarded as perpetually antagonising principles to the pursuit of national power—viz. neglect of shipping and aversion to a fish diet. The mercantile system considers mankind as occupied solely in pursuing and acquiring national power."[6]

5. Cf., for contradiction with the view that power was the predominant objective, *The Growth of English Industry and Commerce in Modern Times*, Vol. II, *In Modern Times, Part I*, Cambridge, 1903, p. 459: "From the Revolution till the revolt of the colonies, the regulation of commerce was considered, not so much with reference to other elements of national power, or even in its bearing on revenue, but chiefly with a view to the promotion of industry." Cf. also, *The Wisdom of the Wise*, Cambridge, 1906: "In the pre-scientific days the end which men of affairs kept in view, when debating economic affairs, was clearly understood; the political power of the realm was the object they put before them, . . ." (p. 21) "We recognize [today] that the defence of the realm is essential to welfare, but we are no longer so much concerned about building up the power of the country, or so ready to engage in aggressive wars *for the sake of commercial advantage*, as Englishmen were in the eighteenth century." (p. 22) The italics are mine. The contradiction the italicized words seem to indicate may not be real, since Cunningham may have had in mind that the "commercial advantages" were sought for the sake of their contribution to British power, but such exposition, ambiguous, if not contradictory, is so common in the literature that it provides of itself a justification for an article such as the present one.

6. In a review of Cunningham's *Growth of English Industry and Commerce* in *The Economic Journal*, II (1892), 696. Cunningham, in a reply to Hewins and other reviewers, *ibid.*, IV (1894), 508-16, permitted this interpretation of his posi-

All the German and English economic historians who found in mercantilism the complete subordination of economic to political considerations seem to have been themselves sympathetic to the subordination of the individual to the state and to the exaltation of vigorous nationalism characteristic of mercantilism, and to have been hostile to nineteenth century liberalism and its revolt against the residues of mercantilist legislation. Where this was combined, as in Schmoller and Cunningham, with a dislike of the rise of the bourgeois and his values to dominance over politics, to attribute to the mercantilists the conception of power as the sole or preponderant end of national policy was to praise rather than to blame them.

Eli Heckscher, the great Swedish economic historian and the outstanding authority on mercantilism today, follows the standard interpretation of the mercantilist objectives, but clearly to add to their shame rather than to praise them. Heckscher is an outstanding liberal, an individualist, a free-trader, and clearly anti-chauvinist. When to the section of his great work dealing with the foreign policy of the mercantilists he gives the heading "Mercantilism as a System of Power,"[7] and applies it to mercantilism in general and not only to the mercantilism of the absolute monarchies or of the non-maritime countries, he is reinforcing the indictment of it which he makes on other grounds, for to him "power" is clearly an ugly name for an ugly fact. More systematically, more learnedly, and more competently than anyone else, he supports his thesis that the mercantilists subordinated plenty to power. His argument calls therefore for detailed examination if this proposition is to be questioned.

Heckscher really presents an assortment of theses, ranging from the proposition (1) that for mercantilists—whether for most, or many, or only some, not being made very clear—power was the *sole* ultimate end of state policy with wealth merely one of the means to the attainment of power, through the "eclectic" thesis (2) that power and plenty were parallel ends for the mercantilists but with much greater emphasis placed on power than was common before or later, to the concession (3) that mercantilists occasionally reversed the usual position and regarded power as a means for securing plenty and treated purely commercial considerations as more

---

tion to pass without comment, although it must have been obvious to him that Hewins regarded it as a *reductio ad absurdum*.

7. *Mercantilism*, translated by Mendel Shapiro, 2 vols., London, 1935, II, 13-52.

important than considerations of power. His central position, however, and to this he returns again and again, is that the mercantilists
expounded a doctrine under which all considerations were subordinated to considerations of power as an end in itself, and that in
doing so they were logically and in their distribution of emphasis
unlike their predecessors and unlike the economists of the nineteenth
century.

It is difficult to support this account of Heckscher's position by
direct quotation from his text, since he presents it more by implication and inference from mercantilist statements than by clear-cut
and explicit formulation in his own words. That mercantilists
according to Heckscher tended to regard power as the *sole* end is
to be inferred by the contrasts he draws between the position he
attributes to Adam Smith—wrongly, I am sure—that "power was
certainly only a means to the end" of "opulence," and the
"reverse" position of the mercantilists,[8] the "reverse," I take it,
being the proposition that wealth was only a means to power. That
there is something special and peculiar to mercantilism in conceiving
power as an end in itself underlies all of Heckscher's exposition,
but the following passages come nearest to being explicit. "The
most vital aspect of the problem is whether power is conceived as
an *end in itself,* or only as a means for gaining something else, such
as the well-being of the nation in this world or its everlasting
salvation in the next."[9] This leaves out of account, as an alternative,
Heckscher's "eclectic" version, where both power and plenty are
ends in themselves. On John Locke's emphasis on the significance
for power of monetary policy, Heckscher comments, with the clear
implication that the injection into economic analysis of considerations of power is not "rational," that it is "interesting as a proof
of how important considerations of power in money policy
appeared even to so advanced a rationalist as Locke."[10]

Heckscher later restated his position in response to criticisms,
but it seems to me that he made no important concession and indeed
ended up with a more extreme position than at times he had taken
in his original exposition.

The second of the aims of mercantilist policy . . . —that of power—
has met with a great deal of criticism from reviewers of my book. . . .

8. *Ibid.,* II, 17.
9. *Ibid.,* II, 16.
10. *Ibid.,* II, 47.

I agree with my critics on that point to the extent of admitting that both "power" and "opulence" . . . have been, and must be, of importance to economic policy of every description. But I do not think there can be any doubt that these two aims changed places in the transition from mercantilism to *laissez-faire*. All countries in the nineteenth century made the creation of wealth their lode-star, with small regard to its effects upon the power of the State, while the opposite had been the case previously.[11]

The evidence which Heckscher presents that the mercantilists considered power as an end in itself and as an important end, and that they considered wealth to be a means of power need not be examined here, since there is no ground for disputing these propositions and, as far as I know, no one has ever disputed them. That the mercantilists overemphasized these propositions I would also not question. Nor will I enter here into extended discussion of the rationality of these concepts beyond stating a few points. In the seventeenth and eighteenth centuries, colonial and other overseas markets, the fisheries, the carrying trade, the slave trade, and open trade routes over the high seas, were all regarded, and rightly, as important sources of national wealth, but were available, or at least assuredly available, only to countries with the ability to acquire or retain them by means of the possession and readiness to use military strength.

In the seventeenth and eighteenth centuries also, "power" meant not only power to conquer and attack, and the prestige and influence which its possession gave, but also power to maintain national security against external attack. "Power as an end in itself" must, therefore, be interpreted to include considerations of national security against external aggression on the nation's territory and its political and religious freedom. Given the nature of human nature, recognition of power as an end in itself was therefore then neither peculiar nor obviously irrational unless there is rational ground for holding that the promotion of economic welfare is the sole sensible objective of national policy to which every other consideration must be completely subordinated.

---

11. "Revisions in Economic History, V, Mercantilism," *The Economic History Review*, VII (November 1936), 48. The foreign policy implications of the nineteenth century economics, I believe, need investigation as much as do the aims of mercantilism. Until such investigation is systematically made, comparisons with mercantilism are liable to be misleading with respect to the true position of both bodies of doctrine.

There remains, therefore, to be examined only whether Heckscher has demonstrated that mercantilists *ever* regarded power as the *sole* end of foreign policy, or ever held that considerations of plenty were *wholly* to be subordinated to considerations of power, or even whether they ever held that a choice has to be made in long-run national policy between power and plenty.

Despite his wide knowledge of the mercantilist literature, Heckscher fails to cite a single passage in which it is asserted that power is or should be the *sole* end of national policy, or that wealth matters *only* as it serves power. I doubt whether any such passage can be cited, or that anyone ever held such views. The nearest thing to such statements which Heckscher does cite are statements maintaining that wealth is a means of power and is important as such, unaccompanied by express acknowledgment that wealth is also important for its own sake. In almost every case he cites, it is possible to cite from the same writer passages which show that wealth was regarded as valuable also for its own sake. The passage of this type which Heckscher most emphasizes is a "passing remark" of Colbert in a letter: "Trade is the source of finance and finance is the vital nerve of war." Heckscher comments that Colbert here "indicates clearly the relationship between means and ends."[12] But argument from silence is notoriously precarious, and if it were to be pressed would work more against than for Heckscher's thesis, since there is a great mass of mercantilist literature in which there is no mention whatsoever, and no overt implication, of considerations of power. Colbert does not here indicate that the relationship was a one-way one. To make a significant point Heckscher would have to show that Colbert would not also have subscribed to the obverse proposition that strength is the vital nerve of trade and trade the source of finance.

Of all the mercantilists Colbert is the most vulnerable, since he carried all the major errors of economic analysis of which they were guilty to their most absurd extremes both in verbal exposition and in practical execution, and since, either as expressing his own sentiments or catering to those of his master, Louis XIV, he developed more elaborately than any other author the serviceability to power of economic warfare, the possibilities of using military power to achieve immediate economic ends, and the possibilities of substitut-

---

12. *Mercantilism*, II, 17.

ing economic warfare for military warfare to attain national ends.
Even in his case, however, it is not possible to demonstrate that he
ever rejected or regarded as unimportant the desirability for its
own sake of a prosperous French people or the desirability of
guiding French foreign policy, military and economic, so as to
augment this prosperity. In many of his official papers he is obviously catering to Louis XIV's obsession with power and prestige,
or perhaps to a conventional fashion of *pretending* that a great
monarch would be so obsessed,[13] so that there is no reason to reject,
as unrepresentative of his genuinely-held views, such passages as
the following:

> . . . comme toutes les alliances entre les grands rois ont toujours deux
> fins principales, l'une leur gloire particulière et quelquefois la jonction
> de leurs intérêts, soit pour conserver, soit pour acquérir . . . et l'autre
> les avantages de leurs sujets . . . Et quoyque, dans l'ordre de le division,
> celuy de l'avantage de leurs sujets soit le dernier, il est néanmoins tou-
> jours le premier dans les esprits de bons princes. . . .
> Les avantages de leurs sujets consistent à les maintenir en repos
> au dedans et à leur procurer par le moyen du commerce, soit plus de
> facilités de vivre aux nécessiteux, soit plus d'abondance aux riches.[14]

Certain peculiar features of mercantilist economic analysis—
features incidentally which modern apologists for mercantilist
economics such as Lipson seem strangely to avoid discussing—do
seem to imply a disregard on the part of mercantilists for economic
welfare.[15] What was apparently a phase of scholastic economics,
that what is one man's gain is necessarily another man's loss, was
taken over by the mercantilists and applied to countries as a whole.

---

13. Cf. the following passage in his famous "Mémoire au Roi sur les Finances"
of 1670: "Il est certain, Sire, que Vostre Majesté . . . a dans son esprit et dans toute
sa nature la guerre par préférence à toute autre chose. . . . Vostre Majesté pense
plus dix fois à la guerre qu'elle ne pense à ses finances." *Lettres Instructions et
Mémoires de Colbert*, P. Clément, ed., Paris, 1870, VII, 252. This long memoir
is a plea to the king to look to his economic policy, including economic warfare,
as an essential instrument for attaining his ends. Even in the case of Louis XIV,
himself, it is easy to show from his writings that the prosperity of his people,
while no doubt inexcusably underemphasized, was a matter of some concern to
him for its own sake.

14. "Dissertation sur la question: quelle des deux alliances de France ou de
Hollande peut estre plus avantageuse à l'Angleterre," March, 1669. *Lettres*, VI,
261. A letter of Colbert to Louis XIV in 1681 contains the following passage: "Ce
qu'il y a de plus important, et sur quoi il y a plus de réflexions à faire, c'est la
misére très-grande des peuples." C. Dareste de la Chavanne, *Histoire de l'Administration en France*, Paris, 1848, II, 258.

15. See Ephraim Lipson, *The Economic History of England*, Vols. II-III, "The
Age of Mercantilism," 3rd edition, London, 1943.

They incorporated this with their tendency to identify wealth with money, and with their doctrine that, as far as money was concerned, what mattered was not the absolute quantity but the relative quantity as compared with other countries. Since the quantity of money in the world could be taken as constant, the quantity of wealth in the world was also a constant, and a country could gain only at the expense of other countries. By sheer analogy with the logic of military power, which is in truth a relative matter, and with the aid of the assumption of a close relationship between "balance of power" and "balance of trade," which, however, they failed intelligently to analyze, the mercantilists were easily led to the conclusion that wealth, like power, also was only a relative matter, a matter of proportions between countries, so that a loss inflicted on a rival country was as good as an absolute gain for one's own country. At least one mercantilist carried this doctrine to its logical conclusion that plague, war, famine, harvest failure, in a neighboring country was of economic advantage to your own country.[16] On such doctrine, Adam Smith's trenchant comment is deserved, although he exaggerates its role in mercantilist thought and practice:

By such maxims as these, however, nations have been taught that their interest consisted in beggaring all their neighbours. Each nation has been made to look with an invidious eye upon the prosperity of all the nations with which it trades, and to consider their gain as its own loss. Commerce, which ought naturally to be, among nations, as among individuals, a bond of union and friendship, has become the most fertile source of discord and animosity. The capricious ambition of kings and ministers has not, during the present and the preceding century, been more fatal to the repose of Europe, than the impertinent jealousy of merchants and manufacturers. The violence and injustice of the rulers of mankind is an ancient evil, for which, I am afraid, the nature of human affairs can scarce admit of a remedy. But the mean rapacity, the monopolizing spirit of merchants and manufacturers, who neither are, nor ought to be, the rulers of mankind, though it cannot perhaps be corrected, may very easily be prevented from disturbing the tranquillity of any body but themselves.[17]

Heckscher cites mercantilist doctrine such as Adam Smith here criticizes as evidence that the mercantilists were not interested in

16. Theodor Ludwig Lau, *Aufrichtiger Vorschlag*, 1719, as reported in Walther Focke, *Die Lehrmeinungen der Kameralisten über den Handel*, Erlangen (dissertation), 1926, p. 59.

17. *Wealth of Nations*, Cannan, ed., London, 1904, I, 457-58.

economic welfare for its own sake, but subordinated it to considerations of power. Adam Smith's assumption that the exposition of
such doctrine was confined to merchants to the exclusion of statesmen (or philosophers) is invalid. But in so far as it was expounded
by merchants, it is scarcely conceivable that these were so different
from merchants at other times that they were governed more by
chauvinist patriotism than by rapacity. The significance of such
doctrine is not that those who adhered to it placed power before
plenty, but that they grossly misunderstood the true means to and
nature of plenty. What they were lacking in was not economic
motivation but economic understanding.

What then is the correct interpretation of mercantilist doctrine
and practice with respect to the roles of power and plenty as ends
of national policy? I believe that practically all mercantilists,
whatever the period, country, or status of the particular individual,
would have subscribed to all of the following propositions: (1)
wealth is an absolutely essential means to power, whether for
security or for aggression; (2) power is essential or valuable as a
means to the acquisition or retention of wealth; (3) wealth and
power are each proper ultimate ends of national policy; (4) there is
long-run harmony between these ends, although in particular
circumstances it may be necessary for a time to make economic
sacrifices in the interest of military security and therefore also of
long-run prosperity.

The omission of any one of these four propositions results in an
incorrect interpretation of mercantilist thought, while additions of
other propositions would probably involve internal dispute among
mercantilists. It is to be noted that no proposition is included as
to the relative weight which the mercantilists attached to power and
to plenty, respectively. Given the general acceptance of the
existence of harmony and mutual support between the pursuit of
power and the pursuit of plenty, there appears to have been little
interest in what must have appeared to them to be an unreal issue.
When apparent conflict between these ends did arise, however,
differences in attitudes, as between persons and countries, did arise
and something will be said on this matter later.

That plenty and power were universally regarded as each
valuable for its own sake there is overwhelming evidence, in the
contemporary writings of all kinds, and what follows is more or less
a random sampling of the available evidence. In the text accom-

panying and interpreting the Frontispiece of Michael Drayton's poem, *Polyolbion*, 1622, there is the following passage:

> Through a Triumphant Arch, see Albion plas't,
> In Happy site, in Neptunes arms embras't,
> In Power and Plenty, on hir Cleevy Throne

In Barbier d'Aucour's *Au Roy sur le Commerce, Ode*, 1665,[18] an early French equivalent of *Rule Britannia*, appear the following lines :

> Vos vaisseaux fendant tous les airs,
> Et cinglant sur toutes les Mers,
> Y porteront vostre puissance;
> Et ce Commerce plein d'honneur,
> Fera naistre dans vostre France,
> Un flus et reflus de bon-heur.

Montchrétien opens his book with this passage: "Ceux qui sont appellez au gouvernement des Estats doyvent en avoir la gloire, l'augmentation et l'enrichissement pour leur principal but."[19] Another Frenchman, writing in 1650 says :

> Deux choses sont principalement necessaires pour rendre un Estat florissant; c'est assavoir le Gouvernement, & le Commerce; & comme sans celuy-là il est impossible qu'il puisse longtemps subsister; de mesme sans celuy-cy on le voit manquer de mille sortes de choses importantes à la vie, & il est impossible que les peuples acquierent de grandes richesses.[20]

John Graunt, in 1662, states that "the art of governing, and the true politiques, is how to preserve the subject in peace, and plenty."[21] An anonymous English writer, in 1677, declares that : "The four main interests of a nation are, religion, reputation, peace, and trade. . . ."[22] William III, in his declaration of war

---

18. The citation from D'Aucour in the text is made from a reprint extracted from J. Carnandet, *Le Trésor des Pièces Rares . . . de la Champagne*, Paris, 1863-1866. D'Aucour was a tutor of Colbert's son. F. C. Palm, *The Economic Policies of Richelieu*, Urbana, 1920, pp. 178-79, quotes from an earlier *Ode à . . . Richelieu*, in much the same vein by Jean de Chapelain (1595-1624), which similarly stresses power and plenty.

19. *Traicté de l'œconomie politique* [1615], Th. Funck-Brentano ed., Paris, 1889, p. 11.

20. Cited from Ch. Vialart dit St. Paul, *Histoire du Ministère d'Armand . . . Duc de Richelieu*, Paris, 1650, I, 332.

21. *Natural and Political Observations made upon the Bills of Mortality* [London, 1662], Johns Hopkins University Reprint, Baltimore, 1939, p. 78.

22. *The Present State of Christendom, and the Interest of England, with Regard to France* [1677], in *The Harleian Miscellany*, London, 1810, VIII, 106.

against France in 1689, gives as one of the reasons that Louis XIV's "forbidding the importation of a great part of the product and manufactures of our Kingdom, and imposing exorbitant customs upon the rest, are sufficient evidence of his design to destroy the trade on which the wealth and safety of this nation so much depends."[23] In the preamble of 3 and 4 Anne, cap. 10, are the following words: "The Royal Navy, and the navigation of England, wherein, under God, the wealth, safety, and strength of this Kingdom is so much concerned, depends on the due supply of stores necessary for the same."[24] An English pamphlet of 1716 on the relations with Russia, after describing the Czar as "a great and enterprizing spirit, and of a genius thoroughly politic" attributes to him and his people "an insatiable desire of opulency, and a boundless thirst for dominion."[25] William Wood, a noted mercantilist writer, refers to the English as "a people . . . who seek no other advantages than such only as may enlarge and secure that, whereby their strength, power, riches and reputation, equally encrease and are preserved. . . ."[26] Bernard Mandeville discusses how "politicians can make a people potent, renown'd and flourishing."[27] An anonymous English writer states in 1771 that:

"Nature, reason and observation all plainly point out to us our true object of national policy, which is commerce; the inexhaustible source of wealth and power to a people."[28] In an undated memoir of Maurepas to Louis XVI, on the commerce of France, occur the following passages: "Le commerce est la source de la félicité, de la force et de la richesse d'un état. . . . La richesse et la puissance sont les vrais intérêts d'une nation, et il n'y a que le commerce qui puisse procurer l'une et l'autre."[29]

Such evidence as the foregoing that in the age of mercantilism

---

23. As cited in *Mercator, or Commerce Retrieved*, No. 1, London; May 26, 1713.

24. Cited in G. S. Graham, *Sea Power and British North America 1783-1820*, Cambridge Mass., 1941, p. 143.

25. *The Northern Crisis; or Impartial Reflections on the Policies of the Czar* [London, 1716], as reprinted in Karl Marx, *Secret Diplomatic History of the Eighteenth Century*, London, 1899, p. 32.

26. *Survey of Trade*, 2nd ed., London, 1719, Dedication, pp. iv-v.

27. *The Fable of the Bees* [6th ed., 1732], F. B. Kaye ed., Oxford, 1924, I, 185.

28. *Considerations on the Policy, Commerce and Circumstances of the Kingdom*, London, 1771, as quoted in the preface to G. S. Graham, *British Policy and Canada, 1774-1791*, London, 1930.

29. *Mémoires du Comte de Maurepas*, Paris, 1792, III, 195.

wealth and power were both sought for their own sakes could easily be multiplied many fold. In English literature of the period of all kinds, from poetry to official documents, the phrases "power and plenty," "wealth and strength," "profit and power," "profit and security," "peace and plenty," or their equivalents, recur as a constant refrain. Nor is there any obvious reason, given the economic and political conditions and views of the seventeenth and eighteenth centuries, why power *and* plenty should not have been the joint objectives of the patriotic citizen of the time, even if he had freed himself from the mercantilist philosophy. Adam Smith, though not a mercantilist, was speaking for mercantilists as well as for himself when he said that "the great object of the political œconomy of every country, is to increase the riches and power of that country."[30]

In all the literature I have examined, I have found only one passage which is seriously embarrassing for my thesis, not because it subordinates in extreme fashion economic to political considerations, but for the reverse reason. The passage, in an anonymous and obscure pamphlet of 1754, whose authorship I have been unable to determine, is as follows:

> You want not, Gentlemen, to be informed by me, that commerce is the nearest and dearest concern of your country. It is what should be the great object of public attention in all national movements, and in every negotiation we enter into with foreign powers. Our neighbours on the continent may, perhaps, wisely scheme or quarrel for an augmentation of dominions; but *Great Britain, of herself, has nothing to fight for, nothing to support, nothing to augment but her commerce.* On our foreign trade, not only our wealth but our mercantile navigation must depend; on that navigation our naval strength, the glory and security of our country.[31]

It is much easier indeed to show that power was not the sole objective of national policy in mercantilist thought than to explain how historians ever came to assert that it was. The evidence they cite in support of this proposition is not only extremely scanty but is generally ambiguous if not wholly irrelevant to their thesis. It would be extremely difficult, I am sure, for them to cite even a single passage which unmistakably rejects wealth as a national objec-

---

30. *Wealth of Nations*, Cannan, ed., London, 1904, I, 351.
31. *Mercator's Letters on Portugal and its Commerce*, London, 1754, p. 5. The italics are not in the original text.

tive worth pursuing for its own sake or unconditionally subordinates it to power as an ultimate end. It is only too probable
that there has been operating here that intellectual "principle of
parsimony" in the identification of causes which, whatever its
serviceability in the natural sciences, has in the history of social
thought worked only for ill.

Cunningham and Heckscher[32] make much of a passage of Francis
Bacon's made famous by modern scholars in which he speaks of
King Henry VII "bowing the ancient policy of this estate from
consideration of plenty to consideration of power" when in the
interest of the navy he ordered that wines from Gascony should
be imported only in English bottoms. As a fifteenth century measure, this falls outside the period of present interest, but Bacon,
no doubt, put much of his own ideas, perhaps more than of Henry
VII's, in his *History of the Reign of King Henry the Seventh*.
It is relevant, therefore, that Bacon speaks of Henry VII as conduct-
ing war for profit, and attributes to him even over-developed
economic objectives. In 1493, Henry VII had declared an embargo
on all trade with the Flemish provinces because the pretender,
Perkin Warbeck, was being harbored there. The embargo after a
time "began to pinch the merchants of both nations very sore,
which moved them by all means they could devise to affect and
dispose their sovereigns respectively to open the intercourse again."
Henry VII, no longer apprehensive about Warbeck, was receptive.
"But that that moved him most was, that being a King that loved
wealth and treasure, he could not endure to have trade sick, nor
any obstruction to continue in the gate-vein, which disperseth that
blood," and by the *intercursus magnus* of 1495-96 with the Arch-
duke of Austria he negotiated the end of the trade war.[33]

---

32. Heckscher refers to this as "a very characteristic passage" (*Mercantilism*,
II, 16), but I find it difficult to cite a duplicate, whether from Bacon's writings
or in the period generally. See also Heckscher, "Revisions in Economic History,
V, Mercantilism," *Economic History Review*, VII (November 1936), 48: "I think
Cunningham was right in stressing the famous saying of Bacon about Henry VII:
'bowing the ancient policy of this Estate from consideration of plenty to consideration of power.'"

33. See *The Works of Francis Bacon*, James Spedding, ed., London, 1858, VI,
95-96; 172-73. Cf. also *Considerations touching a War with Spain* [1624], in *The
Works of Francis Bacon*, Philadelphia, 1852, II, 214, where he says that: "whereas
wars are generally causes of poverty or consumption . . . this war with Spain, if
it be made by sea, is like to be a lucrative and restorative war. So that, if we go
roundly on at the first, the war in continuance will find itself." On the other hand,
in his *Essays or Counsels* [2nd ed., 1625], *Works*, London, 1858, VI, 450-51, he

Not so frequently stated as that power and plenty are properly joint objectives of national policy but undoubtedly a pervasive element in the thought of the period is the proposition that they are also harmonious ends, each reinforcing and promoting the other. The idea is expressed in the maxim attributed to Hobbes: "Wealth is power and power is wealth."[34] There follow some passages in which the idea is spelled out somewhat more fully: "Foreign trade produceth riches, riches power, power preserves our trade and religion."[35] "It is evident that this Kingdom is wonderfully fitted by the bounty of God Almighty, for a great progression in wealth and power; and that the only means to arrive at both, or either of them, is to improve and advance trade. . . ."[36] "For as the honesty of all governments is, so shall be their riches; and as their honour, honesty, and riches are, so will be their strength; and as their honour, honesty, riches, and strength are, so will be their trade. These are five sisters that go hand in hand, and must not be parted."[37] "Your fleet, and your trade, have so near a relation, and such mutual influence upon each other, they cannot well be separated; your trade is the mother and nurse of your seamen; your seamen are the life of your fleet, and your fleet is the security and protection of your trade, and both together are the wealth, strength, security and glory of Britain."[38]

"By trade and commerce we grow a rich and powerful nation,

makes what appears to be a clear-cut statement that the prestige of power ("grandeur") is more important than plenty.

34. J. E. Barker, *Rise and Decline of the Netherlands*, London, 1906. p. 194.

35. Josiah Child, *A Treatise concerning the East India Trade*, London, 1681, p. 29.

36. *Ibid.*, *A New Discourse of Trade*, 4th ed. (ca. 1690), Preface, p. xliii.

37. Andrew Yarranton, *England's Improvement by Sea and Land*, London, 1677, p. 6.

38. Lord Haversham in the House of Lords, November 6, 1707, *Parliamentary History of England*, VI, 598. Cf. also James Whiston, *A Discourse of the Decay of Trade*, London, 1693, p. 3:

"For, since the introduction of the new artillery of powder guns, &c., and the discovery of the wealth of the Indies, &c. war is become rather an expense of money than men, and success attends those that can most and longest spend money: whence it is that prince's armies in Europe are become more proportionable to their purses than to the number of their people; so that it uncontrollably follows that a foreign trade managed to the best advantage, will make our nation so strong and rich, that we may command the trade of the world, the riches of it, and consequently the world itself. . . . Neither will the pursuing these proposals, augment the nation's wealth and power only, but that wealth and power will also preserve our trade and religion, they mutually working for the preservation of each other. . . ."

and by their decay we are growing poor and impotent. As trade
and commerce enrich, so they fortify, our country."

"The wealth of the nation he [the 'Patriot King'] will most
justly esteem to be his wealth, the power his power, the security
and the honor, his security and honor; and by the very means by
which he promotes the two first, he will wisely preserve the two
last."[39]

"De la marine dépendent les colonies, des colonies le commerce,
du commerce la faculté pour l'Etat d'entretenir de nombreuses
armées, d'augmenter la population et de fournir aux enterprises les
plus glorieuses et les plus utiles."[40]

George L. Beer has commented, with particular reference to
the statement from Lord Haversham quoted above, that "The men
of the day argued in a circle of sea power, commerce and colonies.
Sea power enabled England to expand and to protect her foreign
trade, while this increased commerce, in turn, augmented her naval
strength."[41] Circular reasoning this may have been, but it was not,
logically at least, a "vicious circle," since under the circumstances
of the time it was perfectly reasonable to maintain that wealth and
power mutually supported each other, that they were, or could be
made, each a means to the augmentation of the other.[42]

In contending that by the mercantilists power and plenty were
regarded as coexisting ends of national policy which were funda-

---

39. Lord Bolingbroke, "The Idea of a Patriot King," in *Letters on the Spirit of
Patriotism*, London, 1752, pp. 204, 211.

40. Petit, a colleague of the French Foreign Minister, Choiseul, in 1762, as cited
by E. Daubigny, *Choiseul et la France d'Outre-Mer après le Traité de Paris*, Paris,
1892, p. 176.

41. *The Old Colonial System, 1600-1754*, New York, 1912, I, 16.

42. Edmond Silberner, *La Guerre dans la Pensée Économique du XVIᵉ au
XVIIIᵉ Siècle*, Paris, 1939, concentrates on the search for attitudes toward war,
idealizing or pacific, rather than on the motivations of foreign policy, but it
presents a rich collection of extracts from the contemporary literature which in
so far as it is pertinent to the present issue is, I believe, wholly confirmatory of my
thesis. Cf. also, by the same author, *The Problem of War in Nineteenth Century
Economic Thought*, Princeton, 1946, p. 286: "In the protectionist view, there is
a reciprocal action between the economic and war: industrialization facilitates
the conduct of war, and military victories increase the possibilities of industrialization and of economic prosperity. This point of view recalls that of the mercantilists: wealth increases power, and power augments wealth." The thesis
presented in the text above is also supported not only by the title but by the
contents, if I understand his Italian aright, of Jacopo Mazzei's article, "Potenza
Mezzo di Ricchezza e Ricchezza Mezzo di Potenza nel Pensiero dei Mercantilisti,"
Rivista Internazionale di Scienze Sociali, XLI (January 1933), 3-19.

mentally harmonious, I do not mean that they were unaware that in specific instances economic sacrifices might have to be made in order to assure national security or victory in an aggressive war. But as a rule, if not invariably, when making this point they showed their belief that such economic sacrifices in the short run would bring economic as well as political gains in the long run. The selfishness from a patriotic point of view of taxpayers resisting war-time impositions for armament or for war was always a problem for statesmen in the age of mercantilism, and sometimes the parsimony of monarchs was also a problem. It was also necessary at times for statesmen to resist the pressure from merchants to pursue petty commercial ends which promised immediate economic gain but at the possible cost of long-run military security and therefore also of long-run national prosperity. The mercantilist, no doubt, would not have denied that if necessity should arise for choosing, all other things would have to give way to considerations of the national safety; but his practice might not rise to the level of his principles, and his doctrine would not lead him to recognize that such choice was likely to face him frequently. It is not without significance that it was an anti-mercantilist economist, Adam Smith, and not the mercantilists, who laid down the maxim that "defence is more important than opulence." A typical mercantilist might well have replied that ordinarily defense is necessary to opulence and opulence to effective defense, even if momentarily the two ends might appear to be in conflict.

Queen Elizabeth was notoriously parsimonious and one of her diplomatic agents, Buckhurst, in reasoning with her in 1587 when the safety of England against the menace from Spain appeared to call for rearmament, anticipated Adam Smith's maxim:

And alwaies when kinges and kingdomes do stand in dout of daun-ger, their saftie is a thing so far above all price of treasure, as there shold be no sparing to bring them even into certenty of assurans.

He accordingly advised Elizabeth to:

unlock all your cofers and convert your tresure for the advauncing of worthy men and for the arming of ships and men of war, that may defend you, sith princes' treasures serve only to that end and lie they never so fast nor so full in their chests, can no waies so defend them.[43]

---

43. "Correspondentie van Robert Dudley Graaf van Leycester," Part II, *Werken uitgiven door het Historisch Genootschap*, Utrecht, 3rd Series, No. 57 (1931), pp. 239, 240.

Statesmen frequently found it necessary to warn against endangering political ends by unwise pursuit of temporary or petty commercial gains in response to pressure from business interests. This was especially true in connection with the relations between England and France during the Seven Years' War, which to many contemporaries seemed to be conducted with too much attention to economic considerations of minor importance. Just before the outbreak of the conflict, when it was still being debated whether the issue between the two countries should be settled by economic or military means, Lord Granville was reported as "absolutely against meddling with trade—he called it, vexing your neighbours for a little muck."[44] And in the face of the struggle itself, Mirepoix, the French Ambassador to England, is said to have commented "that it was a great pity to cut off so many heads for the sake of a few hats."[45] In the course of controversy over the Newfoundland fisheries after the ending of hostilities, in 1763, Choiseul appealed to Halifax: "mais pour l'amour de Dieu, ne laissons pas des querrelles de pêcheurs dégénérer en querrelles de nations."[46]

To some extent this point of view may have been a reflection of a certain disdain for trade in general which was beginning to affect the aristocratic class who conducted the foreign relations of the time. It would be a mistake, however, to explain it in terms of basic disregard for economic considerations, rather than as belief that the pursuit of temporary and minor economic benefits should not be permitted to dominate foreign policy. Such is the position of John Mitchell, who makes clear elsewhere that "power and prosperity" are the proper ends of policy:

It is well known, that our colonies in America are rather more under the tuition and influence of the merchants in Britain, than the government perhaps, and that all public measures relating to them are very much influenced by the opinions of our merchants about them. But the only things that they seem to attend to are the profits of trade

---

44. *The Diary of the Late George Bubb Dodington*, new ed., London, 1784, pp. 344-45.

45. [William Knox], *Helps to a Right Decision*, London, 1787, p. 35; cf. also a slightly different version in *Letters Military and Political from the Italian of Count A. Algorotti*, Dublin, 1784, p. 129. The hats were involved, of course, because beaver skins were the main prize of the American fur trade, and the hair from these skins was the basic raw material for the men's hats of the time.

46. Cited in *Mélanges d'histoire offerts à M. Charles Bémont*, Paris, 1913, p. 655.

. . . . This, it is true, is necessary to be considered likewise, but it is not the only thing to be attended to. The great thing to be considered by all states is power and dominion, as well as trade. Without that to support and protect our trade, it must soon be at an end.[47]

While mercantilist doctrine, moreover, put great stress on the importance of national economic interests, it put equally great stress on the possibility of lack of harmony between the special economic interests of the individual merchants or particular business groups or economic classes, on the one hand, and the economic interest of the commonwealth as a whole, on the other. Refusal to give weight to *particular* economic interests, therefore, must never be identified with disregard for the national economic interest as they conceived it, in interpreting the thought of the mercantilists. In human affairs, moreover, there is always room for divergence between dogma and practice, between principles and the actual behavior of those who profess them. It is doctrine, and not practice, which is the main concern here. The task of ascertaining how much or how little they corresponded in the age of mercantilism, and what were the forces which caused them to deviate, is the difficult duty of the historian, in whose hands I gladly leave it.

It was the common belief in France, however, that commercial objectives and particular commercial interests played a much greater role in the formulation and administration of British than of French foreign policy, and some Englishmen would have agreed. There was universal agreement, also, that in "Holland" (*i.e.*, the "United Provinces"), where the merchants to a large extent shared directly in government, major political considerations, including the very

---

47. *The Contest in America between Great Britain and France*, London, 1757, Introduction, p. xvii. Cf. also *A Letter to a certain Foreign Minister, in which the grounds of the present war are truly stated*, London, 1745, p. 6: "That we receive great benefits from trade, that trade is a national concern, and that we ought to resent any attempt made to lessen or to injure it, are truths well known and out of dispute, yet sure the British people are not to be treated like a company of merchants, or rather pedlars, who, if they are permitted to sell their goods, are to think themselves well off, whatever treatment they may receive in any other respect. No, surely, the British nation has other great concerns besides their trade, and as she will never sacrifice it, so she will never endure any insult in respect to them, without resenting it as becomes a people jealous of their honour, and punctual in the performance of their engagements."

The occasion for this outburst was a Prussian "rescript" insisting that Britain should not intervene in quarrels between German states, since they had nothing to do with British commerce.

safety of the country or its success in wars in which it was actually participating, had repeatedly to give way to the cupidity of the merchants and their reluctance to contribute adequately to military finance. Whether in the main the influence of the commercial classes, where they had strength, worked more for peace or for war seems to be an open question, but there appears little ground for doubt that with the merchants, whether they pressed for war or for peace, the major consideration was economic gain, either their private gain, or that of their country, or both.

The material available which touches on these strands of thought is boundless, and there can here be cited only a few passages which give the flavor of contemporary discussion. We will begin with material relating to the influence of the merchant and of commercial considerations on British policy.

Sir Francis Bacon, in reporting a discussion in Parliament, in the fifth year of James I's reign, of the petition of the merchants with regard to their grievances against Spain, makes one of the speakers say that: "although he granted that the wealth and welfare of the merchant was not without a sympathy with the general stock and state ["estate?"] of a nation, especially an island; yet, nevertheless, it was a thing too familiar with the merchant, to make the case of his particular profit, the public case of the kingdom." The troubles of the merchants were partly their own fault: they so mismanaged their affairs abroad that "except lieger ambassadors, which are the eyes of kings in foreign parts, should leave their sentinel and become merchants' factors, and solicitors, their causes can hardly prosper." Wars were not to be fought on such minor issues. Another speaker was more sympathetic to the merchants, who were "the convoy of our supplies, the vents of our abundance, Neptune's almsmen, and fortune's adventurers." Nevertheless, the question of war should be dealt with by the King and not by Parliament, presumably because the merchants wielded too much influence there. Members of Parliament were local representatives with local interests; if they took a broader view it was accidental.[48]

Allies or potential allies of England sometimes were troubled by England's supposed obsession with commercial objectives as making her an unreliable ally where other interests were involved. In September, 1704, a minister of the Duke of Savoy issued a memorial

---

48. *The Works of Sir Francis Bacon*, Philadelphia, 1852, II, 193-99.

which the English representative at that Court reported as holding that England and Holland, "the maritime powers, (an injurious term, I think, which goes into fashion,) were so attentive to their interests of trade and commerce, that, perhaps, they would . . . abandon the common interests of Europe" in the defeat of France in the war then under way.[49] When Pitt declared to Catherine the Great of Russia that no Russian conquest could give offense to England, she was skeptical, and replied: "The acquisition of a foot of territory on the Black Sea will at once excite the jealousy of the English, whose whole attention is given to petty interests and who are first and always traders."[50]

Montesquieu and Quesnay both thought that in England, unlike France and other countries, the interests of commerce predominated over other interests:

D'autres nations font céder des intérêts de commerce à des intérêts politiques; celle ci [i.e. England] a toujours fait céder ses intérêts politiques aux intérêts de son commerce.[51]

en Angleterre . . . où les lois du commerce maritime ne se prêtent point aux lois de la politique; où les intérêts de la glèbe et de l'État sont subordonnés aux intérêts des négociants; où le commerce des productions de l'agriculture, la propriété du territoire et l'État même ne sont regardés que comme des accessoires de la métropole, et la métropole comme formée de négociants.[52]

The history of British policy and practice with respect to enemy trade and to trade with the enemy during war provides abundant and occasionally startling evidence that considerations of plenty did not always automatically give way to considerations of power. There is much in British history, as in the history of Holland, of

---

49. *The Diplomatic Correspondence of the Right Hon. Richard Hill*, London, 1845, I, 479; see also II, 751.

50. Cited by Edward Crankshaw, *Russia and Britain*, New York, no date (ca. 1943), pp. 45-46.

51. Montesquieu, *De l'Esprit des Lois*, Book XX, Ch. 7.

52. *Oeuvres Économiques et Philosophiques de F. Quesnay*, Auguste Oncken, ed., Paris, 1888, p. 429. Quesnay is referring here specially to Britain's policy with respect to the trade of the colonies. Adam Smith's comment on the monopolistic aspects of this policy was more acid: "To found a great empire for the sole purpose of raising up a people of customers, may at first sight appear a project fit only for a nation of shopkeepers. It is, however, a project altogether unfit for a nation of shopkeepers; but extremely fit for a nation whose government is influenced by shopkeepers." *Wealth of Nations*, Cannan, ed., II, 114.

France, and of Spain, to support the statement of Carl Brinkmann that: "The history of war trade and trade war is a rich mine of interest to the economic and social historian just for the peculiar ways in which the autonomy of business connexions and traditions is seen cutting across even the sternest decrees and tendencies of political *ultima ratio.*"[53]

That in Holland commercial interests predominated was taken for granted in both France and England when foreign policy was formulated. Thurloe commented, in 1656, that all proposals "of alliances of common and mutual defense, wherein provision was to be made for the good of the Protestant religion" failed "in respect the United Provinces always found it necessary for them to mingle therewith the consideration of trade. . . . The Hollanders had rather His Highness [Oliver Cromwell] be alone in it than that they should lose a tun of sack or a frail of raisins."[54] A French naval officer, writing to Colbert with reference to the failure of the Dutch to provide the fleet which they had promised for the Levant, said that he was not at all surprised: "les Hollandais n'agissent en cette occasion que par leur propre intérêt; et comme ils ont peu ou point de bâtiments en Levant, et qu'en leur pays ils ne regardent qu'au compte des marchands, ils n'ont garde d'envoyer et de faire la dépense d'une escadre de ce côté-là."[55]

In the summary given in Cobbett's *Parliamentary History* of the principal arguments made in Parliament in favor of moderating the peace settlement to be made with France to end the Seven Years' War, a contrast was made as to the policy proper for England and

---

53. *English Historical Review*, XXXIX (April 1924), 287. There is not space here to elaborate on this theme, but reference to one striking instance will serve to bring out the nature of the evidence available. In the 1740's, during the War of the Austrian Succession, English marine insurance companies insured French vessels against capture at sea by the British navy, and Parliament, after protracted debate, refused to make the practice illegal. Cf.: *Parliamentary History* (Cobbett, ed.), XII, 7-26 (for 1741); [Corbyn Morris], *Essay towards Illustrating the Science of Insurance, particularly whether it be Nationally Advantageous to Insure Ships of our Enemies*, London, 1747; Admiral H. W. Richmond, *The Navy in the War of 1739-48*, Cambridge, England, 1920, III, 248-250; C. Ernest Fayle, "The Deflection of Strategy by Commerce in the Eighteenth Century," and "Economic Pressure in the War of 1739-48," *Journal of the Royal United Service Institution*, LXVIII (1923), 281-294, 434-446; Charles Wright and C. Ernest Fayle, *A History of Lloyds*, London, 1928, pp. 80 ff.

54. Cited by F. M. Powicke, "The Economic Motive in Politics," *Economic History Review* XVI (1946), 91.

55. A. Jal, *Abraham du Quesne et la Marine de son Temps*, Paris, 1873, I, 470.

that for a country like Holland. The economic value of the British conquests of French colonies in America was great. Nevertheless it was to be remembered:

. . . that the value of our conquests thereby ought not to be estimated by the present produce, but by their probable increase. Neither ought the value of any country to be solely tried on its commercial advantages; that extent of territory and a number of subjects, are matters of as much consideration to a state attentive to the sources of real grandeur, as the mere advantages of traffic; that such ideas are rather suitable to a limited and petty commonwealth, like Holland, than to a great, powerful, and warlike nation. That on these principles, having made very large demands in North America, it was necessary to relax in other parts.[56]

There was general agreement that in France economic considerations played a lesser role in foreign policy than in England and Holland. In part, this was to be explained by the lesser importance even economically of foreign trade to France and by the lesser role of French merchants in French politics. George Lyttelton, an English observer at the Soissons Congress of 1729, where the question of the maintenance of the alliance with England was at issue, reported to his father:

Affairs are now almost at a crisis, and there is great reason to expect they will take a happy turn. Mr. Walpole has a surprizing influence over the cardinal [Cardinal Fleury, in charge of French foreign policy]; so that, whether peace or war ensue, we may depend upon our ally. In truth, it is the interest of the French court to be faithful to their engagements, though it may not entirely be the nation's. Emulation of trade might incline the people to wish the bond that ties them to us were broke; but the mercantile interest has at no time been much considered by this court. . . . The supposition, that present advantage is the basis and end of state engagements, and that they are only to

---

56. *Parliamentary History of England*, XV (1813), 1271-1272 (for December 9, 1762). For similar views as to the propriety of a country like Holland confining her foreign policy to commercial matters and to defense, without attempting to participate otherwise in *Haute Politique*, see the instructions prepared in 1771 by the French foreign office for the French Ambassador to Holland, *Recueil des Instructions Données aux Ambassadeurs et Ministres de France*, XXIII, Paris, 1924, 308.

For the comments of the Anglophile Prince of Orange in the course of his attempts to keep Holland neutral during the War of the American Revolution, which proved unsuccessful because of both pressure from France and the financial ambitions of the commercial classes in Holland, see *Archives ou Correspondance Inédite de la Maison d'Orange-Nassau*, 5th Series, F. J. L. Kramer, ed., Leyde, 1910, I, 607 ff., 618, 635 ff., 677 ff., *et passim*.

be measured by that rule, is the foundation of all our suspicions against the firmness of our French ally. But the maxim is not just. Much is given to future hopes, much obtained by future fears; and security is, upon many occasions, sought preferably to gain.[57]

Frenchmen in the period occasionally professed readiness to yield to Britain predominance in maritime trade if Britain would give France a free hand on the Continent,[58] but it would be a mistake to conclude that this reflected a readiness to concentrate on political objectives alone. Even on the Continent there were economic prizes to be won, though less glittering ones than those naval power could win overseas.

Historians, moreover, may have been too ready to find sharp differences in kind between the role of economic considerations in the making of foreign policy in England and France, respectively, in the age of mercantilism. The differences, though probably substantial, seem in the matters here relevant to have been differences in degree rather than in kind. In particular, the extent of the influence which commercial interests in France could in one way or another exercise on policy has been seriously underestimated by many historians, and both in theory and in practice absolutist government was not as absolute in power nor as non-commercial in motivation as the school textbooks have taught us. French records have been misleading in this regard because the older generation of historians were not interested in economic issues and tended to leave out of their compilations of documents matter of a markedly economic character, and French historians seem for some time to have been moving toward a reconsideration of the role of economic

---

57. *The Works of George Lord Lyttelton,* G. E. Ayscough, ed., 3rd ed., London, 1776, III, 243-44.

58. An instance in point is in a despatch by Louis XIV to his ambassador in London, in 1668: "Si les Anglais voulaient se contenter d'etre les plus grands marchands de l'Europe, et me laisser pour mon partage ce que je pourrais conquérir dans une juste guerre, rien ne serait si aisé que de nous accommoder ensemble." Cited by C.-G. Picavet, *La Diplomatie Française au Temps de Louis XIV,* Paris, 1930, p. 171.

About a century later, in 1772, George III of England, alarmed by the coalition of Austria, Prussia, and Russia to partition Poland, expressed sympathy for the idea of an alliance between Britain and France despite their traditional enmity: "Commerce the foundation of a marine can never flourish in an absolute monarchy; therefore that branch of grandeur ought to be left to England whilst the great army kept by France gives her a natural preeminence on the Continent." (Sir John Fortescue, ed., *The Correspondence of King George the Third,* London, 1927, II, 428-429.)

factors in the formulation of foreign policy under the Ancien Régime.[59]

There may have been monarchs who recognized no moral obligation to serve their people's interests, and there were no doubt ministers of state who had no loyalties except to their careers and perhaps to their royal masters. Frederick the Great is said to have declared, with brutal frankness, that "Je regarde les hommes comme une horde de cerfs dans le parc d'un grand seigneur et qui n'ont d'autre fonction que de peupler et de remplir l'enclos," and there is little in the King's voluminous writings which makes this incredible.[60] Some monarchs were, to modern taste, childish in the weight they gave to the routine symbols of prestige and protocol.[61]

59. For representative contemporary evidence in support of these points, see: *Mémoires de Louis XIV*, Jean Longnon, ed., Paris, 1927, p. 73; a proclamation of Louis XIV reprinted in P. M. Bondois, "Colbert et l'industrie de la dentelle," *Mémoires et Documents pour Servir à l'Histoire du Commerce et de l'Industrie en France*, VI (1921), 263; Vauban, "Description Géographique de l'Élection de Vézeley" [1696], in A. de Boislisle, *Mémoires des Intendants sur l'État des Généralités*, Paris, 1881, I, 738-49; G. Lacour-Gayet, *L'Éducation Politique de Louis XIV*, 2nd ed., Paris, 1923, pp. 341 ff. For reconsiderations of the traditional views by modern historians, see A. Jal, *Abraham du Quesne et la Marine de son Temps*, Paris, 1883, II, 352-53; P. Muret (a book review), *Revue d'Histoire Moderne et Contemporaine*, IV (1902-3), 39-41; J. Hitier, "La Doctrine de l'Absolutisme," *Annales de l'Université de Grenoble*, XV (1903), 106-113, 121-31; Charles Normand, *La Bourgeoisie Française au XVII° Siècle, 1604-1661*, Paris, 1908, pp. 195, 279-287; Henri Hauser, La *Pensée et l'Action Économiques du Cardinal de Richelieu*, Paris, 1944, pp. 185 ff.; Philip Dur, "The Right of Taxation in the Political Theory of the French Religious Wars," *Journal of Modern History*, XVII (December 1945), 289-303.

60. Frederick the Great did recognize, however, at least in principle and in his better moments, that the economic well-being of his people should be one of the major objectives of a monarch. See his "Essai sur les Formes de Gouvernement et sur les Devoirs des Souverains," of which he had printed a few copies only in 1777, *Oeuvres*, IX (1848), 195-210.

61. To a letter from Louis XIII in 1629 proposing closer commercial relations, Czar Michel Federowitz of Russia replied favorably, but complained about the manner in which he had been addressed: "Mais nous ne savons à quoi attribuer que notre nom, nos titres et nos qualités aient été oubliés à la lettre que vous nous avez écrit. Tous les potentats de la terre ... écrivant à notre grande puissance, mettent notre nom sur les lettres et n'oublient aucun des titres et des qualités que nous possédons. Nous ne pouvons approuver votre coutume de vouloir être notre ami, et de nous dénier et ôter les titres que le Dieu tout-puissant nous a donnés et que nous possédons si justement. Que sí, à l'avenir, vous désirez vivre en bonne amitié et parfaite correspondance avec notre grande puissance, en sorte que nos royales personnes et nos empires joints ensemble donnent de la terreur à tout l'univers, il faudra que vous commandiez qu'aux lettres que vous nous récrirez à l'avenir toute la dignité de nostre grande puissance, notre nom, nos titres et nos qualités soient écrits comme elles sont en cette lettre que nous

The personal idiosyncrasies of rulers and, above all, dynastic ambitions, exerted their influence on the course of events. Occasionally religious differences made the course of diplomacy run a little less smoothly by injecting an ideological factor into the range of matters out of which disputes could arise or by which they could be sharpened. But it seems clear that predominantly diplomacy was centered on and governed by considerations of power and plenty throughout the period and for all of Europe, and that religious considerations were more often invoked for propaganda purposes than genuinely operative in fashioning foreign policy. Even the cardinals, who in some degree monopolized the diplomatic profession on the Continent, granted that religious considerations must not be permitted to get in the way of vital national interests, and even genuine missionary enterprises could get seriously entangled with the pursuit of commercial privileges. When Louis XIII in 1626 sent an emissary to Persia with the primary purpose of promoting the Catholic religion, he instructed him at the same time to seek special privileges for French trade as compensation for the diplomatic difficulties with the English and the Dutch which would result from a French attempt to catholicize Persia. "Sa majesté pensait qu'on ne pouvait éviter cet inconvénient qu'en se rendant maître du commerce du pays, lequel, outre le gain des âmes, qui est celui que sa majesté recherchait, offrirait encore à son royaume de notable avantages."[62]

The role of the religious factor in Cromwell's foreign policy has been much debated. The literature of historical debate on this

---

vous envoyons de notre part. Nous vous ferons la semblable en écrivant tous vos titres et toutes vos qualités dans les lettres que nous vous manderons, étant le propre des amis d'augmenter plutôt réciproquement leurs titres et qualités que de les diminuer ou retrancher." *Recueil des Instructions*, VIII (1890), 29.

62. G. deR. de Flassan, *Histoire Générale et Raisonnée de la Diplomatie Française*, 2nd ed., Paris, 1811, II, 395-6.

In 1713 Charles XII of Sweden wrote to Queen Anne demanding that England, in conformity with her treaty obligations, give him assistance in regaining his territories in the Germanic Empire. "It was not possible," he said, "that Anne could allow her mind to be influenced by the sordid interests of trade; the protectress of the Protestant religion could not fail to support the Protestant power of the north," as against Russia. But Russia at the time was seeking admittance into the Grand Alliance against Louis XIV, and England, alarmed at the ambitions of both monarchs, made no choice. See Mrs. D'Arcy Collyer, "Notes on the Diplomatic Correspondence between England and Russia in the First Half of the Eighteenth Century," *Transactions of the Royal Historical Society*, New Series, XIV (1900), 146 ff.

question is voluminous, but it is not apparent to the layman that any progress toward a definitive decision has been made, unless it is that Cromwell was a complex personality on whom economic, religious, and power considerations all had their influence, but in varying degrees and combinations at different times. George L. Beer quotes Firth as saying about Cromwell that: "Looked at from one point of view, he seemed as practical as a commercial traveller; from another, a Puritan Don Quixote," and gives as his own verdict that "It was 'the commercial traveller' who acted, and the 'Puritan Don Quixote' who dreamt and spoke."[63] Other historians have given other interpretations.[64]

I have unfortunately not been able to find an orthodox neo-Marxian study dealing with these issues for this period. If there were one such, and if it followed the standard pattern, it would argue that "in the last analysis" the end of foreign policy had been not power, and not power and plenty, but plenty alone, and plenty for the privileged classes only, and it would charge that members of these classes would always be there in every major diplomatic epi-

---

63. Cromwell's Policy in its Economic Aspects," *Political Science Quarterly*, XVII (March 1902), 46-47.

64. Cf. John Morley, *Oliver Cromwell*, New York, 1902, p. 434; Guernsey Jones, *The Diplomatic Relations between Cromwell and Charles X. Gustavus of Sweden*, Lincoln, Neb., 1897, pp. 34-35; Frank Strong, "The Causes of Cromwell's West Indian Expedition," *American Historical Review*, IV (January 1899), 245; M. P. Ashley, *Financial and Commercial Policy under the Cromwellian Protectorate*, Oxford, 1934; [Slingsby Bethel], *The World's Mistake in Oliver Cromwell* [1668], in *The Harleian Miscellany*, London, 1810, VII, 356-57.
I have not been able to find any systematic or comprehensive study of the role of the religious factor in power politics. The following references are a fair sample of the material bearing on this which I have come across: Leon Geley, *Fancan et la Politique de Richelieu de 1617 à 1627*, Paris, 1884, pp. 264-290; "Discours sur ce qui peut sembler estre plus expedient, & à moyenner au sujet des guerres entre l'Empereur & le Palatin," [1621], in *Recueil de Quelques Discours Politiques*, no place given, 1632, pp. 314 ff; C. C. Eckhardt, *The Papacy and World Affairs as Reflected in the Secularization of Politics*, Chicago, 1937, p. 89; S. Rojdestvensky and Inna Lubimenko, *Contribution à l'Histoire des Relations Commerciales Franco-Russes au XVIII° Siècle*, Paris, 1929, p. 4; *Mèmoires de Noailles*, Paris, 1777, I, 126; Cheruel, "Le Baron Charles D'Avaugour Ambassadeur de France en Suède, 1654-1657," *Revue d'Histoire Diplomatique*, III (1889), 529; [Jean Rousset de Missy], *The History of Cardinal Alberoni*, London, 1719, p. 105; W. E. Lingelbach, "The Doctrine and Practice of Intervention in Europe," *Annals of the American Academy*, XVI (July 1900), 17, note; "Les Principes Généraux de la Guerre," *Oeuvres de Frédéric le Grand*, XXVIII (Berlin, 1856), 50; C.-G. Picavet, *La Diplomatie Française au Temps de Louis XIV*, Paris, 1930, pp. 8, 160-166; Georges Pagès, *La Monarchie d'Ancien Régime en France*, Paris, 1928, pp. 67 ff.

sode, pulling the strings of foreign policy-making for their own special benefit. Writing a few years ago in criticism of this theory as applied to more recent times, I ventured the following comment: "While I suspect that Marx himself would not have hesitated to resort to the 'scandal' theory of imperialism and war when convenient for propaganda purposes, I am sure that he would basically have despised it for its vulgar or unscientific character."[65] I was "righter" than I deserved to be.

Karl Marx studied the British diplomacy of this period, even making use of the unpublished records in the British Foreign Office, and discussed the role played by commercial objectives in British foreign policy. The ruling oligarchy needed political allies at home, and found them in some section or other of the *haute bourgeoisie.*

As to their *foreign policy,* they wanted to give it the appearance at least of being altogether regulated by the mercantile interest, an appearance the more easily to be produced, as the exclusive interest of one or the other small fraction of that class would, of course, be always identified with this or that Ministerial measure. The interested fraction then raised the commerce and navigation cry, which the nation stupidly re-echoed.

Eighteenth century practice thus "developed on the Cabinet, at least, the *onus* of inventing *mercantile pretexts,* however futile, for their measures of foreign policy." Writing in the 1850's, Marx found that procedure had changed. Palmerston did not bother to find commercial pretexts for his foreign policy measures.

In our own epoch, British ministers have thrown this burden on foreign nations, leaving to the French, the Germans, etc., the irksome task of discovering the *secret* and *hidden* mercantile springs of their actions. Lord Palmerston, for instance, takes a step apparently the most damaging to the material interests of Great Britain. Up starts a State philosopher, on the other side of the Atlantic, or of the Channel, or in the heart of Germany, who puts his head to the rack to dig out the mysteries of the mercantile Machiavelism of "perfide Albion," of which Palmerston is supposed the unscrupulous and unflinching executor.[66]

Marx, in rejecting the economic explanation of British friendship for Russia, fell back upon an explanation of both a sentimental

---

65. "International Relations between State-Controlled National Economies," *American Economic Review Supplement,* XXXIV (March 1944), 324.

66. Karl Marx, *Secret Diplomatic History of the Eighteenth Century,* Eleanor Marx Aveling, ed., London, 1899, pp. 55-56. The italics are in the original.

pro-Russianism in high circles in Britain and an unjustified fear of Russian power. It is a paradox that the father of Marxism should have sponsored a doctrine which now sounds so non-Marxian. I cannot believe, however, that the appeals to economic considerations which played so prominent a part in eighteenth-century British discussions of Anglo-Russian relations were all pretext, and I can find little evidence which makes it credible that friendly sentiment towards foreigners played a significant role in the foreign policy of England in the eighteenth century. Leaving sentiment aside, England's foreign policy towards Russia in the eighteenth century, like English and European foreign policy in general, was governed by joint and harmonized considerations of power and economics. That the economics at least was generally misguided, and that it served to poison international relations, is another matter which, though not relevant *here*, is highly relevant now.

Bentham and J. S. Mill:
The Utilitarian Background*

THE ONE-HUNDREDTH ANNIVERSARY of the publication of J. S. Mill's *Principles of Political Economy* falls in the year 1948, and the American Economic Association in the programming of its meetings takes advantage of anniversaries of births, deaths, and dates of publication to remind its members that our discipline has a past. This is a proper occasion, therefore, for a paper on J. S. Mill. The inclusion of Bentham in the scope of my paper is of my own contriving, but perhaps I can technically legitimatize it by appeal to the fact that British learned circles have been celebrating during 1948 the two-hundredth anniversary of Bentham's birth. There is no intellectual difficulty, however, in associating Bentham with Mill. The intellectual history of Mill is in large part a history, first, of faithful discipleship, then of rebellion from, and finally of substantial return, to the Benthamite set of doctrines.

The general lines of Bentham's thought were wholly of the eighteenth century, as I could demonstrate if there were time. Of English intellectuals who have had great influence, Bentham was perhaps the least original in his stock of general ideas, but clearly the most original in finding means and devices for putting his philosophy to practical use. To the nineteenth century Bentham was important as a carrier of eighteenth century thought and, still more, as a translator of this thought into a program of social reform. It was the seventeenth century which was the Age of Genius. The philosophers of the eighteenth century were, nonetheless, fertile in ideas. They were, however, almost completely devoid of zeal for the application of these ideas to change of institutions, or even of

*A paper presented at the meetings of the American Economic Association, Dec. 29, 1948. Reprinted from *The American Economic Review,* Vol. 39, March 1949, pp. 360-382, by the courtesy of the American Economic Association.

zeal in generating ideas which would call for change in existing institutions.

We economists like to think of Adam Smith as an exception in this regard, but he was so only to a moderate extent. The one social issue on which Adam Smith was a zealot was the issue of freedom of trade *versus* mercantilism. But Smith had little confidence in the ability of ideas to move worlds. It is often overlooked that it was with reference to internal as well as to international free trade that Adam Smith made his famous statement that "To expect, indeed, that the freedom of trade should ever be entirely restored in Great Britain, is as absurd as to expect that an Oceana or Utopia should ever be established in it," and this although when he wrote, by obsolescence rather than by deliberate repeal, the restrictions on internal freedom of trade had already become largely inoperative. There is no evidence that Smith was more optimistic about the prospects for international than for domestic free trade, or that, beyond writing his book and preparing a few memoranda for the government when called upon, he ever felt moved to do anything, and especially to resort to anything rude or, in the eighteenth-century meaning of the term, to "enthusiasm," to obtain acceptance and execution of his reforming ideas.

The eighteenth century, in Britain if not in France, and before the American and the French Revolutions if not after, was the age of social complacency, political, economic, moral, of satisfaction with the *status quo* at least to the extent of belief that the costs of substantial change would exceed the benefits of removal or moderation of whatever evils were recognized to prevail. British eighteenth-century government was oligarchic, corrupt, inefficient, though it was generally not tyrannical in intent and usually too lax, too inert, too decentralized, and too sceptical to be seriously tyrannical in effect. Until the end of the century there was no major figure who even mildly suggested the need for major political reform. Whether the economic condition of the masses of the people was improving or deteriorating, and whatever its trend, whether it was desperately bad or moderately good as compared to later standards, I frankly have no idea. We may rest assured, however, that it was not idyllic, if only because it never is.

Nevertheless, there was not until the very last moments of the century either a single major political debate which turned on the economic conditions of the poor or a single major writer who had important suggestions as to how to improve them, with the sole exception of Adam Smith's plea for freedom of trade. It was even a common doctrine of the century that the poor should never be relieved of their poverty above the level of a bare subsistence plus perhaps a few crumbs of cake, and it was at least the quasi-official doctrine of the Church of England that the poverty of the poor—and the prosperity of the bishops—were in accordance with the Divine Will.

Bentham and the Benthamites, on the other hand, were never complacent about the condition of the people of England. They were "Radical Reformers," and they worked hard at their reforms: by working out detailed blueprints for them; by propaganda, agitation, intrigue, conspiracy; and, if truth be told, by encouragement to revolutionary movements up to—but not beyond—the point where resort to physical force would be the next step. Bentham, moreover, was a successful social reformer, more successful perhaps than anyone else in history except Karl Marx—I have in mind here only the realization and not the merits of programs of change—if he is given credit for those changes which came after his death as the result largely of the efforts of his disciples.

The list of reforms in England which derive largely from Bentham is a truly impressive one, and I present it here only in part: fundamental law reform in many of its branches; prison reform; adult popular suffrage, including woman suffrage; free trade; reform in colonial government; legalization of trade unions; general education at public expense; free speech and free press; the secret ballot; a civil service appointed and promoted on merit; repeal of the usury laws; general registration of titles to property; reform of local government; a safety code for merchant shipping; sanitary reform and preventive medicine at public expense; systematic collection of statistics; free justice for the poor. Bentham was the first person to propose birth-control as a measure of economic reform, and this *before* Malthus had published his first *Essay on the Principle of Population*.[1] The Ministry of Health which he proposed would be made responsible not only for general sanitation and routine public

---

1. See J. Bentham, "Situation and Relief of the Poor," *Annals of Agriculture*, Vol. XXIX (1797), pp. 422-23 (p. 31, in the separate pamphlet version). See also Norman E. Himes, "Jeremy Bentham and the Genesis of English Neo-Malthusianism," *Economic History* (Suppl. of *The Economic Journal*), Vol. III (1936), pp. 267-76.

health work, but also for smoke prevention, local health-museums, and the policing of the medical profession to prevent their formation of monopolies.

Related to the conditions of the time when these reforms were proposed, Bentham's program was comprehensive, radical, and progressive without being visionary. The modern "democratic socialist" would find it wanting, since Bentham did not approve of tampering with the system of private property except through inheritance taxation and insisted on "compensation" where reform measures would involve violation of "reasonable expectations." He apparently never formulated any concrete proposals for social security on an insurance basis, but he approved in principle of government-administered and government-subsidized insurance against every conceivable type of social hazard for which individual prudence could not make adequate provision. It was too early for proposals to stabilize employment through monetary or fiscal measures, although Bentham did explore the possibility of increasing real investment and production through the "forced frugality" induced by the issue of paper money.[2] Pronounced individualist though he was, his specific program of reforms in both the content and the processes of legislation, in governmental organization, and in public administration, made him a major source of inspiration for the Fabian socialists as well as for the laissez-faire liberals.

To belief in political democracy Bentham came only slowly, and only as their failure to adopt his proposals eroded his faith in the good intentions of the British aristocratic politicians. The Benthamite case for political democracy was first elaborately expounded by James Mill in his famous essay on Government first published in 1820. It turned out to be an embarrassment for Bentham and his other disciples because by the scholastic formalism of its argument and the extreme lengths to which it carried Bentham's doctrine it was seriously vulnerable to rebuttal and, even worse, to ridicule. Starting out from the proposition that the sole proper purpose of government is to promote the greatest happiness of mankind, James Mill proceeded by purely *a priori* analysis, without any reference

---

2. Bentham's treatment of this still remains in large part in manuscript. Extracts from these unpublished manuscripts and comments by Ricardo on them have recently been published by Edmund Silberner, "Un Manuscrit Inédit de David Ricardo sur le Problème Monétaire," *Revue d'Histoire Économique et Sociale*, Vol. XXV (1940), 195-259, and were then also already in page proof in Piero Sraffa's long-forthcoming edition of Ricardo's works.

to history or to contemporary fact, from the premise that legislators served *only* their "sinister interests"—a stock Benthamite term for the self-interest of rulers or a ruling class—to the conclusion that good government was therefore obtainable only by making it, through popular suffrage and frequent elections, the self-interest of the elected to serve the interests of the electors.

Bentham, writing in the 1780's, had conceded that if at any time legislators "have suffered the nation to be preyed upon by swarms of idle pensioners, or useless place-men, it has rather been from negligence and imbecility, than from any settled plan for oppressing and plundering of the people," but in 1814 he appended a note withdrawing the concession: "So thought Anno 1780 and 1790.—Not so Anno 1814.—J. Bentham."[3] By that time he had adopted the doctrine of "Sinister Interests." But James Mill carried the doctrine further than was necessary to meet Bentham's requirements and probably further than Bentham's belief in it. As Tawney has remarked: "To [James Mill] the State is not a band of brothers, but a mutual detective society: the principal advantage of popular government is that there are more detectives, and therefore, presumably, fewer thieves."[4] Bentham always, but James Mill rarely, if ever, conceded that men, even legislators, could not only be influenced by the praise and blame of other men, but could even display some measure of pure benevolence. As Barker has commented: ". . . while all—or nearly all—of the theorems of Mill's article may be found in Bentham, they have undergone a change. The egoism is more egoistic; the negativism is more negative,"[5] and it may be added the *a priori* analysis more "high *priori*." In the seventeenth century Harrington had denied that Hobbes could work the miracle of "making you a king by geometry." Macaulay was now to deny that the Benthamites could depose an aristocracy by geometry.

Macaulay, a young man anxiously seeking fame by his fluent and facile pen, found the opportunity in James Mill's essay on Government. Reviewing in 1829, in the magisterial *Edinburgh Review*, a reprint of this essay of James Mill, Macaulay raked it high and low, primarily on the basis of its use, without benefit of historical induc-

---

3. Bentham, "Principles of Morals and Legislation," *Works* (Edinburgh, 1838-1843), I. 5.

4. R. H. Tawney, preface to *Life and Struggles of William Lovett*, new ed. (New York, 1920), p. xxi.

5. Sir Ernest Barker, in the preface of his edition of James Mill, *Essay on Government* (Cambridge, England, 1937), p. xv.

tion or of reference to contemporary facts, of the *a priori* or, in the language of the time and earlier, the geometrical method, but also on the more concrete ground that the proposition that legislators *always* and *invariably* act in terms of their selfish interests was preposterous whatever the method by which it was attempted to establish it.[6]

The Benthamites were shaken by the attack, and J. S. Mill most so, as we shall see later. But Macaulay himself, without withdrawing anything of what he had written, soon thereafter made his peace with James Mill and from then on was an exponent of political democracy on the basis of a line of argument which Paxton in his *Civil Polity* had already presented in 1703, and which should have been the original and was to become the standard line of the Benthamites, namely, that only by democratic voting could there be an adequate guarantee that legislators would *always* or predominantly serve the general interest, without denial that they might sometimes do so even in the absence of democracy.

I come now to deal more systematically with the most difficult and the most controverted aspect of Benthamism, namely, its psychological and ethical justifications for utilitarianism as legislative policy.

Bentham's main concern with ethics was with the ethics which should be followed by moral leaders, not with the ethics of the ordinary man, not with private morals, except as they were data to be operated on by the elite. "The science," he said, "whose foundations we have explored can appeal only to lofty minds with whom the public welfare has become a passion."[7] And by them, Bentham held, its lessons should be pressed on legislators, whether *their* minds were lofty ones or not. As Bentham acknowledged,[8] he sometimes overlooked this, and wrote as if what he had to say was directed at private morals, and critics have made much of this oversight without treating it merely as a lapse from his fundamental purposes. It was Benthamism interpreted as a system of private ethics, didactic as well as descriptive, that has aroused the most

---

6. See the preface, pp. ix-xi and pp. 160 ff. of *The Miscellaneous Writings and Speeches of Lord Macaulay*, Popular Edition (London, 1891).

7. *Theory of Legislation*, C. M. Atkinson, ed. (London, 1914), II. 337.

8. Cf. for example, the preface, first added to the 1823 edition, of his *Introduction to the Principles of Morals and Legislation*, where he says that "an introduction to a plan of a penal code" would have been a title better indicating the nature of its contents.

violent and the most emotional antagonism. Even as private ethics, however, Benthamism has seemed so vulnerable a target to *odium theologicum* and *odium ethicum* only because the private ethics of the critics permitted them to attack Bentham's words without taking pains to ascertain what the thoughts were which these words were intended to communicate.

Bentham starts from the standard eighteenth-century proposition, common to theologians and to sceptical philosophers alike, that man operates "under the governance of two sovereign masters, pain and pleasure." Happiness is a net sum or aggregate of individually experienced pleasures and pains.[9] Man, he claims, acts only in response to his "interests," by which he usually, and fundamentally, means whatever men are interested in, but, unfortunately, frequently allows to mean what men regard as in their self-interest. Men normally are interested to some extent in the happiness of others than themselves, and in exceptional cases are capable of "universal benevolence," or a dominating concern with the happiness of mankind at large, but generally, if they are left to themselves, there will be serious discrepancy between the actual behavior of individuals and the behavior which would conduce to "the greatest happiness of the greatest number." It is the function of legislation to coerce or bribe individuals to make their behavior coincide with that required by the greatest-happiness principle, and of education and moral leaders to mould men's desires so that they spontaneously associate the happiness of others with their own happiness.

Bentham nowhere attempts or asserts the possibility of a positive demonstration that greatest happiness, whether as hedonism or as eudaemonism, is the proper moral objective for the common man, the moral leader, or the legislator, and his only argument in support of the greatest-happiness principle is the negative one that the rival principles proposed by other ethical systems are either resolvable upon scrutiny to verbal variants of the utility principle, or are sheer *ipse dixitism*, or are meaningless patterns of words.

"Pleasure" and "happiness" were to Bentham widely inclusive terms, involving not only the pleasures of the senses but also those

---

9. *Cf.* "Gamaliel Smith" [= Jeremy Bentham], *Not Paul, but Jesus* (London, 1823), p. 394: "happiness, to be anything, must be composed of pleasures: and, be the man who he may, of what it is that gives pleasure to him, he alone can be judge."

of the heart and the mind. Pleasures, moreover, which in their "simple" or primary form, genetically speaking, were pleasures of self could by "association of ideas" become associated with the pleasures of others. Man, by living in society, by education, and by acts of parliament, could be made good. The eighteenth-century utilitarians may have traded, as a German philosopher has put it, "in the small wares of usefulness (*Nutzlichkeitskrämerei*)." Or it may be that to accept the pursuit of pleasure as a proper end of man is "swinish doctrine," if it be proper to assume that man pursues swinish pleasures. But a utilitarian does not have to be a Philistine. If in Bentham's exposition of his psychology there was often undue stress on the selfish sentiments, this fault—which was much more evident in James Mill than in Bentham—was the result of lack of imagination and of feeling, or of faulty observation—itself the consequence of these lacks—rather than any inherent incompatibility of broader views with the logic of his system. One important manifestation of this—systematic on the part of James Mill but only occasional and incidental on the part of Bentham—was the assumption that even when one's own pleasure had through association of ideas become involved in the pleasure of other persons, the affectionate sentiments toward others still contained an element of conscious reference back to one's own pleasures. This, by implication at least, was a proclamation of the universal prevalence of psychological hedonism.[10]

The eighteenth century is often termed the "Age of Reason," and it is correctly so termed if by the phrase is meant that it was the age in which philosophers held that the credibility of all things should be tested by reason. But from the point of view of its prevailing psychological doctrines, it could more properly be called the "Age of the Passions" because of its stress on the emotions and the instincts, the affections and aversions, and its playing down of the role of reason in the behavior of the ordinary man. David Hume was writing in the spirit of his times when he declared that: "Reason is and ought only to be the slave of the passions, and can never pretend to any other office than to serve and obey them." The normal role of reason was that of an obedient servant of the passions, a

10. In notes to his edition of James Mill, *Analysis of the Phenomena of the Human Mind* (London, 1869), J. S. Mill, without fully admitting that his father had held this doctrine, points out passages which could be interpreted as implying it. See II. 217, note; II. 233 ff., note; II. 286 ff. note, etc.

passive agent for the comparison of their relative intensities and for the justification of the choices made between them. "So convenient a thing," said Benjamin Franklin, in his Autobiography, "it is to be a reasonable creature, since it enables one to find or make a reason for everything one has a mind to do."

For the moral philosopher and the properly conditioned legislator, however, Bentham assigned more important roles to reason, first, that of moulding the passions of individuals so that they would contribute more to the augmentation of general happiness, and second, that of providing a technique for the comparison of passions of individuals with a view to making a socially oriented choice between them where choice had to be or could be made. It was for this social purpose, and not for the routine behavior of routine individuals, that Bentham endeavored to construct what he at different times labelled as a "moral thermometer," a "moral arithmetic," a "felicific calculus."

Much amusement has been derived from Bentham's attempt to develop a technique by which the quantities of pleasure and pain could be measured by the legislator or the benevolent philosopher. Wesley Mitchell's well-known essay on "Bentham's Felicific Calculus,"[11] is the fullest and the least unsympathetic account I am acquainted with of Bentham's position on this question. Mitchell points out the excessive degree of hedonism attributed by Bentham to mankind, and comments penetratingly on Bentham's attempt to find a common denominator through money for the pleasures of different persons. Mitchell says that in fact Bentham used the calculus not as an instrument of calculation, but as a basis of ordinal classification. "It pointed out to him what elements should be considered in a given situation, and among these elements *seriatim* he was often able to make comparisons in terms of greater and less." I think this is a somewhat misleading description of Bentham's method. The "classification" was not *seriatim*, was not in terms of higher and lower, but merely of pro and con, of pleasure and pain, and was wholly preliminary to rather than part of the calculus. The "calculus" as he actually used it was merely a mental comparison of the comparative weights of the pros and cons, a technique which neither calls for fancy labels nor is properly conducive either to merriment or to measurement.

---

11. Reprinted in W. C. Mitchell, *The Backward Art of Spending Money* (New York, 1937), pp. 177-202.

Bentham did not invent the concept or the terminology of "moral arithmetic." Play with the idea of measuring the unmeasurable and resort to the language of measurement where it was silly to attempt to apply it goes back to at least the seventeenth century, when the prestige of geometry and later of algebra tended to trap all philosophers with scientific pretensions into casting their analysis into pseudo-mathematical form. Mandeville, as early as 1730, laughed at physicians who studied mathematics because it was fashionable, and cited one who had advised that for certain diseases "the doses of the medicines are to be as the Squares of the Constitutions."[12] Thomas Reid, in his *Essay on Quantity* of 1748, questioned the possibility of reducing to measurement such things as sensations, beauty, pleasure, and the affections and appetites of the mind, even though they "are capable of more and less," and he warned that to apply mathematical language to non-measurable things is "to make a show of mathematical reasoning, without advancing one step in real knowledge."[13]

Bentham never went far afield for the sources of his ideas, and I suspect that Benjamin Franklin was his source, direct or indirect, for this idea of classification by "bipartition" plus "measurement" of the relative weight of the two classes. Franklin a few years earlier, in 1772, had been expounding it in private correspondence with Joseph Priestley and Richard Price—with all three of whom Bentham had personal contacts—in very much the same terms as Bentham was later to use, and under the similar, and already old, label of "moral or prudential algebra."[14]

None of Bentham's immediate disciples showed any interest in this aspect of Bentham's thought, and it was not until Jevons drew attention to it and made it the basis of his subjective theory of economic value that it had any influence, for good or bad. I like to think, more so probably than Wesley Mitchell would have appreciated, that Bentham's felicific calculus was merely one more manifestation of the inferiority complex which practitioners of the social "sciences" had in the eighteenth century, and have reacquired

12. Bernard Mandeville, M.D., *A Treatise of the Hypochondriack and Hysterick Diseases*, 2nd ed. (London, 1730), p. 184. Compare the history of "Lullism."

13. *The Works of Thomas Reid*, Sir William Hamilton, ed., 3rd ed. (Edinburgh, 1852), p. 717.

14. *The Monthly Repository*, Vol. XII (1817), p. 13, and *Proceedings of the Massachusetts Historical Society*, 2nd ser., Vol. XVII (1903), p. 264.

in the twentieth, towards mathematics, towards the exact sciences, and towards quantification as one of the higher virtues. Since with the application of "political arithmetic" to "moral arithmetic" we now all accept without protest the derivation of measured "propensities" from correlations between psychologically and otherwise promiscuous statistical aggregates compiled catch-as-catch-can on anything up to global scale, our readiness to laugh at Bentham's modest and wholly platonic gestures in this direction excites my propensity for amazement.

There remains one question, specially important for economics, where the influence of Bentham on J. S. Mill is obvious, the question of laissez-faire, or the economic role of government. Élie Halévy, in his great but tendentious work on the Benthamites,[15] has made much of the existence in Bentham's system of a conflict between his juristic and his economic doctrines. According to Halévy, Bentham in his juristic theory makes it the primary function of government to create an *artificial* harmony between the interests of individuals and the public interest, whereas in his economic theory he reaches laissez-faire conclusions on the basis of an implied natural or spontaneous harmony of interests. This has become a stereotype of present-day comments on Bentham, and although there may be exceptions to the natural law which proclaims that stereotypes in the field of the history of ideas provide a light which blinds rather than guides, this is not one of them.

Bentham did interpret the function of government, under the influence largely of Helvétius, as that of creating, through the application of rewards and punishments, an approach to harmony between the interests of individuals and the social interests. He did prescribe limits for the field for governmental intervention in economic matters, but these limits were not, as we shall see, very narrow ones, and in any case were not so narrow as to give scope for a doctrine of natural harmony of interests, in the sense of a harmony preordained or inherent in the nature of man living in a society unregulated by government. Of explicit formulation by Bentham of a doctrine of natural harmony I can find not the slightest trace in his writings, and such a doctrine would be in basic conflict not only with his juristic theories but with his whole cosmological outlook. Faith in natural harmony always stems from either faith in the

15. *La Formation du Radicalisme Philosophique*, 3 vols. (Paris, 1901-1904). There is an inferior edition in English in one volume.

continuous intervention of a beneficent Author of Nature or faith in the workings of a natural evolutionary process, and the Benthamites rejected the former and had not yet heard of the latter.

It has been common since Adam Smith's day to take for granted *in economics* the role of the state with reference to the protection of legal property rights and the enforcement of contracts, leaving it to juristic inquiry to explore the problems of theory and of practice in this field. Such was also the procedure of Bentham, and in his juristic writings he keeps very much in mind that "passion . . . from the excesses of which, by reason of its strength, constancy, and universality, society has most to apprehend; I mean that which corresponds to the motive of pecuniary interest."[16] Here he deals with the problem of "repression" of harmful economic activity by means of civil and penal law. If Bentham believed that there was a natural harmony of private and public interests in the economic field, it was one, therefore, which would prevail only after the magistrate and the constable had performed their duties.[17]

But Bentham does not advocate anything like "anarchy plus the constable." His most general proposition of a laissez-faire character is as follows:

With the view of causing an increase to take place in the mass of national wealth, or with a view to increase of the means either of subsistence or enjoyment, without some special reasons, the general rule is, that nothing ought to be done or attempted by government. The motto, or watchword of government, on these occasions, ought to be— *Be Quiet.*[18]

This may sound like a sweeping enough support of laissez-faire, if, as is common though rarely desirable practice in such matters, it be read carelessly and out of its context. There are important qualifications, explicit or implied, within this apparently emphatic text. First, the text deals with "encouragement" and not with "repression" of economic activity. As I have already pointed out, Bentham deals with the problem of repression of harmful economic activity as a problem in law and not in economics. Second, the gen-

---

16. "Introduction to the Principles of Morals and Legislation," *Works*, Vol. I, pp. 90-91.

17. Bentham deals briefly with the relations between political economy and law in "A General View of a Complete Code of Laws," *Works*, Vol. III, pp. 203-4.

18. "Manual of Political Economy," *Works*, Vol. III, p. 33. All subsequent citations of Bentham are from the "Manual."

eral rule of doing nothing positive is applicable only if there is no special reason to the contrary. A rule is not equivalent for him to a principle, nor a "motto" to a dogma.

Bentham presents three grounds for the general rule against governmental activity of a positive kind in the economic field: (1) in this field, individuals know their own interest better than government can; (2) individuals operate more ardently and more skillfully in pursuit of their own interests than government can or will operate on their behalf; (3) governmental intervention means coercion, either directly or indirectly through taxation, and coercion involves "pain" and therefore is an evil.

Bentham is ready to approve of any departure from the general rule, however, if a case can be made for such departure on utility grounds. "Indiscriminate generalizations" are an error, he says, and "In laying down general rules, [even] fortuitous and transient cases ought not to be forgotten." And he lives up to his doctrine as, for instance, when he says that "what ought not to be done with the intention of supporting an unprofitable branch of trade, may yet be proper for preventing the ruin of the workmen employed in such business," or, when opposing in general any restrictions on the introduction of labor-saving machinery, he approves, however, of transitory aid to workmen injured economically by such introduction.

Bentham does not, moreover, limit his exceptions from the non-intervention rule to fortuitous and transient cases, but presents an elaborate analysis of the circumstances under which government should not ("non-agenda") and those under which it should ("agenda") intervene. The argument may, to some tastes, be weighted too heavily on the side of *non-agenda*, but it is free from any dogma except the utilitarian one with which it is supposed by Halévy to clash.

Whether government should intervene, says Bentham, should depend on the extent of the power, intelligence, and inclination, and therefore the spontaneous initiative, possessed by the public, and this will vary as between countries. "In Russia, under Peter the Great, the list of *sponte acta* being a blank, that of *agenda* was proportionally abundant." Government has special responsibilities for providing security against food shortages as well as military security. He approves of government aid in the construction of roads, canals, iron railways, of public hospitals for the sick, hurt and helpless, of public establishments for the "occasional maintenance and employment of able-bodied poor," and, as we have seen, of public health activities on a scale still unknown. He was an ardent advocate of general education at public expense and he urged the extension of governmental registration services to make fraud more hazardous—and also of the systematic collection of economic statistics, but with a proviso which I suspect saps his concession of most of its virtue for modern statisticians, namely, that "no institution should be set on foot for the furnishing any such articles, without a previous indication of the benefit derivable from such knowledge, and a conviction that it will pay for the expense."

Whatever its merits or defects, this treatment of the economic role of government is not in manner or substance doctrinaire, is not in any detail, as far as I can see, inconsistent with his general "principle of utility," and does not have in it, explicitly or implicitly, any trace of a doctrine of natural harmony of interests. It is to be borne in mind, moreover, that the best Bentham hopes for after all that can be done artificially to harmonize private interests with the public interest will still be far from perfect harmony. This has, indeed, been made the basis from another point of view of attack by moral philosophers of other faiths against utilitarianism: it is taken to task for failing to build a bridge between individual and general happiness. But this would be a valid criticism only if either it had professed to have succeeded in doing so and failed, or if it were a proper demand of *any* moral philosophy that it should provide a *practicable* scheme of perfect harmony of interests. Bentham did not completely bridge the gulf between private interests and the general interest, but neither did he deny the existence of such a gulf, and he did propose two ways, education and government, by which the gulf could be somewhat narrowed—with religion, though grudgingly, accepted as a useful part of education in so far as it educates for virtue. Does anyone know of a third way?

I turn now to John Stuart Mill. His famous *Autobiography*—revealing, but not as much so as he no doubt intended—made generally known the extraordinary intellectual régime to which he had been subjected as a boy by his father, and the precocity which resulted from it. In 1822, at the age of sixteen, he was engaging the redoubtable Robert Torrens in battle in the pages of an important newspaper about the theory of (economic) value. Before he was twenty he had edited Bentham's five-volumed work on the *Rationale of Evidence*, had published at least seven major articles in important periodicals on economic, political, and legal matters, had pointed out with great assurance and even less reverence the literary, political, economic, philosophical, and ethical shortcomings of the august *Edinburgh Review*, and had been arrested for distributing birth-control pamphlets.

In this first stage of his career, drilled to a rigid adherence to the Benthamite canon, J. S. Mill was a zealous exponent of Bentham's and of his father's moral and political doctrines and of Ricardo's economics. In 1826, however, when still in his twentieth year, he underwent a mental crisis, which continued intermittently for several years and which brought him sieges of mental depression, as well as an intellectual conversion which he was later, in his *Autobiography*, to describe as akin to a religious "conviction of sin," the sin being in effect Benthamism.

It is conceivable that J. S. Mill's main trouble was primarily due to overwork, but his own explanation was that the sudden realization that the Benthamite doctrines left the nobler human feelings too much out of account and did not offer a sufficiently full prospect for human happiness had proved more than he could take. During these and subsequent years, he manifested the characteristic which was to remain prominent in all the rest of his career, his susceptibility to influence from widely diverse ideas or, as he was later to put it in his *Autobiography*, his "great readiness and eagerness to learn from everybody, and to make room in my opinions for every new acquisition by adjusting the old and the new to one another." New winds of doctrine were impinging on his mind, which was then as open as a prairie: Wordsworth's nature-poetry, with its reverence for beauty and its revelation—for a Benthamite—that there were other fruitful sources of impressions than those provided by syllogisms; the reading of one of Comte's early works and personal associations with Saint-Simonians, which brought him into contact with the new historical approach to social thought; Macaulay's refutation in the *Edinburgh Review* of his father's *a priori* demonstration of the superiority of democracy to aristocratic government; the conservative political views and the more-or-less orthodox religious views of his friends John Sterling and Frederick Maurice; the feudalistic and pre-fascistic doctrines being expounded with fiery moral passion by Carlyle; and so forth. From all of them he borrowed something, although never as much as he then supposed, and for the most part not for keeps.

For a time, while his dour and magerful father still lived, the younger Mill did not break openly with the Benthamites, but his personal relations with the school became strained—more so, in fact, than he was ever to be aware of. Bentham, however, died in 1832 and James Mill in 1836, and freed from the restraint of their disapproval and evident disappointment, J. S. Mill began to explore the new ground on which he not too firmly stood by the hazardous procedure of putting his thoughts in print for the public to read.

The break was sharpest in the field of private ethics, where Bentham's and James Mill's interest had been least. In his economics, J. S. Mill remained faithful to the Ricardian doctrines as he understood them—and, to some extent, improved upon them in the process of interpreting them. In any case, the Ricardian economics was not wholly acceptable to Bentham, nor Bentham's economics at all acceptable to Ricardo. In the fields of politics and of law, J. S. Mill proclaimed some major departures in his thinking from the views of Bentham, but he never specified what they were. I think that, apart from some wavering as to the virtues of political democracy and some approaches to the benevolent Toryism of Coleridge, Wordsworth, Sterling, and Maurice, these were mainly methodological, loss of faith in the adequacy of the "geometrical" method in politics, rather than substantive.[19] With his father's writings he never, it seems to me, dealt with complete frankness, and he reserved for Bentham blows which could more justly have been directed against James Mill. The harshness and vehemence of the attack on Bentham was no doubt a subconscious manifestation of the urge he was under to free himself from what he had come to feel was an intellectual straitjacket, but it had been his father rather than Bentham who had placed it on him.

The attacks on Benthamism began in 1833, while his father was still living but after Bentham had died, with critical "Remarks on Bentham's Philosophy" included, under cover of anonymity, as an appendix to Bulwer Lytton's *England and the English.* In 1838, or

---

19. For his attempt to substitute, under Saint-Simonian influence, a philosophy-of-history approach, see his series of essays on "The Spirit of the Age," originally published anonymously in the *Examiner* in 1831, and reprinted in 1942 by the University of Chicago Press, with a characteristically learned and penetrating introduction by F. A. Hayek.

two years after his father's death, he published in the *London and
Westminster Review* his famous full-dress article on Bentham, again
anonymous, but with the authorship inevitably known at once to
friends and foes. In 1840, he published in the same *Review* an article
on Coleridge, which, by its sympathetic treatment of the latter's
ethical and political views, was indirectly a criticism of Benthamism.

Meanwhile, in 1835, in a review in the *London and Westminster*
of a book by Adam Sedgwick which criticized utilitarian ethics as
expounded by Paley, he had defended the principle of utility when
properly expounded, but without mentioning any names had remarked that for a full exposition of it additional materials were
needed beyond those already to be found in the writings of philosophers.

In these articles Mill was clearly endeavoring to salvage, or at
least shrinking from abandoning, a utilitarian system of ethics while
rejecting such features of Bentham's system as he could no longer
tolerate. There was high praise, therefore, for Bentham as well as
sharp blame. His main criticism of Bentham related to his treatment
of private morals and of psychology, and especially the stress Bentham put on the role played in human behavior by calculation of
gain or loss. He objected also that Bentham, by shifting from a
technical (or broad) meaning of terms—and especially of the term
"interest"—to a popular (or narrow) meaning, often slid into an
account of human behavior which pictured it as inherently selfish.
He explained this—unkindly—in terms of Bentham's personality.
Bentham, said Mill, intellectually recognized the possibility of generous action, of benevolence, but "the incompleteness of his own
mind as a representative of universal human nature" led him to regard genuine benevolence as rare and therefore unimportant in real
life.

> In many of the most natural and strongest feelings of human nature
> he had no sympathy; from many of its graver experiences he was alto-
> gether cut off; and the faculty by which one mind understands a mind
> different from itself, and throws itself into the feelings of that other
> mind, was denied him by his deficiency of Imagination.[20]

There was a basis for Mill's criticisms. That Bentham frequently
fell into language which pictured human behavior as if it consisted
almost solely of action based on calculations of personal gain and

20. "Bentham," reprinted in J. S. Mill, *Dissertations and Discussions*, 3rd ed.,
L. 1875, I. 353.

that his imagination was deficient with respect to the possible range of human emotions is beyond dispute. But Mill goes further in his criticism at some points than the texts he cites, or their context, justify, and in doing so disregards peculiarities of the Benthamite terminology which at other times, when his attitude had changed, he was to invoke against misinterpretations of Bentham at other hands. I can here deal with only one of these misinterpretations. Mill points out that if in Bentham's *Table of the Springs of Action* we find such words as "Conscience," "Principle," "Moral Recti-tude," "Moral Duty," which in the mouths of others represent recognition of such a thing as conscience as a thing distinct from philanthropy, affection, or self-interest in this world or the next, it is as synonymous for "love of reputation," and that the word "self-respect" appears not at all either here or in any of Bentham's writ-ings.[21] The critics of Bentham who have since made the same criticism and cited his *Table of the Springs of Action* as evidence are beyond enumeration.

There is only too much ground for criticism of Bentham for not using words quite as other men do, provided that deviation on his part from the common use of terms is not taken as reliable evidence of deviation from the common run of thought on the questions with which these words are usually associated. But Mill, who should have known better, makes use here of this kind of argument against the one person of all who by his discussions of the logic of language had made himself least vulnerable to it. Moreover, Bentham in his writings does use "conscience" and "duty" very much as other men do, and if he did not use "self-respect," his stock of synonyms was adequate to fill the void.

The *Table of the Springs of Action*, however, itself provides a more direct, though only a partial, answer to Mill's criticism. The psychology of Hartley and of James Mill from which Bentham started distinguished between "simple" pleasures, and "complex" or "compound" pleasures derived from the "simple" ones genetically by the processes of "association of ideas." Benevolence, generosity, duty, justice, conscience, and so forth would be "compound" pleasures. But Bentham expressly says of the *Table*—which is suffi-ciently formidable as it stands—that: "The pleasures and pains here brought to view are, every one of them, *simple* and *elementary*."[22]

---

21. *Ibid.*, I. 359.
22. *Works*, I. 207.

He does cite a few "Compound Pleasures," as illustrative of one broad category of such excluded from the table. One of these, "Love of Justice," has as one of its components "Sympathy for the community at large, in respect of the interest which it has in the maintenance of justice." Mill was later to emphasize love of justice as one of the major virtues. His present refusal to be satisfied with Bentham's recognition of it as one of the "Springs of Action" was perhaps a not too captious suspicion that the words added to it by Bentham made of it a less admirable virtue than if Bentham had written merely "Love of Justice (Period)." But it was common ground among the Benthamites, including J. S. Mill, that the tone and moral significance of "compound pleasures" could be radically different from the tone and original significance of their component elements, the "simple pleasures" from which they had been compounded.

By the time Mill was working on his *Principles of Political Economy*, he had swung back a large part though not all of the way to Bentham's political theory and moral philosophy. What was left of his revolt was confined mostly to a continued insistence on recognition of the complete range of human feelings and a consequent endeavor to avoid exaggerating the role of rationalistic hedonism in human behavior.

William Whewell, an anti-utilitarian professor of moral philosophy at Cambridge University where an even narrower type of utilitarianism with hell-fire trimmings—"theological utilitarianism," it was later to be labeled—had until his advent reigned unchallenged for over a century, in 1838, on the appearance of Mill's article on Bentham, had in private correspondence with a friend welcomed Mill's recantation, but complained—with some justice—of its manner:

It is certainly very encouraging to see on all sides strong tendencies to a reform of the prevalent system of morals. The article [by Mill] in the *London Review* is an indication of this, and appears to me to be in many important points right, and at any rate right in the vigorous rejection of Bentham's doctrines and keen criticism of his character. But I confess I do not look with much respect upon a body of writers, who, after habitually showering the most bitter abuse on those who oppose Bentham's principles, come round to the side of their opponents, without a single word of apology, and with an air of imperturbable complacency, as if they had been right before and after the change.

Nor do I see any security, in their present creed, against a change of equal magnitude hereafter.[23]

This was real prescience on Whewell's part. In 1843, in conversation about the surviving disciples of Bentham, Mill made the remark which "though smilingly uttered . . . was not at all a jest" that as for himself: "And I am Peter, who denied his Master."[24] In 1852 Mill was to write a critical review of Whewell's *Lectures on the History of Moral Philosophy in England*, published in the same year. Conceding very little error in the Benthamite doctrine, Mill rejected vehemently Whewell's objections to utilitarian ethics in general and to Bentham in particular, even when they were very similar indeed to his own criticism of Bentham in 1838.

The final stage in Mill's presentation of his ethical views was in 1863, when his essays on Utilitarianism appeared. In form, these still represented an adherence to the doctrine, but so modified by the admission without obvious absorption of foreign elements that they have been the despair of its friends and the delight of its critics ever since. Acts were to be morally appraised solely in terms of their consequences for happiness—a strictly Benthamite proposition. *All* consequences, however, were to be taken into account, including the effects on the character of the agent—an early doctrine of Mill's, which he derived from Coleridge and which he regarded as contrary to Bentham's views, mistakenly, I think. Happiness was conceived broadly enough to cover every type of wish or aspiration man could experience. Mill—unwisely, I think—went a step further than Bentham ever ventured by offering a "proof" that happiness was the proper criterion of virtue: namely, that competent judges accepted it as such, a type of proof which eighteenth century critics of the "moral sense" school of ethics had exposed to ridicule for its circularity.

Mill now attempted also to incorporate into utilitarianism a novel element for it and one which many moral philosophers hold to be incompatible with it, namely, the recognition of non-homogeneity of pleasures and consequently the existence of qualitative differences of a hierarchial nature, as well as quantitative differences, between pleasures:

---

23. Mrs. Stair Douglas, *Life of William Whewell* (London, 1881), pp. 270-71.
24. David Masson, "Memories of London in the 'Forties'," *Blackwood's*, Vol. CLXXXIII (1908), p. 553.

It is quite compatible with the principle of utility to recognize the fact, that some *kinds* of pleasure are more desirable and more valuable than others. It would be absurd that while, in estimating all other things, quality is considered as well as quantity, the estimation of pleasures should be supposed to depend on quantity alone.[25]

The test of quality as between two pleasures was the preference "by those who are competently acquainted with both" of the one above the other despite the fact that the other represented a much greater quantity of pleasure.[26]

I venture to suggest: (1) that the problem as Mill presents it, that is, within the limits of utilitarianism, is a spurious one; (2) that what he proffers as a solution is even more spurious; and (3) that Bentham and his predecessors to some extent and modern economists using utility theory to a larger extent, have provided a technique which, while it does not solve any fundamental moral problem, suffices to show that a dichotomy and possible clash between ratings of values on the basis of quality and their rating on the basis of quantity is not one of the fundamental moral problems.

Pleasures—or desires—are of course not homogeneous with respect to every conceivable quality they may possess—any more than are any other objects of human attention except abstract numbers. Comparison is—or should be—always with respect to specified qualities of objects, and if there is possibility of and proper occasion for measurement the measurement is also with reference to these specified qualities.

Mill confuses the issue by attempting at the same time to give predominant importance to the ordering of *classes* of pleasures on a higher-lower scale and to leave room for legitimate preference in particular cases of a pleasure of a lower order over one of a higher. This is the famous and ancient false dilemma of the water-*versus*-diamonds problem in economics, extended to the whole field of values. Whatever may be the case for didactic purposes, for actual behavior—including "moral" behavior—the issues arise in the form of necessary choices between units and not between classes of ob-

---

25. J. S. Mill, *Utilitarianism*, 3rd ed. (London, 1867), pp. 11-12.

26. *Ibid.*, p. 12. In an undated manuscript "On Social Freedom," found in Mill's house at Avignon after his death, and published, among other places, in *Living Age*, 7th ser., Vol. XXXVI (1907), pp. 323-36, there is a stronger statement of the higher-lower thesis with the order of rank made a pure matter of "feeling," not subject to demonstration or to argument—a complete swing back to the eighteenth century "moral sense" school.

jects. Bentham's famous dictum "Quantum of pleasure being equal, pushpin [a children's game] is as good as poetry" would meet all the proper requirements of the utilitarian principle if restated somewhat as follows: "Desire being equal at the margin of choice, a marginal unit of pushpin is as good as a marginal unit of poetry." The utilitarian but didactic moralist would still be free to insist that since in fact experienced choosers don't plump for even a first unit of pushpin until they are gorged with poetry, *in that sense* poetry as a class is higher on the scale of values than pushpin as a class.

I come now at long last to Mill's *Principles of Political Economy*. He wrote this two-volume book in less than two years, and when he began it he expected it to take only a few months to write. For at least ten years prior to this, he had not given much attention to economics. It was designed to do for Mill's time what Adam Smith had done for his, and to present what was known of the "Principles of Political Economy" as a science, together with their applications to concrete problems and, in the words of its title page, "some of their Applications to Social Philosophy." By the "science" of political economy Mill meant a body of deductive analysis, resting on psychological premises derived from introspection and observation of one's neighbors, and even with respect to these premises abstracting from all aspects of human behavior except those most intimately and most generally associated with the business of buying and selling. When Malthus, in 1824, objected that the "new school" of Ricardians had "altered the theories of Adam Smith upon pure speculation," Mill had replied: "it would, indeed, have been somewhat surprising if they had altered them on any other ground."[27] Later, as the result of Comtean influence and of his investigations in logical method, Mill was more receptive in principle to the possibilities of historical induction. But it is clear that he never assigned to it the right to an independent role in the "science" of political economy. Writing in 1835 with respect to the historical form of the inductive method, he had said:

History is not the foundation, but the verification, of the social science; it corroborates, and often suggests, political truths, but cannot prove them. The proof of them is drawn from the laws of human

27. In a review of the article by Malthus in the *Quarterly Review*, Vol. 30, January 1824, criticizing McCulloch's "Political Economy" article in the *Supplement* to the fourth edition of the *Encyclopaedia Britannica*, *Westminster Review*, Vol. III (1825), p. 213.

nature; ascertained through the study of ourselves by reflection, and of mankind by actual intercourse with them. . . . The usefulness of history depends upon its being kept in the second place.[28]

This was, of course, standard methodological doctrine, and to a large extent practice, in English social thought since Hobbes. Inquiry was to be pursued by means of deductive reasoning resting on psychological premises obtained empirically, but chiefly through introspection—which, it should always be remembered, was universally regarded in the past, whatever may be the fashion today, as an "empirical" technique of investigation, and sharply distinguished from intuition, or "innate ideas." But in J. S. Mill, as methodological doctrine, it has less significance than for most of his predecessors, since he confines it to the "scientific" part of Political Economy, stresses the importance of "applications" which can proceed by a wider range of logical methods, gives repeatedly at least platonic warnings that any abstraction from reality must be allowed for before the results of such analysis are made the basis for pronouncements on policy, and rejects it for every other established branch of social thought.

Of his earlier rebellion against the psychology of Bentham and of his father, the most important residue for his economics was probably his repeated emphasis on the importance of custom as a rival to the competitive principle, especially in connection with land-tenure and the relations of landlord and tenant. Here he showed the influence of Richard Jones, one of the pioneer advocates of resort to systematic induction in economics. But this presented J. S. Mill with somewhat of a methodological dilemma, which he never succeeded in resolving. "It is unphilosophical," he wrote, "to construct a science out of a few of the agencies by which the phenomena are determined, and leave the rest to the routine of practice or the sagacity of conjecture."[29] On the other hand, "only through the principle of competition has political economy any pretension to the character of a science,"[30] a proposition which F. Y. Edgeworth was later in effect to repeat, when he wrote that if monopoly should prevail over a large part of the economic order:

28. "Professor Sedgwick's Discourse on the Studies of the University of Cambridge," *Dissertations and Discussions*, Vol. I, pp. 112-13.

29. *A System of Logic*, 3rd ed., Vol. II, p. 472.

30. *Principles of Political Economy*, Bk. II, Chap. IV, "Of Competition and Custom."

Among those who would suffer by the new regime there would be [included] . . . the abstract economists, who would be deprived of their occupation, the investigation of the conditions which determine value. There would survive only the empirical school, flourishing in a chaos congenial to their mentality.[31]

We seem, however, to have found another alternative, that of becoming amateur lawyers.

Mill thus had no technique for dealing systematically with the analysis of economic process where competition was encroached upon either by custom or by monopoly, and when he did mention custom—or monopoly—he left it to the reader to estimate its importance and to make the necessary corrections in the conclusions he had reached on the basis of abstractions from these complicating factors. For himself, he assumed the responsibility only for that "uncertain and slippery intermediate region," between "ultimate aims" and "the immediately useful and practically attainable."[32] Logicians and physical scientists have the right, I suppose, to jeer at Mill's failure to extricate himself from this plight. For those among us, however, upon whom the redeeming grace has not as yet been bestowed of that special ideology which takes the form of faith in the capacity of statistical method to perform logical miracles, humility is prescribed, since we are all in the same fix.

The *Principles* thus has no single methodological character. As is the case with the *Wealth of Nations* of Adam Smith, some portions are predominantly abstract and *a priori;* in others, there is a substantial measure of factual data and of inference from history. Its wide range of subject matter; the sucess with which the lucidity of its style and the nobility of its outlook on life divert attention from its lack of logical rigor; the patent honesty and open mindedness with which controversial issues are treated; these and other qualities made it probably the longest-lived textbook our discipline has ever had or ever will have. It was the text used in the first college course in economics I took, over sixty years after its first publication. Francis Walker's *Political Economy* was also assigned to us, and I think we showed good judgment when we labeled the course, as students will, "Milk and Water." Writing in 1832, Mill had presented a forceful case in defense of ambiguity in language,

31. "The Pure Theory of Monopoly," [1897], *Papers Relating to Political Economy* (London, 1925), Vol. I, pp. 138-39.
32. *Autobiography* (London, 1873), p. 189.

on the ground that it was for many persons the price which would have to be paid if important ideas which by their richness and variety of content it is difficult to make clear were not to be sacrificed on the altar of logical clarity.[33] The *Principles*, I think, demonstrate that for Mill himself this was good doctrine; it would have been an inferior book, much less rich in content—and much smaller in size—if Mill had thrown out all that was ambiguous and lacking in strict logical consistency.

What most struck his contemporaries in the contents of the *Principles* was the sympathetic manner in which Mill dealt with proposals for radical change along socialist lines in the economic structure of society. The sympathy was in large degree platonic, for in no major concrete instance did Mill actually commit himself to the desirability of a specific drastic change. Mill aspired after the millennium, but he found abundant reason why it was not and should not be wished to be imminent. He looked forward, mostly on ethical and humanitarian grounds, to substantial socialization of the institution of property at some time in the vague future. Meanwhile, however, he warned against any weakening of the institutions of private property, free competition, and the rule of the market. This combination of hard-headed rules and utopian aspirations was just exactly the doctrine that Victorians of goodwill yearned for, and it made a large contribution to the popular success of the book.

Mill's handling of the problem of laissez-faire was a case in point. Except for the difference in tone and feeling, the fuller expression of lofty ideals and impracticable aspirations, it was substantially similar in method of analysis and nature of conclusions to Bentham's treatment. Like Bentham, and like all the other major classical economists except perhaps Senior—who was not a Benthamite—J. S. Mill gave only a very qualified adherence to laissez-faire. It was for him only a rule of expediency, always subordinate to the principle of utility, and never a dogma. The dogmatic exponents of laissez-faire of the time were the Manchester School, and Mill—like Torrens before him and Cairnes, Jevons, Sidgwick, Marshall, Edgeworth and others after him—denied repeatedly, and forcefully almost to the point of blasphemy, that the Cobdenites had either authority or logic to support them when they invoked the "Laws of

33. Review of G. C. Lewis, *Use and Abuse of Political Terms*, *Tait's Edinburgh Magazine*, Vol. I (1832), pp. 164 ff.

Political Economy" to stop government from coming to the relief of distress.

It is, fortunately, not part of my assignment to appraise the technical economics of Mill's *Principles*. What I have tried to do is to show the intellectual relations between two men important in the history of our discipline. From these two men several generations of British and American—and above all Canadian—economists, and to some extent also "liberal" continental economists, derived in large part the psychological, ethical, political, and methodological presuppositions upon which they built their economic analysis. With the ebbing of liberalism in the profession, the importance of knowing what its intellectual foundations were has become chiefly historical, and to those under fifty the historical is not obviously important. But for those *over* fifty, a comment of Tawney's is relevant. "It is a wise philosopher," he writes, the flatterer really meaning "economist," "who knows the source of his own premises."[34] I would go even further. It is an unusually alert economist who knows what his premises are, regardless of their source. For those over fifty study of Bentham and of Mill can do something to remedy both of these lacks. Beyond this remark, I make no attempt to draw any moral from what I have said. But I believe that in exercising this unaccustomed measure of self-restraint I am conforming to the "Principle of Utility" if broadly enough interpreted.

34. Introduction to Raymond W. Firth, *Primitive Economics of the New Zealand Maori*, (New York, 1929.)

Introduction to Bernard Mandeville, *A Letter to Dion (1732)**

THE *Letter to Dion*, Mandeville's last publication, was, in form, a reply to Bishop Berkeley's *Alciphron: or, the Minute Philosopher*. In *Alciphron*, a series of dialogues directed against "free thinkers" in general, Dion is the presiding host and Alciphron and Lysicles are the expositors of objectionable doctrines. Mandeville's *Fable of the Bees* is attacked in the Second Dialogue, where Lysicles expounds some Mandevillian views but is theologically an atheist, politically a revolutionary, and socially a leveller. In the *Letter to Dion*, however, Mandeville assumes that Berkeley is charging him with all of these views, and accuses Berkeley of unfairness and misrepresentation.

Neither *Alciphron* nor the *Letter to Dion* caused much of a stir. The *Letter* never had a second edition,[1] and is now exceedingly scarce. The significance of the *Letter* would be minor if it were confined to its rôle in the exchange between Berkeley and Mandeville.[2] Berkeley had more sinners in mind than Mandeville, and Mandeville more critics than Berkeley. Berkeley, however, more than any other critic seems to have gotten under Mandeville's skin, perhaps because Berkeley alone made effective use against him of his own weapons of satire and ridicule.[3]

---

*Reprinted from Bernard Mandeville, *A Letter to Dion* (1732), Berkeley, Calif., University of California, William Andrews Clark Memorial Library, 1953. Augustan Reprint Society publication 41, 1953, pp. 1-15, by the courtesy of the publisher.

1. In its only foreign language translation, the *Letter*, somewhat abbreviated, is appended to the German translation of the *Fable of the Bees* by Otto Bobertag, *Mandevilles Bienenfabel*, Munich, 1914, pp. 349-398.

2. Berkeley again criticized Mandeville in *A Discourse Addressed to Magistrates*, [1736], *Works*, A. C. Fraser ed., Oxford, 1871, III. 424.

3. *A Vindication of the Reverend D— B—y*, London, 1734, applies to *Alciphron* the comment of Shaftesbury that reverend authors who resort to dialogue

Berkeley came to closest grips with the *Fable of the Bees* when he rejected Mandeville's grim picture of human nature, and when he met Mandeville's eulogy of luxury by the argument that expenditures on luxuries were no better support of employment than equivalent spending on charity to the poor or than the more lasting life which would result from avoidance of luxury.[4]

Of the few contemporary notices of the *Letter to Dion*, the most important was by John, Lord Hervey. Hervey charged both Berkeley and Mandeville with unfairness, but aimed most of his criticism at Berkeley. He claimed that *Alciphron* displayed the weaknesses of argument in dialogue form, that it tended either to state the opponent's case so strongly that it became difficult afterwards to refute it or so weakly that it was not worth answering. He found fault with Berkeley for denying that Mandeville had told a great many disagreeable truths—presumably about human nature and its mode of operation in society—and with Mandeville for having told them in public. He held, I believe rightly, that Mandeville, in associating vice with prosperity, deliberately blurred the distinction between vice as an incidental consequence of prosperity and vice as its cause: vice, said Hervey, "is the *child* of Prosperity, but not the *Parent;* and . . . the Vices which *grow* upon a flourishing People, are not the Means by which they became so."[5]

T. E. Jessop, in his introduction to his edition of *Alciphron*, characterizes Berkeley's account of the argument of the *Fable of the Bees* as "not unfair," and says: "I can see no reason for whitewashing Mandeville. The content and manner of his writing invite retort rather than argument. Berkeley gives both, in the most sparkling of

---

form may "perhaps, find means to laugh gentlemen into their religion, who have unfortunately been laughed out of it." See Alfred Owen Aldridge, "Shaftesbury and the Deist Manifesto," *Transactions of the American Philosophical Society*, New Series, XLI (1951), Part 2, p. 358.

4. Francis Hutcheson, a fellow-townsman of Berkeley, had previously made these points against Mandeville's treatment of luxury in letters to the *Dublin Journal* in 1726 (reprinted in Hutcheson, *Reflections upon Laughter, and Remarks upon the Fable of the Bees*, Glasgow, 1750, pp. 61-63, and in James Arbuckle, *Hibernicus' Letters*, London, 1729, Letter 46). In the *Fable of the Bees*, Mandeville concedes that gifts to charity would support employment as much as would equivalent expenditures on luxuries, but argues that in practice the gifts would not be made.

5. Lord Hervey, *Some Remarks on the Minute Philosopher*, London, 1732, pp. 22-23, 42-50.

his dialogues. Mandeville wrote a feeble reply, A *Letter to Dion*."[6] F. B. Kaye, on the other hand, says of the exchange between Berkeley and Mandeville that "men like . . . Berkeley, who may be termed the religious-minded . . . in their anguish, threw logic to the winds, and criticized him [i.e., Mandeville] for the most inconsistent reasons."[7]

Objective appraisal of the outcome of the debate between Berkeley and Mandeville would presumably lead to a verdict somewhere between those rendered, with appropriate loyalty to their authors, by their respective editors. It is mainly for other reasons, however, that the *Letter to Dion* is still of interest. There is first its literary merit. More important, the *Letter* presents in more emphatic and sharper form than elsewhere two essential elements of Mandeville's system of thought, the advocacy, real or pretended, of unqualified rigorism in morals, and the stress on the role of the State, of the "skilful Politician," in evoking a flourishing society out of the operations of a community of selfish rogues and sinners. The remainder of this introduction will be confined to comments on these two aspects of Mandeville's doctrine. Since the publication in 1924 of F. B. Kaye's magnificent edition of the *Fable of the Bees*, no one can deal seriously with Mandeville's thought without heavy reliance on it, even when, as is the case here, there is disagreement with Kaye's interpretation of Mandeville's position.

It was Mandeville's central thesis, expressed by the motto, "Private Vices, Publick Benefits," of the *Fable of the Bees*, that the attainment of temporal prosperity has both as prerequisite and as inevitable consequence types of human behavior which fail to meet the requirements of Christian morality and therefore are "vices." He confined "the Name of Virtue to every Performance, by which Man, contrary to the impulse of Nature, should endeavour the Benefit of others, or the Conquest of his own Passions out of a Rational Ambition of being good."[8] If "out of a Rational Ambition of being good" be understood to mean out of "charity" in its theological sense of conscious love of God, this definition of virtue is in strict conformity to Augustinian rigorism as expounded from

6. *Alciphron, or the Minute Philosopher*, T. E. Jessop, ed., in *The Works of George Berkeley, Bishop of Cloyne*. Edited by A. A. Luce and T. E. Jessop. London, etc., III. (1950), 9-10.

7. In his edition of the *Fable of the Bees*, Oxford, 1924, II. 415-416. All subsequent references to the *Fable of the Bees* will be to this edition.

8. *Fable of the Bees*, I. 48-49.

the sixteenth century on by Calvinists and, in the Catholic Church, by Baius, Jansenius, the Jansenists, and others. Mandeville professes also the extreme rigorist doctrine that whatever is not virtue is vice: in Augustinian terms, *aut caritas aut cupiditas*. Man must therefore choose between temporal prosperity and virtue, and Mandeville insists, especially in the *Letter to Dion*, that on his part the choice is always of virtue:

. . . the Kingdom of Christ is not of this World, and . . . the last-named is the very Thing a true Christian ought to renounce. (p. 18)[9]

"Tho' I have shewn the Way to Worldly Greatness, I have, without Hesitation, preferr'd the Road that leads to Virtue." (p. 31)

Kaye concedes: that Mandeville's rigorism "was merely verbal and superficial, and that he would much regret it if the world were run according to rigoristic morality;" that "emotionally" and "practically, if not always theoretically," Mandeville chooses the "utilitarian" side of the dilemma between virtue and prosperity; and that "Mandeville's philosophy, indeed, forms a complete whole without the extraneous rigorism."[10] Kaye nevertheless insists that Mandeville's rigorism was sincere, and that it is necessary so to accept it to understand him. It seems to me, on the contrary, that if Mandeville's rigorism were sincere, the whole satirical structure of his argument, its provocative tone, its obvious fun-making gusto, would be incomprehensible, and there would be manifest inconsistency between his satirical purposes and his procedures as a writer.

Kaye argues that rigorism was not so unusual as of itself to justify doubt as to its genuineness in the case of Mandeville; rigorism was "a contemporary point of view both popular and respected, a view-point not yet extinct." To show that rigorism was "the respectable orthodox position for both Catholics and Protestants," Kaye cites as rigorists, in addition to Bayle, St. Augustine, Luther, Calvin, Daniel Dyke (the author of *Mystery of Selfe-Deceiving*, 1642), Thomas Fuller (1608-1661), William Law, and three Continental moralists, Esprit and Pascal, Jansenists, and J. F. Bernard, a French Calvinist.[11]

Christian rigorism by Mandeville's time had had a long history. From and including St. Augustine on, it had undergone many types

9. All page references placed in the main text of this introduction are to the *Letter to Dion*.
10. *Fable of the Bees*, II. 411, I, lxi, I, lvi.
11. *Ibid.*, I. li, I. lv, I. cxxi.

of doctrinal dilution and moderation even on the part of some of its most ardent exponents. In Mandeville, and in Kaye, it is presented only in its barest and starkest form. Kaye, however, required by his thesis to show that Mandeville's doctrine was "in accord with a great body of contemporary theory,"[12] while accepting it as "the code of rigorism" treats it as if it were identical with any moral system calling for any measure of self-discipline or associated with any type of religious-mindedness.[13] He also identifies it with rationalism in ethics as such, as if any rationalistic ethics, merely because it calls for some measure of discipline of the passions by "reason," is *ipso facto* "rigorist."[14]

Mandeville was presumably directing his satire primarily at contemporary Englishmen, not at men who had been dead for generations nor at participants in Continental theological controversies without real counterpart in England, at least since the Restoration. If this is accepted, then of the men cited by Kaye to show the orthodoxy and the contemporaneity of rigorism only William Law has any relevance. But Law was an avowed "enthusiast," and in the England of Mandeville's time this was almost as heretical as to be an avowed sceptic. Calvinism in its origins had been unquestionably—though not unqualifiedly—rigoristic. By Man-

---

12. *Ibid*. I. cxxiv, note.

13. For example, Kaye cites from Blewitt, a critic of Mandeville, this passage: "nothing can make a Man honest or virtuous but a Regard to *some* religious or moral Principles" and characterizes it as "precisely the rigorist position from which Mandeville was arguing when he asserted that our so-called virtues were really vices, because not based *only* on this regard to principle." (*Ibid*. II. 411. The italics in both cases are mine.) The passage from Blewitt is not, of itself, manifestly rigoristic, while the position attributed to Mandeville is rigorism at its most extreme.

As further evidence of the prevalence of rigorism, Kaye cites from Thomas Fuller the following passage: "corrupt nature (which without thy restraining grace will have a Vent.)" *Ibid*. I. cxxi, note. But in Calvinist theology "restraining grace," which was not a "purifying" grace, operated to make some men who were not purged of sin lead a serviceable social life. (See John Calvin, *Institutes of the Christian Religion*, Bk. II, Ch. III, pp. I. 315-316 of the "Seventh American Edition," Philadelphia, n.d.) As I understand it, the rôle of "restraining grace" in Calvinist doctrine is similar to that of "honnêteté" in Jansenist doctrine, referred to *infra*. The rascals whom Mandeville finds useful to society are not to be identified either with those endowed with the "restraining grace" of the Calvinists or with the "honnêtes hommes" of the Jansenists. For other instances of disregard by Kaye of the variations in substance and degree of the rigorism of genuine rigorists, see *ibid*. II. 403-406, II. 415-416.

14. See especially F. B. Kaye, "The Influence of Bernard Mandeville," *Studies in Philology*, XIX (1922), 90-102.

deville's time, however, avowed Calvinism was almost extinct in England; even in Geneva, in Scotland, in Holland, its rigorism had been much softened by the spread of Arminianism and by a variety of procedures of theological accommodation or mediation between the life of grace and the life of this sinful world. On the Continent, Jansenists were still expounding a severe rigorism. But Jansenist rigorism was not "orthodox." Though not as extreme as Mandeville's rigorism, it had repeatedly been condemned by Catholic authorities as *"rigorisme outré."*[15]

To take seriously Mandeville's rigorism, the narrowness with which he defines "virtue," the broadness with which he defines "vice," his failure to recognize any intermediate ground between "virtue" and outright "vice," or any shades or degrees of either, the positiveness with which he assigns to eternal damnation all who depart in any degree from "virtue" as he defines it, is therefore to accept Mandeville as a genuine exponent of a rigorism too austere and too grim not only for the ordinary run of orthodox Anglicans or Catholics of his time but even for St. Augustine (at times), for the Calvinists, and for the Jansenists.

Kaye justifiably puts great stress on the extent of Mandeville's indebtedness to Pierre Bayle. There is not the space here to elaborate, but it could be shown, I believe, that Mandeville was also indebted greatly, both indirectly through Bayle and directly, to the Jansenist, Pierre Nicole, and that Mandeville's rigorism was a gross distortion of, while Bayle's was essentially faithful to, Nicole's system.[16] Nicole insisted that "true virtue" in the rigorist sense was necessary for salvation, but at the same time expounded the usefulness for society of behavior which theologically was "sinful." But it was the "sinful" behavior of *honnêtes hommes*, of citizens conforming to the prevalent moral standards of their class, not of rogues and rascals, which Nicole conceded to be socially useful.[17] Mande-

---

15. Cf. Denzinger-Bannwart, *Enchiridion Symbolorum.* (See index of any edition under "Baius," "Fénelon," "Iansen," "Iansenistae," "Quesnell.")

16. The most pertinent writings of Nicole for present purposes were his essays, "De la grandeur," "De la charité & de l'amour-propre," and "Sur l'évangile de carême," which in the edition of his works published by Guillaume Desprez, Paris, 1755-1768, under the title *Essais de morale*, are to be found in volumes II, III, and XI.

17. For a similar distinction by Bayle between *honnêtes hommes* who are not of the elect and the outright rascals, see Pierre Bayle, *Dictionaire historique et critique*, 5th ed., Amsterdam, 1740, "Éclaircissement sur les obscenitez," IV. 649.

ville, on the other hand, not only lumped the respectable citizens
with the rogues and rascals, but it was the usefulness for society
of the vices of the rogues and rascals more than—and rather than—
those of honest and respectable citizens which he emphasized. In the
flourishing hive, prior to its reform, there were:

> . . . Sharpers, Parasites, Pimps, Players,
> Pick-pockets, Coiners, Quacks, South-sayers,
>   . . . .
> These were call'd Knaves, but bar the Name,
> The grave Industrious were the same.[18]

The moral reform which brought disaster to the "Grumbling Hive"
consisted merely in abandonment of roguery and adoption of the
standards of the *honnête homme*.[19]

The contrast between his general argument and that of Nicole
or Bayle throws light on the role which Mandeville's professed
rigorism played in the execution of his satirical purposes. It not
only supports the view of all his contemporaries that Mandeville's
rigorism was a sham, but also the view that he was not averse to
having its insincerity be generally detected, provided only that it
should not be subject to clear and unambiguous demonstration. By
lumping together the "vices" of the knave and the honest man,
Mandeville could without serious risk of civil or ecclesiastical penal-
ties make rigorism of any degree seem ridiculous and thus provide
abundant amusement for himself and for like-minded readers; he
could then proceed to undermine all the really important systems
of morality of his time by applying more exacting standards than
they could meet. Against a naturalistic and sentimental system, like
Shaftesbury's, he could argue that it rested on an appraisal of human
nature too optimistic to be realistic. Against current Anglican systems of morality, if they retained elements of older rigoristic doctrine he could level the charge of hypocrisy, and if they were
latitudinarian in their tendencies he could object that they were
expounding an "easy Christianity" inconsistent with Holy Writ and
with tradition.

18. *Fable of the Bees*, I. 19.

19. In the French versions of 1740 and 1750, the title, *The Fable of the
Bees: or, Private Vices, Publick Benefits*, is translated as *La fable des abeilles
ou les fripons devenus honnestes gens*.

For the "honnête homme" in 17th and 18th century usage as intermediate
between a knave and a saint, see M. Magendie, *La politesse mondaine et les
théories de l'honnêteté en France*, Paris. n.d. (ca. 1925), and William Empson,
The Structure of Complex Words, London, 1951, ch. 9, "Honest Man."

Mandeville clearly did not like clergymen, especially hypocritical ones, and there still existed sufficient pulpit rigorism to provide him with an adequate target for satire and a substantial number of readers who would detect and approve the satire. As Fielding's Squire Western said to Parson Supple when the latter reproved him for some misdeed: "At'nt in pulpit now? when art a got up there I never mind what dost say; but I won't be priest-ridden, nor taught how to behave myself by thee." Only if it is read as a satire on rigorist sermons can there be full appreciation of the cleverness of the "parable of small beer" which Mandeville, with obvious contentment with his craftsmanship, reproduces in the *Letter to Dion* (pp. 25-29) from the *Fable of the Bees.* Here the standard rigorist proposition that there is sin both in the lust and in the act of satisfying it is applied to drink, where the thirst and its quenching are both treated as vicious.[20]

Mandeville, as Kaye interprets him, resembles the *"Jansénistes du Salon"* who prided themselves on the fashionable rigor of their doctrine but insisted on the practical impossibility of living up to it in the absence of efficacious grace. In my interpretation, Mandeville was both intellectually and temperamentally a "libertine" patently putting on the mask of rigorism in order to be able at the same time to attack the exponents of austere theological morality from their rear while making a frontal attack on less exacting and more humanistic systems of morality. The phenomenon was not a common one, but it was not unique. Bourdaloue, the great seventeenth-century Jesuit preacher, not very long before had called attention to libertines in France who masqueraded in rigorist clothes in order to deepen the cleavages among the members of the Church: "D'òu il arrive assez souvent, par l'assemblage le plus bizarre et le plus monstrueux, qu'un homme qui ne croit pas en Dieu, se porte pour défenseur du pouvoir invincible de la grâce, et devient à toute outrance le panégyriste de la plus étroite morale."[21]

The *Letter to Dion* has bearing also on another phase of Mandeville's doctrine which is almost universally misinterpreted. Many scholars, including economists who should know better, regard

20. Kaye in a note to this parable, *Fable of the Bees,* I. 238, cites as relevant, *1 Cor. x. 31;* "Whether therefore ye eat, or drink, or whatsoever ye do, do all to the Glory of God." Even more relevant, I believe, is *Deut. xxix. 19,* where, in the King James version, the sinner boasts: "I shall have peace, though I walk in the imagination of mine heart, to add drunkenness to thirst."

21. "Pensées diverses sur la foi, et sur les vices opposés," *Oeuvres de Bourdaloue,* Paris, 1840, III. 362-363.

Mandeville as a pioneer expounder of laissez-faire individualism in
the economic field and as such as an anticipator of Adam Smith.
Kaye accepts this interpretation without argument.

The evidence provided by the *Fable of the Bees* in support of
such an interpretation is confined to these facts: Mandeville stressed
the importance of self-interest, of individual desires and ambitions,
as the driving force of socially useful economic activity; he held
that a better allocation of labor among different occupations would
result, at least in England, if left to individual determination than
if regulated or guided; he rejected some types of sumptuary legislation.

All of this, however, though required for laissez-faire doctrine,
was also consistent with mercantilism, at least of the English type.
The later exponents of laissez-faire did not invent the "economic
man" who pursued only his own interest, but inherited him from
the mercantilists and from the doctrine of original sin. English
analysis of social process had in this sense always been "individualistic," and in this sense both mercantilism and the widely-prevalent
theological utilitarianism were at least as individualistic as later
laissez-faire economics. Englishmen, moreover, had long been jealous
of governmental power, and at the height of English mercantilism
they insisted upon limits to appropriate governmental intervention.
It is not safe, therefore, to label anyone before Adam Smith as an
exponent of laissez-faire merely on the ground that he would
exempt a few specified types of economic activity from interference
by government. It would be misleading also to apply to eighteenth-
century writers modern ideas as to the dividing line between "inter-
ventionists" and exponents of "liberalism" or of "laissez faire." As
compared to modern totalitarianism, or even to modern "central
economic planning," or to "Keynesianism," the English mercantilism of the late seventeenth and the eighteenth century was
essentially libertarian. It is only as compared to Adam Smith, or
to the English classical and the Continental "liberal" schools of economics of the nineteenth century, that it was interventionist.

Adam Smith is regarded as an exponent of laissez-faire because
he laid it down as a general principle (subject in practice to numerous and fairly important specific exceptions) that the activities of
government should be limited to the enforcement of justice, to defense, and to public works of a kind inherently unsuitable for
private enterprise. He based this doctrine partly on natural rights

grounds, partly on the belief that there was a pervasive natural and self-operating harmony, providentially established, between individual interest and the interest of the community, partly on the empirical ground that government was generally inefficient, improvident, and unintelligent.

There is nothing of such doctrine in Mandeville; there is abundant evidence in his writings that Mandeville was a convinced adherent of the prevailing mercantilism of his time. Most English mercantilists disapproved of some or all kinds of sumptuary regulations on the same grounds as Mandeville disapproved of some of them, namely, the existence of more suitable ways of accomplishing their objectives or the mistaken character of their objectives. Mandeville's objection to charity schools on the ground that they would alter for the worse the supplies of labor for different occupations was based on his belief that England, unlike some other countries, already had more tradesmen and skilled artisans than it needed. Mandeville, in contrast to Adam Smith, put great and repeated stress on the importance of the rôle of government in producing a strong and prosperous society, through detailed and systematic regulation of economic activity.

It is a common misinterpretation of Mandeville in this respect to read his motto, "Private Vices, Publick Benefits," as a laissez-faire motto, postulating the natural or spontaneous harmony between individual interests and the public good. The motto as it appeared on title pages of the *Fable of the Bees* was elliptical. In his text, Mandeville repeatedly stated that it was by "the skilful Management of the clever Politician" that private vices could be made to serve the public good, thus ridding the formula of any implication of laissez-faire.

This is made clear beyond reasonable doubt by the *Letter to Dion*. Berkeley, in *Alciphron*, had made Lysicles say: "Leave nature at full freedom to work her own way, and all will be well." Mandeville, taking this as directed against himself, disavows it vigorously, and cites the stress he had put on "laws and governments" in the *Fable of the Bees*. (pp. 3-4; see also 55). He repeats from the *Fable of the Bees* his explanation that when he used as a subtitle the "Private Vices, Publick Benefits" motto, "I understood by it, that Private Vices, by the dexterous Management of a skilful Politician, might be turned into Publick Benefits." (pp. 36-37). Later he refers to the role of the "skilful Management" of the "Legislator" (p. 42), and to "the Wisdom of the Politician, by whose skilful Management the Private Vices of the Worst of Men are made to turn to a Publick Benefit." (p. 45). "They are silly People," he says, "who imagine, that the Good of the Whole is consistent with the Good of every Individual." (p. 49).

A recent work[22] provides indirectly unintentional support to my denial that Mandeville was an exponent of laissez-faire. In this work we are told that "The most famous exponent of what Halévy calls the natural identity of interests is Bernard Mandeville" and that "What Mandeville did for the principle of the natural identity of interests Helvétius did for that of their artificial identity," that is, "that the chief utility of governments consists in their ability to force men to act in their own best interests when they feel disinclined to do so." It so happens, however, that Helvétius as an apostle of state intervention was not only not departing from Mandeville but was echoing him even as to language. Helvétius said that motives of personal temporal interest sufficed for the formation of a good society, provided they were "maniés avec adresse par un législateur habile."[23]

Here also there is a close link between Mandeville, Bayle, and the Jansenists, especially Nicole and Domat. All of them adopted a Hobbesian view of human nature. All of them followed Hobbes in believing that the discipline imposed by positive law and enforced by government was essential if a prosperous and flourishing society was to be derived from communities of individuals vigorously pursuing their self-regarding interests. Mandeville's originality was in pretending that in the interest of true morality he preferred that the individual pursuit of prosperity be abandoned even at the cost of social disaster.

---

22. John Plamenatz, *The English Utilitarians*, Oxford and New York, 1949, pp. 48-49.

23. Helvétius, *De l'esprit*, Discours II. Ch. XXIV. In the French version of the *Fable of the Bees*, the phrasing is almost identical: See *La fable des abeilles*, Paris, 1750, e.g. II. 261; "ménagés avec dexterité par d'habiles politiques." When the Sorbonne, in 1759, condemned *De l'esprit*, it cited the *Fable of the Bees* as among the works which could have inspired it. (F. Grégoire, *Bernard De Mandeville et "La Fable des Abeilles,"* Nancy, 1947, p. 206.)

Kaye, in his "The Influence of Bernard Mandeville" (*loc. cit.*, p. 102), says that *De l'esprit* "is in many ways simply a French paraphrase of the *Fable*." In his edition of the *Fable of the Bees*, however, he says, "I think we may conclude no more than that Helvétius had probably read the *Fable*." (*Fable of the Bees*, I. CXLV. Note.) Kaye systematically fails to notice the significance of Mandeville's emphasis on the rôle of the "skilful Politician."

Schumpeter's *History of Economic Analysis**

The appearance of Schumpeter's *History of Economic Analysis*[1] constitutes a major event in the history of the *Dogmengeschichte* of our discipline. It is a book large in its physical proportions; its text proper amounts to some 1180 large and closely printed pages, much of it in small type. It covers its subject matter from Ancient Greece to Keynes. It aims to account for every writer who made a significant contribution to the development of economic theory. Greek, classical Latin, mediaeval Latin, Italian, Spanish, Swedish, and Dutch contributions, as well as, of course, German, French, and English literature, are reported on from their original texts. Most important of all, this is a history of theory written on the grand scale by an economist who was an original, a powerful, and a versatile theorist on his own account. Schumpeter, moreover, was interested, deeply interested, in apparently the entire range of matters intellectual, was learned beyond the normal capacities of economists, could exercise with facility and with power the whole range of skills which the economic theorist employs: static analysis, dynamic analysis, historical analysis, mathematical and statistical analysis, partial- and general-equilibrium analysis, and so forth without visible end. He was able to deal familiarly with all ages and with the materials of a wide range of disciplines: physics, psychology, history, sociology, mathematics, philosophy, jurisprudence, and perhaps still others. This is a work written in the polymath manner by perhaps the last of the great polymaths.

This is no doubt an over-ambitious book, and it would not be difficult to assemble from it evidence to support the charge that

*Reprinted from *The American Economic Review*, Vol. 44, December 1954, pp. 894-910, by the courtesy of the American Economic Association.

1. Joseph A. Schumpeter, *History of Economic Analysis*, edited from manuscript by Elizabeth Boody Schumpeter. (New York, Oxford University Press, 1954.)

there runs through it a vein of pretentiousness and of intellectual arrogance towards the common run of economists. The fact remains, nevertheless, that Schumpeter did possess learning and skills manifestly exceeding in range those displayed by any other economist of his or our time, and that in this book he applied these endowments to the enlightenment of his readers with a brilliance and a virtuosity which excite and dazzle even when they fail wholly to persuade. There is, as we shall see, much in this book which is redundant, irrelevant, cryptic, strongly biased, paradoxical, or otherwise unhelpful or even harmful to understanding. When all this is set aside, there still remains enough to constitute, by a wide margin, the most constructive, the most original, the most learned, and the most brilliant contribution to the history of the analytical phases of our discipline which has ever been made.

There is evident only one major limitation to the scope of this history which Schumpeter deliberately adopted. This is a history of "economic analysis," not of economics in general. Social doctrines, practical policies, and the application of economic theory to the solution of practical problems, while repeatedly referred to, are brought into the discussion only to show their relation, or, more often, their lack of relation, to economic analysis.

A history of economic analysis can be written, legitimately, according to any one or any combination of a number of patterns: as a history of concepts and of ideas, the intellectual ingredients of theories; as a history of theories, the constituent elements of systems; as a history of systems; as a history of authors, or of schools or near-schools; as a history of the use of particular tools. Although there is a large measure of validity to his claim that "theorems and not persons are the heroes of [his] story" (p. 384), Schumpeter in fact follows to some extent all of these patterns, and moves from one to another freely as he goes along. There results a considerable amount of overlapping material and of repetition, and a highly complex organization of the book as a whole. For the reader these disadvantages are more than compensated for, however, by the richness of insights and the variety of logical relationships and intellectual filiations which this procedure brings into our range of vision.

Repetition creates opportunity for contradiction and inconsistency, and I have found some, especially with reference to attributions and denials of priorities in discovery. The contradictions, however, are extraordinarily small in total and extraordinarily unimportant, if weighed against the amount of material handled and against the fact that this is a posthumous publication, unfinished, and prepared for publication by his widow, the late Elizabeth Boody Schumpeter, from manuscript which was to some extent still in preliminary and tentative shape at the time of Schumpeter's death.

Schumpeter includes, as "techniques" of economic analysis, economic history, statistics, economic theory, and "economic sociology," the role of economic theory being, apparently, to supply the tools of analysis, and of the other three to provide the content, factual and hypothetical, of the propositions to which the tools can be applied for the purpose of deriving statements of causal relations or interdependencies. He makes adequately clear some of the types of intellectual operations which he regards as outside the field of "economic analysis": mere common-sense or unsophisticated explanations of relations between phenomena (p. 9); nonempirical, "mystical," "metaphysical" propositions (p. 8); "philosophic vision or interpretation of meanings" (p. 422); "factual analysis" and the "immediately practical," presumably when pursued without aid of refined tools (p. 497); "the institutional aspects of economic life" (p. 589); "the attempts of men to apply their reason—and volition—to the task of changing [things]" (pp. 757-58); "the ends themselves, that is to say, the kind of society or culture we want" (p. 1145).

All of these are excluded from the area of study for which he assumes responsibility not on the ground that they are unworthy of study, but as an arbitrary delimitation of his task: "analytic or scientific . . . remember: we do not attach any complimentary meaning to either of these words . . ." (p. 55); "He who writes a history of, say, agricultural technology does not thereby prove that he thinks it more important than the history of religion" (p. 1140). This does not suffice, however, to conceal from us the fairly obvious fact that for Schumpeter it is analytic achievement which above all else entitles an economist to honor and brings intellectual distinction to economics.

It is not made quite clear to what extent "good" economic analysis is dependent on the realism of its assumptions. "Scientific truth" at times seems to include propositions which are factually untrue. On the other hand, "associationist socialism is unscientific because these plans involve assumptions about human behavior and administrative and technological possibilities that cannot stand scientific analysis for a moment" (p. 454). A close investigation might show that Schumpeter unconsciously was less exacting in his demand for realism for authors to whom he was favorably disposed than for authors who rubbed him the wrong way. When defending resort to or acceptance of unrealistic assumptions he appeals to what he regards as appropriate parallels in other fields, especially physics: "It is as important to realize the inevitable discrepancies between theory and fact that must result from [reasoning from unrealistic assumptions in economics] as it is to realize that they do not constitute a valid objection to the former; it is no valid objection to the law of gravitation that my watch that lies on my table does not move toward the center of the earth, though economists who are not professionally theorists sometimes argue as if it were" (p. 1031). The problems that may arise for economic analysis because the obstacles to the operation of its theoretical "principles" are more omnipresent and in practice less removable than are tables as obstacles to the operation of the law of gravity are not really explored.

It is a major doctrine of Schumpeter that philosophies, political doctrines, value preferences, psychology, and many other matters, have no contribution to make to economic understanding, which is exclusively the product of acquaintance with facts and of "scientific" analysis. "[David Hume's] economics has nothing whatever to do with either his psychology or his philosophy" (p. 447). The universe of economic analysis and the universe of philosophic discourse "are two different worlds that do not touch anywhere and neither of which can tell us anything about the phenomena . . . in the other without reducing its own arguments to futility" (p. 422, with particular reference to Adam Müller). Beliefs, moral principles, sympathies, preferences, may provide the economic theorists with motivation for finding a logical (and presumably also an illogical) basis for a desired conclusion (p. 383). But economic analysis has nothing to contribute to the choice of ends, which is a wholly subjective affair: "We may, indeed, prefer the world of modern dictatorial socialism to the world of Adam Smith, or vice versa, but any such preference comes within the same category of subjective evaluation as does, to plagiarize Sombart, a man's preference for blondes over brunettes" (p. 40).

Economic theory can serve economic policy, but only by pointing out the appropriate means for attainment of given ends:

To say that pure theory is of no interest for practice is as unreasonable as to say that pure mechanics is of no interest for building the machines we want. The ends themselves, that is to say, the kind of society or culture we want, we must choose ourselves. No science can do more than indicate the means of attaining whatever it is we want (p. 1145).

This picture of economic analysis as a somewhat ethereal intellectual activity, without roots in values, without entanglements with other social disciplines, without any contribution to make to the rational selection of social ends, represents, I suppose, Schumpeter's subjective ideal. In actual life, means and ends are not so sharply distinguishable, and ends are not frozen and impervious to "analysis." Ends can be means to other ends, and what are means from one point of view are ends from another; economic analysis could in particular cases bring this to light, and merely bringing it to light could result in a modification of ends. Systems of ends, moreover, may be—are perhaps certain to be—complex and incompletely harmonious. Economic analysis, by exposing the source and the character of contradictions in systems of ends, can operate, without need for exhortation, to bring about a revision of an established set of ends, for individuals and for societies. Economic analysis can conceivably show that the means requisite for the attainment of certain ends are not available, or are too costly in some sense, and may thus in effect force a revision of ends. There is no method of influencing ends which falls outside the legitimate scope of economic analysis except the employment of the hortatory method, the appeal to the emotions, and the appeal to authority. To deny any influence to economic analysis is to deny any role to reason in the formation by a sensible man of his system of ends. I cannot quite believe that Schumpeter would have rejected these elementary propositions, but he certainly wrote as if he did.

It could well be inferred from what I have said so far about Schumpeter's book that its contents consisted wholly or overwhelmingly of reproduction of and reasoned appraisal of specific analytic performances. Measured in pages, however, I am sure that much less than half of the book fits these specifications. The remainder consists of a very miscellaneous collection of matter, much of it having only the most tenuous or even no visible connection with economic analysis.

In the first place, the book is badly name-ridden. There is a tre-

mendous parading of names associated with meager and casual
bibliographical information, names of all kinds of persons, some
listed for commendation as economic analysts, other listed for commendation of their work in other phases of economics, or in other
fields, others listed for disapproval, or as uninteresting, and others
just listed. There is frequent ranking, and awards of grades for merit
of one kind or another, and comparisons as to merit of men whose
connection with each other is scarcely indicated. The index of
names, on a rough count, lists well over a thousand names, and from
a sample check I gather that probably well over a hundred names
have not won admission to the index.[2]

In this respect the book follows only too closely the model of
Schumpeter's earlier (1914) *Epochen der Dogmen und Methoden-
geschichte,* which in turn followed too closely the model of Cossa's
Guida allo Studio dell'Economia Politica in its various editions and
translations. An orderly annotated bibliography would have served
much better than this clutter of names. It would not be difficult, I
think, to enrich the book by adding fifty or so additional names
at a prescribed ratio of, say, one new name to ten names dropped.
The additions I would propose would be mainly of scholastics, of
contemporary commentators on Ricardo, of members of the Trinity
College, Dublin, school, and, surprisingly enough given Schumpeter's
command and my lack of command of the mathematical literature, of pioneer users of the mathematical, including the graphic,
method in their analysis. Much as I would like to, however, I am
unable to add to Schumpeter's list the name of a single nonliving
author for whom I would claim that as economic analyst he was
in or near the first rank.

There is, second, a good deal of general intellectual history, not
visibly related to economic analysis and frequently described as having no such relation. There is, third, some economic history, some-

2. The major service which this book will perform will be as a book of
reference rather than as a book for continuous reading. The index, therefore,
is all important. I happen to know that Mrs. Schumpeter, who, before her
death, put so much effort, devotion, and skill into the preparation of the manuscript for publication, was at one stage at least acutely dissatisfied with the
quality of an earlier index which had not been prepared by her or under her
direction. I have no criticism of the present index except that it is incomplete,
both in its subject part and in its names part. In both cases the incompleteness
is serious enough to detract significantly from the potential usefulness of a
very important book.

times of supreme quality, but often with no demonstrated relation to economic analysis or its history. There are, fourth, references to or accounts of specifically economic writings, and biographical material concerning their authors, with respect to which there is reported the absence of analytic content, or the absence of meritorious analytic content, or the presence of analytic achievement without description of its nature.

These four categories of material account for the great bulk of the first two hundred pages, for perhaps half of the next three hundred pages, and for a much smaller but still substantial fraction of the remainder of the book. It seems to me a great pity that Schumpeter did not concentrate more on the reporting and reasoned appraisal of important analytical work, which he did so exceedingly well, and did not leave the *Kulturgeschichte* to the encyclopedias and the reporting on the great areas barren of economic analysis to the mythical author of the chapter on snakes in the book on the flora and fauna of Ireland.

On the display of bias in this book I will say little. Schumpeter was not simple-minded nor naive, and I would have to know more about him and to know better than I do the corpus of his other writings to be sure that I had correctly identified the patterns it took. His biases could take the form of exaggerated enthusiasm and praise as well as of undue disdain and contempt. He was basically generous, moreover, and there is much evidence of his disciplining himself to give appropriate praise to analytical work which was of a high quality even when executed by men who used it to support conclusions he did not like. The fact remains that in the case of some authors he emphasizes their defects as analysts and admits their merits only grudgingly whereas with others he draws attention only to their strong points and leaves unmentioned or strains himself to find some sort of defense for the weak points in their analysis.

It is when Schumpeter is dealing with authors whose analytical quality he rates highly and whose economic analysis constituted a complex and coordinated system that he rises to his highest level in his book. His reports of these systems are magnificent feats of summarization. In outlining the analytical framework of these systems, moreover, he brings clearly into the light the fullness of their achievement and enables us to read these authors henceforth with deeper understanding and appreciation. It is the substantial portions of the book which he devotes to exposition, appraisal, and praise, of the economic analysis of Cantillon, Quesnay, Marx, Jevons, Menger and Böhm-Bawerk, Cournot, and Walras—and less enthusiastically, Adam Smith, Marshall, and Fisher—which constitute its most valuable contribution. Nowhere else, I think, in the literature of our discipline, can one find, within comparable limitations of space, as brilliant, and as self-effacing, exposition by one economist, himself a master, of the analytical achievements of other economists. Since I have raised the issue of bias, it is incumbent on me to add that there are hints throughout of disagreement with the conclusions even of the economists he praises most highly, that the basis of this disagreement is often some line of analysis more or less special to Schumpeter himself, that his own special doctrine is never obtruded on the reader or even clearly exposed, and that he never makes any claims to priority on his own account or even refers to any of his own original work.

The remainder of this review will consist mostly of objections of one sort or another, minor and major, to specific positions taken by Schumpeter. It will be a mechanical consequence that the amount of space in this review as a whole given to adverse criticism exceeds the amount given to praise. I would ask the reader to bear in mind, however, that my praise is in general terms and my criticisms are mostly of specific points, and that criticism both calls more for support by appeal to argument and detailed evidence than does praise and is more susceptible of such support than is praise.

Schumpeter's display of command of intellectual history is most impressive in its range and in its apparent depth. My major reaction to it is one of humble and respectful admiration. It may none the less be useful to point out a few instances where I am more or less certain that he has gone astray.

In signaling Petty's pioneer work in introducing "figures" into economic analysis, Schumpeter fails to point out that some of these "figures" were the products of a rather undisciplined imagination or of arbitrary manipulations of data. Partly in consequence of such procedure on the part of Petty, and of other early political arithmeticians, not only was it not true of Political Arithmetic that "nobody attacked" it (p. 211), but it was a frequent subject of satire from the late seventeenth well into the eighteenth century. Among those who made it the butt of their satire were Shaftesbury, Swift, Defoe, Richard Steele, and Mandeville, although it had among its many defenders men who, for our purposes at least, had even greater distinction.

In referring to Tooke and Newmarch's *History of Prices*, excessively factual for the purposes for which it was written, as "*histoire raisonnée*" (p. 690) Schumpeter mistakes the meaning of the term, which was the French equivalent of "conjectural history," or history not factual enough for its purposes.

Schumpeter expresses amusement at the use of the term "experimental" by utilitarians to describe their procedure, and interprets it as an illegitimate attempt at appropriation of a term that, through the successes of physical experimentation, had acquired an eulogistic connotation. Such attempt he says, "runs through the whole history of economics from the seventeenth century" (p. 432; see also pp. 493, 537). "Experimental," however, was commonly used, with no intent to deceive, not only to mean "learning from experiment" but also to mean "learning from experience." This latter is still given as an acceptable meaning by the *Oxford Dictionary*.

Terms like "individualism," "rationalism," "empiricism," "romanticism," the fiat currency of intellectual history, are conceded by Schumpeter not to have stable and uniform meaning, but he nevertheless uses them freely as if they did and without attempt at definition. He states his "strong personal aversion to utilitarianism" (p. 1153). All his references to it, and especially to its Benthamite version, are hostile and abusive. It is associated not only with hedonism, but with a hedonism of "stable and barn" (p. 429). It ruled out, "as contrary to reason, all that really matters to man"; it was "the shallowest of all conceivable philosophies of life" (p. 133). It was "boisterous and vulgar" (p. 66). There is no definition, however, and no argument, and there is, I think, sufficient evidence in this book to show that, surprisingly for him, he had no direct acquaintance with the complex early history of the quite respectable body of doctrine to which, late in its history, was given the name of "utilitarianism."

Schumpeter wrongly identifies Hobbes' "social contract,"—which he explains correctly—with Locke's (p. 119). There is an important difference between them: the monarch is not a party to Hobbes' contract and therefore acquires no obligations to his subjects; the monarch is a party to Locke's contract, and his lawful authority is confined within the limits of the obligations to the citizens which he assumes in entering into that contract.

Schumpeter says of Montesquieu's famous definition of "natural laws" that it is one which "cannot be commended too highly" (p. 232), but quotes only a fragment of it as if it were all of it. High authorities, early and recent, have pointed to Montesquieu's definition as an outstanding example of the survival of confusion between "natural law" as a declaratory statement of observed regularities in the behavior of phenomena and as comprising normative rules of conduct as revealed by "right reason" or as proclaimed by divinely ordained civil authorities.[3]

There follow comments on specific passages in Schumpeter's book more closely related to economic analysis.

On Plato's treatment of division of labor, Schumpeter comments as follows:

He elaborates on this eternal commonplace of economics with unusual care. If there is anything interesting in this, it is that he (and following him, Aristotle) puts the emphasis not upon the increase of efficiency that results from division of labor per se but upon the increase of efficiency that results from allowing everyone to specialize in what he is by nature best fitted for; this recognition of innate differences in abilities is worth mentioning because it was so completely lost later on (p. 56).

The importance of innate differences of abilities was one of Schumpeter's strongest convictions. I know of no one of consequence except Adam Smith who failed to point out as one of the services of division of labor that it enabled tasks to be assigned in accordance with aptitudes. (Even Adam Smith's failure was not a complete one.)

There no doubt has been "commonplace" treatment of division of labor in economic writings, but this has by no means been the invariable rule. I know of no study of the history of discussion of the idea, but such a study would reveal that division of labor was at times made the starting point for pioneer exploration of the technological foundations of economic process, of the role of physical capital, especially machinery, in economic progress, and of the relations between occupational and class differentiations of populations.

---

3. Cf. André Lalande, *Vocabulaire technique et critique de la philosophie* (Paris, 1926), I, 435.

Schumpeter finds very little economic analysis in the ancient Greeks and Romans. I am not qualified to dispute this judgment, although I think it would be possible to add a little to what he has culled.

On the basis of a passage from his *Ethics,* Schumpeter interprets Aristotle as "groping for some labor-cost theory of price" (pp. 60-61). Commentators on and translators of Aristotle have always had a tendency to find in his texts whatever theory of value was fashionable at the time they were writing. The first attribution to Aristotle of a labor-cost theory of value that I have been able to find was by John Gillies, a classical scholar, in 1797, who in fact charged Adam Smith with plagiarizing Aristotle in this respect.[4] In recent years, when an Austrian-type, or a utility- or demand-type of value theory has been dominant, commentators have found in Aristotle an anticipator of such theory.[5] I have failed myself to acquire any conviction as to what Aristotle was driving at, except that, if modern translations are at all adequate, there is nothing in his texts to justify attributing to him any labor theory of value beyond what is involved in the explicit recognition only of labor as a factor of production.

Schumpeter deals with the economic doctrines of the scholastics throughout in a strongly apologetic way, and as if they still stood in urgent need of defense against the neglect or biased attack which was common generations ago. In the process he praises their value and monetary theorizing not only as basically sound, but as innovating and as superior in many respects to later accepted doctrine. The late schoolmen had all the elements for "a full-fledged theory of demand and supply . . . the technical apparatus of schedules and of marginal concepts that developed during the nineteenth century is really all that had to be added to them" (p. 98). He insists in particular that the subjection of the schoolmen to Church authority did not in any way restrict their resort to scientific analysis of economic phenomena. Only where revelation was involved was

4. John Gillies, *Aristotle's Ethics and Politics* (London, 1797), I, 270-71. Gillies, in addition to the passages on value which are commonly cited today from *Ethics* and from *Politics,* refers to Metaphysics, Bk. 1, ch. 9; 1050A-28ff. (Bekker).

5. See, *e.g.,* O. Kraus, "Die Aristotelische Werttheorie in ihren Beziehungen zu den Lehren der moderner Psychologenschule," *Zeitschr. f. die gesamte Staatswiss.* (1905), LXI (4), 573-592, and Josef Soudek, "Aristotle's Theory of Exchange," *Proceedings of the American Philosophical Society,* XCVI, February 1952, pp. 45-75.

Church authority of decisive importance, but "in everything else (and this includes, of course, the whole field of economics) any argument from authority was 'extremely weak' " (pp. 76-77; citing Aquinas).

My direct knowledge of the writings of the schoolmen is fragmentary, but I have read widely the secondary sources, old and recent. On the basis of this reading, my general impression is that Schumpeter is substantially correct in his account of their monetary and value doctrines and that his praise of them, while exaggerated, is largely justified. His selection of particular writers for laudation seems to me rather arbitrary and, despite the profusion of names which he provides, there are some notable omissions.[6]

When it comes, however, to the analytic merits of the scholastic doctrine of usury (interest), it seems to me that Schumpeter carries his apologetics to wholly unreasonable lengths. Here, unlike the question of just price, Church authority, in the form of official interpretations (and translations) of Biblical texts, decisions of Church Councils, Papal Bulls, Church tradition, resolutions of theological faculties, etc., had decisive importance as to what it was permissible not only to practice but to say.

That money capital was sterile—or alternatively that its offspring was illegitimate—was standard doctrine of the Church. All that is of legitimate interest in the present connection is that the prohibition of interest was supported not only on dogmatic grounds but also on economic and utilitarian grounds. In the process of distinguishing between what was licit and what illicit, the doctrine grew progressively in complexity and in subtlety and the arguments supporting the lawfulness of some kinds of transactions were often marked by analytical insight and development. The fact remains that a large part of the scholastic literature on usury consisted of an attempt to demonstrate that there was a sufficiently sharp *economic* difference between the money-loan, or *mutuum*, where if interest was charged it would be (approximately) pure interest

6. Among the secondary sources not referred to by Schumpeter that, I think, provide ample support for this opinion are: Charles Jourdain, "Mémoire sur les commencements de l'économie politique dans les écoles du Moyen Age," Institut National de France, Académie des Inscriptions et Belles Lettres, *Mémoires* (Paris, 1874), XXVIII, Pt. I; Joseph Höffner, *Wirtschaftsethik und Monopole im fünfzehnten und sechzehnten Jahrhundert* (Jena, 1941); A. Sandoz, "La notion de juste prix," *Rev. Thomiste* (Apr.-June 1939), XLV, pp. 285-305; Raymond de Roover, "Monopoly Theory Prior to Adam Smith," *Quart. Jour. Econ.* (Nov. 1951), LXV, pp. 492-524.

only, on the one hand, and transactions in which the interest element was implicit and tied-up with other elements (business ventures involving some participation by the investor in the risks of
loss of the enterprise, purchases of annuities and of perpetual bonds,
leases of durable property, and so forth) on the other hand, to make
reasonable on ethical and economic grounds, as well as necessary
on grounds of religious dogma, the condemnation to eternal damnation of those who practiced the former without repentance and
restitution, and the sanction, as altogether legitimate, of the latter.
In so far as I understand it, the equivalent with reference to English
common law would be to hold that a "loan" at interest was illegal,
socially injurious, and scandalous, whereas a transaction approaching
it as closely as possible in every respect except that it was given
the form of a "bailment" would be completely legal, socially beneficial, and without any odor of scandal. The common argument of
apologists, which Schumpeter accepts, that the historical economic
circumstances were such that this distinction had economic and
welfare merit then which it later lost seems to me unsubstantiated,
highly questionable, and without *raison d'être* except its services
to apologetics.

Schumpeter's defense seems to be in part motivated by the fact
that his own theory of interest has some affinity to that of the
scholastics in that, like the latter, it sharply distinguishes between
interest on money-loans and direct return to durable physical capital. Schumpeter, apparently, would reject the proposition that even
an "idle" cash balance, if held in rational amount in relation to the
circumstances of the holder, would be no less productive—of product, or of consumer's utility—than an inventory of materials awaiting processing or of goods awaiting sale, than a second plough held
in reserve by a farmer, or than the contents of a housewife's deep
freeze, when each of these was of rational dimensions. As far as
this book is concerned, however, no light is afforded to the reader
as to the analytical grounds for such rejection, and I find it difficult
even to conjecture what they are, even with the aid of such acquaintance—far from complete—as I have with Schumpter's handling
elsewhere of the problem of interest.

Schumpeter comes equally vehemently to the defense of the
mercantilist doctrines against later criticism—including that of the
present writer. His defense consists of an acceptance, as reasonable
in the historical circumstances, of the national objectives of the

mercantilists, including the indefinite accumulation—apparently at whatever economic cost—of hard money or "treasure" and the pursuit of self-sufficiency with regard to all products except raw materials, and of a justification of the appropriateness (or effectiveness) of the specific means whereby they thought these ends could be promoted. There are no novelties in Schumpeter's treatment of the issue, and there would be no point in joining debate on it here. I make only one comment. Schumpeter asks whether I would condemn modern arguments and practices of a "mercantilist" character as vigorously as I have criticized those of the past (p. 336). The best answer I can give that would be extremely brief is that the events of recent decades have only strengthened rather than weakened my conviction of the faults, analytical, practical, utilitarian, of the mercantilist approach to international economic problems.

Schumpeter's "Reader's Guide" to Adam Smith's *Wealth of Nations*, although unfinished, is an admirable outline of such theoretical structure or "system" as there is in that book, and would make an extremely useful introduction to any new edition of it. Schumpeter does not like Smith, however, as theorist, as man, or with respect to his social views. The *Wealth of Nations*, although in some unexplained way it was "a great analytic achievement" (p. 38), completely lacks originality. It "does not contain a single *analytic* idea, principle, or method that was entirely new in 1776" (p. 184). Many of his predecessors excelled him as analysts. Verri's concept of economic equilibrium was "as far as this goes, rather above than below A. Smith" (p. 178). It is "not without interest to observe how little, if anything, [Campomanes] stood to learn from the *Wealth of Nations*" (p. 173). Most references to Adam Smith are hostile. He suggests that Smith's criticism of Mandeville's (two-volume!) "pamphlet," *The Fable of the Bees*, may have been due to jealousy of Mandeville as the anticipator of the argument for "Smith's own pure Natural Liberty" (p. 184).[7] "The wooden hands of the Scottish professor" and "the safe side that was so congenial to him" (p. 212), his "feelings of resentful distrust" and his "narrow

---

7. This conforms with the standard interpretation of Mandeville. It is, nevertheless, about as wrong as it could be, because it overlooks the vital role Mandeville assigns to "the dexterous management of the skillful politician." *Cf.* my introduction to the reprint by the Augustan Reprint Society of Mandeville's *A Letter to Dion* [1732] (Los Angeles, 1953). [*Editor's note:* Professor Viner's introduction precedes this review in the present volume.]

views" with respect to big business (pp. 150, 545), these are representative of Schumpeter's reaction to Smith. Smith was writing "in bad faith" when he claimed that the mercantilists "confused" wealth with money (p. 361). It is not, I think, necessary to accept Adam Smith as a hero of our profession to conclude that Schumpeter's objectivity was somewhat undermined here by the conflict between Smith's and his own "ideologies."

It is a major element in Schumpeter's almost complete rejection of Ricardo's analysis that Ricardo accepted the demand-and-supply explanation of the determination of market price but rejected it for "natural" or long-run normal (competitive) price. (See pp. 220, 482, 569-70, 604, 611, 684, 921.)

Two comments which Schumpeter makes in connection with other matters have some relevance for this matter also: first, one should distinguish between "the markets of real life" and "markets that are . . . nothing but highly abstract creations of the observer's mind" (p. 1008); second, "with economists' loose ways of expressing themselves, I find it very difficult to arraign individuals whose statements might be amenable to more favorable interpretations" (p. 1052). In using demand-and-supply *terminology* for the determination of "market price," that is, actual price, or temporary price, or instantaneous price, but rejecting it in his explanation of "natural price," Ricardo was not innovating. This practice goes back to the seventeenth century at least. It can be justified on the ground that it was semantically unfortunate that it later on became common to use the same term "demand" (and correspondingly for "supply") both for *the* quantity that would *actually* be taken in a given historical market at a given *actual* price in a given *actual* moment of time and for "that highly abstract creation of the observer's mind," the long-run normal demand function.

The only evidence that Schumpeter offers—and I am unable to add to it—that the issue is more than a semantic one, is the statement with a reference to Ricardo's *Principles*, Chapter 30, that "in the Ricardian system prices can fall to cost level directly, that is, in a way other than by increase of output" (p. 684). The only thing in this chapter which can conceivably be interpreted as supporting this is the use by Ricardo, presumably as a limiting case, of an illustration where, in modern terminology, a demand curve of zero elasticity intersects a (constant-cost) supply curve of infinite elasticity.

In his *Notes on Malthus,* Ricardo refers to a page of Malthus' *Principles* in which the following propositions are laid down: (1) that an alteration in cost without alteration in output would not result in an alteration of price; (2) that "the relation of the supply to the demand . . . is the dominant principle in the determination of prices whether market or natural, and that the cost of production can do nothing but in subordination to it, that is, merely as this cost affects . . . the relation which the supply bears to the demand." Ricardo comments: "These positions those which have preceded them and those which follow are not that I know of disputed by any body." A few lines earlier, Ricardo had said that in a case where hats are produced at constant cost, "their market price will depend on supply and demand—the supply will be finally determined by the natural price—that is to say by the cost of production."[8] Terminology aside, there did not exist that dual line of price analysis, Ricardian and Malthusian, which Schumpeter insists upon. If there was any significant difference between the two, it was that Ricardo's concentration on constant-cost cases kept him inadvertently from working out an adequate apparatus for explaining the determination of long-run price where both quantity demanded and quantity offered were variables dependent on price. It does not follow, in the absence of supporting evidence, that if such a case were presented to Ricardo, or to any one of his followers, he would have handled it any differently than would Malthus.

Many of Schumpeter's other critical comments on Ricardo's analysis lose their point if Ricardo's major concern in his value theorizing was not the explanation of how a given structure of prices had come to be what it was but the explanation of (a) the effect on a given structure of prices of divergent changes in the amounts of the respective factors, and (b) the effect on the relative amounts of the factors of changes in the structure of prices. This interpretation of Ricardo involves the question of the role of the supply functions of the factors in "Ricardian" as contrasted with "Austrian" theory, to be commented on later. It makes possible, I think, a better explanation of the ability of the Ricardian theory of rent to survive than that offered by Schumpeter (p. 934). It makes

8. David Ricardo, *Notes on Malthus' Principles of Political Economy,* in *The Works and Correspondence of David Ricardo,* Piero Sraffa, ed. (Cambridge, 1951), II, 44-47.

Ricardo's rent theory perform a function in his system more fundamental than that of an ingenious device by which Ricardo could offset his inability to handle simultaneous equations by arbitrarily reducing the number of variables in his model (see p. 569).

Schumpeter does not make clear which of four (or more?) possible explanations of Ricardo's stress on the role of labor costs in the determination of relative prices he accepts: as a device to simplify analysis and with no further intended implications; as providing for most (or for some) purposes an adequate approximation to the truth because of the predominance in fact of labor costs in total costs; as having, per unit of cost, more value-determining significance than other costs; as having, per unit of cost, more welfare or ethical significance than other kinds of costs. (See especially pp. 594-96.)

On the strength of a statement by Ricardo in a letter (to McCulloch, June 13, 1820) that "the great questions of Rent, Wages and Profits . . . are not essentially connected with the doctrine of value," Schumpeter agrees "that there is some truth in Professor Knight's indictment that [in Ricardo's *Principles*] 'the problem of distribution . . . was not approached as a problem of valuation at all.'" Schumpeter concedes that there is material in Ricardo which refutes it (he could have found some in the very letter in question) but concludes that "it does show that the full implications of the fact that capitalist distribution is a value phenomenon were not clearly seen even by Ricardo" (p. 543; *cf.* p. 568). It all depends on what Ricardo meant by "the doctrine of value." It seems clear to me from the context that what Ricardo here meant by these words was not the explanation of the determination of relative prices but the problem of finding a "measure of value" through time which itself had stable value.

I question whether it is true that Ricardo held "that 'real values' of commodities are 'regulated' by the 'real difficulties' encountered by the least-favored firm" (p. 1032). To confirm this it would be necessary to establish that for Ricardo the intensive margin played no or little part and the producers who were on the extensive margin were always or generally the least efficient and lowest-income farmers.

The repeated association by Schumpeter of the Ricardian theory of rent with a "monopoly theory of rent" puts undue weight on what for the most part represents only a change in usage of the word "monopoly" by economists (pp. 263-264, 592, 672, 934). In Ricardo's time the term was widely used to cover: (1) ownership of a scarce commodity by a single holder; (2) ownership by a few; and (3) scarcity of a commodity which, because of zero elasticity of supply, a rise in price would not ameliorate. Land was believed to belong to this third class. I think it more correct to say that Ricardo had an inadequate theory for the determination of price in any of these three classes than to say that he had one theory, and that a definable one, for all three classes. The common element for Ricardo with respect to the determination of prices of all three classes was that demand would determine price in these cases irrespective of costs. We would not today call this a "monopoly theory of value."

Schumpeter maintains that the Malthusian population theory dealt with a fictitious problem and dealt with it in a trivial manner (pp. 578 ff.; see also p. 446). Botero's "path-breaking performance" of 1589 was "the only performance in the whole history of the theory of population to deserve any credit at all" (p. 255). From the seventeenth to the first decades of the nineteenth century, "with unimportant exceptions," it was manifestly correct that *"under prevailing conditions,* increase in heads would increase real income per head" (pp. 251-52).

A look at eighteenth-century England serves, I think, to bring things into truer proportions. English society was then organized so as to check growth of population by "artificial" means. Compulsory poor relief on a parochial basis and financed by local real property taxes together with the settlement laws gave a powerful incentive to the ruling classes to discourage local growth of population. There were in effect deliberate deterrents to marriage of various kinds. There was organized public custody of foundlings and of children of persons on poor relief, and it was common knowledge that this operated so as to ensure that most of them would not survive long. There was nevertheless rapid growth of population and deep and pervasive poverty. If one were to accept Schumpeter's argument, the trouble must have been that there was not enough population.

I am not sure that I grasp Schumpeter's point when he argues that it is wrong to criticize the classical theory of the international mechanism "on the ground that it put an altogether unjustifiable burden upon the price mechanism" since "price variations of the kind the 'classic' theory visualizes imply shifts of demand curves which in turn imply variations in income" (p. 733). A few pages earlier, he had rightly stressed the importance of the distinction between what may be implied in an author's statement and what the author understood by it. Moreover, changes in prices, even when they do imply variations in income, do not account for the nonprice effects of variations in income. Reference to price changes is even more obviously inadequate for the analysis of cases where variations in income are unassociated with any changes in prices, or, as Schumpeter himself puts it, "in patterns in which prices are rigid."

On the question of the validity of the substitution by Jevons, Menger, Böhm-Bawerk, and others of a demand or utility explanation of the determination of price for the Ricardian explanation, Schumpeter, like almost all modern theorists, lines up firmly on the "Austrian" side; the Austrian theory in effect added to the English classical theory what needed to be added and rejected what called for rejection, or, less clearly, what could be rejected without serious loss. Let me distinguish two propositions: first, the need for the introduction into value theory of something like the marginal utility analysis to constitute a fundamental or "ultimate" regulator of value; second, the need, or the permissibility, of rejecting costs in the sense either of disutilities or negative utilities, or of the surrender of leisure, of immediate for future consumption, or of more attractive for less attractive employment, as a second fundamental or "ultimate" regulator or determinant of value. After Jevons, etc., had written, scarcely an economist raised any question about proposition one above. It is only on the second proposition that controversy has not altogether expired, and it is only this second proposition which I question.

Marshall, while adopting, and incorporating into his system, marginal utility analysis, rejected proposition two, as did Edgeworth, Taussig, and others, and as do I. It seems to me impossible logically to accept proposition two and at the same time to grant that the quantities of some or all of the factors of production are not given, but are functions of their rates of remuneration. It also seems to me that this difference in the treatment of the amounts of the factors is the only important difference between the Marshallian and the "Austrian" systems, but it is an important difference.

I present some of Schumpeter's comments on Marshall's system which are relevant to this issue:

> Marshall's theoretical structure, . . . is fundamentally the same as that of Jevons, Menger, and especially Walras, but . . . the rooms in this new house are unnecessarily cluttered up with Ricardian heirlooms, which receive emphasis quite out of proportion to their operational importance (p. 837).

> Thus, we return from this excursion with the same result that we always get when inquiring into the nature and importance of Marshall's deviations, *in what purport to be fundamentals*, from the Jevons-Menger-Walras analysis: they are negligible (p. 924).

> . . . note XXI in the Appendix to Marshall's *Principles* is conclusive proof of the fundamental sameness of his and Walras' models (p. 952).

It is important here to make another distinction: between questions of formal validity and questions of "emphasis," or of practical significance. I confine myself to the former. Marshall's "note XXI" to which Schumpeter refers includes, as one of a list of assumptions: "(iii) *m* supply equations, each of which connects the price of a factor with its amount."[9] In a corresponding Jevonian, or Austrian, or Walrasian listing of assumptions, the amounts of the factors would be listed as constants. In formal analysis, there is surely nothing more "fundamental" than whether a specific quantity whose importance is not questioned is a constant or a variable. When the quantities of the factors are treated as variables, as functions of their prices, a wide area of analytical development is opened up for and demands exploration. This area Ricardo and Marshall did explore and the "Austrians" did not, except as a side issue, under pressure of criticism, belatedly, and, I believe, incorrectly.

Schumpeter adduces what he calls "the Principle of the Negligibility of Indirect Effects" in support of Marshall's treatment of consumer's surplus (pp. 990 ff.). It seems to me that for some at least of Marshall's analysis it is necessary, for the correctness of his findings, not only that particular indirect effects of the change in a particular price shall be negligible, or of a lower order of size than the (total) direct effect, but that the *sum* of all the indirect

9. Alfred Marshall, *Principles of Economics*, 8th ed. (London, 1920), "Mathematical Appendix," p. 855.

effects shall be of a lower order of size, and that Marshall fails to give any reason why this should necessarily or ordinarily be the case.

I can see why, for what I understand to be Schumpeter's own version of static equilibrium under perfect competition, there needs to be atomistic as well as over-all perfect equilibrium and every entrepreneur needs to be a zero-profit entrepreneur. But I cannot see why he thinks this is a necessary condition also for a Marshallian or a Walrasian static equilibrium (pp. 674, 893, 1011). For their systems, I would think, all that is requisite is over-all equilibrium of the balanced aquarium type, in which firms (fish) and factors (plants) come into being, grow and die, and only aggregates remain the same. In such an equilibrium there could be risks for the individual firm. Such a model would be more realistic, and for some purposes at least more useful, than one in which equilibrium is required to be present not only over all but for each unit.

In a Walrasian system, constant coefficients of production need not involve "that there is, for each product, only one technologically possible way of producing it" (p. 1011; *cf.* p. 1027). All that the Walrasian system requires in this connection is that there always shall be available one way of producing each product such that some of its technical coefficients are smaller and none is greater than for any other technologically possible way of producing it.

Pointing out that first-order homogeneity of the production function means that there are constant returns to scale, Schumpeter comments: "In itself this implies nothing, of course, about what happens when only one of the 'factors' is increased, the others remaining constant, i.e., about the shape of each 'factor's' marginal productivity curve" (p. 1034). I would see nothing to question in this if all that was intended was to deny that first-order homogeneity of the production function either sufficed to prescribe the shape of any particular marginal production curve, or was inconsistent with almost any conceivable shape for any one (not too important) marginal productivity curve. It does seem to me, however, that acceptance of first-order homogeneity of the production function imposes important restrictions on the general pattern of marginal productivity functions and that these are such as to support *a priori* belief in the predominantly decreasing-productivity shape of the marginal productivity curves. I say this after giving due consideration to Schumpeter's warning that there are logical pitfalls in deciding what properties of production functions are "obvious" or "evident" (p. 1037), but quite probably without giving adequate weight to unperceived mathematical pitfalls.

As I see it, there cannot be both first-order homogeneity of the production function and, for each or most of the factors, constant marginal productivity, *i.e.*, independence of the marginal productivity of the factor from the quantity of that factor, unless there is also, for each or most of these factors, independence of the marginal productivity of the factor from the quantities of the other factors with which it is associated. Similarly, as I see it, there cannot be both first-order homogeneity of the production function and increasing productivities for each or most of the factors unless there is also over-all net rivalry, instead of complementarity, in production between the factors.

As I find it difficult to believe either that the particular marginal productivities of the factors are ever independent of the quantities of the other factors associated with them, or that there ever is or can be net over-all rivalry in production between the factors, acceptance of the first-order homogeneity hypothesis does carry for me a strong implication of diminishing marginal productivity of the particular factors.

Schumpeter says that *"if there were any sense in speaking of a national production function at all*, first-order homogeneity of this function would supply a very simple explanation of a remarkable fact, namely, the relative constancy of the main relative shares of 'factors,' in the national dividend" (p. 1042). But first-order homogeneity presumably is a property attributable only to *static* production functions. There is moreover a big step, analytical and presumably also factual, from the properties of the production function to the characteristics of the distribution pattern. If unmanipulated historical data do in fact show anything like a close approximation to constancy through historical time of the relative shares of factors in the national dividend, the existence of first-order homogeneity in the production function would not suffice to remove the mystery for me, even if the data were indisputably accurate and comprehensive. I am not certain whether Schumpeter relies wholly, or largely, for the validity of the "fact" of constancy of relative shares on the Cobb-Douglas statistical findings. If he does, then there becomes pertinent the additional difficulty that these findings were based, unavoidably, on historical data of incomplete coverage and highly doubtful accuracy, and therefore should not be regarded as providing strong confirmation of any valid static hypothesis.

It does not seem to me that most exponents of what they regarded as a quantity theory of the value of money would have accepted as a necessary condition for the validity of their theory "that velocity of circulation is an institutional datum that varies slowly or not at all, but in any case is independent of prices and volume of transactions" (p. 703). Most of them, I think, would not find variability of velocity disturbing for their theory, provided the variations in velocity were not inverse to those in quantity—or, perhaps, even if they were, provided the amplitude of variation of velocity was less than that of quantity.

I am not convinced that Schumpeter says anything (pp. 1095-1110) which bears strongly against the validity of the quantity theory of money if the latter is understood as holding only: (1) that an authority powerful enough to make the quantity of money what it pleases can so regulate that quantity as to make the price level approximate to what it pleases, and (2) that the possibility of existence of such power is not inconceivable *a priori*.

PART III

Scholarship and Graduate Training

A Modest Proposal for Some Stress on Scholarship in Graduate Training*

THE TITLE I HAVE CHOSEN for my talk may possibly recall to some of you the somewhat similar form of title which eighteenth-century writers used ironically for brutally satiric essays. Jonathan Swift in his "A Modest Proposal for Preventing the Children of Poor People from being a Burden to their Parents or the Country" recommended that the problem of the starving children be solved by serving the children as food to the rich. Philip Skelton made his irony obvious by the very title of his essay, which read: "Some Proposals for the Revival of Christianity." If, however, there is any irony in the title or satire in the contents of my talk, I would like you to believe that, like M. Jourdain's prose, they are unplanned and unconscious.

My proposal is both sincere and modest. I give also only an old-fashioned and modest meaning to the term "scholarship." I mean by it nothing more than the pursuit of broad and exact knowledge of the history of the working of the human mind as revealed in written records. I exclude from it, as belonging to a higher order of human endeavour, the creative arts and scientific discovery.

What I propose, stated briefly and simply, is that our graduate schools shall assume more responsibility than they ordinarily do, so that the philosophers, economists, mathematicians, physicists, and theologians they turn out as finished teachers, technicians, and practitioners shall have been put under some pressure or seduction to be also scholars.

I do not ask that before economists are turned out from the graduate school assembly line bearing the Ph.D. as a stamp of completion of the training process they be required to have shown that they are finished scholars as well as finished economists. True

*Address before the Graduate Convocation, Brown University, June 3, 1950. Reprinted from *Brown University Papers* XXIV, by the courtesy of Brown University.

scholarship is always an unfinished and an unfinishable process. Scholarship is a commitment to the pursuit of knowledge and understanding, but it can never provide guarantees that these have been attained. A great part of true learning, in fact, takes the form of negative knowledge, of increasing awareness of the range and depth of our unconquered ignorance, and it is one of the major virtues of scholarship that only by means of it, one's own or some-one else's, can one know when it is safe to dispense with it. Learned ignorance, therefore, is often praiseworthy, although ignorant learn-ing, about which I will say something later, never is.

There is so much that needs to be known, and so little time in one's student days for learning it, that it is not a depreciation of the doctor's degree to regard it as merely marking the termination of one advanced stage in one's education, the last stage in which the responsibility is shared with others, to be followed by another stage lasting to the end of one's life in which one is intellectually wholly on one's own. The University of Avignon, in 1650, found itself faced by a candidate for the doctorate who had capacity but who had applied himself less closely to the pursuit of knowledge than to less exacting and more exciting extra-curricular activities. After some hesitation, it conferred the doctoral degree upon him with the notation *sub spe futuri studii,* which I am told can be translated as "in the hope of future study." May I suggest that our doctoral degrees should be granted, and accepted, in this spirit even when there is not occasion to spell it out in the letter of the parchment?

I do not claim much for the pursuit of scholarship for its own sake, either in material rewards to the scholar or in tangible benefit to the community. We live in perilous times, with crucial problems of life and death, of riches and poverty, of freedom and tyranny, awaiting solution. In the social sciences, as in the natural sciences, students tend to seek first for solutions to these problems, or for skills by aid of which they may be attacked. This is as it should be. These are first, and probably also second, and third, and fourth. It is not as an escape from the burning problems of the world that I speak a word for scholarship. Not for me, and not recommended to any of you, is the plea of Joseph Hall during the British civil and religious contentions in the late sixteenth century:

> 'Mongst all these stirs of discontented strife,
> O let me lead an academic life.

> To know much and to think we nothing know;
> Nothing to have, yet think we have enow.[1]

Nor do I wish to suggest that scholarship loses merit of any kind, even as scholarship, as it gains in utility, in relevance to major current problems. Such doctrine was once standard among the learned, but it today smacks of priggishness, of absence of a sense of proportion. A great mathematician, Jacobi, for instance, in a letter to another great mathematician, Legendre, wrote in 1830 of a third great mathematician, Fourier, as follows:

> It is true that M. Fourier had the opinion that the principal purpose of mathematics was public utility and the explanation of natural phenomena; but a philosopher such as he was should have known that the sole end of science was the honor of the human mind, and that by this criterion a question in the theory of numbers was as important as a question of the nature of the universe.[2]

Although I have a sneaking admiration for Jacobi's doctrine of scholarship for scholarship's sake *alone*, judgment and discretion master inclination, and I refrain—not without effort—from subscribing to it. I certainly do not venture to preach it. Given the strength, however, of the prevailing pressures against expenditure of time and thought on learning which cannot demonstrate its relevance to increasing the yield of cotton or winning the cold war, the doctrine is scarcely to be regarded as a dangerous one. It is at least not a doctrine dictated by or approved by Moscow.

The modest proposal I make is that graduate schools make a place in their programs, a modest place, but one not confined to the Humanities departments, for scholarship, and that they require or at least plead with their students, especially those who are destined to be college teachers, to devote to that part of the graduate school program a fraction, a modest fraction, of their attention.

A small place once given to scholarship, moreover, I would not object if it were then confined to its allotted space, or at least not permitted to spread without restraint into areas beyond its proper jurisdiction, where if it intrudes it steals time and other less valuable resources from what are generally acknowledged to be more

---

1. Virgidemiarum, Bk. IV. Satire VI [1599], *The Works of the Right Reverend Joseph Hall, D.D., Bishop of Exeter*, new edition (Oxford, 1863), IX, 649.

2. J. T. Merz, *A History of European Thought in the Nineteenth Century* (Edinburgh, 1903), II, 657.

important activities. A verger of a church, reproved for locking the doors of the church, replied that when they were left open it often resulted in people praying all over the place. I concede that we don't want students and faculty unrestrainedly pursuing scholarship all over our universities while they have so much more urgent business to attend to.

Scholarship may be misplaced, moreover, not only because it distracts attention from more vital matters, but also because the scholar tends to inject himself, his techniques, his values, and his lack of impatience for quick results into problem areas where his contributions are regarded as irrelevant or as not prompt enough to be serviceable. Scholarship out of place brings nothing but embarrassment to the scholar and irritation to his clients—if any. A woman in a shop asked for a drinking bowl for her dog. When the clerk replied that he had no drinking bowls especially for dogs, the woman said that any drinking bowl would do. The clerk, having found one for her, then suggested that he have the word "dog" painted on it. "No, thanks," said the woman. "It is not necessary. My husband doesn't drink water and my dog can't read." Learning should be kept in its place. A university is today many things, very, very many things. As one of these many things, not too low on the list, it should strive to continue to be, or again to become, a place of and for scholarship. But it cannot be expected, and it will not be permitted, to be a place for scholarship only or predominantly.

Aware of the fact that scholarship does not necessarily yield even to the scholar the limited rewards, spiritual or material, sought from it, I thought for a time of choosing for my title: "Lo, the Poor Scholar!" In one of his sermons, Robert South, an eighteenth-century Anglican clergyman, expounds at length, and with traces of complacency, the woes that beset the scholar. He takes as his text, Ecclesiastes I. 18: "In much wisdom there is much grief; and he that increaseth knowledge increaseth sorrow." Among the many perils of learning he lays special emphasis on its hazards for health and prosperity: "Knowledge," he remarks, "rewards its followers with the miseries of poverty, and clothes them with rags. Reading of books consumes the body, and buying of them the estate."

---

3. Robert South, D.D., *Sermons Preached upon Several Occasions* (Library of Old English Divines edition, New York, 1871), V, 11.

Accumulation of knowledge moreover leads by a fatal association to desire to communicate it, and this in turn leads to the desire
to write books, and this in turn to additional woes and pains.
Rousseau once said, as reported by David Hume, that "one half of
a man's life is too little to write a book and the other half to correct
it." Rousseau must have meant a scholarly book, for he himself
wrote many books, and never corrected any of them, as far as I
have been able to discover. The modern scholar spends much more
time in correcting the books of non-scholars which, unfortunately,
took much less than half a lifetime to write, than in writing his
own books. For the writing of books there is little time left to
scholars by their other inescapable tasks. It is still true that of the
writing of books there is no end, but it is also true that most
scholarly manuscripts have no ending. If the scholar does complete
his *opus majus*, there is often too little conversion of even university
presses to the virtues of deficit financing to make its publication
possible. If, nevertheless, the scholar does manage to complete his
manuscript and to find an unworldly publisher, he still reaps little
reward of any sort, except to his vanity if the reviewers are kind.
But the kindness of reviewers, or even the hope of it, let scholars
be frank about it, is often a sufficient reward. Consider the confes-
sion of Pascal, who made it his practice not to conceal from others
his own weaknesses, or theirs:

Vanity is so anchored in the heart of man, that a soldier, a soldier's
servant, a cook, a porter, brags and seeks admirers; and even philosophers
wish for them. And those who write against vanity wish to have the
glory of having written well; and those who read what the latter have
written wish to have the glory of having read it; and I, who write this
attack on vanity, perhaps also have a yearning for this glory; and perhaps
also those who will read this.[4]

Nor is yielding to vanity the only reproach which can be
levelled against the motives of the scholar. Curiosity is an even
more prevalent, and, of course, more serious vice of the true scholar
than vanity. Bernard Mandeville, who read human nature the way
an editor reads proof-sheets or a professor a doctoral thesis, looking
only for errors, faults, and deviations from the standard proprieties,
added avarice to vanity and curiosity as the faults of the scholar.
Book royalties must have been larger in those days! But Mandeville

---

4. *Pensées*, 150.

maintained that private vices are public benefits, and in his *Fable of the Bees* he found illustration for his doctrine in the operations of scholars:

> There is no Part of Learning but some Body or other will look into it, and labour at it, from no better Principles, than some Men are Fox-hunters, and others take delight in Angling. Look upon the mighty Labours of Antiquaries, Botanists, and the Vertuosos in Butterflies, Cockle-shells, and other odd Productions of Nature; and mind the magnificent Terms they all make use of in their respective Provinces, and the pompous Names they often give, to what others, who have no Taste that way, would not think worth any Mortal's Notice. Curiosity is often as bewitching to the Rich, as Lucre is to the Poor; and what Interest does in some, Vanity does in others; and great Wonders are often produced from a happy Mixture of both.[5]

David Hume, perhaps with Mandeville in mind, gave a somewhat different and more realistic, though not obviously more flattering, account of the motivation of authorship. In his account, avarice was not a supplement but a rival to curiosity, and acted as a barrier to the writing of books, presumably because more profitable activities were usually available:

> . . . it is more easy to account for the rise and progress of commerce in any kingdom, than for that of learning. . . . Avarice, or the desire of gain, is an universal passion, which operates at all times, in all places, and upon all persons. But curiosity, or the love of knowledge, has a very limited influence, and requires youth, leisure, education, genius, and example, to make it govern any person. You will never want booksellers, while there are buyers of books. But there may frequently be readers where there are no authors.[6]

Hume, in attributing specially to youth a yearning for knowledge, for scholarship, was generalizing from his own experience. As he wrote to a friend, in 1764:

> I repent heartily my ever having committed anything to Print. Had I a Son I shou'd warn him as carefully against the dangerous Allurements of Literature as K James did his Son against those of Women; tho' if his Inclination was as strong as mine in my Youth, it is likely, that the warning would be to as little Purpose in the one Case as it usually is in the other.[7]

My role today is, of course, the reverse of Hume's. I am plead-

---

5. *Fable of the Bees, Part II* [1729], F. B. Kaye ed. (Oxford, 1924), II, 342.
6. *Essays Moral, Political, and Literary,* Green and Grose eds. (London, 1898), I, 176.
7. *The Letters of David Hume,* J. Y. T. Greig, ed. (Oxford, 1932), I, 461.

ing for planned increase of the allurements of scholarship rather than for increased protection against them. And I plead on behalf of scholarship, not that it will save the world, although this has conceivably happened in the past and may happen again; not that it brings material rewards to the scholar, although this also may have occurred, to the scandal of his academic superiors; not that it is an invariably exciting activity, for it generally involves a great deal of drudgery, and, like diplomacy for Charles G. Dawes, is often indeed harder on the feet than on the head. All that I plead on behalf of scholarship, at least upon this occasion, is that, once the taste for it has been aroused, it gives a sense of largeness even to one's small quests, and a sense of fullness even to the small answers to problems large or small which it yields, a sense which can never in any other way be attained, for which no other source of human gratification can, to the addict, be a satisfying substitute, which gains instead of loses in quality and quantity and in pleasure-yielding capacity by being shared with others—and which, unlike golf, improves with age.

To the objection that other needs are so pressing that we can't afford the time which scholarship calls for, I fear the answer which Robert Browning gave in his *A Grammarian's Funeral* would not now be acceptable:

> What's time? Leave *Now* for dogs and apes!
> Man has Forever.

It is not as easy today as in the good old days of Queen Victoria to believe that Man has Forever. But suppose we do steal from what time we do have some few hours for this less urgent business, surely no clear and present danger to our security or our prosperity or even the prosperity of our universities will result from such larceny.

Not that I would make an unqualified plea for all that is associated with the pursuit of scholarship, even when it is indulged in in only minor doses. So modestly stocked as a rule are the closets of scholars—unless they are of the medical profession—that despite the smallness of these closets there is still room in them to conceal a few skeletons. I propose to say a few words on the skeletons of the scholars. But let those of the fraternity in our midst rest tranquil, for I will speak only of those of our skeletons which we parade before the reading public's gaze.

First, the lay public complains, with something short of complete lack of justification, that scholars have a tendency to pass off obscurity for profundity. A scholar of a kind and poet of a comparable kind, Sir Richard Blackmore, once published an ungenerous couplet on this theme:

> Let idle Students on their Volumes pore
> To cloud with Learning, what was clear before.[8]

To this I can make on behalf of the scholar only this feeble reply in kind:

> Let unlearned laymen not be too sure,
> That what seems simple, is not obscure.

Second, for some reason which I have never quite fathomed, laymen object to footnotes and quotations as if they were always blots ostentatiously or capriciously sprinkled on texts. Perhaps scholars should dispense with footnotes when writing for laymen. They should, of course, dispense with them when they are superfluous or can conveniently to the reader be incorporated in the text. There have been some extraordinary manifestations of what a non-scholar has diagnosed as "foot-and-note-disease," and not all the redundant *infras, op. cits.,* and *loc. cits.* have fallen under the vigilant eye of Frank Sullivan of "A Garland of *Ibids*" fame. Hugo Grotius, for instance, was meticulously careful to append heavy documentation to such propositions of common notoriety as that man embraces woman; the author of "Mother Goose's Melody," said to be Oliver Goldsmith, was poking fun at him when he attached as a footnote to his melody, as an alleged quotation from Grotius, the statement that "It is a mean and scandalous practice in authors to put notes to things that deserve no notice." There is also that somewhat famous footnote in an English book published in 1854, inserted " as a relief to the uniformity and matter of these pages," a footnote to end all footnotes, which extends from page 334 of the book to page 628.[9]

I wish I could persuade laymen, nevertheless, that footnotes and quotations in texts often perform useful functions, and not only for scholars. Footnotes are frequently the only anchor of text

---

8. "Solomon's Irony" [1714], in *A Collection of Poems on Various Subjects* (London, 1718), p. 468.

9. [Christopher Walton], *Notes and Materials for an Adequate Biography of the Celebrated Divine and Theosopher, William Law* (London, 1854).

to fact, the only obstacle to flights of imagination where what is called for is merely soberly accurate reporting. As for quotations, they are often the only tasty plums in the author's pudding, as I would not have to depart far from my present text to provide an illustration. What irritates the laymen, I suspect, is frequently not the presence of the quotations but of the quotation *marks*. But scholars, and especially writers of doctoral dissertations, can omit these little marks only subject to great professional peril, for they are required to enable the reader to distinguish mere scholarship from creative writing.

Third, there is a special product of scholarship for which it is hard to find an excuse except that it is an occupational disease of the scholar which it often requires severe self-discipline, constant vigilance, and the aid of hostile critics completely to avoid. This is what Jeremy Bentham called "nonsense-on-stilts," a type of sophisticated nonsense, of ignorant learning, which only educated men are capable of perpetrating. An eighteenth-century French wit has distinguished two types of learned balderdash, of "galimatias," the simple type, where the author believes he understands what he is saying but cannot make it intelligible to his readers, and the compound type, where neither author nor readers can make anything of the text. It would not be difficult to extend this classification so as to cover still other types, as, for example, where the readers think they understand but the author knows he doesn't, and it would not be difficult to find illustrations, even in the "Great Books," and especially in the commentaries upon them, for all the types distinguished. Even with respect to highly technical subjects the layman can here make his own contribution to good scholarship by keeping his modesty under control; if after due application he fails to find a text addressed to laymen intelligible, he should hold in mind the bare possibility that the fault lies not with him but with the absence of meaningfulness in the text.

With the impatience of the layman or of the members of other disciplines with a particular discipline's technical terms, however, I have only limited patience. True it is that the scholar needs to be watched lest he use technical jargon to conceal the absence of precision, rather than in its service. But technical language, though never a sufficient condition of precision of thought, and sometimes a substitute for it, is often its necessary condition. I have friends who inadequately conceal their incredulity when I plead that to explain to them, for example, my belief that it is sometimes to a country's advantage to have an unfavorable balance of trade, I would have to resort to technical terms. These same friends, however, on the slightest provocation, or even with no provocation at all, will blandly break into a very rash of technical jargon, totally incomprehensible to me, if it is a question of why the runner was out at second base, or how to knit a baby sweater, or how to tell a yellow warbler from a canary.

I come now to the fourth and last of those of the scholar's skeletons which are fit matter for public discussion, at least among friends, to what I regard as the major barrier to the promotion of true scholarship in our graduate schools. This is the ever-growing specialization not only as between departments but even within departments, a specialization carried so far that very often professors within even the same department can scarcely communicate with each other on intellectual matters except through the mediation at seminars and doctoral examinations of their as yet incompletely specialized students. This development has not been capricious or without function. The growth in the accumulation of data, in the refinement and delicacy of tools for their analysis so that great application and concentration are necessary for mastery of their use, has not only ended the day of the polymath with all knowledge for his province, but seems steadily to be cutting down the number of those who would sacrifice even an inch of depth of knowledge for a mile of breadth.

I am told, and do not disbelieve, that this intensive specialization is frequently necessary for discovery, and especially for the improvement of techniques of discovery. To be able to keep on discovering things not known before it seems often to be necessary to work in a narrow groove, and to look always straight ahead in that groove without even glances at the once delectable knowledge in one's scholarly neighbor's rival garden. For our liberal colleges we preach synthesis of disciplines, breadth of view, and historical perspective, and in our liberal colleges there are still teachers who practice it. But when, by fellowships or other blandishments, we have enticed the college graduate into our graduate schools, we at once encourage him to grow the professional blinders which will confine his vision to the narrow research track, and we endeavor —often successfully—to make out of him a trufflehound, or, if you prefer, a race-horse, finely trained for a single small purpose and not much good for any other. We then let him loose on the under-graduates.

There may be a real dilemma here. It may really be true that at least in many cases there is a genuine and sharp conflict between, on the one hand, effective training for discovery, which requires narrow specialization, and, on the other hand, training for broad scholarship, which requires more time, less concentration of interest, less exclusive infatuation with laboratory models whose charms are the product of art rather than of nature, than progress in research can afford.

I yield to no one in recognition of the importance to mankind of the training for research which our graduate schools administer. If in the last generation or so American research over a wide range of fields has come of age, I would claim for the American graduate schools a great share of the credit. If the only relationship between graduate schools and colleges consisted in the recruiting from the colleges of the students for the graduate schools, I could even reconcile myself, though reluctantly, to the existence under modern conditions of an inherent conflict between research and scholarship, between narrowly-specialized skills and broad learning, and I would let the graduate schools go on in their present course, and encourage scholarship to seek refuge elsewhere.

The graduate schools, however, train our college teachers as well as our researchers, and the graduate school faculties also teach in the colleges. The graduate schools, I repeat, tend to mould their students into narrow specialists, who see only from the point of view of their subject, or of a special branch of their special subject, and fail to recognize the importance of looking even at their own subject from other than its own point of view. These students then acquire their doctoral degrees on the strength of theses which have demonstrated to the satisfaction of their supervisors that they have adequately decontaminated their minds from any influences surviving from their undergraduate training in other fields than those occupied by their chosen discipline. They then find their way back to the colleges to transmit to the next generation the graduate school version of a liberal education, or how to see the world through the eye of a needle. I would not pause to emphasize that mechanical shuffling of college curricula or verbal relabeling of courses is not an effective antidote to aggravated specialism in college teaching, were it not for my conviction that we often underestimate how very true, how very important, and how very much neglected, truisms can be.

Men are not narrow in their intellectual interests by nature; it takes special and rigorous training to accomplish that end. And men who have been trained to think only within the limits of one subject, or only from the point of view of one subject, will never make good teachers at the college level even in that subject. They may know exceedingly well the possibilities of that subject, but they will never be conscious of its limitations, or if conscious of them will never have an adequate motive or a good basis for judging as to their consequence or extent.

Samuel Johnson once said, before the urgent need of saying it had become obvious: "the rights of nations and of kings sink into questions of grammar, if grammarians discuss them." Samuel Johnson certainly had no prejudice against grammar. I don't think, therefore, that I am being unduly generous to him, and I am at least making my quotation from him more relevant to my present purposes, if I interpret it as intended only as a warning to specialists not to reduce all issues to *mere* applications of their specialty. Pride in one's special subject matter is a virtue, not a vice. It is right and proper, and good to look upon, to see a tanner in love with leather and a carpenter in love with wood. But what a meager portion of the realm of the mind is covered even by the proudest single subject! If only there is the will, how much of the rich realm of the human mind lies open for invasion, for the physicist beyond, beside, and behind nuclear fission, and for the economist in regions where the circulating medium is of more precious metal than even under the gold standard.

Robert Browning began his *A Grammarian's Funeral* with a dirge for scholarship:

> Let us begin and carry up this Corpse,
> Singing together,
> . . . .
> This is our master, famous calm and dead,
> Borne on our shoulders.

Browning did not end on a mournful note, however, and neither will I. Ways can be found to harmonize training in professional skills with training in scholarship. They must be found. They will be found. They need not involve any change in the declared objectives of our graduate schools. They will involve, however, changes in their actual practice. What the required changes are is a matter for exploration and experimentation.

Our graduate schools are now turning out large new crops of doctors of learning, whose primary task it will be to rescue the world from the perils of war, of disease, of poverty, and of sin. May they be given moments of leisure, and may they use some of these moments to give a little thought to the ways by which scholarship, as an ornament of the peace and the prosperity they will be winning for us, might also be promoted.

PART IV

Shorter Reviews

John R. Commons,
Legal Foundations of Capitalism
New York, The Macmillan Company, 1924*

THE SUPREME COURT OF THE UNITED STATES has upon occasion found it appropriate to express in adequately emphatic terms its failure to discover—and its disinclination to seek—in the classifications and the theories of the economists aid or enlightenment in the accomplishment of its task. The author of this work, who is a distinguished economist with a brilliant, versatile, and quantitatively impressive record of contribution to American economics, repays bad coin with good by finding in the decisions of the Supreme Court not only the development of a sound economics but an economics which is superior in its philosophy, psychology, and realism to that which is currently expounded by the economists themselves. The Supreme Court, though like M. Jourdain (if I may slightly depart from the original) it may not be aware of it, and unlike M. Jourdain may not be flattered to learn it, has been talking economics all of its life. It belongs in economics to the school of "volitional theorists," "whose initial thinkers are Hume, Malthus, Carey, Bastiat, Cassel, Anderson, but especially the Supreme Court of the United States." There are three underlying principles of economics, the principles of "mechanism, scarcity, and working rules," and the discovery of the last-mentioned principle is in large part due to the Supreme Court during the period from 1872 to 1897, as manifested in the changes made by the court in the definitions of the terms "property," "liberty," and "due process of law." The book is in the main a study of the evolution of the principle of the "working rule" by the court as applied to its unit of investigation, the "transactions" of "going concerns." Since it is mainly upon this principle "that modern business is conducted and that American legislatures, executives and inferior courts are held in conformity to the Constitution of the United States," the author

*Reprinted from *Illinois Law Review*, Vol. 19, April 1925, pp. 710-712, by the courtesy of the Northwestern University School of Law.

credits the Supreme Court with occupying "the unique position of the first authoritative faculty of political economy in the world's history"! (pp. 1-10).

The book is at times incomprehensible to me, and I therefore feel incapable of appraising its merits. Almost every page leaves me lost in a maze of novel terminology or of new, and therefore confusing, applications of established terms. The more discerning reader may perhaps find in it a contribution of striking novelty and tremendous significance to economic, or to legal, thought. What most impresses me in it is the prodigious industry with which the author has applied himself to the splitting of innumerable metaphysical hairs of the finest of fineness. As an economist, I remain unconvinced that it is either valid or enlightening to reduce economics to the three principles of mechanism, scarcity, and the working rule. I know of no period in economic thought and no school of economists which failed either to give explicit recognition of what the author calls the "working rule" or else implicitly to assume that the economic behavior they were describing was going on in the midst of the existing environment with its current set of working rules. I hazard the opinion that the Supreme Court was more belated than the economists in discovering this principle, and that the canonists of the Middle Ages applied it in their market-price doctrines more thoroughly than do the American courts.

I suspect that the men learned in the law will in many instances reject the author's interpretations of court terminology, decisions, and dicta. For example, the author declares that the Supreme Court in the *Minnesota Rate Case* (1890 134 U.S. 418) "changed the definition of property from physical things having only use-value to the exchange value of anything" (p. 14), and he defines exchange-value, presumably following the court, as ". . . the market-value expected to be obtained in exchange for the thing in any of the markets where the thing can or might be sold. In the course of time this exchange-value has come to be known as 'intangible property' ": (p. 19). I feel very doubtful whether any judge would hold that a thing's exchange-value is necessarily what the owner expects to be able to sell it for. I am certain also that the legal concept of "intangible property" antedates the 1890 decision, and even the 1865 and 1875 taxation cases later cited by the author (pp. 172ff.), and in the law of taxation, at least, means neither the exchange-value of property nor even the exchange-value of intangible property. I presume that the courts would protect a person in his ownership of intangible property even though it were valueless in the market. The economists, I believe, would go further than the lawyers in their acceptance of the following passage:

"... the court has legislated by definition. It changed the meaning of due process of law and thus amended the federal and every state constitution. It changed the meaning of property and liberty as used in the Fourteenth Amendment, and thus took over from the states the final determination of what was due process of law in the regulation of property and business" (p. 355).

Raymond Sachot, *Les Prix de Monopole d'après les Doctrines et dans les Faits*

Paris, Imprimerie C. Pailhe, 1926*

THE LITERATURE ON THE THEORY of monopoly price is scattered and unsystematic, and there is need for a collection, examination, and restatement of the deductive theory, and even more, for a further extension of inductive work on the objective manifestations of monopoly price. This book is an attempt at this task, but unfortunately, aside from its useful survey of the history of the deductive theorizing with respect to monopoly price, it is possessed of only a very moderate degree of merit. Even the doctrinal history, however, calls for some serious criticisms. The important contributions of Edgeworth and Pigou are represented only by single periodical articles for each, no use being made of Edgeworth's collected *Papers*, or of Pigou's *Economics of Welfare*. The latest references to American books on the monopoly problem are to the 1900 works of Ely and of Jenks, and the most valuable material that exists on the problems of monopoly price, namely, the reports of official investigations, the court records, and the commentaries thereon by American economists, remains unmentioned and unused so far as the period since 1900 is concerned. In the origination of a

*Reprinted from *The Journal of Political Economy*, Vol. 36, June 1928, pp. 411-412, by the courtesy of the University of Chicago Press.

precisely formulated doctrine of monopoly price, the author claims major credit, I believe justifiably, for two of his countrymen, Cournot and Dupuit. An American engineer, writing in the 1830's, however, carried the analysis of monopoly price, especially with reference to the elasticity of demand, the principle of charging what the traffic will bear and the maximum revenue principle, and the advantages of multiple prices, in some respects as far as did Cournot and Dupuit. This was Charles Ellet, and his writings with respect to the transportation problem, and especially his *Essay on the Laws of Trade*, Richmond, 1839, entitle him to rank with Cournot and Dupuit as a pioneer formulator of the pure theory of monopoly price in precise terms.

The author accepts the pseudo-subjective price analysis of Dupuit, as of later writers, which attempts to express "utilities" and "consumer's surpluses" in terms of a monetary unit whose subjective importance is simply a reflection of the subjective importance of what can be gotten in exchange for it, and cannot therefore be either greater or less than the latter, as if it were genuine utility analysis. The "marginal utility" of the writers whom he discusses is not distinguishable from the objective marginal demand price of that much over-rated person, the marginal purchaser. What their consumer's surplus is but the shadow of a non-existent shadow, I cannot see. It calls for comment that while a definite graphic solution of the problem of the fixation of monopoly price is an easy matter, all the graphs reproduced by the author from various sources, with the exception of one taken from Marshall which does present a trial-and-error solution, are only statements of the problem and not geometrical solutions thereof. There is, in the inductive section of the book, an interesting attempt at analysis and explanation of the price-phenomena of the rare-book market, but the inductive work is in general but a mediocre analysis by common-sense methods of scattered and wholly inadequate statistical data. The chief merits of the book lie, therefore, in its really useful history of the pure theory of monopoly price, and in its emphasis upon the importance of a more systematic and thorough study of the problems of monopoly price than has as yet been made.

Edgar Salin and Artur Sommer, *Friedrich List, Schriften, Reden, Briefe,* Volume IV, *Das Natürliche System der politschen Ökonomie*

Berlin, Verlag von Reimar Hobbing, 1927*

THIS PORTLY VOLUME, one of an apparently lengthy series in which List's writings are being collected, analyzed, and appraised, publishes for the first time an essay on commercial policy which List submitted, without success, to a Paris prize contest held in 1837. The original French text, some 200 pages long as here printed, and a German translation made by one of the editors, are given on parallel pages. An elaborate introduction gives the history of the prize contest, biographical notes on the supposed judges, a detailed analysis of the text of the original manuscript, and a careful study of the principal sources used by List. The essay itself is followed by some 90 pages of annotations by the editors. The paper and format are excellent and expensive. No other economist has ever received as devoted study, as elaborate a collation of his various writings, as detailed and worshipful interpretation and exegesis, as List here receives.

The essay here printed seems to differ in no essentials of its reasoning from the book which List published under a slightly different title in 1841, *Das nationale System der politischen Ökonomie,* although I have not thought it worth while to make a detailed comparison. Like the later book, it is a highly partisan and exaggerated plea for protection to manufactures and for free trade with respect to all other commodities. The central idea of the essay is that a country has not reached its optimum stage of national well-being, of maximum development of its "productive forces," until it has developed its manufacturing industries sufficiently not only to take care of its own wants for manufac-

*Reprinted from *The Journal of Political Economy,* Vol. 37, June 1929, pp. 364-366, by the courtesy of the University of Chicago Press.

tured products but also to produce a surplus for export, and that
the competition of industrially more advanced countries is an
insuperable barrier to the attainment of this state of blessedness
unless manufactures are protected against foreign competition
during their period of immaturity. This is, of course, the "infant
industry" argument expounded in the special terminology of the
"theory of the productive forces." The editors of the present work
do not succeed in making clear what List's claims to originality can
be. The infant industry argument had been a commonplace in the
English literature on commercial policy from the 1750's on, and
was known to French writers of the 1830's. The concept of the
"productive forces" was made much of by Chaptal, Dupin, Louis
Say, and other French writers of the period, to whom List acknowl-
edges his indebtedness, and Adam Müller also anticipated him in
this respect. List, it is true, attempted to build up on the basis of
this concept a "theory of the productive forces," explaining their
growth and development, as a counterfoil to the static value theory
of the classical school, with its free-trade tendencies. It is here that
List brings his historical method of approach to bear on the question of commercial policy, but it seems to be the vagueness of his
theory rather than its "genetic" character which has made it so
attractive to Spann and others of the modern German romantic
school. List stresses the importance of urbanization as a product of
industrial development, and of high productive capacity in general
as a product of urbanization, and his plea for manufactures, and for
the development through them of the "productive forces," is really
a plea for urbanization. List is entitled to praise as a pioneer of the
historical point of view in economics. But his actual use of historical
material is not worthy of praise. His sources are meager and second-
hand, he selects and paraphrases therefrom with flagrant bias, and
he uses them to fit the course of economic development into a neat
and simple pattern of economic stages which, providentially, *always*
and in every detail supports his argument. History, unfortunately,
is never actually so kind to theories of historical development.

List does not confine himself to the infant-industry argument
but reinforces it by most of the protectionist fallacies current in his
time in both America and Europe. The home market, saving of
freight, attraction of foreign capital and labor, utilization of by-
products, and diversification of industries arguments, are all to be
found here applied unreservedly in support of protection to manu-

factures. But with respect to raw materials and agricultural products, List is an unqualified free trader, making no concessions whatsoever. Of the case for free trade in terms of the principle of comparative costs, which Ricardo and Torrens had by this time already made *the* argument for free trade which the intelligent protectionist had to meet, List seems to have had no inkling, and Ricardo is not mentioned by him. His references to the doctrines of the free traders, and especially of Adam Smith, are so unfair as to be caricatures, effective enough perhaps for propaganda purposes, but not deserving of serious consideration as objective scientific analysis.

This series should satisfy to the full any reasonable degree of curiosity as to what List thought and wrote and where he acquired his notions. If the other volumes of the series are designed on the same lavish scale, more pages seem to be necessary to do justice to List's contribution than Palgrave's *Dictionary* makes suffice for all economics. List is entitled to homage from patriotic Germans as a pioneer apostle and martyr of German nationalism. German industrialists seeking still further tariff protection should find some profit in the aggrandizement of his reputation. But are not the scholars who, *as economists*, are lavishing their industry and ability on this extravagant enterprise displaying a rather serious lack of sense of proportion?

Merrill K. Bennett, *Farm Cost Studies in the United States*

Stanford, Calif., Stanford University,
Food Research Institute,
Miscellaneous Publication 4, 1928*

THIS BOOK is a somewhat severe criticism of the procedure of agricultural economists in gathering and using farm cost data. Their methods of collecting such data are unnecessarily expensive; the

*Reprinted from *The Journal of the American Statistical Association*, Vol. 25, March 1930, pp. 111-113, by the courtesy of the American Statistical Association.

data which they get are insufficiently representative to be usable; there is a generally inflationary bias in their farm cost data; in many cases there is no clear notion of what purpose they are to be made to serve and no purpose which they can conceivably serve. In part these defects are due to the fact that their collection is not by individual farmers for their private purposes, but by government agencies operating at the public's expense, who are free, therefore, from the constant pressure to show results proportionate to their efforts to which the costing service of private industry is presumably subject. The statistical methods by which these data are analyzed are either too simple and crude to give usable results or too refined and difficult for both those who supply them and those whom the analyses are intended to serve. Finally, there are serious defects in the manner of collection and use of farm cost data which are attributable in large part to the insufficient knowledge and use by farm management experts of economic theory with respect to the relations of costs to price.

This indictment is probably warranted and, accompanied as it is by many constructive suggestions which seem to be sound and practicable, should prove valuable if those to whom it is addressed pay any attention to it. I strongly suspect that similar profit would accrue from similar scrutiny of the extensive mass-research in other fields which is the outstanding characteristic of present-day effort in American economics. I would feel somewhat uncertain, however, about the product which farm management experts would derive from the application of the economic theory which the author expounds for their benefit, even if it were logically impeccable. As in some respects it is involved in confusion and error, it would perhaps be just as well that they should continue innocent of knowledge of economic theory as here presented.

Space limitations permit only a brief summary of the inadequacies of the author's theoretical analysis. The allocation of joint costs must rest on an arbitrary principle from the point of view of serving as a guide to farmer behavior (p. 49) only if the relative proportions in which the joint products shall be produced are not at all within the control of the producer, a situation which I understand is extremely rare. After the correct assertion that "Economists in their discussions of cost-and-price relationships under freely competitive conditions . . . say nothing about 'fair' prices," there follow statements that the economists do call competitive prices "fair." (pp. 188-189. See also pp. 219-220.) The author says that "Economists . . . do not include rent of land as an element of cost," and that ". . . they deny that in the long run the volume of supply would be affected by cost calculations of individuals involving consideration of the amount of rent." (pp. 190, 192.) I do not know of any economists who deny that rent is a part of entrepreneurs' costs, and there are probably many more economists of standing who assert that rent is as much a price-determining cost as any other cost than who deny it. Although I am old-fashioned enough still to maintain that there is an element of truth important enough to be worth salvaging in the Ricardian doctrine, I cannot see any reason why any economist should deny that the rent which land could yield as corn land may affect the extent to which it will be used for wheat and therefore the supply and price of wheat. The author's exposition of economic rent and marginal costs is vague. (pp. 190 ff.) Marginal costs enter into the determination of rent only if price equals marginal cost, and even then rent is not the sum of the differences between marginal cost and other costs, but is the difference between marginal cost and average cost, exclusive of rent, times the number of units of output. When x units are produced, the marginal cost is the increase in aggregate costs of x output as compared to $x-1$ output. Given the output, and the only costs which are distinguishable are the marginal cost and the average costs, farm and crop as a whole. If in an actual year a, there is an output x, and in year b an output $x+1$, the excess in cost, if any, of the second output over the first has no direct bearing on the amount of rent. Fixed costs, to the extent that they are really sunk costs and therefore inescapable and invariable in their aggregate amount regardless of output, do not affect marginal costs, and the same results as to marginal cost will be obtained from a calculation which does and one which does not take them into account. (pp. 203-204.) As the author says: "The general concept of marginalism is by no means easy to grasp."

There is a discussion of "bulk-line" cost curves which is a distinct improvement over most of what has been said about them, but it is not free from error. The statement: "A particular point on a cumulative curve of wheat costs means . . . that a certain proportion of the total amount of wheat grown on the farms under investigation was produced at a cost of $2 per bushel" to be correct should be amended to read: "was produced at a *farm-average* cost of $2 per bushel *or less.*" The theorist need not assume close correspondence between normal price and marginal cost even in a static state, if he grants that even in such a state error, weather variations, etc., would occur. The bulk-line concept—the "statistical" or "accountants' " cost curve, or Marshall's "particular expenses" curve—is usable even in long-run static analysis. Under static conditions the personnel of the extra-bulk-line group of producers would be ever-changing, but the group would be permanent. (pp. 198 ff.). Granting the author's assumption that in the long run price equals marginal cost, it is an erroneous proposition that: "Crops, like oats, which from the point of view of maintenance of soil fertility and employment of available labor fit well into a rotation centering about corn . . . would continue to be produced despite cost-and-price discrepancy." (p. 201.) This is like the argument for a tariff on beet sugar because beet-culture enriches the soil for other crops. Rotation of crops makes the different crops joint products, and demands determination of the rotation on the marginal cost principle, as Longfield pointed out almost a hundred years ago. Price-fixing at the bulk-line cost does not find its justification in the substitution, for the output of the displaced extra-bulk-line producers, of increased output of the other producers (p. 225), for without an increase in price there is no inducement to the latter to increase their output, and without a decrease in price there is no reason why the extra-bulk-line output should decrease. The bulk-line analysis, correctly interpreted, does not "locate a price-determining cost," but locates a price which is consistent with maintenance of existing output. It locates a *point* on the supply curve which corresponds to the prevailing price and the prevailing output. What the bulk-line point is, and if it has stability, could be determined only by collection of bulk-line cost curves over a series of years. In this connection, it should be pointed out that land-rent is an equalizing cost through a conceptual or *timeless* long run and not, as the author has it, through a long *historical* period (p. 254), which he confuses with the economist's long run. The bulk-line comparison of costs in different countries for tariff purposes does not necessarily lead to a higher duty than the comparison of average costs. (pp. 255-256.)

Edwin Cannan,
A Review of Economic Theory
London, P. S. King & Sons, Ltd., 1929*

THIS NEW BOOK by Professor Cannan, essentially a revised version of his famous course of lectures given for many years at the London School of Economics, is a blend of a history of economic thought and of a systematic exposition of the author's own doctrines. Although in his preface Dr. Cannan has attempted to forestall just such impertinent comments, I regret exceedingly that he did not give us instead that comprehensive history of English economic thought which is so much needed, and which he is so pre-eminently—I am almost inclined to say, so exclusively—equipped to write. As it is, this book falls between two stools. It is not comprehensive enough either as a history of doctrine or as a systematic exposition of the author's position to be entirely satisfying in either rôle. But no book by Professor Cannan in the field of economic theory can be devoid of great merits, and we should be grateful, I suppose, for what we get, even if it proves not to be what we had hoped to find it.

The lectures upon which this book is based must have been rich fare for the students to whom they were addressed, unless the maturity of English undergraduates exceeds that of American undergraduates in even greater degree than is commonly supposed to be the case. Its manner and content are such as to make it more suitable to the specialist in economic theory interested in the subtleties of dialectic than to the undergraduate seeking to acquire without undue intellectual strain a bird's-eye view of economic structure and process. In any case, there is solid and important matter in this book for the mature theorist to digest and to ruminate upon, and it is by no means a manual for the young. Although this book covers a wider field chronologically, topically, and in range of men discussed than the author's renowned *History of Theories of Production and Distribution*, it is, like that book, largely concerned with an examination of the doctrines of the English classical school. Professor Cannan is once more exceedingly critical of most of the writers

*Reprinted from *Economica*, No. 28, March 1930, pp. 74-84, by the courtesy of the London School of Economics and Political Science.

with whom he deals, although they have been selected for consideration, I suppose, not because they provide suitable victims
for a massacre on the grand scale, but because they were the
most important contributors to the fruitful development of economic thought that the author could find. In any case, they emerge
from the ordeal with their reputations for skill in analysis and
wisdom of judgment sadly tarnished, and, what is to the author
obviously not at all a trifling matter, even their syntax and punctua-
tion are demonstrated not to have been all that could be asked of
them if they had received, or had adequately benefited from, a good
sound literary education. The author's contemporaries, to their great
good fortune, escape a searching and rigorous examination of their
shortcomings, but they do so as a rule only at the cost of not being
mentioned, or of just being mentioned in passing, which is perhaps
the harshest treatment of all. Even the great Marshall is shown not
to have been wholly incapable of error, but in his case the evidence
is presented with an unusual degree of gentleness. Of non-English
economists there is but scanty mention.

There is need for critical examination of the evolution of English economic thought. The lack of interest of English economists
in the history of the ideas which they manipulate is notorious, and
when they do embark upon ventures in doctrinal history, it is
generally to exalt a hero, and to demonstrate that even if there is
the appearance of error in his work, it is due to faults of exposition
rather than of analysis, to discrepancies between what he said and
what he meant. But here, as elsewhere, there must surely be a golden
mean, and if there is, Dr. Cannan is on the other side of it. Whether
due to its essential soundness or to its lack of immediate relevance
to current problems—both hypotheses have their exponents—the
classical economics has shown extraordinary survival power in the
face of changing circumstance and of rough handling by critics.
But what has survived has been more its technique of analysis than
its specific conclusions, and what the author attacks are its conclusions rather than its methods, which are largely also his own. When
Dr. Cannan criticizes the earlier economists, he is no doubt usually
right. Many of his criticisms have now been before the economic
world challenging rebuttal for many years, and effective rebuttal is
still lacking. His dissatisfaction with their concepts has been shared
by many other economists, and some of his suggestions for their
revision have become part of our present-day equipment, in many

cases without adequate acknowledgment of their source. Nor can it be said of Dr. Cannan, as it can of many other critics of the classical economists, that his criticisms rest on ignorance of their writings or on recognition of the obstacles which their doctrines present to the common acceptance of some cherished fallacies of his own. No one will dispute, I think, that there are few rivals of Dr. Cannan in close and scholarly acquaintance with the economic writings of the English classical period. Nevertheless, I believe that the picture which he gives of the nature of and quality of the classical economists is, because of an over-critical temperament in such matters, one-sided and inaccurate in its emphasis. The classical economists were not wholly free from error, for they were only mortals, even if of a superior species. But Dr. Cannan seems more interested in their mistakes than in their achievements, seems as much interested in their petty mistakes as in their more serious ones, and seems to be much less interested in discovering their virtues than in exposing their frailties.

Dr. Cannan's own work is an unintentional tribute to the merits of the classical school, for it demonstrates what valuable contributions to economic thought can be made by the skilful employment of concepts and methods of analysis of the kind with which it endowed economics in the examination of problems of the sort with which it concerned itself. Merciless critic of the classical economists, he is nevertheless one of them himself, in spirit, in methods of analysis, in range of doctrinal interests, in zest for dialectic and for the niceties of terminological usage. Its sharpest critic, he is also one of the most complete of the posthumous conquests of the classical school, although his attachment to it reminds one of George Eliot's Tom Tulliver, who, it may be remembered, was "very fond of birds, that is of throwing stones at them." His main concern seems to be to correct the errors of the classical school and to amend its concepts in the somewhat conflicting directions of greater precision and closer approach to common usage, and his interest in devising or employing new methods of analysis and finding fresh problems to which to apply them seems quite mild. Not much of importance in economic thought, one gathers, was brought to light after the period of the magnificent, though blundering, classical economists, except such as resulted from the exposure of their blunders. The exercise of a soundly critical common sense, avoidance of technical concepts unintelligible to the intelligent layman, distrust of long chains of abstract reasoning and of highly technical refinements of concepts and procedures, freedom from any yearning to construct a formal and elaborate doctrinal "system," these are the outstanding characteristics of his method. With the paraphernalia of economic inquiry developed since the classical period—demand and supply curves, utility analysis, the translation of economic process into algebraic equations, the concept of general equilibrium, systematic induction by statistical methods, the comprehensive study of the influence of institutional change on economic process, and so forth—he will have commerce only at arm's length or not at all. If the book is a faithful transcript of the lectures, his students could have received from him little stimulus to become master of any of these techniques, and must have been led to an undue degree of contentment with common sense as an adequate instrument of economic investigation, especially if they failed to realize that the common sense which their master was exhibiting was of a very uncommon order, and that though a superior intelligence can do wonders with the simplest of tools, the ordinary student of economics needs training in the skilled use of technical tools if he is to accomplish anything at all.

I have already suggested that the author concentrates unduly on the defects of the classical school. His tendency to put them in the worst light possible leads him, I believe, frequently to find absurdities in their reasoning which are either not there at all or represent shortcomings in their exposition rather than in their logic or judgment. To a number of these instances I feel obliged to call attention.

In his discussion of Malthus's population theory, Dr. Cannan, successfully, I think, maintains: (*a*) that Malthus could not have understood the correct meaning of the terms "arithmetical ratio" and "geometrical ratio," and therefore meant by them as he used them something other than what they would mean to the mathematician, and (*b*) that Malthus attached considerable importance to the contrast between the behavior of these two ratios, one characteristic of food and the other of population unrestrained by positive or negative checks. But instead of endeavoring to find out what idea Malthus was trying to express with the aid of his unfortunately chosen mathematical illustration, our author devotes several pages to showing how ridiculous Malthus's argument was if the ratios are given their strict mathematical meaning (pp. 67-73).

The only use Malthus made of his ratios was to draw a contrast between two rates of increase, one slower than the other. What he was clearly trying to say was that the rate of growth of which any given population was biologically capable, if supplied with unlimited subsistence, was much greater than the rate at which a population could increase its sustenance in the absence of unlimited fertile virgin land, a proposition whose absurdity is at least not glaring.

Dr. Cannan asserts that where Malthus "went wrong was in treating the increase of food production as if it were a kind of natural phenomenon with which the amount of human industry had nothing to do" (p. 72). No passage is cited from any of Malthus's writings, and I am confident that there is none to be cited, which maintains or implies any such thing. It is so obvious and has always been so obvious that the amount of food produced is dependent upon the amount and quality of the labor devoted to its production, that Malthus could reasonably have been pardoned for not taking the pains to elaborate upon it. In at least the later editions of his *Essay on Population*, however, Malthus was sufficiently explicit, as the following citations will demonstrate:

"The effect of ignorance and oppression will therefore be to destroy the springs of industry, and consequently to diminish the annual produce of the land and labour in any country" (Ward, Lock and Co., reprint of sixth edition, p. 432).

"That an increase of population, when it follows in its natural order, is both a great positive good in itself, and absolutely necessary to a further increase in the annual produce of the land and labour of any country, I should be the last to deny" (*Ibid.*).

". . . agriculture may with more propriety be termed the efficient cause of population, than population of agriculture; though they certainly re-act upon each other, and are mutually necessary to each other's support" (*Ibid.*, p. 433).

Dr. Cannan says that "Marshall endeavours to show, in defiance of all evidence, that Ricardo never desired to put forward the pure labour theory of value. He had apparently never looked at the first and second editions of Ricardo's *Principles* . . ." (p. 177, note). But Cannan himself refers to some evidence in support of Marshall's interpretation, when he points out that, "From the first he [i.e. Ricardo] admitted that the fact of the 'fixed capitals employed' being 'of unequal value and unequal duration' in the case of different products does *sometime* affect their value" (p. 176; italics mine). Ricardo's actual words show that from the first he held that the relative values of commodities are *always* partly dependent on the relative amounts of fixed capital employed in their production:

> "Besides the alteration in the relative value of commodities, occasioned by more or less labour being required to produce them, they are also subject to fluctuations from a rise of wages, and consequent fall of profits, if the fixed capitals employed be either of unequal value, or of unequal duration" (*Principles of Political Economy*, first edition, p. 23).

If Ricardo ever held a labor theory of value, it was a wages theory and not a labor quantity theory, since he admitted that differences in rate of pay of different classes of workers were reflected in the relative values of their products. But assuming, as did Ricardo generally, that all labor was remunerated at the same rate, in order to convict him of holding that relative values were determined *only* by relative labor costs, it would be necessary to show that he maintained that the relative amounts of interest or "profits" incurred in connection with the production of different commodities had no influence on their relative values. Ricardo, on the contrary, in his first edition, shows by laborious arithmetical examples not reproduced in the final edition that two products into whose production labor and capital enter in different proportions will have relative values different from their relative labor costs, and that their relative values will change if the common rates of wages and of profits change, even though their relative labor costs remain the same. In his examples, capital costs have, pound for pound, exactly the same influence on relative values as do wages costs (*Principles*, first edition, pp. 31-41).

Dr. Cannan thinks that Ricardo would have been puzzled if he had been asked, "When you say that the quantity of labor required for the production of a commodity alone determines its value, do you mean to deny that the quantity of land required for its production has any influence on its value?" For, "if it takes the same quantity of labor but six times as much land to grow a ton of greengages as it takes to grow a ton of potatoes, greengages will sell for more per pound avoirdupois than potatoes" (p. 180). But this is not as successful a *reductio ad absurdum* of Ricardo's doctrine that rent does not affect price as Dr. Cannan seems to imagine. Ricardo expressly stated that he was arguing for the proportionality of value to highest labor cost economically permissible (in modern terminology, to "marginal labor cost") and not to *average* labor cost (*Principles*, first edition, p. 59). If greengages require on the average six times as much land of given quality as do potatoes per ton, either their values will not be the same, or their average labor costs will not be the same. But if the marginal labor costs of potatoes and greengages are the same per ton, their values will be the same per ton, regardless of how much land each requires on the average.

Dr. Cannan disposes of the Ricardian rent theory as erroneous, because it rests on an untenable distinction between the circumstances determining the supply of land and those determining the supplies of other instruments. "No doubt the earth's surface cannot be increased, but this is a fact of the same nature as the fact that the different kinds of matter provided by Nature cannot be increased. It has exactly the same relevance to the value of land that the fact that there is only a certain amount of iron ore in the world has to the value of steam-engines" (p. 246). The classical economists may have drawn too sharp a contrast between the conditions governing the supply of land and those governing the supplies of other factors of commodities in general, but it would be extraordinary if the supply of land and the supply of steam-engines had identical characteristics. If the demand for steam-engines increases, the amount of steam-engines can be increased by using iron-ore which otherwise would have gone into the production of other commodities or which otherwise would not have been produced at all. And the additional units of steam-engines and of iron-ore will be just as good in quality as any others. None of these possibilities exist, at least to anything like the same degree, in the case of an increase in the demand for land.

Dr. Cannan says that: "The real-cost of production theorists assumed that it was at any rate approximately true that production involved painful effort and sacrifice, and that competition arranged production, and consequently the values of products, so that people were equally 'rewarded' for equal efforts and sacrifices," and goes on to make it appear that this doctrine of the proportionality of rewards to sacrifices was supposed to hold not only (1) among laborers themselves, but also (2) as between laborers and capitalists (p. 213). I can recall only the blundering and reactionary McCulloch who, after Smith, ever maintained the former, and I can find no economists who ever expounded the latter doctrine.

The wage-fund theory is criticized on the familiar, but I believe thoroughly erroneous, ground that wages are paid out of current production, and that no stock of provision has to be accumulated except in the "rather inaccurate" sense that "the amount of wheaten bread, for example, which could be consumed in the months to elapse before the next harvest came in could not exceed what could be made out of the stock of wheat and flour in existence at the beginning of those months" (pp. 350-355). It is easy to show that real wages are advanced out of the output of past, and to a large extent *long* past, production to a degree much greater than this quotation suggests. For the United States, the total amount of the wages bill, including salaries, is for the post-war years usually estimated at from 55 to 60 per cent of the total national income. A glance at the census of production for any one year will show at once that the percentage of the value added by production in any current year which is accounted for by work done on materials and services which will be available within a year for consumption, not only by labor but by *all* classes, is much less than 55 per cent of the total output of the year and in all probability does not exceed 15 per cent. The great bulk of the process of producing what labor consumes as real wages in any one year must have been undergone long before. I do not present this as a defence of the wage-fund theory as a theory of wages, but as a refutation of the common type of attack on it, which in destroying it also destroys the foundations of a sound interest theory. Assuming continuous production, no stock of provision wholly ready for consumption needs to be accumulated in advance of payment of wages. But current wages are paid out of a flow of finished products to which current labor has contributed only the finishing touches. What current labor produces is in the main future and not current real wages.

J. S. Mill's "last and worst fundamental proposition respecting capital," that "a demand for commodities is not a demand for labour," Dr. Cannan ridicules as "perhaps the biggest blunder made in economic theory in modern times" (p. 109). In refutation of it, he asserts only that "no truth in economics could well be more fundamental than that a demand for a particular kind of commodity either is or immediately gives rise to a demand for labour to make that commodity." This proposition is true (subject to certain exceptions), but Mill himself expounded it: "a demand for [particular] commodities . . . determines into a particular channel a portion, more or less considerable, of the demand already existing. It determines that a part of the labour and capital of the community shall be employed in producing certain things instead of other things" (*Principles of Political Economy,* first and second edition, Book I, Chap. V, pp. 99-100). What Mill denied was that a demand for a particular commodity was rightly to be regarded as an addition to the total demand for labor. His thesis was that a person with given spending power can either "spend" it, i.e. use it in the purchase of "commodities," here meaning *commodities for immediate personal consumption,* or "save" it, i.e. use it in the hire of labor to make some durable good, and that labor as a whole benefits from the latter procedure to a greater degree than from the former. I do not think this is a very serious "blunder in economic theory," although it would be hard to match Mill for obscurity of exposition. Under either procedure there would be, at the same money rates of wages, the same employment of labor, but, as Mill points out, under the latter procedure there would be left for consumption by labor (through the mediation of lower prices for those types of commodities which both labor and other classes consumed, and of substitution of production of working-class commodities for production of expensive luxuries, he might have explained) the commodities which other classes were deliberately refraining from consuming themselves.

"It may happen that an hour's work by a business manager or two days' work by a watchmaker or three days' work by a carpenter or ten days' work by an agricultural labourer may all have the same exchange measure, say a guinea. A guinea may also be the exchange measure of the abstinence or sacrifice involved in the loan of 20 guineas for a year. These various efforts and abstinences, these elements of Cost of production, are certainly not equal to one another."

Dr. Cannan comments on the foregoing quotation from Marshall's *Economics of Industry* that, "If there is no way of measuring except by money-cost, the statement that these various efforts and abstinences 'are certainly not equal' is rash; they may be, for all Marshall knows; he is only entitled to say that he does not know that they are equal" (p. 191). Marshall was somewhat rash. Granting complete absence of knowledge as to their comparative dimensions and granting rejection of money as an accurate measure, their inequality is a matter of probability, not of certainty. But the probability that any two quantities of whose dimensions we know nothing will upon accurate measurement be found to be equal is as one to infinity; *a fortiori*, the probability that *all* of a number of quantities of whose dimensions we know nothing will be found to be equal is also as one to infinity. In fact, we all believe that we do know something about their comparative dimensions, and that what we do know points overwhelmingly to their not being equal. Marshall was certainly entitled to say more than that "he does not know that they are equal."

There is little in Dr. Cannan's exposition of his own general position which is not already familiar to students of his previous writings or which is likely to arouse serious dissent. He goes too far, I suspect, in his reaction against the pessimistic views of the classical economists with respect to the effect of increasing population on the average level of economic well-being, when he leaves with his readers the impression that there is not already in any old country sufficient population to exhaust all the possibilities of economic co-operation (pp. 80 ff.). I doubt the soundness of the argument that an invention whereby doubling all our instruments would increase the income of our community fourfold may result in "an increase in the percentage of deductions which might more than counterbalance the advantage of greater produce per head" as far as labor earnings were concerned (p. 367). If the new instruments rained from heaven into the laps of the capitalists, this might be plausible. But if the instruments themselves had to be produced by labor, even though the first effect of their introduction would be a reduction in the marginal importance of the labor using the instruments, it would involve also a great increase in the productivity of the labor making the machines. As long as the machines had great marginal productivity, labor would be drawn from using machines to making them, until the marginal productivity of the machines had fallen and of the labor had risen to new levels in which labor was equally productive making or using the instruments, and until the return to the manufacturers of the machines was no longer so great as to induce any further increase in their rate of production. I cannot see why "relative supplies" is a better term than "reciprocal demand" (p. 189). An adequate term for the concept intended would expressly mention both supply and demand. It is not true that, "when we say bread or diamonds are scarce or plentiful, we are comparing the supply of the moment with the supply of some other period or the supply of bread or diamonds with the supply of other things at the same period" (p. 196). What we are comparing are the relations of supply to demand of the same commodity at different periods or of different commodities at the same period.

The author's suggestion that "it might well be possible to make contracts of assurance which would give larger amounts if the assured died at an age when his family was least likely to be self-supporting, and less and less as it took place at a later age" (p. 426), will have no novelty for the members of the staffs of American universities, to whom such policies have been made available for some time by an insurance company endowed in their interest. Close supervision of private companies or a State monopoly are not the only alternatives, where insurance is compulsory (p. 427). In Ohio, and perhaps in other states, where workmen's compensation insurance is compulsory, the State maintains an insurance fund in competition with private companies.

Robert Livingston Schuyler, editor,
Josiah Tucker: A Selection from His
Economic and Political Writings
New York, Columbia University Press, 1931*

THIS BOOK CONTAINS a reprint of seven of Tucker's writings, and an Introduction by Professor Schuyler giving an account of Tucker's life and of some of his economic and political doctrines. Among the writings here reprinted are two of special economic interest: *The Elements of Commerce and Theory of Taxes*, privately printed in 1755, and with only three copies in its original form known to survive; and *The Instructions to Travellers*, privately printed in in 1757, published in Dublin in 1758, and also extremely rare.

Tucker is more important for the history of ideas in the eighteenth century as a political than as an economic thinker. Judged by present-day standards, he displayed a strange mixture of reactionary and of liberal tendencies, both in economic matters and in politics. Except perhaps for his anti-imperialistic views and his

---

*Reprinted from *The Journal of Political Economy*, Vol. 40, June 1932, pp. 416-418, by the courtesy of the University of Chicago Press.

opposition to war on economic grounds, he was not even abreast of
the most advanced economic thought of his times. Although he had
the advantage of personal correspondence with David Hume, and
it is possible to show convincingly, by a comparison of his economic writings before and after 1752, that he was influenced by and
profited somewhat from Hume's *Political Discourses* (1752), he
never succeeded in seeing clearly or in absorbing Hume's exposure
of the fallacies underlying his own system of economic thought.
His chief interest for the economist lies in the fact that he reveals
with striking clearness the process of internal disintegration of the
mercantilist doctrine which was going on during the eighteenth
century even before Hume and Smith had provided an acceptable
substitute.

Professor Schuyler, however, credits Tucker with having made
important original contributions to economic doctrine and with
having exercised appreciable influence on later writers, including
Adam Smith and the physiocrats. He relies unduly, however, on
the similar claims made on behalf of Tucker by Walter E. Clark
in his mediocre and naïve monograph, *Josiah Tucker: Economist*,
and the evidence which he himself presents both for Tucker's
originality and for his influence on later writers is exceedingly
slender. *"Like the classical economists of later days,"* says Professor
Schuyler, "Tucker regarded self-interest as the psychological basis
of economics" (p. 13; italics mine). With equal accuracy he could
have said: "Like the mercantilist economists of earlier days." Since
economic writings in English first made their appearance, there
has been common emphasis on self-interest as the dominant factor
in economic activity. A large part of the logic of the mercantilist
doctrines rested on the need for governmental control because
otherwise individuals would follow their own interests to the injury of the common welfare. "The similarity of some of the basic
economic ideas expounded in the *Wealth of Nations* to those which
Tucker had previously set forth," writes our author, "would make
it reasonable to suppose that Adam Smith was influenced by his
older contemporary, even if it were not known that he had a copy
of Tucker's *Essay on Trade* in his library." It might, *if* it were
shown that Smith and Tucker had many important ideas in common, *if* it were shown that these ideas were not widely prevalent at
the time, and *if* it were not true that these ideas could readily be
found in writers prior to both, some of them prior by a century.

There is very little economic reasoning in Tucker which was not fairly common property at the time he wrote, and there were few doctrines in which Tucker was at all in advance of his time in which Hume and others had not made even further progress at an earlier date. To cite as further support of Tucker's influence on Smith that "it has been clearly established, moreover, that Smith owed much to the French economists, some of whom were undoubtedly influenced by Tucker" (p. 16), without lending plausibility to it by concrete and detailed evidence is surely conducive to bringing into discredit the art of tracing intellectual influence. To anyone who is at all familiar with the doctrines of Tucker, the physiocrats, and Smith, the notion that Smith was appreciably influenced by Tucker, via the physiocrats, can be regarded as only a blind stab in the dark.

Tucker's writings are of interest for the history of economic thought as documents illustrative of the struggle of mercantilism to survive in the face of what should have proved crushing criticism by means of a superficial change in form while adhering to an outmoded substance. Only fairly comprehensive ignorance of what preceded and what followed Tucker in the evolution of economic ideas can explain the assignment to him of the rôle of an economic innovator. But we can be grateful to Professor Schuyler for making generally available Tucker's scarce writings and for his no doubt more accurate appraisal of the significance of Tucker's political doctrines.

Eli F. Heckscher, *Mercantilism*

(translated by Mendel Shapiro from the
German edition and revised by the author;
first published in Swedish in 1931),
London, George Allen & Unwin, Ltd., 1935*

HIS ADMIRABLE COMMAND of economic theory, of economic history, and of the cultural history of modern Europe, have given Professor Heckscher the ideal equipment for a study of the mercantilist doctrines. He apparently is able, moreover, to take all western European

*Reprinted from *Economic History Review*, Vol. 6, October 1935, pp. 99-101, by the courtesy of Cambridge University Press.

languages in his stride, and this has enabled him to make use of an extraordinarily extensive and varied range of source materials. For the period up to about 1720—beyond which the treatment is admittedly sketchy—this book not only supersedes previous general accounts of the intellectual content of mercantilism and its relation to material, political, and general cultural background of its period, but it presents to both economic theorists and economic historians a model of how such things should be done. The book, moreover, emerges from the double translation process with a precise, idiomatic, and highly readable style, for which no doubt author and translator are jointly responsible.

The primary concern of the book is the system of economic policy of western Europe, and especially England and France, prevailing in the period from the end of the Middle Ages to the beginnings of *laissez-faire*. Professor Heckscher interprets mercantilism as a policy aiming: to substitute State unification for the medieval combination of cosmopolitan universalism and local particularism; to promote the power of the State in relation to other states; and to promote economic welfare in terms of the accumulation of "treasure," the protection of domestic industry, and "provision" of ample supplies of foodstuffs and raw materials. All of these aspects are studied in detail. His demonstration of the importance in mercantilist thought of the survival from the Middle Ages of "provision" considerations, and of the conflict in practice between these considerations and other mercantilist aims, appears to me his most original contribution, and to be especially valuable in making more intelligible than it has hitherto been the simultaneous pursuit by the mercantilists of the conflicting ends of plenty and scarcity of commodities. But fresh and interesting data and interpretations are presented on all of these aspects of mercantilism. Especially deserving of attention are Professor Heckscher's appraisals of the degree of success or failure—usually the latter—of mercantilism in attaining in practice its various ends, and of the impact of mercantilist policy on the rate of technological progress. Since the breach of our present age with its mercantilist past, whether intellectually or in political behaviour, was never as great in fact as in appearance, and now is in many respects no longer great even in appearance, much of what the author has to say has immediate relevance for an understanding of present-day currents of thought and of the problems which result from such thinking.

It seems to me that in his treatment of the power aspects of mercantilist policy Professor Heckscher has been less successful than in the remainder of his book, both in making his position clear and in demonstrating its validity. He seems to contend that for mercantilism wealth was desirable (only?) as a means to power, whereas for the later period power was sought (only?) as a means to wealth. But I find neither in the evidence he presents nor elsewhere much support for the view that there was substantial difference in these respects between the seventeenth and the nineteenth centuries. For both periods power and wealth were both ultimate ends, i.e. valued for their own sakes. In neither period were they ordinarily regarded as conflicting ends, and on the contrary it was the general view in both periods that the attainment of the one was a means to the attainment of the other; power bred wealth, and wealth power. If there was occasional recognition that the maintenance of power was economically costly, this should not be interpreted without clear evidence as a denial that the loss or surrender of power would be even more costly economically. If in nineteenth-century England and Holland there was less talk of power and more of wealth, may this not have been due to the fact that England then felt herself assured of all the power she felt any occasion to use while Holland recognized that power was unattainable for her no matter how much she pursued it?

On a few other points, Professor Heckscher has either failed to state his position clearly, or it appears open to question. Why should protectionism in the English corn trade be regarded as beginning with the export bounty of 1689, rather than with the earlier import duties, or the earlier export bounty (vol. II, p. 229)? Apologists for private hoarding of the precious metals were not by any means non-existent, for a number of writers saw in such hoarding a welcome alternative to export (vol. II, p. 212). Seigniorage always results in less metal in the coins than is required to be given at the mint in return for coin, regardless of whether or not the seigniorage charge exceeds the cost of coinage. Given a seigniorage charge, English coins will rise in value above the value of their silver content, regardless of how the mint disposes of the seigniorage silver, whenever the state of the exchanges and of the bullion market are such as to make silver flow to England and silver bullion flow to the English mint to be coined. Professor Heckscher seems to be expounding contrary doctrine on these points (vol. II, pp. 257-8). But if these are flaws, they are minor flaws in a work which is a magnificent achievement of intelligent scholarship.

This study succeeds in making mercantilism intelligible, not by the usual procedure of economic historians of identifying historical explanation with justification, but by showing that in the historical setting of mercantilism, and with the as yet embryonic stage which economic analysis had reached, the avoidance of certain characteristic mercantilist fallacies and confusions would have been more surprising than their perpetration. While economic theorists will not be forced by this study to make any drastic revision of their notions as to the quality of mercantilist thought, their criticisms can now be based on evidence instead of on intuitions and traditional formulae of questionable accuracy. But for all future students of mercantilism, whatever their special interest, this book will be an absolutely indispensable guide.

Henry Higgs, *Bibliography of Economics, 1751-1775*

prepared for the British Academy, London,
Cambridge University Press; New York,
The Macmillan Company, 1935*

THIS IS THE FIRST INSTALLMENT of what, according to the jacket, aims to be "a comprehensive, chronologically arranged, catalogue of literature of economic interest," covering the period 1751-75, and contains about seven thousand items, giving authorship where known (or suspected), title, as a rule unabbreviated, date and place of publication, format, and in many cases the number of pages. There are numerous annotations giving information as to other editions, and some additional annotations relating to the nature or the quality of the contents or to the authority for attributing authorship, of which many are by Professor Foxwell. The bibliography is to be continued "backward and forward." The entries under each year are divided into twelve groups in accordance with a rough but fairly serviceable classification.

*Reprinted from *The Journal of Political Economy*, Vol. 43, December 1935, pp. 817-820, by the courtesy of the University of Chicago Press.

This enterprise is a worthy one, and deserving of the fullest encouragement. Those who have attempted serious bibliographical work will appreciate how much painstaking labor must have entered into the preparation of this volume. There has not hitherto been any guide to the economic literature of the period with any claims to completeness, and to investigators of the history and theory of the period, to librarians, to book collectors and the antiquarian book trade, this will be an indispensable tool. As far as my check goes, Mr. Higgs seems to have maintained as nearly perfect a standard of accuracy in the compilation of his material as is humanly possible, and the compositors and proofreaders appear also to have done no damage to his workmanship. While there are errors, no doubt, almost all of them are probably to be attributed to the bibliographical sources which Mr. Higgs was forced to use when actual copies of the items were not available for examination. The succeeding sections of this enterprise, and especially those dealing with the period 1650-1750, for which bibliographical aids are especially lacking, will be awaited with impatience.

Since, however, this volume is but the first product of a continuing enterprise, so that modification of procedure should within limits still be feasible for subsequent volumes, I presume to offer some suggestions of possible improvements in procedure. There should be a fuller, more informative, more specific, explanation of the rules followed in including or omitting items, in noting variant editions, in defining place of publication, and in assigning authorship to items published anonymously. There should especially be a fuller statement of the sources of bibliographical information used, in order that the scholar hunting for omitted items may know what ground has been covered. There are two indexes, one of authors, and one labeled "Index of Anonymous Titles," but the latter is really only an index of anonymous titles of items to which no authorship has been ascribed in the text. There should be either a complete index of titles, or, if this is asking too much, there should at least be a complete index of titles of items which, as listed in the text, were published anonymously. Under the present arrangement an anonymous item whose authorship, actual or suspected, is unknown to the reader cannot be traced from the index if an authorship is attributed to it in the text. Recourse must be had to examination of all the entries for the year in question. Even for this period the entries per year are sufficiently numerous to make this a heavy task, and since the number of entries per year increases rapidly as we move forward in time, this procedure will cease to be at all practicable for the volumes covering later years. For the many anonymous items, moreover, which were issued without indication of the exact year of publication even this procedure is unavailable.

It seems to me also that this work would gain in value if the available resources of time and money were concentrated on a greater approach to completeness of the British entries with abandonment of the attempt to cover other languages or American and colonial imprints in English. A completely exhaustive bibliography is, of course, unattainable, and as the number of items found grows, the search for additional items inevitably encounters steeply and progressively diminishing returns per unit of effort. But there has not here been as great an endeavor to approach completeness, even for British items, as would have been worth while or even as should have been regarded by the sponsors of this enterprise as a reasonable minimum, considering the supreme importance of comprehensiveness in the fields of use in which such a bibliography must find its justification. Mr. Higgs, in his Introduction, expresses the hope that "nothing of primary importance has been omitted," but the first demand on a bibliography of this sort is that it shall be all-inclusive, and that everything has been done which it is reasonably possible to do to catch every item which for whatever reason peculiar to himself the student of the economic literature of the period may regard as important. The coverage in this volume of non-British publications in languages other than English, with the possible exception of French, appears too incomplete to warrant their inclusion at all, and there is even no clear indication of what languages or countries are supposed to be covered. For American imprints the failure to use the outstanding source, Charles Evans, *American Bibliography* (for the period covered by this volume, Vols. III-V), is fatal. The non-British bibliographies, it would seem, could be much more fully and conveniently handled on the spot, especially as British libraries are on the whole not richly endowed with Continental or American material.

But even for the British items too restricted a set of bibliographical sources has been used, if the list of "main sources" given and the results of a few hours of examination of the text are a fair test. There is inadequate listing of the contents of the British periodicals of the period, and not enough use has been made of the printed catalogues of libraries and of the special bibliographies to be found in such works—to take the particular instances which I have examined for this purpose—as Barnes, *History of the English Corn Laws;* Furniss, *The Position of the Laborer in a System of Nationalism;* Seligman, *The Shifting and Incidence of Taxation;* and Kaye's edition of Mandeville, *Fable of the Bees.* Incomplete examination of the bibliographies in these four books alone has yielded over forty items apparently omitted from this volume, including, incidentally, items of such interest as Adam Smith's letter to the Authors of the *Edinburgh Review* (1755), and of such great importance for the history of utilitarianism as Abraham Tucker's *The Light of Nature Pursued* (1768). A further casual check in the card catalogues of the University of Chicago Libraries and the John Crerar Library, Chicago, indicates that several weeks' search in these libraries alone would reveal several hundred British items wholly omitted from this bibliography, and would make possible the actual examination of many items listed in the bibliography on the basis solely of secondary sources. Where so much has been given I feel ungracious in asking for still more, but it would seem to require only a moderate increase in effort to make possible so nearly complete a performance of this task as, for the British field at least, would render its repetition forever unnecessary.

Harvard Graduate School of Business Administration. Baker Library; Kress Library of Business and Economics

Catalogue Covering Materials Published through 1776.
With Data upon Cognate Items in Other Harvard Libraries, with Preface by Arthur H. Cole, Boston, Soldier's Field, 1940*

THIS IS A CATALOGUE of a magnificent collection of economic material published up to 1776. It includes both the collections of the Kress Library of Business and Economics, of which the second

*Reprinted from *The Journal of Political Economy*, Vol. 49, August 1941, pp. 629-631, by the courtesy of the University of Chicago Press. In order to present in a group the three reviews of bibliographies, this and the following review have not been put in chronological order.

Foxwell collection provided the core, and the related holdings of all other Harvard University libraries. As a published catalogue, it has no close rival in its field. The Higgs *Bibliography of Economics, 1751 to 1775*, will with the second volume, for the period of 1701-55, announced as soon to be published, cover substantially the same field. For the years 1751-75, common to both the Kress Library *Catalogue* and the Higgs *Bibliography*, the former lists 2,186 items, while the latter lists 6,741 items. The Higgs *Bibliography*, however, is not a catalogue; and as a collection, chronologically arranged, of bibliographical information derived from a variety of miscellaneous sources, including even booksellers' catalogues, and inadequately indexed, it is neither a convenient nor a wholly reliable tool of research.[1] The Kress Library *Catalogue* has over the *London Bibliography of the Social Sciences* and the British Museum *Catalogue* the advantage of chronological arrangement, of better indexing, and of inclusion only of items of special interest to economists.

For scholars in the period covered, the Kress Library *Catalogue* will be an exceedingly valuable bibliographical tool. The Harvard collections are rich, especially in British, and to a lesser extent in French, literature. A very large proportion of the British items of primary importance are undoubtedly included. The arrangement is excellent, and probably the best available without undue enlargement of the volume. The items are arranged by years, and alphabetically within years, which seems to me the ideal general-purpose arrangement, provided, as is the case here, that there is also a complete index: by author, for items of acknowledged authorship; by title, for anonymous items; and by author *and* title for anonymous items for which attributions of authorship are made.

There are few points on which even the most exacting critic could base complaints. The catalogue makes a bulky volume and will, by its nature, receive heavy use; the soft paper covers in which some, at least, of the copies are bound are therefore less than it deserves or needs. The noninclusion of post-1776 editions (or facsimiles) of works first published before 1777 seems a mistake, at least for scarce items and especially for items, if such there be, of which no pre-1777 copy is listed in this catalogue. This applies also

---

1. *Bibliography of Economics, 1751-1755*, prepared for the British Academy by Henry Higgs (New York, 1935). Cf. my review, *Journal of Political Economy*, XLIII (1935), 817-20, and Hayek's review, *Economica*, new ser., III (1936), 99-100.

to post-1776 publications of early manuscripts hitherto unpublished. No special enterprise has been shown in attributing authorship to items published anonymously, and no general explanation is given as to what authorities were followed in attributing authorship to anonymous works where such attribution was made—a common, but serious, defect in bibliographies and catalogues. The volume is excellently printed, but the printer's (and publisher's?) light is nevertheless kept hidden under a bushel. Presumably, the Harvard University Press deserves the credit.

We are told in the Preface by the librarian, Mr. Arthur H. Cole, that the Kress Library hopes to publish additional volumes, comparable to this one, carrying the catalogue down to the middle of the nineteenth century. It will be splendid if this can be done. British bibliographical work in the economics field has always been, for the most part, an amateurish, sketchy, and hit-and-miss affair, especially for the period after 1776. As far as economics is concerned, the new *Cambridge Bibliography of English Literature*, in scope and in quality of execution, has for this period fallen below even the mediocre British standards; and it is to be regretted that, if a good job were not to be done, it made any attempt at all to deal with this field. The economic bibliography in Volume II of the *Cambridge History of the British Empire*, which deals with the nineteenth century, is even worse in quality of execution. Good bibliography is a prime requisite for good historical work. For British economics, the period 1776-1850—important as it is for students of economic theory and economic history—still remains bibliographically very nearly a trackless desert. There is no comprehensive bibliography of the period, and, with the exception of the bibliographical information in Miss Williams' excellent but highly selective *Guide*,[2] there is even no brief bibliography which is both well selected and reasonably accurate. The service which the Kress Library would render to scholars if it carried publication of its *Catalogue* through this period on the same plan and scale as for the earlier period would therefore be very great indeed.

---

2. Judith Blow Williams, *A Guide to the Printed Materials for English Social and Economic History, 1750-1850* (New York, 1926). Cf. my review, *Journal of Political Economy*, XXXVI (1928), 177-78.

Bibliography of the Published
Writings of John Stuart Mill

Edited from his manuscript by Nay McMinn, J. R. Hainds, and
James McNab McCrimmon, Northwestern University Studies in
the Humanities, No. 12, Evanston, Ill., Northwestern University,
1945*

THIS VOLUME reproduces a bibliography of the works of John
Stuart Mill contained in a notebook found in the portion of the
collection of Mill manuscripts which was acquired by the London
School of Economics after the collection was sold in the 1920's by
the estate of a niece of Helen Taylor, daughter of Mrs. Mill. The
original is not in Mill's own hand, but it was obviously prepared
under his direction and was probably dictated by him from notes
to some person of limited education, if one may judge from the
spelling, especially of proper names.

The editors provide for each entry more exact and fuller bibliographical information. In all but two or three instances they are
able to locate the items referred to, although in many cases the
information provided by the original manuscript was incomplete.
They also give for each item a brief note descriptive of its contents.
These notes are generally helpful; but, as is usual in such cases, they
cannot be unqualifiedly relied upon for accuracy, at least where the
subject matter is not within the fields of specialization of the editors.
In one instance at least—the letter on Absenteeism in the *Morning
Chronicle* (1825) (p. 7)—the editors' note attributes to Mill very
nearly the exact reverse of his actual position.

The bibliography within its limits seems to be substantially complete and to be wholly free from improper inclusions. But the editors in their preface go somewhat too far when they say that it
accounts for "practically everything that Mill had put into print"
(p. ix) and that it accounts for "practically everything from his pen
that got into print" (p. xii). This latter statement should, of course,
be read as intended to apply only to Mill's lifetime. The editors
provide a list of posthumously published works (p. xii n.), but it is

*Reprinted from *Modern Philology*, Vol. 43, November 1945, pp. 149-150,
by the courtesy of the University of Chicago Press.

not a complete one. Even with respect to writings of Mill printed during his lifetime, some omissions can be cited, and it would not be safe to assume that others are not discoverable. The editors apparently relied mainly upon a checking of the notebook with the allusions to published writings in Mill's *Autobiography* for their appraisal of its completeness (cf. preface, p. ix n.). But as the bibliography, according to their own testimony, was probably prepared as an aid to writing the *Autobiography*, this cannot be regarded as an independent check. Moreover, Mill deliberately left out letters and speeches which appeared in print after 1865 (cf. Preface, pp. ix n. and 96); reprints and new editions during his lifetime are only partially accounted for in the original bibliography and in the editors' notes; and at least one item written by Mill was published between the apparent time of preparation of this bibliography and his death (a review of an Italian book on taxation which appeared in the *Fortnightly Review*, March, 1873, pp. 396-98).

As indications of still other omissions, the following notes may be of interest. In his *Autobiography*, Mill gives the number of articles contributed by him to the *Westminster Review* as thirteen, but the notebook records only twelve (cf. p. 10, n.). The additional items in the *Westminster Review*, attributed to Mill by Alexander Bain in his *John Stuart Mill: A Criticism* (London, 1882), seem on internal and other evidence not likely to be from his pen. But Mill wrote jointly with William Ellis the article on McCulloch's *Discourse on Political Economy* in the July, 1825, number of the *Westminster Review* (cf. E. K. Blyth, *Life of William Ellis* [2d ed.; London, 1892], p. 352). The attributions to Mill of contributions to the *Monthly Repository*, made in Francis E. Mineka, *The Dissidence of Dissent: the Monthly Repository, 1806-1838* (Chapel Hill, 1944), p. 417, include several items not listed in the notebook but, from their character, plausibly to be regarded as his. G. J. Holyoake (*Sixty Years of an Agitator's Life* [London, 1892], I, 216) attributes to Mill the obituary of Francis Place in the *Spectator* in 1854. Mill contributed some paragraphs to the article by Bisset on his father, James Mill, in the seventh edition of the *Encyclopaedia Britannica* (cf. Andrew Bisset, *Essays on Historical Truth* [London, 1871], pp. 12 n. and 103 n.). The listing in the notebook of Mill's botanical writings seems to be incomplete (cf. Henry Triman, "His [i.e., Mill's] Botanical Studies," in *John Stuart Mill, His Life and Works* [New York, 1873], pp. 44-45).

Alexander Bain (*Autobiography* [London, 1904], p. 197 n.) states that John Stuart Mill prepared for the *Examiner* in 1848 a notice of Bain's lecture "On the applications of science to human health and well-being." This volume of the *Examiner* has not been available to me for checking.

The editors have failed to locate an item in the notebook listed as an "article on wages and profits, capital & prices, which appeared in the Edinburgh Times of 1 May 1825" because of inability to find any record of a periodical by this name. My colleague, Professor George L. Marsh, has drawn my attention to the following advertisement which appeared in the *Examiner* of January 16, 1825, p. 48: "New Weekly Paper. On Saturday, the 22d instant, will be published, the First Number of the Edinburgh Times, a Weekly Newspaper, to be conducted on liberal principles, etc."

Marian Bowley, *Nassau Senior and Classical Economics*

London, George Allen & Unwin, Ltd., 1937*

THIS CAREFUL AND INTELLIGENT STUDY of the contribution of Senior as economic theorist and poor-law reformer is to be warmly welcomed as an addition to the short list of comprehensive and analytically competent studies of the works of English classical economists. Miss Bowley has evidently read the great mass of Senior's writings in the economics field, printed and unprinted, with painstaking care, and has skilfully summarized and organized her material and related it in an enlightening manner to previous and subsequent currents of economic thought. She has treated Senior a little too sympathetically, perhaps, and as one reads her paraphrases of what he said, the suspicion arises that in endowing him with a Houghton Street vocabulary, she has also occasionally introduced other modern improvements into his analysis. That Senior was an economist of high merit, deserving of more intensive study than he has received, is, however, demonstrated beyond question by this

*Reprinted from *The Economic Journal*, Vol. 48, June 1938, pp. 283-285, by the courtesy of the Royal Economic Society.

book, which will, moreover, make such study much more feasible than it has hitherto been.

The prevalent impression that Senior's merit lay rather in his capacity for brilliant flashes of insight than in systematic execution of original analysis is substantially confirmed by this study. But the character and occasion of most of Senior's economic writings suggest that his relative failure to carry through any substantial inquiry to a satisfactory conclusion was due more to the absence of sufficient stimulus and leisure than to incapacity for sustained rigorous analysis. Senior was obviously a busy man, aside from his academic activities; he wrote extensively—and to little purpose—on non-economic matters of the most varied sort; and his economic writings were mostly by-products of his duties as a civil servant or—still worse—were prepared for delivery as formal university lectures to nondescript audiences at a then backward university. For such purposes, rigorous and thorough theoretical analysis is not, as a rule, the commodity in most urgent demand.

That Senior wrought less well than he could is supported by the following bit of evidence which I have come across. Miss Bowley notes that, while Senior was interested in and commented intelligently on the motives to saving, even in his later lectures his treatment was not as penetrating as that in Rae's *New Principles*, a book with which Senior was acquainted, or in J. S. Mill's *Principles*, where indebtedness to Rae was freely acknowledged. That Senior's failure in this instance to carry the analysis even as far as others had previously carried it was not owing to lack of appreciation of Rae's contribution is indicated by contemporary testimony that at the time Senior was delivering his lectures he was not only speaking with enthusiasm of Rae's discussion of saving, but was also claiming credit for having drawn Mill's attention to it.

There are only a few points, and these not major ones, on which I would seriously question Miss Bowley's doctrinal verdicts or be disposed to find fault with her manner of handling her difficult task. In her comparison of the doctrines of Senior and of the strict Ricardians, Miss Bowley has made no use at all of the replies of the Ricardians to their critics, and has examined too restricted a range of the literature of criticism of Ricardo antedating Senior's contributions. This has resulted in her failing to see that some of the criticisms directed against the Ricardian analysis were either based on misinterpretations of it or would have been accepted by the

Ricardians, and in her overrating Senior's originality—especially
with reference to the generalization of the rent concept, the rejection of the labor-cost theory of value, and the rejection of the
pessimistic implications of the Malthusian population theory. Miss
Bowley fails to note also that much of the later dissatisfaction—and
perhaps most conspicuously that of Senior—with the Ricardian
analysis can be explained by the shift of interest, from the application of economic analysis to the answer of "practical" questions, to
the development of an academic economic theory concerned with
finding solutions to manufactured problems of "pure" intellectual
concern, a shift of interest which Karl Marx was acute enough to
note, but which, in his pleasant manner, he explained in terms of
the naïve objectivity of the Ricardians and the deliberate capitalistic
apologetics of the later economists, Senior included. In any case,
Miss Bowley rates more highly than I would the merits of Senior's
introduction, as a major aspect of economic theorizing, of classifica-
tory patter divorced from all discussion of what uses the classifications could be put to after they had been rendered free of all
realistic confusion and logically impeccable.

Miss Bowley errs also in accepting the standard myth, which
Senior helped to establish, that the Ricardians—or anyone else—ever
believed that labor costs—or any other species of cost—"determined"
values in any other way or degree than by influencing supplies of
products. She greatly overrates Senior's contribution to the theory
of international trade, which was wholly confined to effectiveness
of exposition, and she distributes unfairly the laurels of victory in
the controversies in this field between Senior, on the one hand, and
Torrens and J. S. Mill, on the other, by ascribing obscure virtues to
Senior's errors of analysis.

The absence of a general bibliography is hard to excuse, except
as adherence to an ancient national custom. The collation of
Senior's surviving manuscripts with his printed works is a useful
service, but it does not result in, and is not an adequate substitute
for, a "complete" list of Senior's printed economic contributions.
Even apart from omitted variant editions, and from possible other
omissions unknown to me, several items are to be added to her list.
The intended preface to the fourth edition of his pamphlet on
National Property, which Miss Bowley could not find among
Senior's manuscripts, is in the University of Chicago Library in
printed form. Also in this library, and unmentioned by Miss Bow-

ley, is a copy of Senior's *Remarks on Emigration, with a Draft of a Bill*, 1831, with the *Draft* amended in manuscript in what may be Senior's hand. There is no mention of Senior's *Letters on the Corn Laws, 1839* (which I have never seen, but have several times seen listed).*

These are small defects, however, in what is, both taken as a whole and in its separate parts, a highly meritorious contribution to the history of economic thought. As an author's first book, it is a truly distinguished performance.

W. H. Hutt, *Economists and the Public: A Study of Competition and Opinion*

London, Jonathan Cape, Ltd., 1936†

THIS BOOK IS PRIMARILY a tract for the times, defending the orthodox economic case for individualistic competition and explaining the failure of orthodox economists to convert the public to their views by the lack of sound mental habits on the part of the public, by the biased ignorance on the part of sociologists and political scientists as to the nature of the economist's argument, and by treason within the ranks of the economic profession itself resulting from its corruption by political ambitions, financial entanglements, and the craving for popularity.

The author claims on behalf of competition that it gives maximum scope to "consumer's sovereignty"—the essential economic element in individual freedom—which latter is treated as an ultimate value. Consumer's sovereignty is, in this connection, frequently compared with political sovereignty of the individual as exercised through the ballot—to the disadvantage of the latter. The obvious objection to this comparison—namely, that consumer's sovereignty is sovereignty of the dollar and resembles more closely the plural

---

*[This was not by Senior.—J. V. 1951.]

†Reprinted from *The Journal of Political Economy*, Vol. 46, August 1938, pp. 571-575, by the courtesy of the University of Chicago Press.

voting of the Anglican vestry than the one-adult–one-vote of political democracy—is met, though at a surprisingly late stage of
his argument, by presentation of a program for minimization of
unearned inequalities of wealth through drastic restriction of private
inheritance, steeply progressive taxation, public support of education, and removal wherever possible of sources of special privilege.

Competition is defended not only as essential to individual liberty but also as serving more effectively than any other mode of
economic organization the economic welfare of the community.
The argument here, however, is unduly sketchy and dogmatic in
tone and relies more than is expedient on bare references to other
writings of the author. The possibility that the interests of the
individual in "liberty" in the economic field may not be confined
to his activity as a consumer and may to a large extent be of such a
nature as not to be adequately protected, even in a substantially
competitive economy, merely by exercise of his "consumer's sovereignty," is given scant and generally hostile consideration. The
entrepreneur is treated throughout as merely a medium through
whom the edicts of the sovereign consumers are transmitted to the
productive agents. That in addition to the market the internal government of the workshop provides another legitimate field for
struggle for "sovereignty," for individual status and freedom, the
author would apparently deny. That he sees no important difference between the status of the individual worker in a modern giant
factory and the status of an independent artisan in the eighteenth
century is indicated by his approving citation (p. 261), as if it applied to the modern world, of Adam Smith's dictum: "The real and
effectual discipline which is exercised over a workman is not that
of his corporation, but that of his customers." Trade-unions are referred to only incidentally, mainly as agencies operating to restrict
competition. If an instance is found of their having fought for a
defensible cause, it is explained that they did so for indefensible
reasons (pp. 174 ff., 279-80). The possibility of benefit from state
or trade-union interference with the wage-determination process is
disposed of quite in the manner of a papal encyclical: "A frank
admission of the futility of private or State wage-fixation as a remedial agency ought to be the starting-point of all social studies
concerned with the problem of relative poverty" (p. 202).

The author does concede the propriety of protecting the individual from the results of his own mistakes or ignorance, but not

as protection against exploitation, on the ground, apparently, that if the worker knew and hence insisted upon "those things that are really necessary for his well-being" he would be bound to get them (p. 275). Even where the worker was ignorant as to his true interests, the author would support state interference only reluctantly, if at all, since time usually remedies such ignorance and experience is therefore a better servant than restraint (pp. 278-79). The lessons of the history of social legislation can scarcely be so easy of unambiguous reading as this would imply. Even if it be granted that what is learned from experience is always the truth and never error, is it admissible to assume, without argument, that the cost of restraint exceeds the gain from escaping the time lag inherent in "learning from experience"?

While the author strongly favors measures which would minimize unearned inequalities of wealth, he denies that the existence of such inequalities affords any justification for interference with competitive market processes on the ground that the allocation of productive resources according to the dictates of consumers' demands will still be "just" or "defensible" or "advantageous," presumably as compared to any other conceivable allocation (p. 269). But all that his argument even begins to demonstrate is that, given inequality of wealth distribution, allocation according to competitive prices is more desirable than would be *random* interference with such allocation. Reasoning by analogy from the admitted distortions of values from the optimum resulting from a protective tariff, he claims that, nevertheless, given the tariff, "the competitive adjustment of internal prices within the sheltered market will be to the consumers' benefit" (p. 269). As compared to what? Assuredly not, or not necessarily, as compared to the system of prices which would result from a pattern of interference designed to offset the distortions of values resulting from a tariff which was politically not directly touchable. Having asserted the impossibility of mitigating by state interference "distortions" in the price structure resulting from inequalities, the author easily reaches the conclusion "that the problem of inequalities must be tackled separately" (p. 269). He then cites —presumably approvingly, and presumably to indicate that the problem of inequality is not so urgent or so pervasive as to render of doubtful expediency, while inequality persists, a plea for individual economic liberty, including the liberty to profit from existing inequalities—an unfortunate utterance by Marshall in defense of his abstraction from inequality in his discussion of the welfare significance of market prices: "On the whole . . . it happens that the greater number of the events with which economics deals affect in about equal proportions all the different classes of society" (p. 269n. in Hutt). Since, however, "events" are not of co-ordinate importance, the results of "counting" them are not of much significance. If the "orthodox" economic tradition is to be followed, the economist will lay special stress on those events which affect very differently the different social classes.

The author presents as an additional consideration against the appeal to inequality as justification for interference with a competitive price structure the ingenious argument that since the poor and the moderately well-off have much greater aggregate demand than the rich, and since the demand of the poor is largely directed toward commodities produced under conditions of decreasing cost (food?, shelter?, clothing?), the inequality of wealth tends to produce a price structure favorable to the poor rather than otherwise (p. 287). It seems to me that if the poor were to have half of their income transferred to the rich, the buying power per dollar of the remainder of their dollars would be more likely to rise than to fall, even if all the products consumed by the poor were subject to technological economies of large-scale production. The evil of poverty to the poor is, of course, a matter much more of the smallness in number of their dollars than of what their dollars can buy per dollar relative to the buying power of the dollars of the rich. But even if it be granted that the relative purchasing powers of the poor man's and the rich man's dollars are important, and if it also be granted that inequality of itself tends to raise the relative purchasing power of the poor man's dollar, this still leaves it an open question whether or not it is desirable by deliberate interference with the price structure still further to raise the relative purchasing power of the poor man's dollar.

That "consumer's sovereignty" would be an imperfect regulator of an economy heavily infested with monopoly, the author fully recognizes, and the solution of this difficulty which he proposes is antimonopoly legislation of the American type (plus, I take it, anti-collective-bargaining legislation in the labor field), with compensation for injured vested interests on expediency grounds to weaken their opposition and to create a more favorable atmosphere for effective enforcement.

The author makes it fairly clear that it is consumer's sovereignty per se that is the major object of his affection and that he is not enamored of some of the economic or other products of its exercise. He appears, for instance, to hold pecuniary emulation in low esteem, although in terms of his own analysis it can be shown to constitute in a competitive economy an essential aspect of efficient dedication to the task of responding to the dictates of the consumer. It is apparently unqualifiedly good for the consumer to have the power to give orders, but not at all good that the producer should fully respond to them, given the nature of the orders which consumers actually give. There is probably no inconsistency here, except in appearance, since an apostle of individual freedom might well desire a world in which the consumer's power to give orders is qualified by the power of producers to disobey them subject to paying a known penalty. It does suggest, however, that the author's major thesis would have gained in apparent consistency and in persuasiveness if it had been couched throughout in the familiar terms of "individual" sovereignty instead of in terms of "consumer's" sovereignty.

While the author is unqualifiedly opposed to any direct interference by the state (or by trade-unions or monopolistic associations) with the price structure, it would be a gratuitous departure from traditional usage to label this book as a plea for laissez faire. Prices are sacrosanct, but the state is asked to plan and to maintain a framework within which individual preferences are to regulate prices, which is substantially different from that which now prevails anywhere. I subscribe heartily to all the major items of his specific program, but I fear that his manner of presenting it will afford the enemies of "consumer's sovereignty" more ammunition for attack than occasion for retreat. The most effective modern exponents of an authoritarian economy are careful to pay lip service to the virtues of economic individualism in a world without gross inequalities of wealth, without monopolies, and without the cost rigidities resulting from collective bargaining and other modern institutions. To their taunts to the effect that the exponents of individualism fail to indicate by what practicable and politically conceivable procedures these obstacles to even the tolerable working of an unregulated market can be eliminated or even substantially reduced in importance, this book contributes scarcely any materials for an effective rejoinder.

A word, finally, on the considerable amount of material in the book purporting to contrast the views on competition of the early classical economists with those of the later English economists—from J. S. Mill on—to the disadvantage of the latter. The author explains that the book was written after some years of absence from the source material (see p. 162), and the result, as might have been expected, is largely conjectural history unfair to the early economists in the apologies made for their supposed mistakes and unfair, I hope, to the later economists, and especially to J. S. Mill, in the explanation of their deviations from the author's views as the result of political ambitions and the craving for popular approval.

Etienne Mantoux, *The Carthaginian Peace—Or the Economic Consequences of Mr. Keynes*

New York, Oxford University Press, 1946*

THIS IS AN EXTREMELY SEARCHING CRITICISM of the writings of Maynard Keynes on the German reparations problem after the first World War. It was written by a young French economist, who had already given promise of affording much-needed leadership to French economics in his doctor's thesis on "forced saving" but who died in action in Germany in the service of his country before he could get this second book to press. It was first published in England only a few weeks after the death of Lord Keynes. There is a tragic note about this book, written by a passionately patriotic young Frenchman soon to die in the war against Hitler, in criticism of the earlier economic and political views of a patriotic Englishman who had given all his great intellectual resources and more of his physical resources than he could spare in statesmanlike contribution to the same cause.

The book consists, for the most part, of a detailed critique of the economics of Keynes's *Economic Consequences of the Peace* (Lon-

---

*Reprinted from *The Journal of Modern History*, Vol. 19, March 1947, pp. 69-70, by the courtesy of the University of Chicago Press.

don, 1919). Keynes's book met with a *succès fou* among the English and the American lay reading public when it first came out, and Mantoux may not exaggerate when he attributes great importance to it in determining English and American attitudes toward Germany, reparations, and the Treaty of Versailles from 1919 to the advent of Hitler. It is rather remarkable that so important a book should have had to wait for a quarter of a century before it was subjected to a full-scale, competent economic scrutiny from any quarter. As I recall it, economists at the time regarded its economics as undistinguished in general and technically defective at some crucial points, especially in its treatment of the alleged difficulties of "transfer" of reparations. But the political views which Keynes expounded with great force of exposition were those which Anglo-Saxon liberals of the 1920's, including the economists, shared almost to a man, and I suppose there then seemed little point in exposing technical flaws in an economic argument which had the virtue of leading to the desired political conclusions. My own record may be pertinent here. On several occasions I expressed complete disagreement with Keynes's argument on the *economic* impossibility of levy and transfer of large German reparations. But I shared Keynes's skepticism of the *political* possibility of levy and transfer, since this would depend on the will of the German government and people to pay and, if such will were lacking, on the will of the Allies to apply the necessary coercion. And I am ashamed to say that I shared to the full Keynes's sympathy with the plight of the Germans if they did pay and his impatience with the French insistence that their own economic and political plight in the event that Germany were let off lightly had even greater claims to sympathy. Such a position proved unintelligible to some of the American liberals of the time—notably to the *New Republic* editors—who could not see how anyone who held the "right" doctrine that Germany should not be forced to pay heavily could at the same time insist that Germany was economically capable of making—and transferring—heavy payments. With the hindsight available when he wrote, Mantoux was able to show that Keynes's political views were unsound. He apparently shows also that there were serious errors of bias and inconsistency in Keynes's financial arithmetic, which, I fear, most of us then took on faith.

Like the later Keynes, the early Keynes was a brilliant expositor and dialectician. But the early Keynes—and the Keynes also of his second great period, the period of the Great Depression—was intellectually arrogant, unscrupulous in debate, and addicted to argument *ad hominem,* and, as a rule, he overwhelmed and even humiliated his less nimble opponents in public debate. Mantoux in his own well-mannered and restrained way now delivers a less favorable but sadly belated verdict. But the guilt complex toward Germany and toward the Treaty of Versailles, which Keynes helped to establish in England and America; the grossly unfair caricature of the personality, the character, and the intellect of Woodrow Wilson, which is the most widely remembered part of his book on the Peace; his exaggerated account of the greed and intransigence of the French and of their obsession with a security bogy—these had long before contributed their weight to easing the path to world hegemony for a resurgent and reparations-free Nazi Germany.

On one point, at least, however, Mantoux fails to do full justice to the case against German reparations. The Treaty of Versailles, when requiring Germany to pay heavy reparations, should also have required the Allies to refrain from commercial policies which would make such payment difficult and could even make it impossible economically. Instead, the treaty freed the Allies from all obligations of nondiscrimination against German exports, and for a time most of the Allies, including France and the British Dominions, levied specially high duties on imports from Germany. It is only fair to the memory of Lord Keynes to add also that in the third phase of his career, from Munich to his death, he rose to the highest levels of maturity, balance of judgment, and responsible and world-oriented statesmanship. If there is a successful outcome of the present effort of the great Western democracies to find a common platform from which to promote a postwar world in which peace, freedom, and plenty can all prevail, to Keynes will be due a significant fraction of the credit. Had both Keynes and Mantoux lived and gotten to know each other, I feel sure that they would now be working together on this great project, in perfect harmony and in mutual respect and affection.

H. S. Ellis, editor, *A Survey of Contemporary Economics*

Philadelphia, P. Blakiston's Sons & Company,
for the American Economic Association, 1948*

THIS VOLUME, read apart from the editor's preface, is not obviously much more than a collection of thirteen essays by as many economists of repute on as many different topics having in common little more than that all the topics dealt with have claims of some kind or degree on the attention of some economists. There is a real temptation to the reviewer to appraise the volume on this basis, since he can then follow the easy procedure usual in dealing with collections of miscellaneous essays of picking and choosing for comment the topics or the details with which he is most familiar. This volume, however, is the product of a serious and large-scale experiment by our Association, and in the official journal of the Association it should be reviewed in the light of the specific purposes which it was planned to serve.

The volume itself, unfortunately, gives much too scanty and vague information as to the nature of the original plan, the procedures by which the plan was formulated, the instructions given to the participants by the editor, and the extent to which the contributors adhered to these instructions. Each essay was commented on by two "critics." We are told nothing of transactions between editor, contributors, and critics. Such information might be dull reading for the ordinary reader, but since this is an experiment, to be repeated if the results are judged to be promising, it is information vital for judicious appraisal of the original plan and for elicitation of anything but random suggestions for revision of plan and procedures in case the venture should be repeated.

We are given two rather vague statements as to the purpose of the volume. According to the editor's preface, "The primary purpose of the present volume is to provide the economist outside a particular field an intelligible and reliable account of its main ideas—both analytical devices and their practical application to public

---

*Reprinted from *The American Economic Review,* Vol. 40, September 1950, pp. 649-653, by the courtesy of the American Economic Association.

policy—which have evolved during the last ten or fifteen years." According to a foreword, the purpose the American Economic Association had in mind in sponsoring and financing this volume was that it should serve as "a periodic review of economics."

These seem to be quite distinguishable purposes, both no doubt highly commendable, but unlikely to be well served by a single plan and a single volume. For appraisal of the final outcome, it would have helped if we had been told whether the contributors and critics were made aware of both purposes, and if not, which one they were asked to attend to.

The contents of the volume suggest that it was the first purpose which the contributors were asked to serve, and it is only the first purpose which the volume does serve with any substantial measure of effectiveness. It does incidentally provide material for the second purpose, but so would even a random collection of essays by competent specialists in a variety of economic "fields." Even with respect to the first purpose, however, the contents of the volume suggest that the contributors were left great latitude as to the period to be covered, as to the definition of "fields," as to whether only *American* literature or only literature in *English* was to be treated as relevant, as to the extent to which appraisal as well as recording was expected, as to the stress to be put on novelties of analysis or of policy-conclusions as distinguished from survivals of earlier thought, and as to the scope which the contributors could appropriately give to riding their more-or-less private hobbies.

More unity of design and purpose should, I think, have been pressed upon the contributors. Several of the contributions are too much a mere record or catalogue of activities or concepts, or are too narrow exercises in particular techniques, or too much confined to the exposition of the personal views of the contributors with respect to a particular problem or particular tools of analysis used in particular fields, to be at all satisfactory as accounts for non-specialists of recent developments in analysis and in applications to policy-problems in the fields concerned.

Most of the essays, however, have performed this task commendably, and several have managed at the same time to do adequate justice to the record while making a substantial contribution by tracing the conflicts and the possibilities of synthesis between different prevalent approaches to the problems of their field. The ideal performance would call for a large measure of self-abnegation, of objective reporting of what was prevalent, even if what prevailed was not wholly approved of by the contributor, but with aid provided to the non-specialist so that he could reach some judgment of his own as to the merits of recent developments in the various fields. More than half of the contributions, in my judgment, either meet this test or come fairly close to meeting it. There are not more than three of the essays which I would be inclined to regard as definitely unsatisfactory, because too narrow in scope to be informative to non-specialists as to the major lines of recent development in particular fields, or because they do not reveal what it is in their fields of work which make them significant and presumably interesting to substantial subdivisions of our fragmented profession. On the whole, I regard the experiment as fairly successful and as one which with more advance planning and more exercise of discipline over the contributors would be well worth repeating every decade or so.

If my experience is typical, there is enlightenment in this volume for economists, and food for fresh thought, not only with respect to the fields in which they are not specialists but also with respect to their own fields of concentration. More extensive annotated bibliographical information, however, would for most of the essays have been well worth the space it would have entailed, both for specialist and for non-specialist readers. Not even the full-fledged specialist nowadays becomes aware of all the important contributions to his field while they are still comparatively fresh.

The contributors, moreover, were chosen predominantly, perhaps wholly and deliberately, from among the safe, middle-of-the-road members of the profession, with respect both to their policy-attitudes and their methodological predilections. The result is that the volume is representative only of the patterns of value-judgment and the methods of analysis adhered to by the "center" portion of our profession. The social reactionaries and the Marxians, the fortune-tellers and mechanical quantifiers, the apostles of anti-intellectual institutionalism as gospel and program, the Veblenians, the extreme Keynesians and the extreme anti-Keynesians, the exponents of uninhibited central planning and the exponents of extreme *laissez-faire*, get scanty mention where mentioned at all. Even with the aid of the index I cannot find any reference to what are assuredly the important facts that during the period covered work in the various fields was being carried on and government policy strongly influenced by "scientific" forecasts that the end of the War would be followed by anywhere from 8 to 12 million unemployed unless huge federal deficits were planned, and that American population would soon reach its peak, although the "stagnant economy" thesis does get some attention. Whether we like them or not, these are all significant phases of the record in recent years of our profession. For non-specialists and for laymen, moreover, it was these phases of our operations which attracted most attention, sympathetic or hostile, while they were under way, and they were significant factors in determining the opinions of our profession which outsiders reached. The editor hopes that "for most of the less abstruse and technical subjects . . . the qualified layman . . . will also read with profit." I would not deny the profit, but I predict that it will be accompanied by amazement at how different the predominant activities of the profession apparently were from what he had supposed.

The selection of "fields" to be covered must beyond doubt have been a difficult task for those who planned the enterprise, and anything like complete coverage was obviously impracticable. It seems to me, however, that the "fields" chosen involved an excessive amount of duplication, and that merging of several of these fields was readily feasible, and would have left room, without enlargement of the volume and with an increase in its value and interest, for such omissions as general welfare theory, population, regional economics, location theory, and theories of economic development. Except for reference to a limited treatment of welfare analysis in the essay on "socialist economics," none of these topics even gets notice in the detailed subject index. In these and other fields fresh and interesting work, with new concepts and new tools of analysis, has, I am sure, been done in recent years, and the non-specialists should have been told about it. There is meager reflection in the volume of the great influence of the Knightian ideas during this period on important groups of American and English economists.

The volume clearly does not succeed in providing a "periodic review of economics" if by that is meant a review of the state of our discipline as in some sense and degree a unified and coherent discipline. This would have required a different plan, different procedures, and no doubt in large part different contributors. It would probably also have been a more difficult task, more liable to complete failure. Were it successfully accomplished, however, it would, I believe, have been more valuable than the present volume to the profession and especially more valuable to those not of the profession who have curiosity as to what we try to do and why, and how what we do is related to what they do. Instead of separate essays in different fields, treated as autonomous, it would have had separate essays on general objectives, on general techniques, on the relations of theoretical analysis to policy-formulation, on the contributions economics can make to public administration, on the relations of economics to political theory, to sociology and anthropology, to ethics, and to history, and so forth. It could have dealt with the grounds, if any, on which economists start from the psychological and other preconceptions which constitute the normally unscrutinized substructure of our discipline, and with the borrowings from logic, mathematics, mechanics, statistical theory, and elsewhere, which we apply, as our tools of analysis, to problems which perhaps have peculiarities of their own requiring specially adapted tools of analysis.

In a now far distant past J. S. Mill, Cairnes, J. N. Keynes, Sidgwick, and others, made single-handed attempts, which in their time were universally regarded as valuable, to cope with this task. If it could be done at all now it would, like this volume, have to be the product of teamwork, and for the best results it would require cooperation from experts in other disciplines who were willing seriously to examine the nature of the problems economics deals with and of the tools it uses to deal with them. Without reflection on the worthwhileness of the present experiment and without prejudice to the desirability of its repetition at a proper interval of time, I suggest that a large-scale "review" of the methodological state of our discipline is a project which our Association might well take in hand as its next major experiment.

That such a survey is needed, this very volume provides abundant evidence. There is scarcely a hint in it of discussion of how economists should choose their premises, or as to what are the criteria by which an economist advises as to the goodness or badness of policy, and the mere fact of use of particular tools of analysis, whether with tested fruitfulness or not, is often quietly presented or treated as evidence that the use is justified. One contributor cites in support of resort to a particular arbitrary assumption its use by another economist; that other economist, who happens also to be a contributor, in his own contribution concedes, with a frankness

sufficiently uncommon to call for special commendation, that resort to that assumption, having as its only justification its ease of
use, is a fundamental weakness in his own work. One contributor
presents the fact that the American economy has survived its
oligopolistic features without collapsing as apparently a weighty
argument against taking this problem seriously, although perhaps
it is only against hysteria that he is making his point. Most of us may
be busily engaged in applying the discarded or inappropriate tools
of other disciplines to problems of our own manufacture, and it
may take a survey of the kind I propose both to find this out and to
discover better procedures and more significant problems to apply
them to. A philosopher has recently commented on the social
sciences that they are moving "hither and yon between meaningless
facts and doubtful meanings" and has complained that social scientists borrow their methods uncritically from other sciences instead
of letting their subject matter determine their methods. Even this
volume, I believe, provides considerable evidence supporting this
criticism. We need seriously to examine to what extent the criticism
is justified and to explore the availability of remedies.

The Works and Correspondence
of David Ricardo

Edited by Piero Sraffa with the Collaboration of M. H. Dobb:
Volume I, *On the Principles of Political Economy and Taxation;*
Volume II, *Notes on Malthus' Principles of Political Economy,*
New York, Cambridge University Press, for the Royal Economic
Society, 1951*

THESE TWO VOLUMES are the first installment of a ten-volume edition
of the writings of David Ricardo, the great English classical economist. This is substantially the one-man enterprise of Piero Sraffa, a
Cambridge University don of Italian nativity and education, who
has been at work at it for over twenty years.

The two books, together with what I have seen, in preliminary

*Reprinted from *The New York Times Book Review*, Oct. 14, 1951, p. 30,
by the courtesy of the publisher.

shape, of the contents of the forthcoming volumes, justify the highest acclaim that can be given true scholarship. All that Ricardo wrote, whether published or surviving in manuscript, has been discovered, collated, edited and interpreted, with application and ingenuity. There is nothing to match it in scale or in craftsmanship in the history of economic scholarship.

Tribute is also due Cambridge University Press and the Royal Economic Society and especially Lord Keynes for their sustained and loyal support of the enterprise.

There is comparatively little of Ricardo's writings in these first two books that was not already in print. Sraffa's important discoveries of unknown or lost materials are mainly to be revealed in subsequent volumes. Yet what is presented here is made available for more accurate and intelligent use than had hitherto been possible. Volume I contains a variorum edition of Ricardo's major work, the "Principles," most helpfully annotated, and with an introduction by the editor which aids greatly to the understanding of this difficult book.

Volume II contains Ricardo's critical notes on the "Principles" of his friend and intellectual opponent, Malthus. This had been printed before, in 1928, but here the relevant passages from Malthus and Ricardo's comments thereon are for the first time printed in juxtaposition, so that the reader can readily follow the details of this historic debate.

Ricardo has always had a great influence and a bad press. He was a businessman conscious of his clumsiness in use of the pen, and yielding reluctantly to the insistence of his friends, and especially James Mill, that he put his ideas into systematic book form. His argument is often difficult, often subtle, and almost always obscurely expounded. He has consequently been grossly and systematically misinterpreted. Even his few avowed disciples did not always understand him.

After his death in 1823, he was frequently characterized even by economists as a dangerous radical and demagogue, from whom Marx had inherited the intellectual dynamite with which to explode capitalism. Later, he was more often pictured as the rich stockbroker, preaching the inevitability and perpetuity of miserable poverty for the working class. Modern commentators have attributed to him "willful pessimism" and "coldness and cruelty."

Both pictures of him are gross caricatures. Ricardo was a kindly man, if anything overoptimistic as to the prospects for English labor, provided certain conditions were met.

Having, as he believed, found certain obstacles to the easing of laborers' poverty, Ricardo directed the public attention to them. He did not regard them as irremovable obstacles. They were eventually to be removed, for a time, and only then did the English masses really begin to prosper. Marx did borrow heavily from Ricardo to demonstrate inherent contradictions in capitalism which could be resolved only by socialist revolution—yet he was able to use his borrowings for this purpose only by misinterpreting them or converting them into radically different matter.

Sraffa has in these two volumes already made it more difficult to adhere to the standard misinterpretations of Ricardo. To those who are willing to take reasonable pains to understand him, what Ricardo meant to his time and what he still means to us today will be clear when the whole edition is available. In these two volumes, Sraffa is always the objective editor, neither eulogizing nor dressing up his author nor fighting him, but only trying to display him accurately.

Still I hope that in the final volume—which is to give an account of Ricardo's life and personality—Sraffa will not refrain from acting as arbitrator between Ricardo and his early and late critics.

Publications by Jacob Viner

TRANSLATIONS into foreign languages of items originally published in English are not included in this list. Also excluded are reprints in journals other than those of original publication, in volumes of readings, etc., unless the item was reprinted in substantially revised or extended form. Items marked † are reprinted in the present volume. Items marked * were reprinted in *International Economics*, Glencoe, Ill., Free Press, 1951.

1917
"Some Problems of Logical Method in Political Economy," *Journal of Political Economy*, Vol. 25, March 1917, pp. 236-260.

1919
Reciprocity and Commercial Treaties (in collaboration with others), Washington, D. C., United States Tariff Commission, 1919. Pp. 535.

1920
Tax Reform in Illinois, Chicago, Illinois State Teachers Association, 1920. Pp. 15.

"The Self-Governing Dominions and the British Empire," *Pacific Review*, Vol. 1, December 1920, pp. 235-250.

"Who Paid for the War?" *Journal of Political Economy*, Vol. 28, January 1920, pp. 46-76.

REVIEWS OF:

F. W. Taussig, *Free Trade, the Tariff and Reciprocity*, in *New York Evening Post* (Book Section), May 15, 1920, p. 7.

E. M. Friedman, *International Commerce and Reconstruction*, in *Journal of Political Economy*, Vol. 28, December 1920, pp. 853-855.

1921
"The International Aspect of Tariff Legislation," *The Pacific Review*, Vol. 2, September 1921, pp. 276-286.

"Must the United States as a Creditor Nation Modify Its Traditional Attitude toward a Protective Tariff?" *Annals of the American Academy of Political and Social Science*, Vol. 94, March 1921, pp. 47-51.

†"Price Policies: The Determination of Market Price," in *Business Administration* (L. C. Marshall, ed.), Chicago, University of Chicago Press, 1921, pp. 343-347.

"Tax Reform Proposals at the Illinois Constitutional Convention," *Journal of Political Economy*, Vol. 24, July 1921, pp. 608-611.

REVIEWS OF:
P. Ashley, *Modern Tariff History*, in *Journal of Political Economy*, Vol. 29, March 1921, p. 259.
C. J. Bullock, *Selected Readings in Public Finance*, in *Journal of Political Economy*, Vol. 29, March 1921, pp. 262-263.
R. M. Haig., ed., *The Federal Income Tax*, in *Journal of Political Economy*, Vol. 29, December 1921, pp. 842-844.

1922

Colonial Tariff Policies (in collaboration with others), Washington, D. C., United States Tariff Commission, 1922. Pp. 869.
"Dumping as a Method of Competition in International Trade," *University Journal of Business*, Vol. 1, November 1922, pp. 34-53, and February 1923, pp. 182-190. (Included in *Dumping: A Problem in International Trade*, 1923.)
"The Prevalence of Dumping in International Trade," *Journal of Political Economy*, Vol. 30, October 1922, pp. 655-680, and December 1922, pp. 796-826. (Included in *Dumping: A Problem in International Trade*, 1923.)
†"The Relation between Economics and Ethics" (Discussion), *The American Economic Review, Supplement*, Vol. 12, March 1922, pp. 198-200.
"Textbooks in Government Finance" (Review), *Journal of Political Economy*, Vol. 30, April 1922, pp. 241-256.
REVIEWS OF:
E. R. A. Seligman, *Essays in Taxation*, in *Bulletin of the National Tax Association*, Vol. 7, March 1922, pp. 201-202.
T. E. Gregory, *Tariffs: A Study in Method*, in *Journal of the American Statistical Association*, Vol. 18, March 1922, pp. 127-132.

1923

Dumping: A Problem in International Trade, Chicago, University of Chicago Press, 1923. Pp. iii/343.
†"Taxation and Changes in Price Levels," *Journal of Political Economy*, Vol. 31, August 1923, pp. 494-520.

1924

Canada's Balance of International Indebtedness, 1900-1913, Cambridge, Harvard University Press, 1924. Pp. x/318.
"Economic Factors in International Relations," *Proceedings*, Conference on International Relations of Chicago Council on Foreign Relations, 1924, pp. 41-45.
"Forecasting the Future Trend of Business," *Finance and Industry*, Vol. 46, 1924, pp. 21-22, 38.
"The Mellon Tax Program," *Bulletin Illinois League of Women Voters*, Vol. 4, May 1924, pp. 5, 14-15.
*"The Most-Favored-Nation Clause in American Commercial Treaties," *Journal of Political Economy*, Vol. 32, February 1924, pp. 101-129.
"The Problems of Highway Finance" (in collaboration with others),

Proceedings of the Seventeenth Annual Conference on Taxation, National Tax Association, Vol. 17, September 1924, pp. 411-431.
"Revenue and Taxation in Kentucky," *Report of the Efficiency Commission of Kentucky*, Vol. 1, 1924, pp. 221-342.

REVIEWS OF:

H. B. Hastings, *Costs and Profits: Their Relation to Business Cycles*, in *Journal of the American Statistical Association*, Vol. 19, June 1924, pp. 262-264.

A. F. Macdonald, *Federal Subsidies to the States*, in *Journal of Political Economy*, Vol. 32, October 1924, pp. 617-618.

L. Lancaster, *State Supervision of Municipal Indebtedness*, in *Journal of Political Economy*, Vol. 32, December 1924, p. 734.

P. G. Wright, *Sugar in Relation to the Tariff*, in *Journal of the American Statistical Association*, Vol. 19, December 1924, pp. 544-546.

1925

A Report on the Proposed Amendment to the Revenue Clause of the Illinois Constitution, in Its Bearing upon Real Estate, Chicago, Building Managers' Association of Chicago, 1925. Pp. 12.

"Branch Banking in the United States and Canada," *The Economist* (London), Apr. 18, 1925, pp. 745-746.

†"Objective Tests of Competitive Price Applied to the Cement Industry," *Journal of Political Economy*, Vol. 33, February 1925, pp. 107-111.

"Some Recent Changes in American Commercial Policy," *The Economist* (London) June 6, 1925, pp. 1124-1125.

"The Tariff in Relation to Agriculture," *Journal of Farm Economics*, Vol. 7, January 1925, pp. 115-123.

†"The Utility Concept in Value Theory and Its Critics," *Journal of Political Economy*, Vol. 33, August 1925, pp. 369-387 and December 1925, pp. 638-659.

REVIEWS OF:

†J. R. Commons, *Legal Foundations of Capitalism*, in *Illinois Law Review*, Vol. 19, April 1925, pp. 710-712.

W. McClure, *A New American Commercial Policy*, in *American Journal of International Law*, Vol. 19, April 1925, pp. 442-443.

1926

Memorandum on Dumping, Publications of the League of Nations, II, Economic and Financial, Geneva, 1926, II, 63. Pp. 19.

"American Export Trade and the Tariff," *Annals of the American Academy of Political and Social Sciences*, Vol. 127, September 1926, pp. 128-133.

"Angell's Theory of International Prices," *Journal of Political Economy*, Vol. 34, October 1926, pp. 597-623.

"Economic Problems Involved in the Payment of International Debts," *American Economic Review, Supplement*, Vol. 16, March 1926, pp. 91-97.

"Financing Highway Construction and Maintenance," *Journal of the*

Western Society of Engineers (Chicago), Vol. 31, April 1926, pp. 163-171.

"International Free Trade in Capital," *Scientia* (Milan), Vol. 39, Annus XX, 1926, pp. 39-48.

"National Monopolies of Raw Materials," *Foreign Affairs*, Vol. 4, July 1926, pp. 585-600.

"Urban Aspects of the Highway Finance Problem," *Proceedings of the Highway Research Board*, National Research Council, 1926, Part I, pp. 208-238.

1927

†"Adam Smith and Laissez Faire," *Journal of Political Economy*, Vol. 35, April 1927, pp. 198-232.

REVIEWS OF:

S. Nearing and J. Freeman, *Dollar Diplomacy: A Study in American Imperialism*, in *Journal of the American Statistical Association*, Vol. 22, March 1927, pp. 125-126.

L. H. Jenks, *The Migration of British Capital to 1875*, in *Journal of Political Economy*, Vol. 35, October 1927, pp. 716-718.

1928

"Comparative Costs: A Rejoinder [to Arthur F. Burns]," *Quarterly Journal of Economics*, Vol. 42, August 1928, pp. 697-701.

"Political Aspects of International Finance," *Journal of Business of the University of Chicago*, Vol. 1, April 1928, pp. 141-173, and July 1928, pp. 324-363.

†"The Present Status and Future Prospects of Quantitative Economics," (Discussion) *American Economic Review, Supplement*, Vol. 18, March 1928, pp. 30-36.

*"Die Theorie des auswärtigen Handels," in *Die Wirtschaftstheorie der Gegenwart*, Vienna, Verlag von Julius Springer, 1928, Vol. IV, pp. 106-125. (Part III, "The Theory of International Values," reprinted in *International Economics*, 1951.)

REVIEWS OF:

J. B. Williams, *A Guide to the Printed Materials for English Social and Economic History, 1750-1850*, in *Journal of Political Economy*, Vol. 36, February 1928, pp. 177-178.

†R. Sachot, *Les Prix de Monopole, d'après les Doctrines et dans les Faits*, in *Journal of Political Economy*, Vol. 36, June 1928, pp. 411-412.

1929

"The Commercial Policy and the Foreign Trade of the United States," *Index Svenska Handelsbanken* (Stockholm), No. 37, January 1929, pp. 3-17.

"Inter-Ally Debts and Reparations," *Report of the Round Tables and General Conferences at the Ninth Session* (R. A. Newhall, ed.), Williamstown, Mass., Institute of Politics, 1929, pp. 86-110 ff.

*"International Finance and Balance of Power Diplomacy, 1880-1914," *Southwestern Political and Social Science Quarterly*, Vol. 9, March 1929, pp. 407-451.

REVIEWS OF:

F. C. Mills, *Behavior of Prices*, in *Quarterly Journal of Economics*, Vol. 34, February 1929, pp. 337-352.

†E. Salin and A. Sommer, *Friedrich List, Schriften, Reden, Briefe*, Vol. IV, in *Journal of Political Economy*, Vol. 37, June 1929, pp. 364-366.

J. B. Brigden and others, *The Australian Tariff: An Economic Inquiry*, in *Economic Record* (Melbourne), Vol. 5, November 1929, pp. 306-315.

D. C. Blaisdell, *European Financial Control in the Ottoman Empire*, in *Journal of Political Economy*, Vol. 37, December 1929, pp. 745-747.

1930

"Balance of Trade," *Encyclopedia of the Social Sciences*, Vol. II, 1930, pp. 399-406.

"English Theories of Foreign Trade before Adam Smith, I, II," *Journal of Political Economy*, Vol. 38, June 1930, pp. 249-301, and August 1930, pp. 404-457. (Included in revised form in *Studies in the Theory of International Trade*, 1937).

"Problems of Commercial Policy in the Pacific Area," *Proceedings of the Institute of International Relations*, Sixth Session, Berkeley, Calif., University of California, 1930, Vol. VI, pp. 16-20.

"Self-Interest and the Tariff," *Century Magazine*, Vol. 120, Winter 1930, pp. 45-57.

REVIEWS OF:

†M. K. Bennett, *Farm Cost Studies in the United States*, in *Journal of the American Statistical Association*, Vol. 25, March 1930, pp. 111-113.

†E. Cannan, *A Review of Economic Theory*, in *Economica* (London), No. 28, March 1930, pp. 74-84.

D. G. Barnes, *A History of the English Corn Laws 1660-1846*, in *Journal of Political Economy*, Vol. 38, December 1930, pp. 710-712.

W. Grotkopp, *Amerikas Schutzzollpolitik und Europa*, in *Weltwirtschaftliches Archiv* (Jena), Vol. 31, 1930-I, pp. 221*-222*.

1931

"Cost," *Encyclopedia of Social Sciences*, Vol. IV, 1931, pp. 466-475.

†"Cost Curves and Supply Curves," *Zeitschrift fur Nationalökonomie* (Vienna), Vol. III, 1931-I, pp. 23-46. (Included in R. V. Clemence, ed., *Readings in Economic Analysis*, 1950, Vol. II, with a Supplementary Note.)

"Dumping," *Encyclopedia of the Social Sciences*, Vol. V, 1931, pp. 275-278.

*"The Most-Favored-Nation Clause," *Index Svenska Handelsbanken* (Stockholm), Vol. 6, No. 61, February 1931, pp. 2-17.

"Das Prinzip des Kostenausgleichs in der Zollpolitik der Vereinigten Staaten," *Magazin der Wirtschaft* (Berlin), No. 5, Jan. 30, 1931, pp. 244-247.

"Problems of International Commercial and Financial Policy," *Report of the Round Tables and General Conferences at the Eleventh*

Session (A. H. Buffinton, ed.), Williamstown, Mass., Institute of Politics, 1931, pp. 165-193.

*"The Tariff Question and the Economist," *The Nation and Athenaeum* (London), Vol. 48, Feb. 7, 1931, pp. 592-594 and Feb. 14, 1931, pp. 626-628.

REVIEW OF:

Ausschuss zur Untersuchung der Erzeugungs—und Absatzbedingungen der deutschen Wirtschaft, *Die deutsche Zahlungsbilanz*, in *Weltwirtschaftliches Archiv* (Jena), Vol. 39, 1931, II, pp. 51*-53*.

1932

"The Doctrine of Comparative Costs," *Weltwirtschaftliches Archiv* (Jena), Vol. 36, 1932-II, pp. 356-414. (Included in *Studies in the Theory of International Trade*, 1937, in revised form.)

*"International Aspects of the Gold Standard," in *Gold and Monetary Stabilization* (Quincy Wright, ed.), Chicago, University of Chicago Press, 1932, pp. 3-39.

"International Trade: Theory," *Encyclopedia of the Social Sciences*, Vol. VIII, 1932, pp. 200-208.

*"National Monopolies of Raw Materials," in *The Causes of War* (Arthur Porritt, ed.), London, Macmillan & Co., Ltd., 1932, pp. 185-202.

Testimony before the Public Service Commission of Wisconsin, . . . Investigation of . . . Wisconsin Telephone Company, 2-U-35, taken May 16, 1932, pp. 1194-1249. (Testimony on public utility rates and deflation.)

REVIEWS OF:

J. H. Rogers, *America Weighs Her Gold*, in *The Survey Graphic Number*, Vol. 67, Jan. 1, 1932, pp. 387-389.

J. M. Keynes, *Essays in Persuasion*, in *Saturday Review of Literature*, Vol. 8, Feb. 6, 1932, p. 504.

M. Manoilesco, *The Theory of Protection and International Trade*, in *Journal of Political Economy*, Vol. 40, February 1932, pp. 121-125.

P. W. Martin, *The Problem of Maintaining Purchasing Power*, in *Journal of Political Economy*, Vol. 40, June 1932, pp. 418-419.

†R. L. Schuyler, ed., *Josiah Tucker: A Selection from His Economic and Political Writings*, in *Journal of Political Economy*, Vol. 40, June 1932, pp. 416-418.

1933

"Balanced Deflation, Inflation, or More Depression," *The Day and Hour Series of the University of Minnesota*, No. 3, 1933, pp. 1-30.

"Inflation as a Possible Remedy for the Depression," *Proceedings of the Institute of Public Affairs*, Athens, Ga., University of Georgia, 1933, pp. 120-135.

"Samuel Mountifort Longfield," *Encyclopedia of the Social Sciences*, Vol. IX, 1933, pp. 605-606.

"Sir Dudley North," *Encyclopedia of the Social Sciences*, Vol. XI, 1933, pp. 397-398.

The State and Economic Life, Sixth International Studies Conference, 1933, Paris, International Institute of Intellectual Cooperation, 1934, pp. 48-50, 58-62, 81-83, 116-122, 129-131, and *passim.*

"Tariff Reduction by International Agreement," *Proceedings of the Institute of Public Affairs*, Athens, Ga., University of Georgia, 1933, pp. 108-119.

"An Unpublished Letter of Ricardo to Malthus," *Journal of Political Economy*, Vol. 41, February 1933, pp. 117-120.

"War Debts," *Report of the Eighth Conference of the Cause and Cure of War*, Washington, National Committee on the Cause and Cure of War, 1933, pp. 207-211, 218-229.

REVIEW OF:

J. H. Hollander, ed., *Minor Papers on the Currency Question, 1809-1823, by David Ricardo*, in *Journal of Political Economy*, Vol. 41, April 1933, pp. 272-273.

1934

"Economics," in *The Study of International Relations in the United States: Survey for 1934* (Edith E. Ware, ed.), New York, Columbia University Press, 1934, pp. 180-188.

"Tariff," *Encyclopedia of the Social Sciences*, Vol. XIV, 1934, pp. 514-522.

1935

Report on the Availability of Bank Credit in the Seventh Federal Reserve District (with C. O. Hardy), Washington, U. S. Treasury Department, 1935. Pp. viii/109.

REVIEWS OF:

†E. F. Heckscher, *Mercantilism*, in *Economic History Review*, Vol. 6, October 1935, pp. 99-101.

†H. Higgs, *Bibliography of Economics, 1751-1775*, in *Journal of Political Economy*, Vol. 43, December 1935, pp. 817-820.

1936

"The American Tariff-Bargaining Program and Canadian-American Tariff Relations," *Proceedings of the Conference on Canadian-American Affairs, June 1935*, Carnegie Endowment, Boston, Ginn & Company, 1936, pp. 22-31, 41-44.

"Can Depressions Be Tempered or Avoided?" *Lectures in Current Economic Problems*, Washington, U. S. Department of Agriculture Graduate School, 1936, pp. 31-45. (Multigraphed.)

"The Economic Factor in International Organization," *Interdependence: Quarterly Journal of the League of Nations Society in Canada* (Ottawa), Vol. 13, No. 3, 1936, pp. 218-229.

*"Memorandum on the Technique of Present-Day Protectionism," and "Comments on the Improvement of Commercial Relations between Nations," in *Separate Memoranda . . . on the Improvement of Commercial Relations between Nations*, by the Joint Committee of the Carnegie Endowment and the International Chamber of Commerce, Paris, International Chamber of Commerce, 1936, pp. 58-79, 88-100.

†"Mr. Keynes on the Causes of Unemployment," *Quarterly Journal of Economics*, Vol. 51, November 1936, pp. 147-167.

*"Professor Taussig's Contribution to the Theory of International Trade," in *Explorations in Economics . . . in Honor of F. W. Taussig* (E. S. Mason, ed.), New York, McGraw-Hill Book Company, Inc., 1936, pp. 3-12.

"Recent Legislation and the Banking Situation," *American Economic Review, Supplement*, Vol. 26, March 1936, pp. 106-119.

1937

Studies in the Theory of International Trade, New York, Harper & Brothers, 1937. Pp. xv/650.

1938

Manitoba's Argument with Respect to the Burden on the Prairie Provinces as a Result of Dominion Tariff Policy: A Supplementary Statement, Ottawa, November 1938, p. 42. (Mimeographed).

REVIEWS OF:

†M. Bowley, *Nassau Senior and Classical Economics*, in *Economic Journal*, Vol. 48, June 1938, pp. 283-285.

†W. H. Hutt, *Economists and the Public: A Study of Competition and Opinion*, in *Journal of Political Economy*, Vol. 46, August 1938, pp. 571-575.

1939

The Debt Problem of the Government of the Province of Alberta, report submitted to the Provincial Treasurer, July 1939, pp. 140. (Photostated, Library of Congress; also printed in summary form in various Canadian newspapers.)

"Indemnity Payments and Gold Movements, A Reply [to D. H. Robertson]," *Quarterly Journal of Economics*, Vol. 53, February 1939, pp. 314-317.

1940

"The Centenary of the American Statistical Association," *Journal of the American Statistical Association*, Vol. 35, March 1940, pp. 273-274.

"Mills, 'The Behavior of Prices,' " in *An Appraisal of Frederick C. Mills' The Behavior of Prices* (R. T. Bye, ed.), New York, Social Science Research Council, *Critiques of Research in the Social Sciences*, II, 1940, pp. 165-180 and *passim*.

†"The Short View and the Long in Economic Policy," *American Economic Review*, Vol. 30, March 1940, pp. 1-15.

REVIEW OF:

H. J. Tasca, *The Reciprocal Trade Policy of the United States*, in *The American Historical Review*, Vol. 45, January 1940, pp. 429-430.

1941

"Bibliography of English Economic Theory, 1660-1800," in *The Cambridge Bibliography of English Literature*, Vol. II, Cambridge, England, Cambridge University Press, 1941, pp. 957-959.

"Capital Investment in Latin America," *Proceedings of the Seventeenth*

Institute . . . of the Norman Wait Harris Memorial Foundation, Chicago, 1941, pp. 90-123. (Planographed.)

"Financing the Defense Program," *Commerce* (Chicago), Vol. 38, April 1941, pp. 19-21, 35-36.

"International Economic Relations and the World Order," in *The Foundations of a More Stable World Order* (W. H. C. Laves, ed.), Lectures on the Harris Foundation, 1940, Chicago, University of Chicago Press, 1941, pp. 35-73.

"Letter Addressed to Brazilian Ambassador to the United States, October 17, 1940" (on selective credit control), in Octavio Gouvea de Bulhoes, *Orientação e Controle em Económia,* Rio de Janeiro, 1941, pp. 89-94.

†"Marshall's Economics, in Relation to the Man and to His Times," *American Economic Review,* Vol. 31, June 1941, pp. 223-235.

REVIEW OF:

†Harvard Graduate School of Business Administration. Baker Library, Kress Library of Business and Economics. *Catalogue Covering Material Published through 1776,* in *Journal of Political Economy,* Vol. 49, August 1941, pp. 629-631.

1942

"Inflation: Menace or Bogey?" *The Yale Review,* Vol. 31, Summer 1942, pp. 684-702.

"The International Economic Organization of the Future," in *Toward International Organization,* Oberlin College Lectures, New York, Harper & Brothers, 1942, pp. 110-137.

"International Economic Reconstruction," in Canadian Institute on Public Affairs, *War and Reconstruction, Some Canadian Issues,* Toronto, Ryerson Press, 1942, pp. 39-43. (Summary of a lecture.)

"Objectives of Post-War International Economic Reconstruction," in *American Economic Objectives,* New Wilmington, Pa., The Economic and Business Foundation, 1942, pp. 159-185.

REVIEW OF:

W. K. Hancock, *Survey of British Commonwealth Affairs,* Vol. II: *Problems of Economic Policy, 1918-1939,* Part I, in *Journal of Political Economy,* Vol. 50, February 1942, pp. 143-144.

1943

Trade Relations between Free-Market and Controlled Economies, Geneva, League of Nations, 1943. Pp. 92.

*"German Reparations Once More," *Foreign Affairs,* Vol. 21, July 1943, pp. 659-673.

Testimony in United States Circuit Court of Appeals for the Seventh Circuit in matter of *Aetna Portland Cement Co., et al., Cement Institute, et al. v. Federal Trade Commission, Transcript of Record,* Chicago, 1943-1946, Vol. 8, pp. 5198-5272.

*"Two Plans for International Monetary Stabilization," *The Yale Review,* Vol. 33, Autumn 1943, pp. 77-107.

"What about the Trade Agreements?" a radio discussion by Ralph E. Flanders, T. W. Schultz, and Jacob Viner, *The University of Chicago Round Table*, Transcript 265, Apr. 18, 1943.

1944

*"The Case for the Bretton Woods Agreements," in *International Financial Stabilization* (M. Shields, ed.), New York, Irving Trust Company, 1944, pp. 53-68.

"Economic Reporting by the American Foreign Service," *American Foreign Service Journal*, Vol. 21, November 1944, pp. 595-597, 630-635.

*"International Relations between State-Controlled National Economies," *American Economic Review, Supplement*, Vol. 34, March 1944, pp. 315-329.

*"Peace as an Economic Problem," in *New Perspectives on Peace* (G. B. Huszar, ed.), Chicago, University of Chicago Press, 1944, pp. 85-114.

REVIEWS OF:

J. H. Williams, *Post-War Monetary Plans and Other Essays*, in *The New York Times Book Review*, Aug. 20, 1944, pp. 6, 20.

H. M. Groves, *Production, Jobs and Taxes*, A. D. H. Kaplan, *The Liquidation of War Production*, and S. M. Fine, *Public Spending and Post-War Economic Policy*, in *The New York Times Book Review*, Sept. 17, 1944, pp. 5, 19.

1945

*"The American Interest in the Colonial Problem," in *The United States in a Multi-National Economy*, Studies in American Foreign Relations No. 4, New York, Council on Foreign Relations, 1945, pp. 1-17.

†"Clapham on the Bank of England," *Economica* (London), New Series, Vol. 12, May 1945, pp. 61-68.

"Commercial Policy in the Post-War World," *Proceedings of the Twenty-First Institute ... of the Norman Wait Harris Memorial Foundation*, Chicago, 1945, pp. 139-144.

"The Treatment of Germany," *Foreign Affairs*, Vol. 23, July 1945, pp. 567-581.

REVIEW OF:

†N. MacMinn, J. R. Hainds, J. M. McCrimmon, eds., *Bibliography of the Published Writings of John Stuart Mill*, in *Modern Philology*, Vol. 43, November 1945, pp. 149-150.

1946

*"The Implications of the Atomic Bomb for International Relations," *Proceedings of the American Philosophical Society*, Vol. 90, Jan. 29, 1946, pp. 53-58.

*"International Finance in the Post-War World," *Lloyd's Bank Review*, Vol. 1, October 1946, pp. 3-17.

"The Place of the United States in the World Economy," in *The Evolution of Social Institutions in America*, Princeton, N. J., Princeton University Bicentennial Conference IV, Oct. 8, 1946. (Planographed.)

"We Should Practice Dollar Diplomacy," *Commercial and Financial Chronicle*, Nov. 14, 1946, pp. 2458, 2495-2496.

1947

*"America's Lending Policy," *Academy of Political Science Proceedings*, Vol. 22, January 1947, pp. 57-66.

"An American View of the British Economic Crisis," *Lloyd's Bank Review*, New Series No. 6, October 1947, pp. 28-38.

"Can We Check Inflation?" *The Yale Review*, Vol. 37, December 1947, pp. 193-211.

*"Conflicts of Principle in Drafting a Trade Charter," *Foreign Affairs*, Vol. 25, July 1947, pp. 612-628.

"The Employment Act of 1946 in Operation," *The Review of Economic Statistics*, Vol. 24, May 1947, pp. 74-79.

*"In Defense of 'Dollar Diplomacy'," The New York Times Magazine, Mar. 23, 1947, pp. 11, 66-67.

*"International Economic Cooperation," in *United States in the Postwar World* (W. B. Willcox and R. B. Hall, eds.), Ann Arbor, University of Michigan Press, 1947, pp. 15-36.

*"The Prospects for Foreign Trade in the Post-War World," *Manchester School of Economics and Social Studies* (Manchester), Vol. 15, May 1947, pp. 123-138.

†"The Role of Costs in a System of Economic Liberalism," in *Economic Institute on Wage Determination and the Economics of Liberalism*, Washington, Chamber of Commerce of the United States, 1947, pp. 15-33.

REVIEWS OF:

†E. Mantoux, *The Carthaginian Peace—or the Economic Consequences of Mr. Keynes*, in *Journal of Modern History*, Vol. 19, March 1947, pp. 69-70.

O. J. McDiarmid, *Commercial Policy in the Canadian Economy*, in *Journal of Political Economy*, Vol. 55, June 1947, pp. 265-266.

1948

†"Power versus Plenty as Objectives of Foreign Policy in the Seventeenth and Eighteenth Centuries," *World Politics*, Vol. 1, October 1948, pp. 1-29.

REVIEWS OF:

R. G. Hawtrey, *Bretton Woods for Better or Worse*, in *American Economic Review*, Vol. 38, June 1948, pp. 437-438.

B. U. Ratchford and William D. Ross, *Berlin Reparations Assignment: Round One of the German Peace Settlement*, in *American Historical Review*, Vol. 54, October 1948, pp. 104-105.

1949

†"Bentham and J. S. Mill: The Utilitarian Background," *American Economic Review*, Vol. 39, March 1949, pp. 360-382.

†"Government-Business Tension in Relation to Business Outlook," *Commercial and Financial Chronicle*, Sept. 29, 1949, pp. 1252, 1273.

Speech discussing the President's Economic Program, in Trade and Industry Law Institute, *Current Business Studies*, No. 3, June 1949, pp. 32-58.

1950

The Customs Union Issue, New York, Carnegie Endowment for International Peace, 1950. Pp. 221.

†*A Modest Proposal for Some Stress on Scholarship in Graduate Training*, address before the Graduate Convocation, Brown University, June 3, 1950, Brown University Papers XXIV. Pp. 14.

†"Cost Curves and Supply Curves" and "Supplementary Note (1950)," in *Readings in Economic Analysis* (R. V. Clemence, ed.), Cambridge, Mass., Addison-Wesley Publishing Company, 1950, Vol. II, pp. 8-35.

*"Economic Foundations of International Organization," in *Perspectives on a Troubled Decade: Science, Philosophy, and Religion 1939-1949* (Conference on Science, Philosophy, and Religion in their relation to the Democratic Way of Life, Tenth Symposium), New York, Harper & Brothers, 1950, Appendix II, pp. 816-832.

†"Full Employment at Whatever Cost," *Quarterly Journal of Economics*, Vol. 64, August 1950, pp. 385-407.

REVIEW OF:

†H. S. Ellis, ed., *Survey of Contemporary Economics*, in *American Economic Review*, Vol. 40, September 1950, pp. 649-653.

1951

International Economics, Glencoe, Ill., Free Press, 1951. Pp. 381.

Rearmament and International Commercial Policies, Washington, D. C., U. S. Department of State, Foreign Service Institute, 1951. Pp. 43.

"Seis Conferencias do Professor Jacob Viner," *Revista Brasileira de Economia*, Ano 5, June 1951, pp. 11-225. (Six lectures on the theory of international trade delivered at the National University of Brazil, Rio de Janeiro, July-August, 1950. Published in this country in 1952 and in England in 1953 under the title *International Trade and Economic Development*.)

REVIEW OF:

†P. Sraffa and M. H. Dobb, *The Works and Correspondence of David Ricardo*, in *The New York Times Book Review*, Oct. 14, 1951, p. 30.

1952

International Trade and Economic Development (lectures delivered at the National University of Brazil, 1950), Glencoe, Ill., Free Press, 1952. Pp. 154.

"America's Aims and the Progress of Underdeveloped Countries," in *The Progress of Underdeveloped Areas* (B. F. Hoselitz, ed.), Chicago, University of Chicago Press, 1952, pp. 175-202.

Defense, Controls, and Inflation (with others, A. Director, ed.), Chicago, University of Chicago Press, 1952, pp. 59-60, 115, 178-179, 335-339.

Testimony in *Hearings on Monetary Policy and the Management of the Public Debt*, U. S. Congress, Joint Committee on the Economic Report, March 1952, pp. 754-796.

1953

International Trade and Economic Development (lectures delivered at the National University of Brazil), Oxford, England, Clarendon Press, 1953. Pp. 121.

†Introduction to Bernard Mandeville, *A Letter to Dion* (1732), Los Angeles, University of California, William Andrews Clark Memorial Library, Augustan Reprint Society publication 41, 1953, pp. 1-15.

"The New Deal under Republican Management," *The Yale Review*, Vol. 42, March 1953, pp. 321-332.

1954

Foreword in Isaac Gervaise, *The System or Theory of the Trade of the World* (J. M. Letiche, ed.), Baltimore, Johns Hopkins Press, 1954. Pp. v-vi. (A Reprint of Economic Tracts.)

"The Role of the United States in the World Economy," in *National Policy for Economic Welfare at Home and Abroad* (Robert Lekachman, ed.), report of Columbia University Bicentennial Conference, May 1954, pp. 175-210, 230-234.

†"Schumpeter's History of Economic Analysis, a review article," *American Economic Review*, Vol. 44, December 1954, pp. 894-910.

1955

"International Trade Theory and Its Present Day Relevance," in *Economics and Public Policy*, Washington, The Brookings Institution, 1955, pp. 100-130.

"The Need for External Assistance of Underdeveloped Countries," *Confluence*, Vol. 4, October 1955, pp. 347-357.

Testimony in *Hearings on the January 1955 Economic Report of the President*, U. S. Congress, Joint Committee on the Economic Report, January and February, 1955, pp. 893-899.

Testimony in *Hearings on Foreign Economic Policy*, U. S. Congress, Joint Committee on the Economic Report, November 1955, pp. 595-618.

REVIEW OF:

S. E. Harris, *John Maynard Keynes*, in *Saturday Review*, Vol. 38, Mar. 5, 1955, p. 21.

1956

"Some International Aspects of Economic Stabilization," in *The State of the Social Sciences* (L. D. White, ed.), Chicago, University of Chicago Press, 1956. (Papers presented at the 25th Anniversary of the Social Science Research Building, the University of Chicago, November 10-12, 1955), pp. 283-298.

1957

"The Gordon Commission Report" (a review article on Royal Commission on Canada's Economic Prospects, *Preliminary Report*, Ottawa, 1956), *Queen's Quarterly*, Vol. 64, Autumn, 1957, pp. 305-325.

"The Scope of Economic Activity in International Income Comparisons Comment," in *Problems in the International Comparison of Economic Accounts*, National Bureau of Economic Research Studies in Income and Wealth, Vol. 20, Princeton, Princeton University Press, 1957, pp. 388-398.

"Some Reflections on the Concept of Disguised Unemployment," in *Contribuções A Analise Do Desenvolvimento Econômico*, Rio de Janeiro, Livraria Agir Editôra, 1957, pp. 345-354.

Index of Persons

Index of Subjects

Absolute monarchy and mercantilism, 301-2.

Advertising: and price-making, 6; the free-enterprise system and, 143-4; and distortion of consumption patterns, 204.

Anglo-American economics, 52, 113-4, 179.

Anti-trust laws, 145-7.

Apprenticeship regulations, Adam Smith on, 227.

Arminianism, 337.

Artificial harmony of interests, 316.

Atomistic competition, 3-6, 56, 67, 110, 363.

Austrian theory of value, 51-2, 177-8, 179, 205-6, 209, 358, 361-2.

Backward-rising supply curves, see rising-backward supply curves.

Balance of payments equilibrium, 162-6.

Balance of power, and balance of trade, 285.

Balance of trade in mercantilist thought, 285.

Bank of England: Clapham on, 262-275; longevity of, 262; prestige of, 263; remarkable constitution of, 263-4; as manager of debt service, 265; as regulator of money market, 266; as reputed manager of international gold standard, 266-9; relations with other central banks, 268; and "Subscription for the Circulation," 270-2; and suspension of cash payments, 273; Ricardo and, 273-4; and relations with Treasury, 274-6.

Benevolence, Adam Smith on, 218, 221, 223, 224-6.

Benthamism, 249, 253, 310-1, 321-25.

See also Jeremy Bentham, utilitarianism.

Bibliographical method: Henry Higgs and, 410-3, 414; Kress Library *Catalogue* and, 413-5; Judith B. Williams' *Guide* and, 415; J. S. Mill's *Writings* and, 416-8.

Birmingham School, 152-3.

Birth-control, advocacy of: by Jeremy Bentham, 308; by J. S. Mill as young man, 320.

Budget-balancing as dogma, 114-15.

Built-in stabilizers, 161-2.

Bulk-line costs, 74-8, 393-4.

Business, tension between government and, 140-9.

Calvinism and rigorism, 336-7.

Cambridge University, and theological utilitarianism, 324.

Capital gains, taxation of, 13-5.

Capital levies, 23-6.

Cement prices, 36-40.

"Chronic" international disequilibrium, 163.

Classical school: and supplies of factors, 52, 361-2; use of "classical" by Keynes to mean neo-classical, 86n.; and utility theory, 177-9; Marshall and, 247-55; J. A. Schumpeter on, 356-61; Edwin Cannan on, 395-405. See also Anglo-American economics.

Cobdenites, 330.

Competition: and free-enterprise system, 116-7, 127-8; as necessary basis for economic theory, 328-9; W. H. Hutt on, 422. See also atomistic competition, monopoly.

Conjectural history, 351.

Consumer's sovereignty, W. H. Hutt on, 421-5.